THE COMING
INTERSPIRITUAL AGE

THE COMING
INTERSPIRITUAL
AGE

KURT JOHNSON
DAVID ROBERT ORD

namaste

PUBLISHING

Vancouver, Canada

Library and Archives Canada Cataloguing in Publication

Johnson, Kurt, 1946-
    The coming interspiritual age / Kurt Johnson & David
Robert Ord.

Includes bibliographical references.
ISBN 978-1-897238-74-5

    1. Spirituality. 2. Religious pluralism. I. Ord, David
Robert II. Title.

BL624.J63 2012   204   C2012-905641-3

Published in Canada by
Namaste Publishing
P. O. Box 62084
Vancouver, British Columbia V6J 4A3
www.namastepublishing.com

Distributed in North America by PGW, Berkeley, CA USA
Typesetting by Steve Amarillo, Urban Design LLC
Cover Design by Diane McIntosh

Printed and bound in Canada by Friesens

Advance Praise and Perspective on
The Coming Interspiritual Age
from Across the World's Religions

Integral

The Coming Interspiritual Age is in part about just that—the emergence, happening now and gaining momentum—of an interspiritually unified world. It has its basis in a background coming transformation—that of the Integral Age. Kurt Johnson and David Robert Ord give a clear, compelling, highly readable account of this coming transformation, which indeed could prove world changing. If you're not sure what all this means—and even if you are—get this visionary book and find out what all the excitement and enthusiasm is about. It might very well change your world!

— Ken Wilber, *The Integral Vision*

A new integral world has begun to come into view, and a new human being is beginning to be called forth. This new humanity is capable of living responsibly and cooperatively in this radically self-transforming world. The implications will be world-changing. Drawing from the inspiring legacy of Brother Wayne Teasdale, Kurt Johnson and David Robert Ord do us all a great service by bringing the sweep of this panoramic vision into focus in this wide-ranging volume.

— Terry Patten, author *Integral Life Practice*;
Founder, Beyond Awakening

The Coming Interspiritual Age is at once an insightful historical overview of the burgeoning interspiritual movement, an urgent call for transformation in the face of the many pressing social, ecological, and spiritual challenges of our time, and a passionate manifesto for the flowering of a new, integral culture that embodies the highest ideals of all the world's great wisdom traditions, ancient and modern. I am happy to recommend this book to readers from any religious background, or none, who are inspired by the possibility that a better, more just and enlightened world awaits us in and through the miracle of "We." This text promises to be a valuable resource for all interfaith and integral religious students and practitioners; it is one I will be using in my classes on these topics going forward.

— Bruce Alderman, John F. Kennedy University

Evolutionary Consciousness

The Coming Interspiritual Age presents a magnificent post–postmodern integral vision, heralding a new kind of spirituality already aborning. While it is written with passion, the authors Kurt Johnson and David Robert Ord are well-grounded in the knowledge of science and of integral and evolutionary theories to make the book at once a systematic narrative of the past, both cosmic and human, a systemic interpretation of the present, and a splendid vision of the future. At the heart of all spiritual traditions is the "Mystic Heart" that connects us to the Heart of the Kosmos and enables us to unconditionally embrace all beings with Love and Compassion. The authors propose that in this New Axial Age it is time for the Mystic Heart to be luminously lit in the hearts of all humanity to transcend the differences and disagreements that have plagued the human family through spiritual alignment eternally existing in the Heart of our hearts. This is a timely book that transcends time.

— Yasuhiko Genku Kimura, Founder, Vision In Action

Kurt Johnson and David Robert Ord set a wide context of the evolutionary development of man and the earth, setting spirituality in a global and historical developmental context with hints as to its future potential. Backed up by abundant scientific evidence and global polls, they make the case for the marriage of science and religion. But the main message shining through is that of an experiential spirituality of the heart that beats through every living being and is the basis of the new emerging Interspirituality. If you want to keep abreast of the leading edge of spirituality, this book is a must read.

— Nancy Roof, Founder, *Kosmos* Journal

This book will simply astonish you. It is not only a beautiful and powerful tribute to the work and vision of Brother Wayne Teasdale, it is also an Interspiritual Akashic Record that will help prepare the way for the Interspiritual Age to be ushered in…one where we will see with the eyes of the heart.

— Diane Williams, Founder, The Source of Synergy Foundation

This remarkable pioneering book, *The Coming Interspiritual Age*, taps and brings to the fore this deeper evolutionary narrative that is the lead event facing humanity today. This evolutionary drama of our maturation as a species takes the reader through a holistic and comprehensive journey into the emergent frontier of Interspirituality. The authors, deeply inspired by the groundbreaking lifework of Brother Wayne Teasdale, brilliantly help the reader read the "signs of our time" and experience the enormity of our current shift to the long-emerging Age of Interspirituality. Building on advances from Brother Wayne's life in global and interreligious dialogue—the awakening of the global heart-mind—the authors focus our attention on the most profound evolutionary moment facing humanity today, our individual and collective crossing into the dilated global space of Interspirituality. In this respect the supreme activism of our time is to be in touch with this lead event in our human journey, to awaken our hearts to our primal unifying source, to our deep interconnectivity, to the challenges of entering a higher form of shared nonviolent culture through the literacy of global dialogue in which our entire human family may flourish together sharing our sacred earth. This book deserves to be widely read on a global scale as we discover, enter, and co-create our new shared story of our human evolutionary journey.

— Ashok Gangadean, PhD, Co-Convenor of the World Commission on Global Consciousness and Spirituality, Margaret Gest, Professor of Global Philosophy (Haverford College), Director of the Margaret Gest Center for Interreligious Dialogue, Founder-Director of the Global Dialogue Institute; author *Awakening Global Enlightenment: The Maturation of our Species*

As a colleague of Dr. Jonas Salk, whose famous "bio-philosophy" held that our survival as a species depends on our capacity to imagine and anticipate the future and, choosing among clear alternatives, thus co-creating, with nature, our destiny—I see this same wisdom in the message of *The Coming Interspiritual Age*. Like Johnson and Ord, Salk predicted that the most important adaptive mechanism for humankind would be a growing ability to collaborate and cooperate. If the religions of the world can apply this evolutionary point of view to their philosophical, cultural, social, and psychological problems, and experientially draw wisdom from the primordial ground of being that underlies them all, indeed there may be hope that the Great Traditions can make a positive contribution to our human future.

— Michael Jaliman, Founder, True North Advisers

A major contribution to the emerging interface of science, evolution, and spirituality—and its vast implications for the human race.

— Stephan Rechtschaffen MD, and Annette Knopp Founders, Blue Spirit Costa Rica

Modernity has become obsessed with slicing, dicing, chopping, and dividing reality into tiny bits of data and, as a result, our world has become increasingly polarized, fragmented, and fractured. It hurts to be alive today. This magnificent book includes a sweeping diagnosis of our imbalanced condition and offers a powerful vision to heal the broken heart of humanity and unify the spirit of our species.

— Rafael Nasser, author *Under One Sky*

Sacred Activism

Profound heart and deep intellect inform every page of this rich and beautiful book. May it have the success it deserves and open the minds and hearts who come to it.

— Andrew Harvey, author
The Hope: a Guide to Sacred Activism and Radical Passion

The Coming Interspiritual Age by Kurt Johnson and David Robert Ord is simply extraordinary. This much-needed book will change the discourse on religion and spirituality. Especially for the younger generation, who no longer recognize themselves in the traditional narratives that world religions are offering them, this book provides hope. It offers a new vision of spirituality and addresses the personal and societal implications of the possibilities that arise from this new way. The future will be interspiritual and this will be our textbook.

— Adam Bucko, Founder, Reciprocity Foundation,
co-author *New Monasticism Manifesto* and, with Matthew Fox,
Occupy Spirituality: A Radical Vision for a New Generation

The Coming Interspiritual Age is a timely gift for a world facing environmental, economic, and geopolitical crises—all of which can be seen as a spiritual crisis. There is a spiritual awakening organically happening amidst this, transcending cultures and religions and giving birth to new possibilities for all of humanity. *The Coming Interspiritual Age* is a brilliant and comprehensive exploration of the complexity, dangers, and promise of this chaotic and profound time.

— Phillip M. Hellmich, author *God and Conflict: a Search for Peace in a Time of Crisis*; Director of Peace, The Shift Network

Islam

Br Wayne Teasdale's momentous legacy of mystical ecumenism is powerfully amplified and elaborated in this sprawling work of historical, scientific and spiritual synthesis.

— Pir Zia Inayat-Khan, Spiritual Leader, the Sufi Order International

In this truly panoramic book, Kurt Johnson and David Robert Ord place Interspirituality within the whole vista of our global human history. They continue Wayne Teasdale's heart-centered vision of our underlying mystical unity, showing how it naturally belongs to the evolution of human consciousness. The challenge facing us all is how to implement this vital vision in our present time of collective crisis. This valuable book helps us to understand why Interspirituality is so central to our shared destiny.

— Llewellyn Vaughan-Lee PhD, Sufi teacher, author *The Prayer of the Heart in Christian and Sufi Mysticism* and many other books

Good News for Postmodern Humanity! Dancing through millennia of human biological and spiritual evolution, *The Coming Interspiritual Age* offers a compelling and comprehensive peek towards a positive future: stories shared rather than dogmas dividing, consciousness expanding to include global compassion rather than globalized consumerism. This is a book for all who are looking beyond interfaith (bare) tolerance to a larger vision of what makes us all human.

— Neil Douglas-Klotz, author *Desert Wisdom: A Nomad's Guide to Life's Big Questions from the Heart of the Native Middle East* and *The Sufi Book of Life*

Christianity

A significant sign of our times is the quest to make a leap of consciousness from religious ideologies to a deeper spiritual consciousness and practice. As Jung warned, "only the mystics bring creativity to religion itself." This book contributes to that important leap by celebrating our mystical roots that the authors believe can heal the split of science and religion and of religions against religions. This ambitious book joins the multiple efforts at interspirituality in our time to celebrate a mystical awakening that can move us from the religions of consumerism and materialism that dominate our culture with the cynicism and despair and addiction they spawn to something more resembling a full-hearted life. It invites us to new and more ancient ways of living our sacred lives in and on behalf of this sacred earth. I welcome it!

— Matthew Fox, author of the inter-religious classics
Coming of the Cosmic Christ and *One River, Many Wells*,
and recently *The Pope's War, The Hidden Spirituality of Men,
Hildegard of Bingen: A Saint for Our Times*, and other books

In the face of life on the precipice of unimaginable calamity, here is a book of authentic hope—a work of expansive, integrative scholarship woven through and through with heart and spirit; a visionary book with its feet on the ground. *The Coming Interspiritual Age* is a compelling read, an engaging experience; a book to be lived with; a book with the potential to change your life, to change our lives, and with them the future of humanity. If I were you, I'd start reading it today.

— Rev Canon Charles P. Gibbs,
Executive Director, United Religions Initiative

I really cannot exaggerate the value and importance of this book. This is where we are going, and we might as well go informed and enlightened! My heart leaps, and my mind expands as I read this book.

— Fr Richard Rohr, OFM, author *The Naked Now* and *Everything Belongs*; Center for Action and Contemplation and Rohr Institute

If some scholars insist that "God is Not One," Johnson and Ord respond "Oh yes He/She/It is!" Religious differences are real, but they do not obstruct, indeed they nurture, religious dialogue. Drawing on contemporary science (biology, physics, and brain studies), philosophy, the teachings of mystics and of religious activists, this book makes a strong case that an "interspiritual age" is both coming and needs to come soon. For both seekers and academics, this is a rewarding, challenging, and inspiring read.

— Paul F. Knitter, Paul Tillich Professor of Theology,
World Religions, and Culture, Union Theological Seminary

The Coming Interspiritual Age provides an essential understanding of the roots of the current spiritual-religious context and the evolution of consciousness affecting every sector of society and culture. It inspires deeper contemplative awareness of the inherent interrelatedness of all being and a vision for the future of the global human family. A book to be shared and discussed!

— Robert G. Toth, Past Executive Director,
Merton Institute for Contemplative Living

Judaism

The Coming Interspiritual Age is a masterful blend of science and heart. It serves as both a wake-up call to the urgency of our global predicament and a potent dose of hope in our ability to come together to repair the world. Kurt Johnson and David Robert Ord eloquently build a case not only for the evolutionary imperative of interspirituality but the great joy that comes when we remember that we already are interconnected, and ever shall be.

— Mirabai Starr, author *God of Love, A Guide
to the Heart of Judaism, Christianity and Islam*

A new world needs a new worldview and Kurt Johnson and David Robert Ord's *The Coming Interspiritual Age* is just that. If you are looking for a map of the unfolding spiritual landscape of tomorrow, this is it. Read this book. Then read it again.

— Rabbi Rami Shapiro, author
The Sacred Art of Lovingkindness and *Rabbi Rami's Guide to God*

Hinduism

"Man is a transitional being. He is not final. The step from man to superman is the next approaching achievement in the earth's evolution." Sri Aurobindo wrote these words a century ago. The FUTURE presses and will not let us lag behind. Its Presence is palpable. The authors of this book sense the urgency of our destiny...and bring together the myriad strands that could hasten the process.

— Aster Patel, Governing Board,
the Auroville (India) Foundation and author *The Presence of Time*

Panoramic in scope and profound in its incisive probing, *The Coming Interspiritual Age* offers us a vision of hope and unity to shape this millennium. The authors identify Wayne Teasdale as a visionary who helped crystalize the interspiritual movement that seeks to develop a progressive spiritual template for our human advancement. Read it and act on it, for, through understanding the role of "consciousness" in the evolutionary process, you will not only shape history but perhaps life itself. This is a pivotal moment in history, and this book is meant to help us understand the awesome power we hold in our minds, hearts, and hands. Reading it will turn on the bulb of spiritual enlightenment for you!

— Russill Paul, author, *Jesus in the Lotus* and *The Yoga of Sound*

Buddhism

This compelling and accessible new work is a tremendous contribution to the emerging field of global spirituality and the evolution of enlightened wisdom for us today. I am moved and impressed by the breadth and depth of the authors' offering here, and recommend it heartily to anyone interested in spirituality and consciousness. In the context of inevitable globalization and multiculturalism, this brilliant and inspiring book comprehensively documents the trend toward a global unity consciousness, makes crystal clear the gifts the Wisdom Traditions can bring to this global discussion, and challenges all domains—religion, science, economics, governance—to develop a profound sense of responsibility to the collective heart and soul, body and mind of humanity.

I highly commend the authors, dedicated spiritual practitioners themselves, for directly challenging the established religions and their adherents to go deeply into the experiential heart and mystical consciousness of their traditions and refine their understanding of their place in our diverse yet interdependent world. In making available a comprehensive view of developmental history and how the characteristics of this current time reflect the past, it reveals how we can profoundly learn from those integral dynamics, laying out how a modern interspiritual outlook and journey can be accomplished both within traditions as well as in new and innovative structures. Read this book and you'll be better for it.

— Lama Surya Das, author *Awakening the Buddha Within,*
Buddha Standard Time, and other books;
Founder, Dzogchen Center and Dzogchen Osel Ling

This is a beautifully written panorama of the spiritual zeitgeist of our times and an eloquent description of the emerging interspiritual aesthetic and ethic that is bubbling up throughout the world. As the authors put it: "…interspirituality is a call for radical and universal exploration into the subtle realms of consciousness and the deepest regions of the heart. This involves plumbing exactly what unifying principles—what Archimedean points of unity—lie beneath the societal history of our species." This book echoes the intention of the Spiritual Paths Foundation and the Snowmass Interspiritual Dialog work that bring together contemplative teachers from many traditions. In our meditations we experience the marvelous diversity of contemplative method and experience. Our merging consciousness feels like circular ripples of water intersecting and overlapping from multiple pebbles dropped in the same pond.

— Ed Bastian, PhD, Spiritual Paths Foundation,
author *InterSpiritual Meditation* and *Living Fully Dying Well;*
publisher *Meditations for InterSpiritual Practice*

Indigenous

The Coming Interspiritual Age is sublime in vision, prophetic in wisdom, an inherently contemplative exploration into the most salient evolutionary choices we face as humankind. A masterful refined interdisciplinary book, I consider Kurt Johnson and David Robert Ord's scholarship a decisive word on the a-priori role of self-reflexive consciousness in the process of human spiritualization. I foresee the widespread reading of *The Coming Interspiritual Age* catalyzing beneficent societal transformation on a global scale of service beyond our seven generations. This book is a heartfelt contribution to re-Membering ourselves as a compassionate and peacefully cooperative planetary species. I enthusiastically recommend it to all earnest seekers and servers of the Great Work!

— Don Oscar Miro-Quesada, Founder,
The Heart of the Healer (THOTH) Foundation

Humanism

Humanists will read this book with interest and appreciate its wide coverage of many writers who work to distinguish spirituality from religions. They will also appreciate the very readable treatment of the development of the sciences and the treatment of the evolution of our planet currently most complex in the *Homo sapiens* species. Humanists will have more difficulty, however, when the authors speak of scientific as well as spiritual "knowing." They will also have difficulty reading of consciousness as a oneness state and also as an interconnected state in the same sentence. Some humanists, after this extensive exposure to "developmental" and "integral" thinking may be even less likely to favor "spirituality." Another way of putting this would be to say that humanists are much more likely to spend time with Julian Huxley than with Aldous Huxley. Felix Adler was indeed a key figure in moving beyond traditional religion to an ethical movement, and his Kantian idealism may have some mystical elements. Those who have built upon him in different humanist movements, however, retain much more of his stress on ethics. Their nontheism is a starting point, certainly not central or a goal. Universal human rights are a goal rather than an inference from mystical or spiritual experiences.

— Robert Tapp, Dean & Faculty
Chair Emeritus, The Humanist Institute

The Coming Interspiritual Age sensitively teases from ethical culture's message of infinite interdependence its special contribution to the 21st century discourse in the coming Age. Emphasizing the visionary aspect of ethical culture founder Felix Adler, the book cogently articulates a possible roadmap for humanists along the path of humanity's quickening higher consciousness.

— Martha Gallahue, Ethical Culture Leader, National Ethical
Service at The United Nations; Faculty, National Peace Academy USA

Interfaith

The Coming Interspiritual Age is a hugely ambitious project—an extended apologia for interspirituality. Extremely readable, it draws widely from history and literature, ancient and modern, and builds on the work of Teilhard de Chardin, Brother Wayne Teasdale, and Ken Wilber, among others. Johnson, a distinguished scientist who has spent much of his life as a monk, is a student of evolutionary biology with a vast background in anthropology, philosophy, and comparative religion. The book comes with its own strong point of view and will be cut to pieces by predictable critics decrying more new age religion. Whether or not you agree with it, though, the writing is immaculate, the arguments compelling, the vision hopeful. Anyone interested in the future of religion (and why so much religion isn't working today) will enjoy reading this book.

— Paul Chaffee, Editor *The Interfaith Observer*

If one can use *The Coming Interspirituality Age* as a map and guidepost, then there exists the possibility that it will light the way towards a global interfaith and intercultural peaceful future for humankind.

— Alison van Dyk, Chair and
Executive Director, Temple of Understanding

The arc of religious history bends toward what the authors of this book call 'interspirituality.' In breathtaking detail, the book chronicles that long and continuing narrative and documents the transformation of consciousness—individual and collective—that it entails. We desperately need that transformation, and we need this book to fully comprehend it.

— Philip Goldberg, author *American Veda: From Emerson and the Beatles to Yoga and Meditation, How Indian Spirituality Changed the West*

The Coming Interspiritual Age is a very valuable contribution, articulating contexts for understanding the emergence of interspiritualities, acknowledging some of the key contributors, and providing many reference points for further study and exploration.

— Neill Walker, Co-Founder and Co-Director, Edinburgh
International Centre for Spirituality and Peace

Wondering what is happening in the interfaith/integral/interspirituality world? Then this is the book for you. It offers a grand perspective, a way of seeing our human journey, a heart-felt vision of what is happening now, and hope for the future. You'll learn a lot and gain direction!

— M. Darrol Bryant PhD, Huston Smith Award winner 2011,
Director, Centre for Dialogue and Spirituality in the World Religions,
Renison University College/University of Waterloo, Canada;
author *Religion in a New Key*

As founder of a seminary that trains Interspiritual ministers, I am deeply grateful to Kurt Johnson and David Robert Ord, who offer a comprehensive and panoramic view of the landscape that gave rise to the emergence of interspirituality and insightful glimpses of where we may be going. Anyone who cares about the evolution of consciousness and spirituality should read this book.

— Rev. Diane Berke, Founder,
One Spirit Learning Alliance/One Spirit Seminary

Birthed in this unprecedented time of breakdown/revolution/ awakening/ and transformation—sometimes referred to as the divine chaos of creation—this remarkable work both individually and collectively reminds us of where we came from and expressively defines where we are going. *The Coming Interspiritual Age* focuses on the shift of human consciousness, the shift in the heart and anticipates what the Heavens are asking Humanity to become in the here and now. Trailblazing the way forward, the authors—grounded in science and guided by intuition—present with clarity, thoroughness, and grace a framework for us to co-create our new spiritual narrative from a place of one heart, one mind. This book is a *must read!*

— Marshia Glazebrook,
Temple of Understanding and Founder, MetanoiaNow

Divine Feminine

The Coming Interspirtual Age identifies one of the most important evolutionary shifts in human religious life—the move away from doctrine and blind belief to the embrace of experiential knowledge, a turning inward to the source of knowledge. The book describes the shift from a paradigm of separation, exclusiveness, and religious competition to one of unity, inclusiveness, and cooperation, one that allows an integration of the practices of multiple religious traditions, without threatening any. This burgeoning spirituality brings great hope and promise for the future.

— Dena Merriam, Founder, The Global Peace
Initiative of Women; Founding Member and
Convener, The Contemplative Alliance

Science and Religion

A comprehensive overview of the central themes, history, cosmology, and key leaders in the nascent field of interspirituality. Full of vital information that remains as yet too little known, *The Coming Interspiritual Age* is an apt title for the evolutionary transformation that is rapidly emerging across spirituality, religion, and science today.

— William Keepin PhD, co-editor,
The Song of the Earth: A Synthesis of the Scientific and Spiritual Worldviews; author, *Divine Duality*

Teachers of Awakened Awareness

The Coming Interspiritual Age is an important new book and enjoyable to read. Often religious beliefs that all proclaim love, forgiveness, and unity have ended up dividing us and even turning us to war. Here in this book we can read about the past history and the new inner and outer movements of hope emerging today. This book highlights the importance of unity consciousness that can be developed by all people to be able to recognize and embrace our particular cultural and religious beliefs and yet recognize our underlying unity and our common community.

— Loch Kelly, Founder, Awake Awareness Institute

A comprehensive handbook to move from tribal-based, sectarian religion to the actual perennial wisdom based in mystical experiences that give rise to love for all creatures. It is a welcome perspective, coming as it is at a time when life and death for our species, as well as many others, are on the line.

— Catherine Ingram, author *In the Footsteps of Gandhi, Passionate Presence,* and *A Crack in Everything*

The Coming Interspiritual Age explores the impact of awakening to our true nature of unlimited, ever-present Awareness in great detail, exploring its social, political, environmental, and economic implications with depth, clarity and honesty. This book brings the perennial understanding of the reality that all beings and things share to the core issues that face our world culture today, holding up a mirror to society and asking questions that we cannot afford to ignore. It is a beautiful and courageous work which will, I'm sure, have far reaching implications.

— Rupert Spira, author *Presence, The Transparency of Things, Conversations on Nonduality,* and other books

Contents

Acknowledgments

OVER THE LAST DECADE, THE INTERSPIRITUAL PATH HAS INVOLVED THE authors of this book with hundreds of spiritual leaders, teachers, practitioners, and supporters. This involvement is in large measure responsible for the present work, coupled with our connection with Constance Kellough, President and Publisher of Namaste Publishing, who caught the vision for such a book and brought us together for this enterprise.

The collaboration involves Kurt Johnson, who is known as an evolutionary biologist (PhD), comparative religionist, contemplative, and former monastic, together with David Robert Ord, a writer who is editorial director for Namaste Publishing and a former minister. Both have in their different ways journeyed toward interspirituality, so that the insights shared here are insights they hold in common. Kurt prepared the original manuscript, with David using his writing skills to produce a book that could be accessible to a wide readership.

Kurt Johnson in particular has many people to thank from his decades in interfaith and interspiritual work; the list is long but has been required to sustain the interspiritual vision—most deeply, of course, Brother Wayne Teasdale for hours of chatting about the vision of interspirituality (after *The Mystic Heart*, in preparation for their program at the 2004 Parliament of the World's Religions, Barcelona, and thereafter in the few months before his transition). Special debt is owed the original founders, with Brother Wayne, of his New York "interspiritual association," incorporated as Interspiritual Dialogue in 2002. Cofounders with Brother Wayne remain associated—Kurt Johnson, Martha Gallahue, Thomas Downes, Matt Mitler, Michael

Stone, Dorothy Cunha, Lisa Lerner, Robert Trabold, Celia Macedo, and Max Kramer.

Special mention must be made of Martha Gallahue, who introduced Kurt to Brother Wayne's work; and special thanks to Kurt's root teachers in Advaita Vedanta—Pamela Wilson, Neelam and Annette Knopp. Deep acknowledgment to the founders of One Spirit Interfaith Seminary in New York City, who invited Kurt's joining with their Board and Faculty in 2005—Diane Berke, Ingrid Scott, Sara Kendall, Karen Watt, and their dear friend Andrew Harvey.

A special thanks to friends of Brother Wayne who strongly urged the writing of this book, particularly Rory McEntee, Adam Bucko, and Timothy Miner, and to individuals who, in 2011-2012, provided hospitality while this book was being written—Constance Kellough and David Ord, in Phoenix, AZ; in New York, NY, Diane Berke, Joyce Liechenstein, Emily Squires and Len Belzer, Cameron Bossert and Maureen Eggington; and the founders of Blue Spirit retreat center, Costa Rica (where most of the outlines for this book were completed)—Omega Institute cofounder Stephan Rechtschaffen and Annette Knopp. For friendships and spiritual support at a personal level, creating energy for this book, special thanks to family— Elizabeth, Ricardo and Alicia, and dear personal friends. Jody Lotito-Levine was particularly influential. Dafna Mordecai added constant support and Erin Kurnik a remarkable inspiring energy. Without these this book would not have gotten drafted. Particular thanks to the many endorsers of *The Coming Interspiritual Age* whose comments have been printed heretofore. Many of them gave substantial feedback that greatly improved our text.

For spiritual and directive counsel after Brother Wayne's transition, deep gratitude to Llewellyn Vaughan-Lee, Lama Surya Das, Loch Kelly, and Diane Berke. For communications on Integral and Spiral Dynamics, special thanks to Ken Wilber and integral colleagues Aster Patel, Terry Patten, Deborah Boyar, Lynne Feldman, Rafi Nassar, Nomi Naeem, Barbara Larisch, Steve Nadel, and Gilles Herrada.

Deep acknowledgment to participants in the 2004 Barcelona parliament program planned around Brother Wayne, who subsequently became long-term companions in this work. This includes many already listed above, but also Gorakh Hayashi, Joyce Liechenstein, Will Keepin, Martha Foster, members of Theatre Group Dzieci, Brother Wayne's close friends Russill and Asha Paul, and his Parliament colleague Ashok Gangadean; for the 2005 expansion of Interspiritual Dialogue into Interspiritual Dialogue in Action (ISDnA) after Brother Wayne's transition—the original "ISDnA Organizer Group" Joyce and Ken Beck, Gorakh Hayashi, Luca Valentino, Chuck Ragland, Adam Blatner, and Deanne Quarrie. Special thanks to Gorakh Hayashi for his cooperation in writing early works on Brother Wayne's thinking after *The Mystic Heart* and before his transition, and to Yasuhiko Genku Kimura for supporting it; to Martha Foster for carrying communications to Brother Wayne during his last months.

Deep thanks to those who arranged the 2005 tribute event to Brother Wayne at "Common Ground" (The Crossings, Austin, Texas), many already listed above, but also Father Thomas Keating, Joan Borysenko, Betty Sue Flowers, Oscar Miro-Quesada, Cindy Wieber, Diane Dunn, and Estaryia Venus; to Aaron Froehlich who built and donated the www.isdna.org website; to those who supported ISDnA through the spiritual and values caucuses of the NGO Community of the United Nations, Rick Ulfik, Steve Nation, Nancy Roof, Barbara Valocore, and later the Executive Council members of the NGO Committee for Spirituality, Values and Global Concerns at the UN, Diane Williams, Sharon Hamilton-Getz, Genie Kagawa, and Parameshananda.

To those supporters, and fellow teachers with Brother Wayne, who became the official "Friends of ISDnA," many already listed above but also Ronit Singer, Catherine Ingram, Stuart Schwartz, Dasarath Davidson, Calvin Chatlos, Lewis Richmond, Philip Goldberg, Neill Walker, Ruth Frei, Emmanuel Vaughan-Lee, Richard Schiffman, Michael Johnson, and Barbara Cushing and Barbara Sargent of the Kalliopeia Foundation, and my fellows in the Advisory Board of Evolutionary Leaders. Particular thanks to the sponsors of ISDnA at the United Nations, the National Ethical Service of the American Ethical Union, Martha Gallahue, Phyllis and Sylvain Ehrenfeld,

Kay Dundorf, Jacqueline and Sharon Pope; thanks to the Humanist Institute (H.I.) for encouraging the relationship of Brother Wayne Teasdale's vision and that of Ethical Culture founder Felix Adler— Anne Klaeysen, Martha Gallahue, Robert Tapp, and the Board and Faculty of H.I.

Warm and collegial thanks to Brother Wayne's colleagues in Father Keating's Spiritual Paths Foundation—Thomas Keating, Ed Bastian, Cynthia Bourgeault, Kabir and Camille Helminski, Rami Shapiro and Atmarupananda; to founders and members of The Contemplative Alliance who have long been a part of this conversation—the convener Dena Merriam and fellow Steering Committee members Mirabai Bush, Pir Zia Inayat-Khan, Adam Bucko, Mohammed Bashar, Joan Chittester, Joan Brown Campbell, Sraddhalu Ranade, Ed Bastian, Philip Hellmich, Robert Toth, Judy Lief, Barbara Sargent, Linda Grdina, and Atmarupananda; to New York Contemplative Alliance fellows Michael Holleran and Sam Joanna Ghiggeri; to founders and members of The Aspen Grove circle for fellow pioneering of interspiritual circles—Lori Warmington, Michael Abdo, Michael Fuller and the Aspen Grove stewards; to the Snowmass Initiative organizers associated with Father Keating for three sets of meetings over the years, particularly the 2012 "New Monastic Conversation"—Father Keating, Rory McEntee, Adam Bucko, Rob Renehan, Janet Quinn and Matthew Wright; to other ecumenical colleagues Charles Gibbs, Deborah Moldow, and Monica Willard of The United Religions Initiative, Alison van Dyk, Sr. Joan Kirby and Marshia Glazebrook of the Temple of Understanding and, along with many listed above, Lawrence Troster, Mirabai Starr, Ralph Singh, Robert Forman, Howie Elmer, Mudra Lipari, Willa Bassen, T. S. Pennington, Jeff Rubin, Rohini Verma, Robert Levine, Rory Pinto, Nita Renfrew, Bernard Starr, Mitchell Rabin, Ellen Friedman, and Ernest Wachter of the New York, NY and other associated interspiritual circles.

Warm gratitude to fellow members of the Community of The Mystic Heart—all 300—founded as Brother Wayne's Universal Order of Sannyasa in 2010 and its Advisory Council spiritual teachers Ken Wilber, Andrew Harvey, Parameshananda, Vidyananda, Ramananda,

Lama Surya Das, Thomas Keating, Pir Zia Inayat-Khan, H. H. Sai Maa Lakshimi Devi, Ashok Gangadean, Nina Meyerhof, J. J. and Desiree Hurtak, Ken "Bear Hawk" Cohen, Philip Hellmich, Terry Patten, Philip Goldberg, Grace Sesma, Lucinda Vardey, and Miranda MacPherson; a special thanks to Timothy Miner and Jean Leone for the founding of the Order of Universal Interfaith to support this work. Thanks to our friends at Sri Aurobindo Ashram and Auroville, India, especially Sri Aurobindo Ashram Trust for permissions to quote from the *Collected Works of Sri Aurobindo* and *Collected Works of the Mother* (gratitude to Sraddhalu Ranade, Aster Patel, Manoj Das Gupta, Matri Bhai and Rohini Verma); similar thanks for permissions to quote to Gord McFee of the Holocaust History Project, to New World Library for *The Mystic Heart* by Wayne Teasdale, Penguin Group (USA) for *A New Earth* by Eckhart Tolle, Random House (Vintage) for "Adagia" by Wallace Stevens, Lantern for *The Common Heart* edited by Netanel Miles-Yepez, and the Foundation for Inner Peace (Mill Valley, CA) to quote from *A Course in Miracles*.

Deep gratitude to long-term monastic associates and ecumenical friends in the Anglican Order of the Holy Cross and Sisters of St. Helena, especially Father Roy Parker and Sister Ellen Stephen, and Sister Edith Raphael of the Sisters of St Mary; also, old friends in interfaith work during the stormy years of monastic renewal and early ecumenism, James Parks Morton, Ninian Smart, M. Darroll Bryant, David S. C. Kim, Sebastian Matczak, Herbert Richardson, Rachel Spang, Shawn Byrne, Traudl Bachman, Kevin Brabazon, and Bruce Casino; Dorset Graves for his very early introductions to Eastern spirituality and the poetry of Wallace Stevens, and to poet friends Lucien Stryk, William Stafford, Bill Witt, Norman Macleod, Richard Rackstraw, and Norman Holmes Pearson of the Yale Collection of American Literature for pursuing these discussions over the years and collecting letters.

In science, special thanks to mentors in the professional sciences of evolution, ecology, systematics, and comparative biology (too numerous to mention), but especially major professors and scientific mentors at Wisconsin, Iowa, and the Graduate Center of the City University of New York: John C. Downey, Charles A. Long, and Frederick H. Rindge. Thanks to the administration and staff of the American Museum of Natural History and the McGuire Center for tropical biology and Florida Collection of Arthropods at the University of Florida for years of productive collegiality. To those who supported the important work developed around the consciousness and science of Vladimir Nabokov, including Dmitri Nabokov, Brian Boyd, Don Johnson, Stephen Blackwell, Dieter Zimmer, Steve Coates and, at Harvard's museum and DNA labs, Stephen Jay Gould, and Naomi Pierce; to Maurizio and Zaya Banazzo for their innovating conferences on Science and Nonduality.

Kurt Johnson
David Robert Ord

1

The Horizon

"A house divided against itself cannot stand"

Abraham Lincoln, quoting Mark 3:25

THE DAWN OF THE THIRD MILLENNIUM PRESENTED HUMANKIND WITH a dilemma. Will the skill that has characterized our species and propelled its development continue to sustain us, or will competition for power and resources lead to escalating conflict and our eventual extinction?

The seriousness of the situation facing us is symbolized by the attack on the World Trade Center in 2001, carried out by a well-organized group trumpeting an extreme religious ideology. The event triggered a wave of conflict in which millions of adherents of one religious and cultural identity have been pitted against another. The calamitous events of 9/11 deepened a long history of intercultural and interreligious distrust, misunderstanding, and even outright hatred.

By the start of the second decade of the millennium, the global financial industry—absent any sense of accountability to the collective—capped an unsustainable cycle of greed and corruption, leaving the world's economies close to financial collapse. Only the governments these commercial establishments appear to control prevented a disaster. The earnings of ordinary citizens were subsequently hijacked to bail out the perpetrators, none of whom were held accountable, thus buying time instead of enacting substantial change, not to mention increasing the disparity of the world's haves and have-nots.

With the arrival of this Third Millennium, something else also began to crest. Throughout the Middle East, millions took to the streets—their only venue of enfranchisement in their cultures—demanding fundamental rights. By 2012 the demand for equitable sharing of resources had spread planet-wide. Forming a counterclaim on the world financial process, it sought to reverse consolidation of wealth in the hands of a few—a phenomenon that had been proceeding apace for at least a half century. The message was for everyone: what has been transpiring is simply unsustainable.

These eruptions parallel a wave that crested in the 18th century. After hundreds of years of unbridled monarchy and totalitarianism, there dawned a universal recognition of the self-evident rights of individuals. Sweeping through the 19th and 20th centuries, this tide of realization either removed monarchies or rendered them principally ceremonial.

Today we are witnessing a fresh eruption of self-evident truths, this time centered on what sharing implies within a community, with implications for access to resources.

As disconcerting as the current wave of social eruptions may be, such eruptions are to be expected in the context of our longer history. By at least the 18th century, with the rise of an evolutionary view of the world, humans had come to realize that our level of consciousness, self-awareness, and intelligence distinguished us from other species—most notably our ability to problem-solve by identifying the relationship of cause and effect. This ability separated us from Earth's other creatures, allowing us to out-compete all our competitors and extend our civilization to nearly every corner of the planet.

As we face an array of new challenges, the same conscious potential that enabled us to fashion spears and arrowheads, master fire, and transform grunts and gestures into language stands ready to serve us as it did in primordial times.

An Uptick in Consciousness

Until recently the insights that can enable us to remake ourselves in the face of our present challenges remained the domain of academics and think tanks. The other 7 billion of us on this planet continued to just "keep on living," in extremes ranging from subsistence in poverty on the one hand to engaging in rampant consumerism and a culture of waste on the other. Overall, the masses had no reason to concern themselves with the planet's larger problems. This is what has begun to change.

Some 13.75 billion years of development have followed the birth of the cosmos in the Big Bang. On our little way station in the Milky Way, planet Earth began its own journey some 4.45 billion years ago, with life arising around 3.8 billion years ago to challenge the eternal ticking down inherent in the universe's physical properties.

At just the right distance from our star the Sun, with the ideal size and mass, and protected from most space debris by the gravity of the gas giant Jupiter, we have enjoyed 60 million unimpeded years of evolution since the last major asteroid collision that wiped out the dinosaurs and permitted the emergence of our species. However, only in the last 10,000 years have we witnessed the arising of what we call "civilization"—the crucible in which all of our present challenges are unfolding.

The uptick in consciousness on our planet at this moment is happening irrespective of station or calling. The masses are feeling things they can barely articulate. Two years ago, in the streets of first Tunisia, then Egypt, people were willing to die for a dream they had only begun to glimpse. In Cairo's Tahrir Square, Christians and Moslems prayed together, using expressions such as "oneness" and "interconnectedness."

While these uprisings didn't miraculously remove the realities of the political and economic regimes under which people lived, the resonance was identical to that generated by expressions such as "freedom" and "human dignity" during the Renaissance of the 14th and 15th centuries—and again when much of the world turned from centuries of monarchy to experiments in democracy a few centuries later.

By 2011, beginning in New York and spreading globally, a new banner had been planted in the streets proclaiming "Occupy." Other street signs were emblazoned with terms such as "we," "us," "ours," and "collective." Again, this didn't immediately lessen the grip of institutions over the common person, but it points toward the arising of a new consciousness at the street level. That the Occupy movement racked up over half a billion entries on Google within a month of its inception is a reflection of this powerful current.

Let's not forget that we mammals, which today dominate the world, once were small, barely noticeable creatures scurrying around at the feet of the ruling dinosaurs. When realizations permeate the street, change is afoot, even if it may still be long coming. A new unity consciousness, a sense of the collective, of "we," is arising on the planet. What its structures and cultures will be is as yet anyone's guess.

The Arising Globalization and Multiculturalism

In tandem with the move toward the democratization of the world, we are witnessing a trend toward globalization and multiculturalism. Of the world's 7 billion people, at least 70% believe globalization is inevitable. Worldwide, more than 60% believe that mutual understanding and multiculturalism will be important to making this transition a smooth one for our planet.

The big question is whether the global era that's dawning will be kind to the world's masses or take the form of an economic tyranny, extending the unsustainable runaway consumerism that propels the wealth of just a few. Will it foster a climate of caring for the world's resources, or of profiteering under the rubric of "grow, grow, grow"? Unless there is a sense that we are a single people, we will undoubtedly end with a catastrophe in which not even the elite will be safe.

The issue is how to create a sense of identity larger than "my interests," "my nation," "my religion," "my ethnic group." A holistic world-centric view would be a tall order for much of the world. Yet terms such as "transnational," "transcultural," and "trans-traditional" are becoming the clarion calls of our generation.

Movements of oneness—of unity consciousness—are afoot in nearly every arena, from the protests in the streets to the emergence of a new science and technology. The quantum world, string theory, and now M-theory in physics are introducing us to a "vibratory" view of reality. A cosmology of potential multiverses and additional dimensions is also being proposed. With the heralded discovery of the universal Higgs-Boson energy field announced by physicists in 2012, science may be closer to understanding how "things" manifest "out of nothing." New frontiers open before us that are immensely creative and promising, offering a vision of a world in which humanity's capacity for self-consciousness is explored for the benefit of all, including the planet itself.

Religion and Spirituality

Although many of us tend to think of religion and spirituality in terms of what we know of churches, synagogues, temples, mosques, and ashrams, anthropologically the panorama of religion and spirituality represents the accumulated narratives of our species' long epochs of development.

That one or another of these narratives is regarded by many as uniquely true is to be expected and perfectly natural, given that such narratives are subjective to the populations in which they have been handed down through millennia. This accounts for the self-satisfying feeling of possessing absolute truth as in the case, for instance, of the 9/11 suicide pilots as they plunged their hundreds of hapless victims into their targets.

Such narratives are anchored in a lens through which we all to some degree look, which we will refer to as magic-mythic. Having been part of who we are from the time of our hunter-gathering era, this lens originates in a world forgotten but still very much alive in our subconscious. The mindset of primeval peoples who communed with nature spirits and ancestors still compels us, which is part of the attraction of stories such as Harry Potter, Star Wars, Star Trek, Lord of the Rings, and Narnia.

Today this lens abuts and impinges upon a different lens, one that emerged some six centuries ago: the scientific lens of the rational, testable, and verifiable. This more recent lens, which is the world of science and technology, has served us well, in many cases affording us improved health and wellbeing, not to mention greater comfort.

Simultaneously, the scientific lens has sometimes robbed us of the deeper world of wonder, including a sense of the magical, instead of skillfully integrating the two worlds so that both might enrich us, since each is fundamental to our makeup and hence to our potential.

It's also important to recognize that spirituality and religion, often confused, aren't the same. Spirituality differs from religion in its sense of unconditional value that's unaffected by circumstances. In spirituality, seen through the heart's unconditional lens, God is one.

Although historically the offspring of spirituality, religion is more focused on whose view of reality is correct. In religion, God isn't one. This is the antithesis of a prescription for a world that is both good and concerned for the interests and wellbeing of every creature.

However, as the millennium turned, a vision of *interspirituality* was emerging from within the world's religions. The result of the inner exploration of contemplatives, meditators, and mystics, along with those who seek to foster the advancement of their fellow humans, the vision draws on the commonality embedded in nearly all the world's Great Wisdom Traditions, both religious and spiritual.

As those who seeded the vision began talking to each other across continents and oceans, and between traditions and cultures, they discerned that their experience, though hugely diverse, was ultimately much the same. All shared a sense of profound interconnectedness, oneness, and a unity that transcended the boundaries of their theological traditions, cultural backgrounds, and historical narratives.

The commonality came as a surprise—and yet not a surprise, given that science and technology were also heading in the same direction. A new unity was emerging among the scientific disciplines, epitomized by the new physics and reflected in new modalities in the philosophy of science and the emerging integral theories of the interrelationship of *everything*.

As if serving as a harbinger of what was to come, the first book to clearly identify this trend and name it "interspirituality" appeared in 1999, at the cusp of the new millennium. As doors were opening worldwide and millions were stepping into the streets to imagine a new world, the stage had been set for a global dialogue.

The Journey

The word "interspirituality" was nonexistent until it was coined in 1999 by a Roman Catholic lay monk and pioneer interfaith leader, Brother Wayne Teasdale, in a book aptly entitled _The Mystic Heart: Discovering a Universal Spirituality in the World's Religions_. By 2004, when Brother Teasdale and colleagues introduced the perspective at the Parliament of the World's Religions in Barcelona, Spain, the term was still hardly known. Yet today an internet search for "interspirituality" or "interspiritual" calls up over 100,000 hits.

It's obvious to many that interspirituality—a more universal experience of the world's religions, emphasizing shared experiences of heart and unity consciousness—represents part of the world's ongoing movement toward globalization and multiculturalism. It can be seen as an inevitable response to globalization—be it welcomed, as in the case of advocates of an unfolding world culture and planetary economic system, or pushed back against by religious fundamentalists and parochialists of all kinds, including terrorists.[1]

Brother Teasdale predicted that interspirituality would become the global spiritual view of our era:

> The real religion of humankind can be said to be spirituality itself, because mystical spirituality is the origin of all the world religions. If this is so, and we believe it is, we might also say that interspirituality—the sharing of ultimate experiences across traditions—is the religion of the third millennium.

[1] Surveys show that it's difficult to measure how many people worldwide hold uncompromising fundamentalist viewpoints. This is because about 50% of those polled believe in only one religion and think they are right, while the other 50% view dedication to one religion as a potential social danger (Gallup, Pew 2005/2007).

> Interspirituality is the foundation that can prepare the way for a planet-wide enlightened culture, and a continuing community among the religions that is substantial, vital, and creative.[2]

Today there are parallel discussions concerning globalization in all fields of human discourse, whether governance, economics, science, or sociology. Since all are interrelated, it's important we share some basic understanding of the many threads that are part of this unfolding. All stem from the fundamental basis of consciousness itself: the ability to recognize the relationship of cause and effect. There is a rather universal perception that many things are not well with the planet right now, leading to the question of what actions—indeed, what major shifts—might set matters right.

One of the goals of this book is to examine the roles of religion and spirituality in the globalization process in light of this wider international discussion. Such a mandate requires attention to many fields simultaneously, encompassing our current knowledge of cosmology, the breadth of scientific knowledge and consciousness studies, the fields of sociology, politics, history, and economics, and even pertinent statistics about what the world's citizenry (the pivotal "person on the street") actually believes about the world in terms of why we are here and where we may be going.

Our hope is to place the vision of an emerging interspirituality in a wider international and cosmopolitan context for the first time. While such an understanding is important to the overall characterization of globalization and multiculturalism itself, it's also important to discerning whether the trend toward interspirituality is real and what it may imply for the future of religion and spirituality. Plus, it provides the first opportunity since 1999 to examine interspirituality, as identified by Brother Teasdale, as a phenomenon in itself.

We particularly wish to explore the experiential aspects of interspirituality. Not only may it change your life in a personal way; it may do so as part of the unfolding planetary trend toward globalization.

---

[2] *The Mystic Heart* [hereafter, "MH"] p 26; quotations from the book *The Mystic Heart* (copyright 1999 by Wayne Teasdale) reprinted with permission of New World Library, Novato, CA. www.newworldlibrary.com; see Teasdale, W. 1999 in Bibliography.

What is Interspirituality?

When one looks with what the early French aviator and author Antoine de Saint-Exupery referred to as "the eyes of the heart," one's vision is tempered with understanding, love, and compassion for one's fellow creatures. One sees the absolute value, which we might refer to as divinity, of everything.

In other words, one looks beyond categories—deeper than labels such as Christian, Jew, Muslim, Buddhist, black, white, gay, straight. Saints, sages, and heroes across the centuries have always understood that seeing with the eyes of the heart allows the greatest potential for understanding, thereby fostering unity consciousness.

Interspirituality is the natural discussion among human beings about what we are experiencing. In academic terms, it's the intersubjective discussion among us all about who we are, why we are here, and where we are going. In the context of religion, interspirituality is the common heritage of humankind's spiritual wisdom and the sharing of wisdom resources across traditions. In terms of our developing human consciousness, interspirituality is the movement of all these discussions toward the experience of profound interconnectedness, unity consciousness, and oneness.

A more heartfelt and experiential definition focuses on the deepest implications of these phrases, rolling them into a statement such as "a spirituality so based on the heart and unconditional love that it would be impossible to feel separate from anything." This definition has profound ethical implications.

The recognition of interspirtuality as recorded in *The Mystic Heart* was the result of the world's religious and spiritual leaders talking to each other, a discussion long overdue. In a very real way, interspirituality represents the culmination of years of international interfaith and ecumenical exchanges centered on the recognition of a common experience within all spiritual traditions—a sense of profound interconnectedness, and what this implies for how humans should behave both individually and collectively. This recognition is in no way divorced from the universal sense of unity that underpins the world's advance toward globalization and multiculturalism. There is a growing appreciation of the value of the world's religions talking to each other. In fact, a recent poll indicated that 80% of Americans felt it was important.[3]

The central challenge of the interspiritual experience is whether doctrinal and theological differences, which have traditionally pitted religious traditions against one another, can be considered secondary—or even left behind—in favor of an emphasis on the common understanding of love, service, and ethics that underpins all religions. This is a tall order, on a par with whether nationalistic allegiances, with their tendency toward competition and conflict ("fighting for your flag"), might fade, to be gradually replaced by an authentic world-centric holism.

Hope may be drawn from the fact that spiritual leaders in all the world's religious traditions point to interspirituality as the deepest of all spiritual exploration, testifying experientially to a sense of profound interconnectedness and oneness. They also claim this experience ultimately renders secondary the importance of beliefs, creeds, and theologies. It is enough, they say, to truly discover and live in loving recognition of one another.

Thus the leaders at the heart of interspirituality challenge adherents to traditions worldwide to step up to this new understanding of religion and spirituality—a frontier not unlike the ideals of true economic egalitarianism, the abandonment of militant nationalism, nuclear disarmament, and other ethical gold standards advanced by the secular voices of globalization and multiculturalism. They are the ideals that propel the defining edge of human development. Although they could be considered utopian, the question is: how high are we willing to raise our bar?

Differences

Central to globalization is the fact that our two primary ways of knowing—the external explorations of science and the internal explorations of religion and spirituality—don't as yet agree much about

---

[3] PRRI/RNS Religion News, 2011.

reality. There are important crossovers between these distinctive ways of knowing, most of which are relatively new and part of the arising globalization process itself. There has also been a long-term trend toward holism. Again, such trends are only now coming to fruition in this time of globalization.

The diversity of social structures and belief systems on planet Earth is astounding. Central to the current planetary dynamic is the reality that the world's major cultures, whether defined by political systems or religious foundations, often don't agree about basic aspects of day-to-day reality. This is mostly because each is also struggling to balance the historical elements of its religious or political heritages with the scientific and technological advances of its particular region.

On the surface, at the level of creeds and apocalyptic predictions, the various traditions appear to have little in common, so that even their everyday religious practices fundamentally differ. But with the advent of international communication systems, we have become acutely aware not only of the startling diversity in the views of the citizenries of individual nations, but also of striking similarities among citizens across all kinds of national and ethnic boundaries. This reflects a world in transition from ethnocentric identities to a world-centric identity.

Those religions steeped in creeds and theologies tend to offer a primarily magic-mythic narrative of reality. This is only natural given the ancient underpinnings of human consciousness and the social structures that arose to reflect these. Many of the historic religious narratives provide a cast of celestial characters, governances, and systems of reward and punishment that lay claim to entire populations' belief in absolute truth. This is one kind of religion. There are also religions that explore consciousness and its relationship to the pursuit of love and high ethical ideals, but that provide no narratives of celestial characters or end-time scenarios. There are of course mixings of these two general modalities.

It's important to remember that religion and spirituality are far from identical, as is apparent from the statistic that more than a third of the world's population define themselves as "spiritual but not religious."[4] In general, the tendency of religion is to value creed over deed, whereas the tendency of spirituality is to emphasize deed over creed. This is a conundrum.

Part of the dynamic of today's globalization is the fact that the person on the street often subscribes to ideas that are entirely different from either their region's science or their local religiously based culture. One of the biggest surprises in preparing this book has been to learn from opinion polls that what would seem to have been proven by science or claimed by various religions holds little sway among the world's citizens. This has been a startling revelation. The implications can be seen in the eruptions of fresh thought that have characterized the beginning of this millennium—from the Arab Spring to the Occupy Wall Street movement. In such movements we are receiving a glimpse with new gravitas of what might be possible for our species.

Why Humans Disagree

While myriads worldwide can agree on common patterns we all observe, we tend to differ greatly about what accounts for these patterns. Most of the differences in our views of reality, including those that have led to wars, boil down to how successfully we are able to link an effect with a cause. Discerning the process that has accounted for a pattern should be the goal not only of science but also of common sense. The crises we face on the planet today differ only in complexity and degree from the challenges that faced our cave-dwelling ancestors. If spear or arrow tips were designed to kill game, and a certain tip didn't penetrate a creature sufficiently, an appropriate change was made to the fashioning of the tip—a change on which the survival of the tribe depended.

The right diagnosis is key to arriving at solutions. In seeking the cause, our point of entry is crucial, for the lens through which we view the problem will influence what we see, especially in cultural and religious terms. As an example, the 14th century person viewed the great plague of that century—the Black Death—either as God's

---

4 PRRI/RNS Religion News, 2011.

wrath (the magic-mythic lens) or as caused by a germ (the rational scientific lens). Today we are still navigating between these two lenses as we move into the current millennium.

The capacity we most need, which is the ability to investigate issues from multiple perspectives, is the capacity we often most lack. Yet the ability to diagnose from a variety of perspectives would prove one of the greatest boons for the successful advancement of globalization and multiculturalism.

The international debate centered on biological evolution versus theistic creation is a classic example. While all can agree that *Homo sapiens* is a mammal, we differ on the process that accounts for this—biological evolution, creationism, or a blend of the two.

Another example is experiences in consciousness. Historically, many have reported seeing visions of Jesus, Mary, Buddha, and a variety of religious figures. Others report seeing pink elephants after long bouts of drinking or while taking drugs. Depending on who you consult, you'll either be told these are *all* visual hallucinations, or hallucinations in the case of pink elephants but not the religious figures.

In reviewing the relatively new field of consciousness studies, it turns out that most findings are still based on asking individuals what they experience, then extrapolating from there. The diversity in this is astounding. The question is how we will move toward a global holism, given the confusion and disagreement.

The dilemma is no different in global problem solving. Although the rational scientific paradigm proclaims itself capable of solving the world's immense challenges, problems continue to spiral out of control. Nevertheless, the rationalist establishment is hard-pressed to agree with the spiritual traditions that what's needed is a post-rational conversation combining the fruits of the scientific (external) and spiritual (internal) ways of "knowing." The rational establishment often identifies the claims of spirituality in terms of "inner knowing" as superstition belonging to the pre-rational, and there is no further progress.

We can agree with the rationalist position that for most of human history, humankind has viewed reality through a magic-mythic lens that in so many ways has stymied progress and led to conflict instead of moving our species forward on the path of consciousness. This lens still commands most of the world's artistic and entertainment modalities, as witnessed by our bestselling superheroes and sagas, from Superman to Star Wars and Harry Potter.

When the strictly rational lens developed, it became just as deeply entrenched as the magic-mythic, so that over time the two ways of knowing separated into two conflicting cultures that are at total loggerheads in their understanding of reality and their resulting public policies.

What is trying to arise now in the world globalization process is an integrative or holistic lens that combines the best aspects of both of its precursors. Yet the need for a new holistic discussion is still widely unacknowledged.

Healthy Change, Unhealthy Change

Every historical change contains the seeds of a positive or negative result, and history seems to have meandered between these extremes. This is especially the case for the person on the street, who has so often been the casualty of war. A revolution based on high ideals one day is hijacked the next day, sending the energy in a totally different direction—a phenomenon seen in the French and Russian revolutions, which were enveloped in tragedy. Even America's 9/11 moment of unity, when there was so much international goodwill toward the United States, was hijacked for political ends, resulting in greater division instead of a coming together.

Worldwide, humans individually and collectively long for change. We seek something truly new, even at the cost of great consequence, not excluding death. This desire for change is what's driving the phenomenon of the street protestor, chosen as *Time* magazine's 2011 Person of the Year. What this new reality would be is far from clear, its precise structures undefined, requiring well thought-out solutions. Currently this global movement exists on the edge of a precipice, sustained only by a sense that something new is trying to arise from some deep gravitas erupting in our species collectively.

The interspiritual trend emerging as part of globalization and multiculturalism is born of incremental steps from interfaith and ecumenical exchange, raising the potential of a trans-traditional experience of spirituality. However, this trend could still have variously fruitful results. Just as economic globalization could result not in a growing egalitarianism but in a shift of most of the wealth to relatively few (which currently seems to be the case), religious globalization could take a pathological turn and result in a dangerous faceoff between conflicting views of reality and the societies that foster them.

However, if interspirituality could take root in a heart-based experiential discovery of the "universal spirituality within the world's religions"—the claim of Brother Teasdale—this could be a momentous positive. It could make religion an asset for humanity's future and not the liability it has so often proven to be.

③ Three doomsday scenarios currently confront our species: being 1. wiped out by wars based on religious allegiance, 2. wiped out by wars based on national allegiance, or wiped out by the 3. polluting and warming of our planet to the point that it becomes unlivable. How religious experience plays out in the world is linked to all of these.

2

The Modern Discussion

"A universal theology is impossible.
But a universal experience is not
only possible, but necessary!"

A Course in Miracles

IF THERE IS AN EMERGING INTERSPIRITUAL AGE, AS BROTHER TEASDALE suggested, it will be in the context of a religious and spiritual discussion that can't be separated from the secular, non-religious discussion. It also can't be separated from the worldwide academic developmental discussion about whether there are identifiable historical trends that suggest where our future may be headed.

Neither can the religious and spiritual discussion be separated from cosmology and what it tells us about our origin, the arising of the human brain, and the nature of consciousness. Given that all of these are inextricably interrelated, a comprehensive understanding spanning the time from our cosmic origin to the current complex difficulties that face our species is essential.

To have such a discussion, we are required to embrace all of the emergent threads that are relevant today: the evolutionary consciousness

SCIENCE
ALL FACETS

AND ADVANCES...

movement, the outgrowths of the developmentalist[5] movement (Integral theory and Spiral Dynamics), the scientific debates on the new physics and the search for a workable modern metaphysic, and the implications of the grassroots revolution in social movements,[6] and see where an emerging interspirituality might play a pivotal role.

The Essence of Interspirituality Isn't New

Interspirituality itself isn't new—just as evolution wasn't new when its great synthesizer, Charles Darwin, changed history by popularizing the phrase "evolution by means of natural selection." Darwin's synthesis had many precursors, combining at least a half dozen earlier hypotheses and drawing on the ideas of many, from the great Swiss scientist Augustin de Candolle (who cast it all as "Nature's War") to Alfred Russell Wallace (with whom Darwin shared the announcement at the Linnaean Society in 1858). In any event, what followed was a global gamechanger.

Brother Teasdale's naming of interspirituality was preceded by a host of earlier visionaries and leaders in all the world's religious and spiritual traditions. Interestingly, the names on this roster aren't the same as the names of the founders of the great religions, which all arose in what has become known as the Axial Age, the period from 800–200 BCE.

The forerunners of interspirituality were visionaries who realized that a common experiential thread underpins all spiritual experience and is the harbinger of an eventual "great coming together." As Brother Wayne Teasdale wrote in 1999:

> We are at the dawn of a new consciousness, a radically fresh approach to our life as the human family in a fragile world. This journey is what spirituality is really about. We are not

---

[5] "Developmentalist movement" refers to Integral theory (Ken Wilber) and Spiral Dynamics (Don Beck and Chris Cowan). As can be seen in Appendix I, Integral uses colors for the various periods of development so that representative institutions and behaviors can readily be discussed ("red behaviors," "amber institutions," etc.). Some colors originating with the Spiral Dynamics historical scheme were altered later by Integral to provide a closer relationship to the actual color spectrum and levels of developing consciousness.

[6] Detailed in Paul Hawken's *Blessed Unrest* (2007).

meant to remain just where we are. We cannot depend on our culture either to guide and support us in our quest. We must do the hard work of clarification together ourselves.

This revolution will be the task of the Interspiritual Age. The necessary shifts in consciousness require a new approach to spirituality that transcends past religious cultures of fragmentation and isolation. We need to understand, to really grasp at an elemental level that the definitive revolution is the spiritual awakening of humankind."[7]

Teasdale recognized that this emerging paradigm would need to embrace all of humanity's experience, knowledge, and capacities, including the intellect and deep subjective experience. It would need to make available to the world, at last, all of the fruits of the millennia of inquiry and discovery. It was a sweeping vision, and Teasdale's book, with a Foreword by His Holiness the Dalai Lama, was an instant success.

The Mystic Heart

How do we account for such a burgeoning phenomenon? Dr José Argüelles, author of *The Transformative Vision: Reflections on the Nature and History of Human Expression,* writes that subjective visionaries are people ahead of their time who cognize reality. Later the truth of their vision is recognized ("re-cognized") by the wider world.

Convinced that the primary vector of our species' ultimate spiritual and ethical development wasn't any one of the world's countless spiritual paths, but the shared direction of all of them, Teasdale coined the words "interspirituality" and "intermysticism" and put forward the view that their historical development has been a single experience on behalf of all humankind—an unfolding existential convergence continuing to this day and defining an aspect of the maturation of our species. After the publication of his books, he worked tirelessly to initiate institutions and structures that could support this historic anthropological recognition concerning human development.

As with all humans, Brother Teasdale was influenced by the social circumstances and assumptions of his day. The world's interreligious

---

[7] Words from Brother Wayne Teasdale's *The Mystic Heart* (p. 4 forward) read at the founding of the Universal Order of Sannyasa, January 9, 2010 (http://www.orderofsannyasa.org/joinus.htm).

and ecumenical discussions were then in relative infancy, peopled by pioneers from the ecclesiastical ranks of the world's religions. Ultimately living as a solitary lay monk under the auspices of the Roman Catholic Diocese of Chicago, Brother Teasdale explored the contemplative environments of monastic settings across a number of traditions both in the United States and India. Mentored closely by interfaith pioneers Father Bede Griffiths[8] in India and Father Thomas Keating of the American Cistercian order, he also became a close friend of His Holiness the Dalai Lama. Although the call of his writing is clear, its style and settings reflect an atmosphere unfamiliar to most outside certain Christian, Hindu, and Buddhist monastic circles. Brother Teasdale's *sannyasa* lifestyle as a religious renunciant—replete with the wearing of monastic robes and use of other ecclesiastical formalities typical of the period—brought him into the circles of great religious contemplatives and mystics of his day. Paradoxically, this seemed to many to suggest that he was seeking out the very world his writings aimed to make obsolete. However, in *A Monk in the World* he envisioned a role for monastics in which they are completely engaged in the world, leading an interspiritual movement. Still, they were monastics nonetheless, and in that sense set apart.

To those who knew him, Brother Teasdale's complete dedication to the trans-traditional contemplative life and its relationship to sacred service was obvious. In his everyday demeanor, he was extremely humble, never overawed or impressed by what he himself was experiencing or the vision he was putting forward, and often asked friends what these might mean. He had a keen sense of humor and was a jokester to the amusement of many of his friends. Even with the subsequent explosion of interspirituality, it's likely he would have continued his own monastic lifestyle had he lived. It's equally likely that had he entered the interfaith–interspiritual scene as it appears across the world today, he might have pioneered the many forms of experimental interspirituality that now eclipse the monastic setting. A "holy" man by whatever standard people have historically understood this

---

[8] Teasdale wrote on Griffith's interspiritual views for his theology doctorate at Fordham University in New York; see Teasdale, W. 2003 in Bibliography.

term, he had the ability to see the big picture—or what futurists call the "meta level."

Brother Teasdale wished to address head-on whether, through cooperation and co-creation, the diverse inner experiences and wisdom of our species would become a transformational asset for our future or a further source of competition and discord, contributing to our biological extinction. An outspoken and challenging voice, he insisted it would take great courage for members of any world religion or spiritual tradition to follow a more universal path. Nevertheless, he was convinced that this path is the destiny of all the world's religions.

This commitment undoubtedly explains his devotion to monasticism, because it appeared to him that only by living a sacrificial life, with full devotion to this interspiritual vision, could he advance his cause. He wanted to bring spirituality back to its experiential essence, most particularly those aspects that result in exemplary ethical and world-serving behavior. He believed that in the third millennium interspirituality and intermysticism would become the norm for humankind.

The Core of Deepest Spiritual Experience Is Always the Same

At the core of Brother Teasdale's vision was his conviction that a universal unity consciousness lies at the heart of all inner exploration. Since it arises naturally from all spiritual paths, he believed it would prove to be the great globalizer, bringing to a culmination the world's millennia of spiritual journeying.

Awareness of unity consciousness gained new impetus in the 20th century when it was at last possible for the first time in human history for mystics and contemplatives from the world's traditions to cross continents and oceans in a matter of hours to meet and discuss their experiences. Central to this discussion was the discovery that the core of the deepest spiritual experiences is always the same—unity consciousness. This profound experience of oneness turned out not to be a complicated phantasmagoric mystical occurrence involving bells, whistles, lights, and cosmic beings (although these can occur), but a life-changing experience of unity that seemed to arise from authentic inner inquiry. In the wake of the experience of profound interconnectedness, the sensation of separateness simply drops away.

Though the experience wasn't new, Brother Teasdale's ability to recognize that this experience is universal and could therefore be the basis for a new kind of dialogue among the world's religions was new. What he called the "interspiritual dialogue" might be capable of underpinning a new era of interreligious dialogue and religious harmony.

Historically, it was precisely the lack of this discussion that caused the world's religions, with all their competition, conflict, and bad behavior, not to be acknowledged as the Great Wisdom Traditions they claimed to be. But if the world's millennia of spiritual inquiry had essentially been a single existential journey aiming toward a convergence of what humans could be as elevated ethical beings, there was still a chance for religion to play this role. This was the message that rang like a clarion call from *The Mystic Heart*.

If this vision for religion is possible at all, it will be because the unitive type of consciousness becomes the norm in human experience. If this occurs, it may well be because, at least from the scientific view, the human brain is continuing to develop and, consistent with its long history, acquiring new skills.

Needed Shifts in Global Awareness

Brother Teasdale was also aware that changes going on in humans at the individual level needed to be reflected in the collective. In an imperiled world, where time might well be of the essence, some of these changes likely need to come to the collective quite directly. This is why Brother Teasdale emphasized the importance of simultaneous individual and collective interspiritual education. Not every individual might be able to access unity consciousness at this moment, but the challenge to the religions is to educate about their shared values and lofty ethical goals, not to emphasize their differences in terms of theologies, creeds, or apocalyptic scenarios.

Brother Teasdale pointed to needed fundamental shifts in global awareness, some of which were already arising:

- Appreciation of the interdependence of all realms of human life and the surrounding cosmos

- Growing ecological awareness, with recognition of the interdependence of humankind and the biosphere, including the rights of all biological species

- Dedication to nonviolence, with a commitment to transcend militancy and violence tied to national or religious identities

- Embracing of the shared wisdom in all the world's religious and spiritual traditions, past and present

- Growing friendship and actual community among the individual followers of the world's religious and spiritual paths

- Commitment to the depths of the contemplative pursuit and the mutual sharing of the fruits of this ongoing journey

- Creative cultivation of transnational, transcultural, trans-traditional, and world-centric understanding

- Receptivity to a cosmic vision, realizing humanity is only one life form and part of a larger community, the universe.

For Brother Teasdale these elements marked the threshold required for a healthy globalization and the participation of the world's religions through an unfolding Interspiritual Age.

A Final Marker

Brother Teasdale was a proponent of the experience commonly referred to as "nondualism," and for him unity consciousness refers to a nondual experience. The massively popular books by Eckhart Tolle, *The Power of Now* and *A New Earth*—the latter taught worldwide through the auspices of Oprah Winfrey—are similarly popular testaments to the nondual message.

In popular literature, nondual consciousness—Brother Teasdale's "unitive awareness"—is referred to by numerous terms and phrases such as awakened awareness, oneness awareness, enlightenment, and God- or Christ-consciousness. In the organized religions, it's equated with capitalized words referring to the divine nature, such as Spirit (Hinduism viz Sri Aurobindo), Brahman (Hinduism viz Shankara), God (the Abrahamic religions), Ein Sof (Judaism's Infinite Nothingness), Shunyata (Buddhism's Emptiness), The One (Greek viz Plotinus), The Self (Hindu Advaita Vedanta viz Ramana Maharshi), The Dao (Taoism viz Lao Tzu), The Absolute (German Idealism viz Schelling), The Nondual (British Idealism viz Bradley), and most recently The Totality (Integral and Systems philosophers).

We only include the above list to illustrate the rich ancient and modern heritage of this term. One could offer the following definition to satisfy all of the above contexts: Nondualism points to unity rather than duality or separateness, in the special sense that things can appear distinct while not being ultimately separate.

Because of the relationship between the search for unity consciousness and the earth's rapid globalization, today there are several arenas of human pursuit in which the nondual view of reality is central. Three of the most well known are quantum mechanics and string theory in the new physics, various areas of cognitive psychology, and the core unitive mystic experience described in all the world's Great Wisdom Traditions. This is important for our discussion of the dynamic kind of thinking that may best serve a global integrative age.

Historically, nondual experience has been more common in Eastern cultures than in the West. Abrahamic religions tend to be focused on a creator God who brought forth the creation, suggesting a dualism between the godhead (the Creator) and everything else (the creation). Much of 20th century Protestant theology, influenced by Karl Barth, focused on God as totally "other," one of several issues we'll be examining to understand dualism. In Western religions, nondual spiritual writing can be found but tends to represent a minority voice, coming from mystically inclined theologians like Meister Eckhart and poets like Rumi. Today the interest in nondual resources has dramatically increased in the West. Rumi, the Sufi poet of unity consciousness who lived a thousand years ago, is often cited as the most widely read poet in the West. The Centering Prayer Movement, based on the writings of Cistercian Fr Thomas Keating, is another example, along with popular books like Jay Michaelson's *Everything is God: The Radical Path of Nondual Judaism* and *The Naked Now* and *Everything Belongs* by Franciscan Fr Richard Rohr.

Equally important, nondualism isn't readily comprehended by the intellect, since intellect, speech, narrative, and so on, tend to be tools of separation, identifying things as this or that. Comprehending nondualism is essentially experiential. Intellectual approaches to it have, historically, been complicated and particularly thorny in relation to what philosophy refers to as monism on the one hand and existentialism on the other, or to monism and dualism as radically different explanations of reality.

When associated with nondualism, language is paradoxical—as in quantum mechanics or a Zen koan. In quantum mechanics, one can speak of apparently opposite phenomena not only happening simultaneously, but together providing a clearer metaphor for a deeper understanding of the holistic phenomenon taking place. The Zen koan (such as "what is the sound of one hand clapping?") also attempts to let the mind see wider phenomena in a holistic way.

Perhaps the easiest example to understand is our common use of the term "brain-mind," referring to how our brain and human intelligence work. We sense that brain and mind aren't the same. We also sense that whatever brain and mind are, their interrelatedness provides us with a feel for how our intelligence functions. The structure we know as the brain simply isn't, in and of itself, able to account for intelligence. There is also mind, which is a function of the brain's electrical fields. The two ideas together, woven in paradoxical language, give us a sense of what's actually going on. Brain-mind is one of the best examples of the paradoxical language that accompanies our understanding of the subtler realm of the nondual.

Nondualism isn't abstract. A practical example of nondual thinking on the street, pertinent to the age of globalization, appears in the side comments of an unidentified rock singer at the 2007 Live Earth concert: "I need to be simultaneously aware that, yes, I am an American or an Arab, and, yes, in that context there are appropriate things for me to do to keep that particular culture honored and whole. Yet I must also simultaneously know that I am absolutely no different at all from anyone else in the world."

Christians often recognize that Jesus' words are full of nondual allusions, of which there are many examples such as, "And now I am no more in the world, but they are in the world, and I am coming to thee. Holy Father, keep them in thy name, which thou hast given me, that they may be one, even as we are one."[9]

The enigmatic Parable of the Vineyard is often cited as reflecting Jesus' nondual conciousness. In this parable, why is the wage paid to the workers the same whether they have worked the whole day or just the final hour of the day? The nondual response would be because there's ultimately only a single consciousness.

It's probably no accident that some academic treatises on nondualism refer to Brother Teasdale's own mentor Father Bede Griffiths who, aside from his religious credentials, was widely respected as a western scholar and person of wide-ranging knowledge. One of these treatises by Bruno Barnhart, a scholar of the Camaldolese monastic order, contains the prediction that nonduality might engender a modern Christian renaissance. This was Brother Teasdale's vision.

Taking Wing

To launch our journey across the interspiritual landscape, we can summarize the heart of Brother Wayne Teasdale's vision thus:

- Human consciousness and heart have been evolving toward a maximum potential regarding the kind of being that humans can be and what kind of an earth we can create

- This has been going on since the known origin of the cosmos as material evolution and as evolution of consciousness

[9] John 17:11, Revised Standard Version.

- This is recognized in a fundamental tenant of the interspiritual vision, that the evolution of world religions has been one unfolding experience reflecting the gradual growth of human maturity

- This trend is anchored in the universally unfolding experience of "unity consciousness" or "awakening," the experience of profound interconnectedness, no separation, and the world of the heart

- This unity consciousness has been emerging through all the world's spiritual traditions

- Historically we have witnessed this unfolding in myriad identifiable threads in the world's philosophies and religions

- This unfolding has implications for how we develop our collective skills so that this consciousness can manifest in the world in tangible skill-sets working toward global transformation

- This has implications for the innumerable realms and arenas of endeavor, represented by all humanity.

If these interest you, in addition to continuing with us through the interspiritual journey of this book, take the time to read Brother Wayne Teasdale's three most influential books: *The Mystic Heart: Discovering a Universal Spirituality in the World's Religions*, *A Monk in the World*, and *Bede Griffiths: An Introduction to His Interspiritual Thought*.

Brother Teasdale spoke regularly about his developing vision with those who created the Interspiritual Dialogue association[10] along with him in 2001 (founded in New York City because of his interest in the United Nations). These discussions were particularly important during the last years of his life when, struggling with cancer, he was increasingly unable to write and speak publicly. The last meetings he participated in with the New York association were to plan a program introducing interspirituality and his vision of the Universal Order of Sannyasa at the 2004 Parliament of the World's Religions. Slated to be both host and keynote speaker, he was too ill to attend. After his transition in October 2004, friends and caregivers gathered for a tribute

---

[10] www.isdna.org.

in Austin, Texas, the site of many of his pioneer interfaith discussions with such figures as the Dalai Lama and Father Keating.

At Brother Teasdale's last meeting of the New York association in 2003, he described in detail what he called his Omega Vision. He himself was never able to write about it, though an account of this vision was published later by two of his friends, Gorakh Hayashi and Kurt Johnson in *Vision in Action,* the internet journal of integralist Yasuhiko Kimura. The essence of the Omega Vision captures Brother Teasdale's global interspiritual vision. It says simply: Omega (be that God, The Totality, or the highest spiritual knowledge of any spiritual tradition or individual) always exceeds the sum of all the experiences of it. If such a premise is accepted as the basis of all spiritual exploration, humans might be able to take a humble seat together on planet Earth. In his usual humor, Brother Teasdale said that night of the vision, "Maybe this means something; maybe it is the $E=mc^2$ of spirituality."

3

Everyone Is a Mystic

"We need to understand, to really grasp at an elemental level, that the definitive revolution is the spiritual awakening of humankind"

Wayne Teasdale

WHILE BROTHER TEASDALE EXPLORED MONASTIC MYSTICISM, IN THE early 1970s a promising graduate student felt called to leave first his medical studies, then his doctoral studies in biochemistry, to take up the search for a "theory of everything." As Brother Teasdale was convinced there was a common experience in the daily living of consciousness and love, Ken Wilber—and a host of eventual colleagues, such as Chris Cowan and Don Beck—searched for a common understanding of how human beings experience things and what this might mean for the future. Drawing on material from an academic movement that had arisen in the late 19th century called the "structuralists" or "developmentalists," these pioneers were inspired by the Darwinian revolution to apply the implications of development to wider concerns of humanity.

Not without stiff opposition from the academic establishment— often because they circumvented conventional peer review to get their ideas to the public—Wilber and his colleagues were to become pivotal figures in our current understanding of how consciousness, spirituality, science, and everything else may be interrelated. Wilber's first book *The Spectrum of Consciousness* was penned around 1973 but was rejected by twenty publishers, so that it didn't appear until 1977.

Pioneers like Wilber, Cowan, and Beck are sometimes considered either lucky to have eventually been heard or lauded for their perseverance against overwhelming odds. Such has often been the case. For instance, in the 1950s an isolated Venezuelan scientist, Léon Croizat (who was also writing only in Spanish!), was a biological champion of the generally scoffed-at theory of continental drift, known as plate tectonics. Like Wilber, he had left the scientific mainstream to make time to "read everything," subsequently coming up with his own synthesis. His critics referred to him as "idiosyncratic" and "from the lunatic fringe." Unable to publish his ideas through respectable channels, Croizat married a wealthy widow and turned to self-publication. Even more ironically, it wasn't until geophysics (not biology) proved plate tectonics to be correct a decade later that Croizat became an honored man (with his works finally translated into English).

The integralists took a gamble in choosing an independent path of exploration. Although still not viewed as authentic scholarship by some in the traditional academic establishment, their books appear today in 39 different languages.

This pursuit of a new view by Wilber and the integralists yielded many surprises. Wilber came to see that unity is even more deeply embedded in how humans understand reality than he expected, noting that all humans experience four simultaneous worlds.

A normal day for everyone in the world is a simple meeting with three of these worlds: "I" (individual), "We" (collective), and "It" (institutional), coupled with our attempt to make sense of them. Getting along with the institutional world (or "It") is the rub for just about everyone. But if you wrapped all the institutions together— everything that goes on from institutional structures themselves to ideas and belief systems—you got a fourth, even more potentially intimidating arena: "Its." How often do the bulk of our struggles come down to dealing with "Its"? Truly, it's a small world.

In further clarifying the implications of the worlds of "I", "We", "It," and "Its," the integralists were quick to realize that the familiarity humans have with "I", "We", "It", and "Its" derives from the way we have structured our languages. It's actually the way we think—what, in grammar, is called 1st person (I), 2nd person (You, We), and 3rd person (It). Wilber, Beck, and others realized that this world of relationships is expressed in every aspect of our complex existence.

The Everyday Reality of "I," "We," and "It"

An easy exercise allows us to see that there are three arenas in everyone's life. One can understand these experientially by thinking through the three following steps:

Step 1: Your individual or "I" space. Close your eyes and walk yourself through getting up in the morning. This is when you are completely by yourself, coming out of sleep, going into the bathroom to go through all the "wake-up and get going" chores. This is your solitary "I" bubble, which you will carry with you as you move through your day.

Step 2: Your collective or "We" space. Move your attention to the first people you meet each day. They may be your family, friends, people on public transport, or colleagues at work. Suddenly your "I" bubble expands as you enter your particular world of "We." Your "We" space is peopled with circles of individuals with whom you have a measure of intimacy or familiarity.

Step 3: The institutional or "It" space. Move your attention to the fact that when you go to work, to a store, or to the post office—in other words, when you engage in all the activities that connect you with the rest of the world—you become involved in an arena that's less personal or even impersonal. These less personal situations are most often the source of your instructions concerning what to do. You are told what to do at work, what to do by the IRS, what to do by your bank, what to do to get your driver's license. This is the institutional space, where you act as expected. It's the world of your church or political party, the ideas to which you subscribe, and the groups that represent them.

Step 4: Move your attention from your "I" space to your "We" space to your "It" or institutional space, getting a feeling for what your life is like. Then realize that every single one of the 7 billion people on this planet does this same thing every day. Their institutional or "It" space tells them what's true, what to believe, and how to behave. Take some time to imagine yourself in different countries and cultures. What's possible for you in terms of freedom and civil rights? What's okay or not okay in terms of books or entertainment? What political system is forced on you? What religious beliefs are you expected to hold? These dynamics confront you and your 7 billion fellow humans on a daily basis.

Steps 1-4 describe what's going on in the world—and everything that's been going on in the world for the 106.5 billion people who are estimated to have lived on this planet since humans emerged. Each of them has just been dealing with their "I," "We," and "It" spaces on a daily basis.

Throughout history, the trend has been for "I" and "We" to create an "It" space that then controls us. Have you ever realized to what degree the institutional or "It" space calls the shots in the world, telling the "I" and "We" that created this "It" space what to do?

In the "I" and "We" spaces, not only is life more personal with some sense of heart connection, but there is also accountability and responsibility. When we enter the myriad institutional settings that surround us—our job, the shopping center, the bank, our relationships with authorities ranging from the police to the IRS—we are in much less personal territory that's also less accountable to us and less responsible, feeling, or caring. Not only can such arenas be impersonal, they can also prove downright demanding, pushy, and even hostile. Yet it's these arenas that tell us how we should behave, what we should buy, and what we should believe.

Almost everything wrong with the world is the result of the way the institutional space is misaligned and out of control.

When was the last time your bank did you a favor? What was your opinion of the "no questions asked" multi-trillion dollar bailout of the financial industry? When you examine social structures anywhere in the world, the most obvious disconnect is between the needs and wants of the "I" and "We" that built the institutional space, and the way the institutional space behaves toward us.

The insensitivity of the institutional space varies from mostly tolerable in open, free societies such as democracies, to downright intolerable in dictatorships. This is the case not only in terms of political systems but also economies. Where do we see responsibility, let alone sensitivity, to the public in much of the economic establishment, such as banks and corporations? The unaccountability of the financial sector is brokered by a political establishment that's dramatically misaligned with the "I" and "We" who created these institutions.

As grassroots social change guru Paul Hawken pointed out in his bestseller *Blessed Unrest*, across the world goods have more rights than people. The health of goods and money are generally put ahead of the wellbeing of people. Value is measured by wealth and power, not by wisdom or contribution to the general good of the community.

How does a world headed toward globalization begin to correct this misalignment?

Fruits of the Integrative View

During the last two years of his life, Brother Teasdale engaged Ken Wilber closely. The last public discussion he took part in, against the advice of his doctors, was with Wilber.[11] It was natural that Brother Teasdale's understanding of interspirituality should connect with the views of the integralists. Indeed, he recognized that his own vision of a better future for humanity through interspirituality isn't only implied in the developmental view, but that interspirituality might need to adopt the integralist map of where the future may be going. Everyone needs a map. Whether driving down the highway, entering the subway, or going to Disney World, everything is easier when one has a map.

---

[11] The provocative discussions between Teasdale and Wilber, which can be viewed on YouTube, are characterized by their emphasis on the world's emerging unity consciousness and its relationship to a positive global future.

A major fruit of the integrative map is the exploration of common ground between science and religion—the external way of knowing and the internal way of knowing. As well as assisting us in elaborating the difference between religion and spirituality, this also predicts the nature of the consciousness that might be possible for our species.

How Religion and Spirituality Differ

It's often joked that religion is for people who are afraid of going to hell, whereas spirituality is for people who have been there. In everyday life, the distinction between religion and spirituality is mostly overlooked, especially by the media, which seems to seldom distinguish them—and thereby renders both a great disservice.

In the beginning, spiritual paths involve a founder or founders who deliver a compelling message that attracts a following. In terms of our integral map, this is a simple I-We dynamic, straightforward and interpersonal. It remains so until the founder either creates an institution or departs the scene. The followers who remain behind develop written records, directives, and creeds that define the institutional or "It" space. The vital experience of spirituality is thus subsumed in the institutional religion. This divergence becomes even more dramatic as the founder's life fades into the past. The question then becomes whether followers will seek to emulate the essence of the founder's life or focus on adherence to beliefs, creeds, dogmas, and rituals.

Adherence to the institution is often fostered by the threat of punishment or the promise of reward. Religions of this "ticket to heaven" variety stress belonging to the right group above one's personal behavior. Ultimately religion is about right belief, with the institution telling the individual how reality should be understood and placing the highest value on allegiance to this understanding. This is why religion tends to value creed over deed. Spirituality concerns right being and right action, which is why it tends to value deed over creed.

These explain why fundamentalism is usually connected to religion and not spirituality, since spirituality is inclusive and pluralistic. It's also easy to see how terrorism can be justified by religion but not by spirituality. Terrorism justified by religion reflects behavior from an early epoch of human development that linked religious belief with authoritarianism and placed a higher value on loyalty to the religious authority than on how people were treated.

The more deeply one pursues spirituality—the inquiry, values, and essence of any of the great founders of spiritual traditions—the more likely it is that one will experience profound interconnectedness and the dropping away of a sense of separation.

It's Ultimately the Same Experience

Picture a tree whose branches are all the religions and spiritual paths of the world. This illustration appeared in a chapter entitled "The Paths Are Many But the Goal is the Same" in Brother Teasdale's book *The Mystic Heart*.

The world's religions are often viewed horizontally, not vertically like a tree with its trunk and branches—as if the religions on Earth at the present time were the sum total of religions. This is akin to considering the plants and animals currently found in nature as the sum total of flora and fauna in the entire history of the planet, forgetting that all these organisms have histories as more primitive species, not to mention the countless extinct species that played a role in the evolution of life. Similarly, thousands of religions have come and gone.

The history of religions is a history of compelling narratives. We might liken these narratives to books, some of which are current bestsellers, some of which enjoyed a wide readership in the past, others of which were read by only a small number, and still others of which are out of print. Today there are five current "bestsellers" in terms of religious narratives: Hinduism, Buddhism, Judaism, Christianity, and Islam. Many lesser sellers are also current, such as Taoism, Confucianism, Shinto, the Sikh faith, Baha'i, Jainism, Babism, and the Latter Day Saints.

Brother Teasdale viewed the trunk, branches, and twigs of the tree of religion as part of a single existential human search that has been unfolding through our history as a species—a search that leads ultimately to our potential to manifest an interspiritual consciousness. He saw authentic awakening as the outcome of seeking along any of these branches. It was his firm belief that the world's religious experience has been one experience on behalf of our destiny as a species united in oneness. Hence it isn't a matter of picking which path is best, even though paths may have varying efficacy, but of realizing that the ultimate awakening is possible in any tradition. The same view is taken by the developmentalists.

The Mystical Pursuit

Brother Teasdale's statement that "everyone is a mystic" shouldn't come as a surprise. Writing in *The Mystic Heart*, he commented, "The real religion of humankind can be said to be spirituality itself, because mystical spirituality is the origin of all the world religions." He further stated, "How we make this journey is what spirituality is really about," adding, "There is nothing else in life more worth doing."[12]

The mystical pursuit is often associated solely with religion and spirituality. This is because the word "mystical" is often confused with "magical" in secular and scientific contexts, and thus easily dismissed. Fundamentally, mysticism involves the same kind of inquiry, the same kind of attention to direct experience, that permeates the everyday consciousness of all humans—particularly the pursuit of insight into how reality functions. It's the same inquiry that science engages in using a different set of tools. If we can say that mysticism is essentially the exploration of consciousness, we need only repeat the words of scientists such as James Watson (the co-discoverer of DNA), E. O. Wilson (the father of sociobiology), and David Gross (physicist and founding string theorist), who each assert that understanding consciousness is the next frontier for science.

The other essential element that connects everyone with the mystical pursuit is its relationship to ethics. Brother Teasdale states in *The Mystic Heart* that the mystical journey concerns the highest ethical

[12] MH, p 26, 18, 124.

understanding possible in this life. The elements he listed in that journey reflect the aspirations of all humans, no matter what their beliefs and background. These are the highest fruits of consciousness: will, creativity, feeling, character, imagination, and behavior. Brother Teasdale focused on universal aspirations such as wisdom, sensitivity, other-centeredness, acceptance of others as they are, self-transcendence, openness, presence, listening, being, seeing, spontaneity, and joy. Such aspirations characterize the foundational documents of our modern world, such as the Universal Declaration of Human Rights, the UN Charter, and the Earth Charter.

Humans are also united in their yearning for a constructive vision. Worldwide, polls on globalization indicate that on average 80% believe the world should be moving toward a global vision. Some 80% of those who believe this assert that basic skills of understanding and working together are necessary to achieve this objective.[13]

If the planet is ultimately seeking a comprehensive "theory of everything," as mathematician and cosmologist Roger Penrose believes, this pursuit is precisely that of mysticism—when mysticism is truly understood.

Reversing a Dangerous Course

Eckhart Tolle challenges in his bestseller *A New Earth*, "Our species now faces a stark choice: Evolve further our comprehensive and integral sense of interconnectedness, and our mutually shared sense of the inherent value of all humanity and planet earth which hosts us, or die."

The shared directions much of the world has taken so far for securing our future appear quite counterproductive. In fact our actions have bequeathed to us the problems that now threaten catastrophe.[14] This is why a holistic, unitive approach must emerge.

Globalization is inevitable, as leaders from Kofi Anan (former UN Secretary General) to Carlos Salinas de Gortari (economist and former

---

[13] FT & Harris polls, 2007; Yankelovich & Pew polls, 1998, 1999.
[14] A quick reread of our list of needed shifts in global awareness enumerates how this is the case. See page 56.

President of Mexico) and Jian Zemin (former General Secretary and President of China) have publically declared. World opinion polls show at least 70% of people believe the ramifications of ongoing globalization must be sorted out or we will face more serious consequences.[15]

On the positive side, a 1998 Yankelovich poll—the world's largest consumer and marketing research group—showed that 91% of the people in their international sample agreed that globalization means it's even more important for people to understand each other. A 1999 Pew poll found that 71% of Americans agreed that success in terms of cultural diversification can lead to a better life for all.

On the negative side, the same poll of six nations showed that an average of 50% or more in richer countries fear globalization because it may dilute their wealth. In the United States, this fear is higher in conservative, less ethnically diverse areas, with up to 64% expressing concern about globalization and multiculturalism. On the other hand, an average of 63% in poorer countries[16] embrace globalization, hoping it will ensure they receive their piece of the pie.

Experts throughout the world debate what globalization itself will produce. Will it mean westernization, Americanization, capitalization? Will it bring rampant materialism and consumerism? If so, are such results sustainable?

Nearly all futurists and social scientists are emphatic that a successful future can only be achieved if there are multiple points of analysis and feedback. The debilitating legacy of the Iraq War for America's financial health reveals the fallacy of making decisions based on faulty information. Our future direction as a world must either involve moving decision making to where accurate information can be found, or moving information to where the decision making is taking place.

This is generally not the world we live in today. Few decisions are based on multiple points of view. Most measures of nearly everything revolve around gross domestic product, currency values, economic

---

[15] Poll for United States, Germany, France, Italy, Spain, Britain (FT/Harris Poll, 2007).
[16] Egypt, Turkey, Azerbaijan, Iran, Indonesia, Nigeria, and the Palestinian Territories (University of Maryland, International Policy Program at WorldPublicOpinion.org).

growth, and the number of millionaires and billionaires. Only one nation in the world, the tiny country of Bhutan, includes a measure of "human happiness" in its evaluation of national life.

The situation is even more precarious if, as so many sense, the world financial establishment essentially rigged the "world financial casino." It's well known that wealth and financial power have shifted into the hands of a tiny minority, perhaps as few as one percent of the world's population, essentially disenfranchising everyone else. The system, which is mostly beyond the jurisdiction of the world's governments and collective regulatory institutions, is in the hands of an elite minority who have no sense of a world collective. Propelled by completely Darwinian views of survival of the fittest, their mentality is one of "take no prisoners" and "give nothing back."

Aligned with or in collusion with governments and world leaders who are controlled by the elite's wealth, or at least under the influence of countless paid lobbyists (if not subject to out-and-out bribery), the "too big to fail" expect their downside risk to be covered by the masses of average taxpayers who will be required to pay up when their greed has gone too far. With no sense of a collective, and living in the illusion that their world touches no other, they simply take again with no compunction to ever give back.

Even if this elite can't be touched, the system isn't sustainable, so that if it collapses across its entirety, it will take down the elite as well. We might liken it to the pesticide DDT, which wasn't banned until everyone understood it could cripple the entire planetary ecosystem. We have to ask what it will take to generate some sense of accountability to the collective in the financial industry, before the house of cards comes toppling down.

How did we get into this predicament of moving from the relative happiness and prosperity that followed World War II, to facing the many doomsday scenarios currently before us?

If we have been brought up to value exterior things more than the interior, we will clamor for external things and won't shrink from escalating competition into conflict to achieve our ends. Our sense of wellbeing will be bought at the expense of someone else's.

On the other hand, if we have been brought up to value our interior world more than exterior things, we will be happy with interior resources and have less need to compete for externals. Our sense of wellbeing will be intertwined with the wellbeing of others. Most of the moral codes stemming from the Great Wisdom Traditions have attempted to teach these values. While there has been an overall failure to achieve such ideals, our species has shown gradual improvement.

Although many of us hold high values in terms of "I" and "We," the degree of misalignment with and unaccountability to "I" and "We" on the part of the institutional "It" space threatens to lead us down a destructive path.

Centuries of the Materialistic and Mental

In recent centuries our species has gone through a major "mentalization," placing most of its eggs in the basket of intellectual and technological endeavor. As we modernized, we unwittingly moved away from our inner, more subjective nature, as modernism labeled much of our ancient subjectivity "superstition." This process has uprooted us from other elemental qualities in ourselves, resulting in a disconnect between individuals and institutions.

By placing an emphasis on the intellectual and material, we have created heartless institutional spaces. This is the source of paradoxes such as the fact we can put men on the moon but can't even get along in our own neighborhoods, while many with wealth or celebrity status are so unhappy that some even end up killing themselves.

Religions, instead of emphasizing the authentic elements of the spiritual and ethical journey, turned also to the mental, promulgating dogma and proffering rewards in an afterlife. Meanwhile the intellectual, academic, and scientific establishments satisfied themselves that the new skills of modernism were sufficient to secure a bright future. Consequently, despite a noble intent to improve our lives materially, we lost our balance—a situation that couldn't go on forever. A period of prosperity after the world wars ended abruptly in the 1960s and 70s, with the emergence of a string of menaces touching personal human happiness, political confrontation, environmental health, resource availability, energy issues, population stability, economic sustainability, and global governance.

No sooner did the good life seem to be within our grasp than the possibility of destroying ourselves presented itself. The bell tolled an end to living for the external only. When a life lived in exteriority implodes, the only hope is a creative stepping up from our interiority—our vast, largely untapped inner resources.

Of the world's top 100 economies, 51 aren't nations but corporations. Given this, it's easy to see why the need for fundamental adjustment puts the world of "I" and "We" in conflict with the "It" of these big corporations and financial institutions.

For a healthy world future, we needed to develop through these past centuries of materialism and exteriority. Undoubtedly they resulted in many wonderful improvements for humankind. But now there must be a readjustment, or the outcome will be catastrophic. As Brother Teasdale explained, "We need to understand, to really grasp at an elemental level, that the definitive revolution is the spiritual awakening of humankind. This revolution will be the task of the Interspiritual Age. The necessary shifts in consciousness require a new approach to spirituality that transcends past religious cultures of fragmentation and isolation." He added, "Taken together, they are preparing the way for a universal civilization, a civilization with a heart."[17]

This is the message of all the religious and secular futurists, from Wayne Teasdale to such luminaries as Eckhart Tolle, Ken Wilber, Don Beck, Willis Harman, and Paul Hawken.

[17] MH, p 12, 5.

4

Framing the Big Picture

"To the Creative, all things owe their beginning"

Lao Tzu, Chinese Philosopher

IN BUDDHISM'S AGGANCHCHA SUTRA, THE GREAT BRAHMA SETS EVERY-thing in motion. In Hinduism, the Day and Night of Brahma initiate lila—the divine play—in which Brahman transforms himself into the world. In the Abrahamic religions—Islam, Judaism, and Christianity—everything begins on a day without a yesterday, streaming forth from a singularity. Underlying the philosophies and metaphysics of these religions is a first cause.

For the myriad indigenous traditions, there appears also to be a common core. Everything is upheld by "the great mystery," and what we are made of is billions of years old.

Belief in a first cause is one thing. But when it comes to what happened as a result of the first cause, science and some fairly large segments of religion have parted company, especially when it comes to a discussion of our species' origin. Humanity is divided between widespread belief in creationism and the evolutionary view supported by modern rational inquiry. The implications of this disagreement are far-reaching, impacting human survival.

Process and Common Sense

All of us are familiar with process, which is in essence cause and effect. If we want to buy groceries, we make our way to the grocery store, pick out and purchase the groceries we need, then bring them home. Or we sit at our computer, go through the steps of ordering online, and someone brings our order to our door. What we can't do is snap our fingers and magically have the groceries appear in our kitchen.

None of us would disagree that buying groceries involves a process. Yet when it comes to how we got here in a biological sense, the gradual process known as "evolution" gets bad press among fundamentalists.

Curiously, current discoveries in the fields of chemistry and physics—both of which support evolutionary understanding—are more readily accepted. For instance, who has any difficulty with the notion that humans are made up of atoms and molecules? It's also widely accepted that when we consume the groceries for which we go through the process of shopping, they undergo the gradual process of digestion by which they are changed into forms that provide the body with sustenance. These are matters of such common sense that no poll has ever been taken on "who believes in atoms" or "who believes in digestion." Further, the synergy of atoms and molecules forming more complex combinations and hierarchies—evolution in the most general sense—is generally understood by the public.

Polls indicate that 41% of chemists and 40% of physicists have no problem with the idea of God,[18] while 40% of professional astronomers list a religious affiliation.[19] Physics and chemistry don't seem to be in conflict with religious belief, whereas the biology of evolution is a different matter. A 2011 Reuters poll ranked the United States 18th among countries that accept biological evolution. A Gallup poll conducted annually since 2007 reveals that only about 13% of Americans believe in naturalistic evolution in which a deity played no part, whereas 48% believe that a deity created "humans pretty

---

[18] *The Los Angeles Times.*
[19] The prestigious scientific journal *Nature.*

much in their present form at sometime in the last 10,000 years or so." A poll of strict creationists, numbering 48% of Americans, by The Skeptical Society indicated 95% think belief in God and science are incompatible.

Taking a middle road, 30% of those polled believe "humans developed over millions of years from less advanced forms of life, but God guided this process." Another 9% are unsure. The 78% who see God in the process stand in contrast to the 93% of trained biologists who reject any idea of creationism or its close ally, intelligent design. Note that pollsters didn't ask whether the God people believe in is a God within the system or acting from outside the system—two very different phenomena.

Science, which is humankind's most public way of collectively inquiring, evaluating, and developing a consensus about what's true, wins only mixed results with the public when it comes to culturally controversial issues. While virtually no one is able to magically snap their fingers and cause groceries to materialize in their kitchen, a large percentage of people are convinced that the 5-10 million species estimated to inhabit the earth got here with just that kind of magic. Perhaps nothing better illustrates the persistence of the magic-mythic viewpoint.

As expected, the Gallup poll also correlated anti-evolution sentiment with highly religious cultures that host significant fundamentalist populations. Several Islamic countries lead the list,[20] followed closely by the United States, while those favoring evolution include largely secular or atheistic regions such as Western Europe and China. India, whose Hindu religion favors stories of process, was solidly in the evolutionary camp, whereas Italy, the civilly conflicted home of Roman Catholicism, ranked high among those "unsure."

Of interest economically, public education prowess paralleled these results, with anti-evolution countries turning out to be less competitive in overall educational skills, especially technology, whereas pro-evolutionary societies were the most adept.

---

[20] However, academic Islam's view of evolution is quite positive.

The Two Cultures of Knowing

The root of this conflict over our origins is to be found in the different ways in which humans come to know things, both individually and at the cultural level. In philosophy this is the complex domain of epistemology, which is the study of knowledge. This is a realm that becomes even more specialized and multifaceted when science and philosophy consider how relationships between parts generate collective action, and how systems interact with the larger environment. Humanity and Earth are obviously such a system.

We can discern the truth of a matter from our uniquely personal ways of inquiring. We think of this as a subjective, inner way of knowing something. We can also discern the truth of a matter from our collective, public ways of inquiring, including science. This we think of as an observational, outer way of inquiring that's more objective.

If we return to the matter of grocery shopping, we can decide which groceries to buy by reading a list at a store or on our computer, then checking off the items we require. This can be a useful approach to stocking the larder. But when it comes to finding a romantic partner, although we might use internet sites to "match" us with someone initially, few of us are going to select such a partner solely by perusing a list of characteristics. In the end we want to fall in love. In other words, head-knowing and heart-knowing both have their place. Subjective and objective ways of knowing can also complement and inform each other, especially in matters of personal import.

There is of course a place for much deeper inquiry, of which our everyday level of experience is but a microcosm. The nature of science, religion, philosophy, the arts—all these can be inquired into at the level of the larger landscape, as indeed they have been investigated by such famous names as Kant, Spinoza, Goethe, Schelling, and Schiller (to speak only of the West). At the heart of the matter is the challenge of how humankind can plumb the depths of its subjective, inner reality (Kant's "secret springs of action"), coupling this with understanding provided by science (which must understand its limitations when it comes to the investigation of the nature of reality).

Our lives are governed every day by standards determined by the collective, public method of inquiring into matters and arriving at a consensus. Some such matters that immediately spring to mind are which side of the road to drive on, or the value of coins and bank notes. In a similar manner, we naturally trust the workings of science in such matters as the change given by the cash register at the grocery store or the bills dispensed by the ATM at the bank. If we need surgery, we obviously choose a doctor who has performed the needed operation successfully on other occasions, not someone who is a novice—let alone someone who has never attended medical school.

No one seems to have a problem with the consensus required in these areas of everyday life. Yet when it comes to evolution, and particularly the question of human origin, there's a disconnect. In the United States at least, we rely on DNA evidence in a trial, with 95% of us regarding it as conclusive.[21] Why then do 48% of us not accept that same DNA evidence of the relationships between various animals and plants?

This divide is particularly intriguing when it comes to what people are curious about. While 91% of atheists are college graduates[22], a recent survey inquiring of college students what questions they most want science to answer didn't include either the causes of cancer or AIDS.[23] Instead it included a list of more fanciful issues, such as the placebo effect, psychic powers, extrasensory perception, near death experiences, UFOs, deja vu, ghosts, mysterious disappearances, intuition and gut feelings, and persistent reports of unknown creatures such as Bigfoot, the Loch Ness monster, and aliens.

We can't underestimate the hold that subjective knowing exerts. A classic example was the Cargo Cults that arose in the South Pacific after local natives first observed planes and ships delivering cargo in World War II. On the basis of their culture's magic-mythic lens, islanders believed such objects were divined from the spirit world. Crowds therefore dressed up as soldiers, created crude airfields, hangars, and

---

[21] According to a CNN poll.
[22] Who's Who (ukwhoswho.com).
[23] science.com.

docks, and marched about singing and chanting, waiting for cargo to appear. When authorities tried to curtail the activity, it led to violence. People were willing to go to jail for their belief in magic cargo! Even odder, "cargo messiahs" arose. This is an extreme case, but it parallels the insight of interspirituality that it's completely natural for anyone having spiritual experiences to believe their insight is correct. The history of religious wars reflects the pathology that can develop from this simple fact.

Pattern Versus Process

While we don't think twice about stopping on red and going on green, understanding that it rained because gravity-prone droplets of water formed in the clouds, or knowing that oxygen enters and exits our lungs throughout the time we are asleep, the simple matter-of-fact realities of process become difficult when we try to determine what kind of process accounts for a certain pattern we observe.

The issue becomes even more complicated when we confuse the *pattern* with the *process* we use to explain it. For instance, if you planned to use the ATM machine during your trip to buy groceries and found it no longer there, you could imagine any number of reasons for this, ranging from the bank moving it, to thieves making off with it, or extraterrestrials visiting in a UFO and confiscating it for investigation.

Questions of human identity are especially complex. It's one thing to agree we are composed of atoms and molecules, but quite another to believe we share a common ancestor with apes. It becomes trickier still when the suggested relationship with apes, couched in terms of random competition and Darwin's "survival of the fittest," could be taken to mean that humans can no longer regard themselves as special, with our attendant fears of meaninglessness. Darwin was careful in his books and published letters to emphasize that his theory was concerned with cause and effect in the observable world, not with how life and the universe came into being.

Less sensitive to the issues than Darwin, the intellectually advanced often identify religious and spiritual experiences as primitive superstition, dismissing them out of hand—of course, all under the guise of critical thinking. Confusing pattern with process, a predetermined "why" often determines the explanation of "how."

We can't forget that the world's most recent collective paradigm shift came precisely from such a violent collision—the events and aftermath of September 11, 2001. The ensuing era has pitted radical allegiance to simplistic fundamentalist notions of process in the Third World against secular and eclectic views of process in the economically rich First World.

Public disagreement about what an observed pattern means comes down to the variety of explanations that can be chosen to account for such patterns. In the matter of evolution, an obvious example is the undisputed fact that millions of fossils have been found, if not a billion. Ways of accounting for such fossils might range from leftovers from the Genesis seven-day creation process, to a pattern of gradual change over millions of years. No one argues about whether T rex existed, only about whether such creatures lived at the same time as humans.

Crop circles are another provocative example of the difference between pattern and process. They're there to see, no doubt about it. But are they created by hoaxers, extraterrestrials, or some other phenomenon? The implications attached to the various processes that could explain the circles are huge.

There are also examples of pattern and process that lie somewhere in between when it comes to the question of "what's true." Try acupuncture. A therapeutic method legally licensed throughout much of the world, it's widely thought to work. However, the original medieval metaphysical explanation for its success was based on mythic elements of earth, air, fire, and water, which makes little sense by modern scientific standards. The result is a compromise, in that many scientists agree that it works and support the politics to license it for public use, while simultaneously seeking an understanding of the process behind it that's compatible with our modern concepts of physics and neurobiology. It's good news that modern science clearly distinguishes between pattern and process—an indication that common sense can prevail.

The topic of evolution continues to fuel dissent because, while there's not much question about the pattern, there's a lot of disagreement about the process that produced the pattern—particularly among the less-educated and religious fundamentalists. Is it comforting that, demographically, the matter appears to reflect levels of education? Perhaps—and perhaps not, when the statistics show that the fundamentalist view has proven more pervasive globally.

Paradoxically, the world's major religious traditions require of their clergy a robust general education, yet are divided on the matter of evolution, with the more educated tending to accommodate both evolution and religion—usually referred to as "theistic evolution"—by distinguishing the kinds of inquiry that science and religion each engage in. A quick web search produces statements concerning theistic evolution by nearly every major liberal Christian denomination. Seminaries associated with those denominations that welcome a synthesis of faith and evolution also tend to teach "the new criticism," an approach developed in the 1960s that treats the scriptures of Christianity as cultural products that arose in particular historical settings.

In moderate and liberally educated Islam, there have been vigorous attempts to synthesize faith and evolution—even classic Darwinism. Hinduism, always a friend to process, has had little difficulty with evolution, and a number of its classic thinkers, such as the late Sri Aurobindo, have been champions of process thinking both scientifically and socially. Buddhism, a spirituality rooted in the recognition of change, joins Hinduism in having a host of classical and modern thinkers working compatibly with the evolutionary model. Reform, Conservative, and Modern Orthodox Judaism, like liberal Islam, also tend to hold views of evolution that are generally compatible with theistic evolution.

What's There to See in the Pattern?

We can't make sense of the phenomenon of spirituality in humankind apart from the arising of consciousness in our species. Neither can we understand the arising of consciousness apart from the biological development of humankind—especially that most remarkable feature of our species, our brain. Not without reason do we classify ourselves as *Homo sapiens*, meaning the "knowing" or "intelligent" human.

Similarly, neither can we make sense of spirituality without understanding how our species wove from our internal diversity and complexity a web of cultural diversity and complexity through the creation of things, then told stories about our creations—and, ultimately, about ourselves.

To go further, whether we will continue to advance or go extinct as a species depends on our ability to appreciate the journey from which our biological makeup has arisen, not to mention the nature of the universe within which we may be among the first to be aware, if not its consummate explorer.

Everything we know of organization, structure, order, relationships, and even leadership comes from—or certainly in an integrative age should come from—our understanding of nature and the cosmology by which it all works and fits together. We can't appreciate any of this without a brief tour of this grand landscape, summarizing what our species has surmised in its 200,000 years of intelligent activity.

During the course of human history, the field of inquiry known as "science" has produced some 50 million scientific articles and books. A recent survey by Learned Publishers indicated the number is about 10 million for highly technical science and mathematics, moves up toward 40 million if you include the medical fields, and is around 50 million if you add a number of other scientific disciplines. That's the source of the pattern information available to modern humankind—not an easy body of information to ignore!

Confronted by the relative flatland of scientific information and the panoramic abilities of the human mind and consciousness, how will we ever distinguish the simple factual paths of data from the spontaneous wellspring of adjectives and metaphors that naturally arise to convey this data? Will this be worked out in an integrative epoch, the coming Interspiritual Age?

Currently some 30-40% of people worldwide embrace a religion that incorporates both science and religion in a theistic evolutionary view, sometimes referred to as "recognizing the Epic of Evolution." This suggests that when we portray the findings of science in an inspiring way, in context with the central themes of most religions' accounts of creation, we generate a compelling context that deepens both religious faith and secular knowledge.

5

Fourteen Billion Years in a Few Pages

"To know your origins is to know your life"

Lao Tzu

LONG BEFORE MODERN PHYSICS, THE 17TH CENTURY ENGLISH POET Francis Quarles declared it was "God's all producing blast which blew up the bubble of the world." Today we refer to this blast as the "Big Bang," a phenomenon discovered in the 20th century.

Imagine early humans standing under the stars at night, wondering about the panorama they beheld. It's not that long ago when modern scientists likewise peered into the night sky without any sense that they were looking at something far vaster than merely our galaxy. Until 1923, when Edward Hubble determined that some of the points of light he saw using the large Mount Wilson telescope in California were too distant to be part of the Milky Way, we imagined that what we today recognize as galaxies were simply stars. Now we know there are in excess of 100 billion galaxies—indeed, a German supercomputer has estimated that the number may be more like 500 billion—with each galaxy containing up to hundreds of billions of suns.

As scientists examine these galaxies with the help of the latest technology, it's evident that each galaxy is moving away not just from us but also from each other. This raises a perplexing question: How can every galaxy be moving away from every other?

If you blow up a balloon with polka dots on it, the dots become further apart. This isn't because the dots are moving away from each other, but because the balloon's surface is expanding. In a similar manner, the space in which the galaxies exist appears to be expanding. Because space itself is inflating, the galaxies are growing further and further apart, but without the individual galaxies moving.

Light travels at roughly 186,000 miles a second, and the distance it travels in a year is called a "light year." As humans peer up at the stars, the distances are so great that by the time light reaches the Earth, it's already millions, and in many cases billions, of years old. This has a surprise bonus, for it allows us to look back in time.

Our ability to look backward in time invites us to ask the question of how it all looks if we "rewind the tape," a favorite saying of the famous biologist Stephen J. Gould. When we roll back the tape, although there's some disagreement about the details of the *process* involved in what we then see, there is undeniable information about the *pattern*.

The initial moment, when everything in the presently expanded universe was all packed into an infinitesimally small point, appears to have lasted something like: .00000000000000000000000000000 00000000000000001 of a second. That's 1 with 43 zeros after the decimal point. This initial moment of the Big Bang is known as the "Planck epoch," named after the great German physicist Max Planck. The estimated temperature of the universe in that moment was 100,000,000,000,000,000,000,000,000,000,000,000 on the international Kelvin scale. That's 1 followed by 32 zeros. You can figure this in degrees Fahrenheit by multiplying by 1.8. Obviously this is unimaginably hot.

Ticking up from 43 zeros after the decimal point, the universe expanded to the size of billions of light years. The evidence for this is that by the time there were 35 zeros after the decimal point, the distribution of matter and energy in the universe was already uniform across its observable breadth. This means that the expansion (called the "Great Inflation") occurred far faster than the speed of light.

Light, whose speed appears to be the only "constant" we know, appears not to have been visible until some 400 million years into the scenario we are investigating. This is because during those first epochs after the Big Bang, the universe was so hot that it was a plasma. Photons, which are the makings of light, moved freely, since there was nothing to reflect off. To an observer, the universe would have appeared dark.

During that first second of the Big Bang, matter and anti-matter formed, consisting of electrons, quarks and anti-quarks, protons and neutrons, photons, neutrinos, and a host of other elementary building blocks. Significant amounts of your tax money have gone into building the cyclotrons and colliders used to study these infinitesimally small particles. This is because the public activity known as science convinced the public activity known as politics that this was important.

After the Big Bang

After the initial inflation, the universe began to cool. By the time that first second had ticked to a minute, the first two elements of the 118 elements we know of today—hydrogen and helium—were loose in the universe, which had cooled to about a billion degrees. As a comparison, our sun burns at a paltry 14 million degrees. The ongoing cooling and clumping provided the seeds for star and galaxy formation. It also gave us the cosmic microwave background radiation (CMB), which at -4 degrees Kelvin is the temperature to which the universe has now cooled.

The first 400 million years of darkness in the universe were succeeded by 600 million years during which the universe cooled to the point that gravity could pull atoms together to form dwarf galaxies, which led to larger and larger galaxies. The formation of each galaxy followed a similar pattern—gas at the center condensed into a black hole, which is an infinitely compact collection of matter with such strong gravity that even light can't escape from it. The rest of the gas around this black hole condensed into small clumps dense enough to foster nuclear reactions in which hydrogen and helium combined into heavier elements, releasing cataclysmic amounts of energy. These dense nuclear reactors are what we call stars. After a further two billion years, stars were growing so large they experienced their own violent explosion, known as a supernova. These explosions were so powerful they ejected heavier elements—carbon, oxygen, iron—into space, where gravitation led to further clumping. These new stars swirled in the midst of incomprehensible seas of hot debris. As this debris congealed, planets formed to orbit such stars. Our solar system formed during this process, almost 4.6 billion years ago.

It would still be several billion years before *Homo sapiens* would experience nights of wonder out under the stars, eventually leading us to seek an understanding of this grand panorama. In us, the universe had become conscious of itself. The "Great Radiance," a term used by evangelical Christians who embrace evolution to refer to the Big Bang, would finally find both its reflection and recognition in humankind.

Even as consciousness was dawning in our species, galaxies beyond our ability to see or dream continued to clump into larger galactic clusters, our own being the largest of some 30 adjacent galaxies. These clusters would become parts of super clusters, which in turn make up the seemingly endless filaments of such super clusters as the Hubble Telescope has revealed—the highest level of cosmic organization currently known. Some 90% of this expansive universe is still empty, its star systems lying in unimaginably huge gulfs. Yet here we are—an island of matter and an island of solitary consciousness.

The Arising of Life on Earth

We don't know how many planets in the universe host life, but it's unlikely we are alone. However, even the possibility of life elsewhere has implications for our interspiritual journey, for it affects our concept of who we are.

In recent years we discovered that life doesn't necessarily need oxygen in order to arise—that in the right combination with other chemicals, methane, hydrogen sulfide, and even arsenic will do. This has expanded our appreciation of what life is. A 2011 report by NASA lists seven different independent natural processes by which life could arise. Our finding of life in habitats of unimaginably challenging conditions of heat or cold, or even lack of light and kilometers underground—including deep below the ocean floor—has drastically changed our appreciation of life's tenacity, adaptability, and ability to innovate.

It shouldn't surprise us that two of our greatest recent scientists, E.O. Wilson (the father of sociobiology) and Theodocius Dobzhansky (the pioneer geneticist), both claimed life's evolutionary process to be the consummate "creative" act, and that Christian clergyman and "creatheist" Michael Dowd entitled his recent book *Thank God for Evolution*. Dowd notes, as do many others, that in connecting to our origins in cosmology, the most unifying theme is the subtle delight of knowing we are all the descendants of stardust.

Since life is what allows us to ask questions, it's worth asking what life is. There is a simple definition common to biology, chemistry, and physics. Ever since the Big Bang, the universe as a whole has been ticking down, a phenomenon known as the second law of thermodynamics. Hence if you buy a watch or a car, they eventually wear out, even as our bodies wear out. However, living things are able to process materials from their environment and create new energy to reverse this inevitable ticking down—for a while. When something is able to reverse this inevitable trend by generating new energy within itself, we say it's alive. Biologically, living things all demonstrate a capacity within themselves for metabolism, growth, reproduction, response to stimuli, and the ability to adapt to their environment. When your car's engine springs to life as you turn the ignition, it's a very different phenomenon because it can't generate this state within itself.

When we rewind the tape on our particular planet, life's advent turns out to have been a slow process. After a long period of congealing into a planet, Earth remained a molten body, only gradually developing a solid outer crust. When we in due course ventured to the Moon, we were surprised to learn that its makeup was the same as Earth's, leading us to the conclusion that a collision split our planet. We believe that in its infant stage, Earth was hit by a huge Mars-sized asteroid, gouging out a chunk that formed the Moon.

The debris of this collision continued to bombard the Earth in the form of meteorites. However, the Roman Catholic Church didn't acknowledge that objects fell to earth from the sky until 1751, producing a scientific document to this effect in 1794. To understand that things could fall from the sky—that is, come from another place—was quite an epiphany. In the worldview of that era, the canopy of blue sky by day and black sky by night was the "dome of heaven," above which God and the angels lived. The stars were peepholes.

After a few hundred million years, the majority of volcanoes on our planet became inactive. The gravitational pull of Jupiter, coupled with ongoing depletion of the asteroid belt that lies between it and Mars, resulted in fewer and fewer meteorites showering Earth. This allowed the planet to cool, which led to H_2O condensing into liquid, creating oceans, lakes, and rivers.

Earth's First Green Revolution

Earth's air and oceans were full of chemicals, especially complex molecules of hydrogen and carbon. Over the next few hundred million years, these hydrocarbons began joining together in diverse ways. In a particularly opportunistic case, a string of hydrocarbons gained the ability to create a mirror image of itself by pulling the chemicals it needed to do so out of the surrounding chemical soup. For the first time in our planet's history, something had reproduced itself! This was the building block of life—precursor DNA. Technically, it was probably a form of RNA, since this reproducing process (known as "transcription," as in copying) is the process of generating a complementary RNA copy of a sequence of DNA.

These earliest building blocks of life gradually became organized into configurations that proved advantageous for survival, which led to bursts of complexification among primitive life forms. One particularly successful combination involved the development of an external "shield" or "skin" that protected an inner region where sophisticated chemical reactions could take place in safety. This was the cell, the fundamental structural element of all plants and animals, including humans. It wasn't long before cells also began combining to form increasingly successful structures—first as colonies, in which each cell did the same thing but gained protection from togetherness, then in arrangements within which different cells not only divided up the work required for survival but also specialized as subparts supporting a larger whole. This was the birth of organisms.

Our world has arisen as a combination of just such natural hierarchies that cooperate together, commonly known as "holarchies." As in our biological past, the key to a successful future lies in working together along the lines of the patterns nature has taken billions of years to perfect. There's way too much hierarchy on the planet at the present time. We need to learn sharing and holarchy from the structure of our own planetary ecosystem.

Our knowledge of DNA provides ways to project our future by learning from our past. Knowing the inner workings of early so-called "primitive" organisms gives us the ability to intentionally engineer our future. Comprehending how each building block of life set the stage for fresh development serves as a guide to the future.

It's in the finer details of nature that we are discovering revolutionary ways of moving into the future. A compelling example involves energy. After long seeing themselves as separate from nature, propulsion scientists have at last noticed that only humans work against their environment to produce energy. For example, fish don't generate energy in order to move, but interact with water to produce the energy for movement. Birds do likewise in the air. This has modern physicists thinking about our potential interactions with the quantum field that surrounds us.

Quite different from even a decade ago, earth's oldest life forms are today grouped under three scientific terms: archaea, bacteria, and eukaryotes. Whether the archaea, bacteria, and eukaryotes had a common ancestor or arose independently is one of the tantalizing questions in our examination of pattern and process. What we do know is that each of these ancient life systems set the stage for the next one. This is crucial to understanding how our current system of life, based mostly on oxygen, developed.

We know that archaea (Greek, meaning "ancient") used a far greater variety of sources of energy than subsequent life forms, ranging from sugars to ammonia, elemental metals, and even hydrogen. Ancient forms in particular produced, of all things, methane from the CO_2 in the air. As the methane warmed the planet in a greenhouse effect, it created the advantageous conditions for a new set of early life forms.

One of these, a simple cell that would lead to a diverse array of bacteria (Greek, meaning "rod-like"), produced oxygen as a waste product. Now we were on our way to the oxygen-based life system we all know today. This waste oxygen also combined with non-living minerals, producing most of the foundational rock forms that would build the continents, granite being the most widespread.

By 2.2 billion years ago, considerable waste oxygen from the sea was escaping into the atmosphere. Although this initially destroyed life forms that weren't oxygen friendly, others developed innovative ways to control the use of oxygen, producing organisms that were even more energetic. These further seeded a budding biosphere.

Around 1.7 billion years ago, a more complicated cell appeared with multiple components, including a centralized nucleus to hold its DNA. It also featured a component specialized in respiration—mitochondria.[24] These new cells were the eukaryotes, named from Greek roots referring to centralized structures. The vitality of the eukaryotes resulted in a life form with the capacity to become increasingly more advanced, leading to multicellular organisms.

Multicellular Creatures Like Us— Sex, Holarchy, and Hierarchy

The way in which multicellular organisms work so skillfully is key to much of what we know about natural organization and interaction, holarchy, hierarchy, and even leadership. These natural models for truly skillful organization developed and diversified over the next billion years, their diversification accelerated by the constant breaking up

---

[24] These are contained within us, too, and have become one of the sources of DNA testing in criminology and the study of relationships in nature.

of landmasses large and small, splitting populations into new varieties and kinds.

We can trace the history of this landmass splitting back to a single super continent known as Pangaea. The division of this landmass advanced biological diversity by drastically separating interbreeding populations of both plants and animals. The increasing mobility of multicellular organisms led to using each other as nourishment, thus establishing the early hierarchies of nature—the various kinds of ecosystems.

Some organisms reproduced through sex, allowing frequent exchange of their DNA building blocks. This kept their genes robust against the constant down-ticking of the second law of thermodynamics. By increasing the variety of genes being exchanged, vitality and diversity were added, utilizing constant recombination of diverse DNA elements and the characteristics their coding implied.

Most spectacular among the organisms that then developed were those which, when showered by the photons that stream to earth as sunlight, could convert chemicals within themselves into new foods. This was earth's first green revolution, the origin of photosynthesis. It was on the basis of these green plants that a new layer of life developed: animals that utilize plants for nourishment.

However, the period of planetary collisions wasn't over. Nor were episodes of cataclysmic volcanism, the possibility of wobbles and shifts in the earth's planetary axis, and drastic changes in the energy coming from our star. Each disrupted the atmosphere, the tides, and ocean temperatures in ways that sometimes proved fatal for myriads of early organisms. Some of these collisions were nearly fatal for all life on the planet.

Such collisions resulted in epochs we might think of as bottlenecks, followed by periods of recovery and fresh creativity. Times of crisis seem to punctuate nearly every advance in human history. In the early epochs, such setbacks, bottlenecks, and recovery periods could last millions of years, before leading to dramatic innovation in terms of the kind of life forms that inhabited the planet and set the stage for what was to come.

Some of these early periods showed conditions barely imaginable today. We know that by 800 million years ago, earth was even colder than what we would later know as the ice ages. Snow and ice were almost everywhere. This period of "snowball earth" lasted until 600 million years ago. Some 70% of primitive multicellular life, both plant and animal, perished in successive fluctuations of diversification and extinction. Nevertheless, as with all cataclysms, the old cliché would hold true: necessity became the mother of invention.

In our time, as an integrative age unfolds, the prediction is that humans will turn to learning more from the natural structures of our universe and how they interact, and from this develop crucial skill sets for the future.

Disaster Leads to New Opportunities

As earth gradually warmed once more, it allowed for the development of organisms that displayed both increased complexity and greater mobility. By 670 million years ago, the undulating movement of jellyfish and the crawling patterns of many wormlike creatures were in evidence.

Two important characteristics then appeared: hard shells for protection, which allowed for larger bodies, and—by 600 million years ago—early versions of light-sensing eyes. Can you imagine a world without eyes, not to mention cameras? Obviously the implications of these developments were huge—so much so that scientists speculating about advanced life elsewhere in the cosmos universally assure us that sight has to be a standard feature.

Facilitating larger and larger bodies, the ozone layer surrounding the earth had now thickened, blocking out more and more of the sun's harmful ultraviolet rays. Consequently the oxygen content of the atmosphere increased by some ten times. These circumstances allowed life to develop on land—and develop in abundance. Ancestors of most of the major groups of animals known appeared in a relatively short time. This burst of abundance is known as the Cambrian Explosion, lasting from 540 to 490 million years ago.

Life spread across land first with invertebrates, then vertebrates, which became the ancestors of most of our familiar creatures, including ourselves. Utilization of this new zone would lead to the era of dinosaurs, beginning 500 million years ago.

In the ensuing period, the land itself underwent great change, as one of the two pieces of the former megacontinent Pangaea, the southern supercontinent Gondwanaland, slowly drifted to the South Pole. The creation there of massive ice sheets caused sea levels, temperatures, and chemistry to alter drastically. Some 60% of known marine life was wiped out.

A warming that followed caused the seas to alter yet again, allowing life both in the sea and on land to respond with another burst of fecundity. Invertebrates flourished, along with the first complex plants—those filled with organized internal tubing that readily moved water and nourishment about, known as "vascular plants."

The oxygen content of the air soared, reaching 35% (compared to 20% today), resulting in plants as tall as 100 feet, along with spiders and insects as large as two to three feet by 420 million years ago. Capping off this era, around 300 million years ago, was a major development—the amniotic egg (the egg as we know it today). The laying of eggs, in which the next generation could be both protected and nurtured prior to emerging fully developed, led to a further explosion of the ability to reproduce on land.

Just as life was booming, an apparently multifaceted catastrophe resulted in the largest mass extinction in our planet's history. This was the great extinction called the Permian-Triassic transition, or the Great Dying. Most likely involving an asteroid collision, it was of such magnitude that massive volcanism was unleashed globally, drastically altering the chemistry of air and sea. Some 70% of land life and 95% of oceanic life appears to have perished.

Every dying is a rebirth. In the millions of years that followed, paradoxically it was this extinction that would open the way for entire new lineages, many of which foreshadowed the kinds of animal and plant forms required for the emergence of humans, and with which we are familiar today. Among these changes was a crucial innovation that would become perhaps the most important to the eventual growth of intelligent life on the planet. The great forests of fern-like plants were replaced by plants with offspring enclosed in seeds, allowing unparalleled protection and mobility for the purpose of reproduction. Appearing 245 million years ago, these gymnosperms would prove to be the key to agriculture millions of years later. They are known to us today as conifers and pines.

It was in this environment that, 215 million years ago, the first small mammals appeared, so meager as to be completely overlooked at first, but in hindsight foreshadowing not only the entire panorama of humankind's now familiar environment but also humankind themselves. Dinosaurs dominated for the next 150 million years, while these lowly forebears of mammals endured underfoot. This was the epoch during which the oil fields were deposited, beginning around 200 million years ago. It was also the advent of the organisms that would eventually remain the only vestiges of our dinosaur heritage— the birds. During this time, modern conifers (or pines) first appeared in their currently recognizable forms. The climate remained warm, a global warming nurtured by carbon dioxide levels some three times those today.

The megacontinent Pangaea completed its breakup, with the southern supercontinent Gondwanaland separating as South America and Africa, creating the great Atlantic Ocean. India and Madagascar broke away from the western margins of Australia and Antarctica, forming the Indian Ocean. North America and Eurasia began separating also. In this spreading, some 90 million years ago, shallow seaways invaded many of the continents, including North and South America, Africa, and Eurasia.

At 65 million years ago, just as *Tyrannosaurus rex* became an invincible predator, a huge asteroid crashed into the Gulf of Mexico, throwing up so much dirt that it blocked out the light and warmth of the sun. Plants began to disappear, followed by the demise of plant-eating, then meat-eating, animals. For the ruling dinosaurs, the result was cataclysmic. In all, 65% of all marine species and nearly 15% of other terrestrial species—including many early mammals—went extinct.

The Advent of Intelligent Life

The mammals started out in a meager fashion. After the asteroid collision that led to extinction of the dinosaurs, all land animals larger than about 50 lbs (20 kg), roughly the size of a large dog, disappeared. Only those that required relatively little food survived.

These crafty mammals, warm blooded and bearing their young alive, came to occupy nearly all parts of the ecological landscape—filling the niches, places where you can "make a living." The landscape teemed with insectivores and rodent-like mammals. While medium sized mammals searched the forests for any food they could find, the first larger—but not yet gigantic—mammals foraged the increasingly abundant vegetation. Some 65 million to 55 million years ago, larger carnivores began stalking their prey. By now the average temperature was about 85°F, the hottest for the last 65 million years. From the North Pole to the South Pole, temperature varied little, so that there was virtually no ice and precipitation was high.

By 50 million years ago, the continents as we recognize them today were moving toward their current positions. Australia split from Antarctica at that time, while India collided with Asia 45 million years ago, pushing up the Himalayas.

Mammals remained small, which was perhaps fortuitous because, by 41 million years ago, changes on the planet ushered in renewed epochs of cold, most likely as a result of the new continental positions and oceans. This was to be the landscape onto which humankind would eventually step.

The idea of intelligent life anywhere in the universe is fascinating to us.[25] On our own planet, the period from 50-45 million years ago produced the unique circumstances in which the creature we call human could arise.

Distinctive of this time period were regular fluctuations between relatively warm and relatively cold periods. Although it might not be apparent, these oscillations created a wider variety of habitats, and thus a far broader opportunity for new kinds of animals and

---

[25] A 2010 CNN poll indicated 86% of respondents shared this fascination.

plants to arise, interacting with each other and utilizing each other's resources.

A dramatically different creature that arose on the planet during this period was the primate—the apes and their relatives. Among other innovations evident in the primate was the shape of the hand, with a thumb and fingers, allowing a potentially wide array of new behavioral activities.

By 30 million years ago, anthropoids—higher primates—appeared in Africa, direct ancestors of the monkeys and other modern apes. This lineage diversified rapidly, with those monkeys that migrated to what was to become South America from still nearby Africa becoming purely New World creatures as the continents drifted further and further apart. By 22 million years ago, the Old World monkeys and New World monkeys had completely separated, to the point that some apes no longer had tails!

Something else occurred during this period of climatic oscillations that was to become of prime importance to the advent of humankind. By 25 million years ago, a new type of plant appeared: grass. This allowed new kinds of animals to appear and prosper, especially those that would become part of the landscape that supported the rise of higher apes. Concomitant with the development of grass, around 19 million years ago many grazing animals, including those ancestral to the ones humankind would later hunt, arose and prospered.

By 18 million years ago, apes also migrated from Africa to Asia where they split into Lesser Apes (small apes) and Great Apes (large apes). There followed a period of exchange of lineages between these land areas, resulting in further diversification for some ten million years, leading to orangutans, gibbons, siamangs, and so on. By seven million years ago, gorillas were arising in Africa. By six million years ago, the Great Apes had split into chimpanzees and hominids—the precursors of humans.

As if in some kind of cosmic choreography, the eventual "best friends" of humans—domestic cats and dogs—also saw the advent of their ancestors at this time. By eight million years ago, modern cats appeared, with dogs following by six million years ago, along with the horse, beaver, deer, camel, and whale. Some 95% of modern seed plant families existed at the six million year point, and none are known to have gone extinct.

These time periods were characterized by fluctuating temperatures, causing various ecosystems worldwide to spread out and retreat. Seasonality developed on massive scales. Temperatures had again dropped sharply by six million years ago, leading to the near present-day expanses of ice at the poles.

Of huge significance for the advent of humans, Africa and Arabia—riding on the African and Arabian tectonic plates—abutted with Eurasia, enabling a great exchange of flora and fauna. Land uplifts in Africa, the ancestral home of humanity's foundational population, caused central West Africa to be wet and East Africa to be dryer. At the six million year point, the Mediterranean Sea also became isolated, cut off from the ocean by the abutment of Gibraltar and North Africa. The crucible was in place for the development of early humans.

The Riddle of Humankind

It's startling how the scientific view of the advent of humans has changed in only a few decades. No longer is there a simple debate about the characteristics of a single distinct lineage, with our ancestors following each other in vertical sequence. Instead there are now a diverse number of precursors to *Homo sapiens*, with a number of earlier species considered to be members of our immediate genus *Homo*. These are quite scattered through time and space, especially vis-a-vis the availability of fossils, in a patchwork quilt of uncertain overlaps and connections.

One of the downsides of science is that there aren't often common names for many of these ancients. In order to make some sense of who they were and where they lived, we'll need to give their scientific names, along with the location of their fossils. *Homo sapiens* is the only survivor of all these pioneers: *Homo antecessor* (Spain), *H. cepranensis* (Italy), *H. erectus* (Africa, Eurasia, Java, China, India, Caucasus), *H. ergaster* (Eastern and Southern Africa), *H. floresiensis* (Indonesia),

H. gautengensis (South Africa), *H. georgicus* (Georgia), *H. habilis* (Africa), *H. heidelbergensis* (Europe, Africa, China), *H. neanderthalensis* (Europe, Western Asia), *H. rhodesiensis* (Zambia), *H. rudolfensis* (Kenya), and *H. sapiens idaltu* (Ethiopia).

In the modern view, our species is now often referred to as "the last man standing." For as recently as 70,000 years ago, there appear to have been at least four "men standing." Two of these were ourselves, early *Homo sapiens*, and a rogue-like cousin, *Homo neanderthalensis*—Neanderthal Man), which current evidence, including DNA, suggests was a distinct species but occasionally interbred with early humans. Two others are very recent additions to the scientific rosters. One is *Homo floresiensis* (Flores Man), a three-foot tall hobbit-like humanoid wiped out by volcanoes in Indonesia as recently as 70,000 years ago. It's likely that Flores Man had contact with our ancestors as we spread to Australia. The other recent addition is *Denisova hominin* (Denisova Man), discovered as recently as 2008—a surprise of great import, because in its remains we discovered testable DNA, which revealed its identity as an early human cousin.

Two views vie in an informative debate concerning our direct origin—the Out of Africa or recent single origin view, which has until recently enjoyed the most support, and the alternative multiregional view. The former holds that *Homo sapiens* originated in Africa and migrated out of the continent between 50,000 and 100,000 years ago, replacing populations of *Homo erectus* in Asia and Neanderthal Man in Europe. The latter view posits that *Homo sapiens* evolved geographically separately but interbreeding, so that populations arose from a worldwide migration of *Homo erectus* out of Africa some 2.5 million years ago.

The crux of the argument seems to rest on how one evaluates ancillary evidence. On the one hand, there is the tightness of the genome (DNA) connected to *Homo sapiens* as of the time of our emergence from Africa. On the other hand, there is evidence that additional ancient genomes (DNA complexes), including Neanderthal and the recently discovered Denisova Man, were also in interplay across the land. A big surprise in the discovery of Neanderthal and Denisova

DNA was that their components were well indicated within the DNA of modern humans.

Aside from this debate, there is concurrence that there was a great leap forward in the emergence of early humans following a serious evolutionary bottleneck. This bottleneck was a widespread extinction among early humans due to a sweeping climatic change after a calamitous regional volcanic eruption of Indonesia's super volcano Toba. Atmospheric dust after the Toba eruption plunged the earth into a centuries-long frigid epoch.

The scientific agreement about this catastrophe seems to explain the evidence that the genome of modern humans is extremely homogeneous. For example, DNA from among humans is far more alike than is usual for most animal species. In humans, external differences such as facial traits, skin color, and various respiratory adaptations to high altitude aren't reflected in significant DNA differences.

This is seen as evidence of a precipitous population bottleneck among early humans some 70,000 years ago. Its effect was to radically constrict the variety of genetic inheritance in subsequent generations. A compelling metaphor arising from the Out of Africa model is science's identification of a Mitochondrial Eve. From research using female mitochondrial DNA and the male Y chromosome, it has been suggested that all humans that emerged from this population bottleneck might have been the offspring of one woman. This created an interesting moment in the religious versus scientific debate over the origin of humankind.

Kinds of Creationism

While clearly identifying the trend toward growing unity consciousness in the evolution of our species, we have also noted the divided views of the world's peoples concerning the process that accounts for our origin and place in the universe. This leads us to ask if there's an endgame in which division ceases, especially in the light of the unfolding Interspiritual Age.

It's one thing to equate evolution with the simple everyday reality of patterns and process, making the volatility of the word more palatable to common sense, and quite another to address the real-time implications of the worldwide divide over the question—especially as it plays out internationally on a stage of stark polarity and even conflict.

While nearly every religious tradition that involves some level of general education for its clergy has accommodated evolution, and scientific philosophy is reasonably clear about the limits of its inquiry, the mass of world citizenry is still locked in this divisive battle that could threaten the survival of our species.

A disturbing aspect of the creation-evolution debate is the portrayal of the two camps as widely divided, having no common ground. The differences between the various players such as creation science, intelligent design, reductionist science, and theistic evolution lie not in the details, but in their elemental "ways of knowing"—in other words, which cultural lens they look through.

Because the battle between the combatants has been waged mainly through the media of politics, law, and education, the international debate has ended up pitting the equivalent of sophisticated lobbies against each other. For example, on the creationist side is the Center for Science and Culture, which now advocates for intelligent design after courts ruled that creation science is a form of religious belief. On the secular side is a diverse coalition under the banner of the National Center for Science Education. We single out these two because they represent several decades of coalescing within and across the creationist and evolutionist advocacy movements.

The God of the Gaps

The basic argument of anti-evolutionists from their inception has been what's known as "the God of the gaps." The idea is that if one can identify areas of doubt, incompleteness, or even complexity within the scientific view, one can argue that only the action of God (or some other metaphysical agent) can suitably explain such gaps.

An example of this way of thinking is a clock. It's argued that if something as complex as a clock requires a clockmaker, something as complex as the earth must have a maker also, since many processes in nature are far more complex than clocks. Say the proponents of this view, only the intelligence of a maker could account for such fine-tuned complexity.

One of the problems with creationist arguments is that their general points, no matter how modernized in phrasing, have histories dating back to the 19th century. Most are built on the same views voiced in Darwin's day, employing standard British theological and philosophical propositions of the time, such as the famous "argument from design" (from the early Greeks and Romans, to the Islamic Averroes, Thomas Aquinas, John Locke, and finally David Hume in his famous *Dialogues Concerning Natural Religion*).

Another strategy central to the approach of some creationists[26] is to portray the discussion in terms of dramatic opposites, such as, "Can one believe in both God and evolution? Can one accept scientific teachings and engage in religious belief and practice?" Coupled with this, they play on western Christian fears of materialism, Communism, scientific reductionism, paganism, and morals and ethics of which they disapprove. Such views are particularly influential among those who believe in magical end-time scenarios.

Virtually all the world's religions have some kind of subculture or lobby that advocates creationism or intelligent design. In Islam, there is the BAV (Science Research Foundation), a relatively recent counter stream to Islam's long history of skillful accommodation of science, particularly in the classic periods (Nasir al-Din al-Tusi, Al-Dinawari, Ibn Maskawayh, and Ibn Khaldun, not to overgeneralize)—and since the 19th century, Jamal-al-Din al-Afghāni and Ghulam Ahmad Pervez. All of these views are in the theistic evolutionary mode. Significantly, the prominent journal *Science* recently indicated that the view of evolution across current Islamic societies is mixed, with general acceptance of cosmology, chemistry, physics, and genetics, but push back when it comes to the shared ancestry of humans and primates. There's definitely something about those apes!

---

[26] As laid out in the document The Wedge, from the Center for Science and Culture.

Judaism has been outspokenly against intelligent design, with a large number of Jewish organizations and academic institutions identifying it as pseudoscience. An exception to this nearly unanimous trend has been Moshe Tendler, a rabbi and biology professor at Yeshiva University in New York.

Buddhism and Hinduism, which are both centered on deep understandings of process and change, have also opposed intelligent design with near unanimity. International Society for Science and Religion publications have included arguments against intelligent design by V. V. Subbarayappa from Hinduism and Trinh Xuan Thuan from Buddhism.

The large population globally whose religions support a view of theistic evolution underscores the fact that purely anti-evolution views operate mainly in the domain of world politics, where they hope to exert and fix their influence by political means. It will be a primary test of the Interspiritual Age and the emerging unity consciousness to see whether such information-proof beliefs can yield to a more inclusive, holistic view, which spirituality would define as the view of the heart.

A Biological Endgame?

Although it's doubtful any scientific evidence could persuade an information-proof fundamentalist, we must see if we can identify any strains of scientific data that are so convincing, so apparent at the level of common sense, that they make the view of evolution all but undeniable.

Advocates of the modern evolutionary view list 23 lines of evidence, not counting major subcategories, that they believe corroborate the scientific view. In terms of arguments for rejecting evolution, two aspects of modern biological discoveries are often not acknowledged or understood by those who spend countless hours claiming they have reasonable and rational arguments against modern evolutionary science.

Evidence from molecular sequencing (DNA, RNA, and their related ERV "retrovirus" strands) provides the most compelling and possibly irrefutable evidence for the genealogical relatedness of all life, which shares the genetic code based on the molecule DNA and its related molecule RNA.

These methods offer extremely impressive probability calculations that demonstrate how well predictions of common descent with modification match our observations. Information from biological molecular mechanisms and structures, along with modern evolutionary theory, gives us precise testable biomolecular predictions. Such arguments take on a uniqueness because they are an instance in which one can directly conclude that linkage implies relatedness, the term for which is genetic fingerprinting.

Once genetic elements could be analyzed and sequences compared, a whole new avenue opened up for scientists to examine gene sequences and identify their relationships. Even if scientists are working blind in terms of where a genetic sample comes from, they can still evaluate its relationships using this methodology.

Because one can go right to the source—the genetic code itself—today it's more possible than ever to test evolution versus other theories of origins. Having said this, there's no doubt the precision and complexity of modern science is itself a problem in terms of public relations. The level of detail and jargon is so intricate that even the short summary above was difficult to compose. The same is the case when we attempt to discuss science's various theories of consciousness. With science, often much more could be said and many more examples given, but sometimes there are no common terms available for what the scientist seeks to convey, only jargon. As a result, much of the world continues to adhere to simplistic answers, since such answers are comforting. As with public doubt about climate change and global warming in the developed world, and belief that AIDS is caused by spirits in the Third World, sadly such adherence carries with it the potential for tragic consequences.

Long before our knowledge of DNA, the understanding of how countless elements of genetic material act within and across equally countless populations of individual plants and animals convinced virtually every biologist who understood it (generally taught only at the

PhD level) that it accounted for how evolution does its work. This complex and dynamic field might be called "the mathematics beneath what you think you see."

The problem is, absent this understanding, those working from the standpoint of "the God of the gaps" continue to claim their simplistic understanding of genetic material and natural selection couldn't possibly account for many of the amazing things we see in the natural world. There have been countless meetings of creationists and evolutionists, even friendly ones, when the latter had to leave at the end of the day saying things as "they don't understand population genetics." It's like having someone tell you that the spectrum of visible light in a room is all that exists, when you know by putting on a certain set of goggles you can readily see both infrared and ultraviolet light.

Perhaps the simplest way to understand population genetics is to imagine a complex card game. Only about 15% of genetic material is actually used within an organism to produce the characteristics we observe, not to mention what that organism is exchanging with others in its wider population reproduction. Imagine only 15% of the cards in a card game being in the game at any one time, with the other 85% held out for the player to cheat. If we further allow that the 15% of the cards in the game can be changed without the other player knowing, he or she will also be in for some big surprises.

Another metaphor that might help is to think about what you are seeing when you view a sonogram. Most everyone is familiar with sonograms, and many have watched the monitor while one was being performed. Imagine that the individual bursts of sound sent to the object of the sonogram, reflected back, and finally composed by the monitor into a moving image, represent the genetic material available in a population. As with the sonogram, you see dynamic movement on the screen. The operator can vary the focus, going deeper or shallower, as well as shifting to the right or left, to reveal the movement of different anatomical features. It's this dynamic movement of elements in the gargantuan shared genetic pool of populations that in any instance shows very different things. This illustrates how drastically different-looking forms arise in nature over time. The math of population genetics envisions and tracks these dynamic changes, which account for radical developments not easily understood by a simplistic view of the process.

A Happy Ending?

One result of the lack of an endgame in the divide over evolution has been the increasing polarization between "cold" and "hot" religions. Cold religions and cooling religions that are no longer strident about their metaphysical claims, most especially their end-time scenarios, have adapted to accommodating differences of opinion. These religions include most of the traditions characterized by high levels of education among their clergy, who are often involved in ecumenical activities. The behavior of hot religions is quite the opposite, as we have witnessed since 9/11 in the movement of the political "right" in American politics.

During the 18th century "enlightenment" when democracy was replacing monarchy globally, some of the world's great leaders were unable to reconcile how the God of their past—an involved God—seemed no longer directly active in their lives. The result was Deism, which was the religion of Jefferson, Hamilton, Madison, Paine, Franklin, and other American founders. A cooling religious view, it rationalized that after God created everything, the creator then stepped away, leaving humankind to its own devices. Though it compelled some of the most gifted men of the time, this view seems outdated to us today. Similarly there have been outbreaks of hot religion throughout history, ranging from episodes of extreme zealotry—such as the Jewish Maccabees, the Crusades, and the Chinese Taiping Rebellions—to the emergence of vigorous new religions (such as Mormonism and Baha'i) and charismatic cult figures (such as David Koresh and Jim Jones).

Today we see evolution-friendly movements even within evangelical Christianity attempting a new kind of discussion around the compelling data of science, without jettisoning a faith whose texts are anchored in millennially old ways of life. We also see recognition across many religious constituencies worldwide of the value of evolutionary psychology. Since the problems of real people, in real time, are being successfully addressed by a psychology built on much of the modern evolutionary view of science, many have to admit there must be some truth to it. Fundamentally, evolution involves adaptation—the process of surviving and thriving that inevitably, whether in nature or human society, leads to revolution upon revolution, trending ultimately toward the Interspiritual Age.

Another critical advent is analytic philosophy, which approaches philosophical problems from the vantage of the scientific method with its conception of sophisticated, holistic, integral worldviews. Both these perspectives offer the possibility of not only understanding complex systems, but also of appreciating the prospect that entirely new ("emergent") qualities may arise as such systems evolve.

The transformational potential of integral worldviews—such as Integral, Spiral Dynamics, and similar systems—is their presentation of comprehensive and dynamic approaches in which many even seemingly conflicting activities can be seen acting simultaneously. In this context, the place, value, and integrity of each can be discerned (like the place of scientific and spiritual insight), and potential complementarities and synergies recognized. In these lies tremendous hope for the future.

Once *Homo sapiens* emerged from Africa, we are somewhat off the hook in relation to the perennial creation-evolution controversy, even though details about the relationship of modern humans to other primitives (Neanderthal, Flores, and Denisova man) are uncertain. True, western scriptural literalists argue we're not on common ground until about 10,000 years ago from the point of view of Judaic and Islamic scriptures, but at least humankind is finally on stage. From this point on, there appears to be little argument that the development of our species simply follows the common sense rules of cause and effect. Consequently, the debate about origins can take a back seat to what happens next.

6

The Dawn of Spirituality

"I feel, therefore I am"

**Neurologist Antonio Damasio on Spinoza's
retort to Descartes**

IT'S POSSIBLE TO SEE THE RELATIONSHIP BETWEEN BRAIN-MIND DEVELOP-ment, the emergence of consciousness, and the beginning of religious and spiritual activity. What we call "consciousness" arose when early humans began to grasp the relationship between cause and effect. First came the general awareness of cause and effect, then action related to this recognition, such as the fashioning of tools.

In brain-mind studies, this direct relationship of a recognition or awareness followed by action is often called "integration consensus." Whenever animals recognize the relation of cause and effect, actions and skills arise. This relationship between awareness and skills wasn't only crucial to the unfolding of our history, but is relevant to whether, in the current millennium, we can recognize and solve the problems that confront us.

Consistent with this understanding of consciousness, a number of acquired skill sets point to the gradual arising of consciousness in humans, including tool making, fire making, burial of the dead, prehistoric art, and the origin and the transition from speech and gestures to full languages. Especially important is the relationship of language to the development of an analytical mind, with the projection of this ability into attributes such as introspection and reflection.

This suggests the development first of what we call "mind," which might be seen as a reflexive cause-effect loop between brain and body—and, as this complexified over time, what we have come to call "consciousness." The latter involves skills such as introspection, reflection, analysis of multiple options, and projection of these as a sense of self, together with an awareness of past and future.

With the latter came naming things, including ourselves and other items, which was accompanied by narrating stories about all these. Once there is a world of stories, it's possible for a being to sense, or actually create, an existence larger than just their present state. If you are sensing spirituality and religion here, you are sensing correctly.

Most scientists date the dawn of these skill sets—what they call "full behavioral modernity"—at some 50,000 years ago, even ranging upward toward 100,000 years ago. This is about the time *Homo sapiens* was migrating out of Africa and meeting with other primitive members of the genus *Homo*.

As with the divide over biological evolution, there's also a divide over what consciousness is. The two main views both recognize qualities generally considered a part of consciousness: subjectivity, awareness, experience of feelings, wakefulness, a sense of individual selfhood, and a command of mental faculties. But is consciousness to be seen as only the qualities produced by the individual brain of individual humans and animals? With some exceptions, this would be the strictly scientific view. Or can there be acknowledgment of a wider collective field, of which the individual's experience is a part? The latter would be the view familiar to religion and spirituality.

As with evolution, the educated elite of science are once more in the minority. While science itself has at least half a dozen very different and equally complex views of consciousness, most of the world has gone its merry way, embracing other assumptions without much critical examination. For general purposes, we will refer to these two different understandings of consciousness as "The Consciousness of Science" (consciousness occurs only in individual body-mind) and

"The Consciousness of Spirituality" (consciousness occurs in a wider collective field).

Consciousness—the Power of a Name

Irrespective of how we view consciousness, what's unique about us is that each of us is distinctly self-identified, yet each of us also exists simultaneously as an inherent part of an interdependent and communicating collective, traditionally the clan or tribe. From self-awareness, particularly in the sense of having a personal name whose existence in language can live longer than the actual person, arises the sense of identity-permanence, with its implications of past and future that lead to recognizable spiritual or religious activities.

Naming is the first evidence of the subjective world, the world of an "idea" held within humankind independent of the world around it. Burying the dead, particularly with ritual, is another mark of personal identity. Also, we can point to the creation of art, especially as an object of devotion. Inherent in these activities is the suggestion of dialogical, reflective, and introspective thinking. In the scientific view, it's these that are most often used to distinguish consciousness.

Scientists point out that unique to our species is an inherent affinity for teaching and learning. When primitive learning experiments are presented to adult apes and children, apes seldom if ever have an inclination to pass on, collectively, what they themselves learn. Even chimpanzees that discover something may not pass this learning on. If they do, it's only to a member of their immediate group. In contrast, human children habitually pass what they learn on to the collective, often with excitement and bravado.

Anthropologists suggest our proclivity for teaching and learning is what defined our species as "the last man standing." We can't really know about the little Hobbit-like Flores Man, since the species was wiped out. But it appears our European cousins, Neanderthal Man, failed to change their habits much during the Ice Age, which caused them to ultimately succumb to extinction. In contrast, we devised clothing, shelter, and hunting techniques to weather that deadly era.

These behaviors help us ask the question of whether, facing the challenges of the current millennium, we will once again be able to adapt in the face of challenge.

It's precisely these ever-expanding activities, as they complexify over time, that become recognizable as spiritual or religious activity.

Toolmaking, Use of Fire, and the Growth of Consciousness

The use of tools implies that the user recognizes the relationship between objects and their effects. Across the animal kingdom, tool use has been observed in various apes, dolphins, elephants, otters, birds, and even octopi. In apes, tools are used in a variety of ways, from hunting to preparing food, self-support (walking sticks and perhaps even primitive measuring rods), and defense. Chimpanzees are known to fashion long sticks with pointed ends as weapons. For example, Bonobo chimps attack laboratory mannequins in a manner that indicates they know how to cause serious injury or death. It's therefore no surprise that in the early forms of *Homo*, tool use was widespread and varied.

A measure of advancement in tool use involves the flexibility to change one's use of tools to accommodate different circumstances. Primitive tools of stone (wooden tools would not have been preserved) is dated as far back in the primitive African *Homo* ancestors as 2.6 to 1.5 million years ago, with increasing sophistication until 300,000 years ago. The fashioning of bone and antlers into more complex tools (fishhooks, buttons, needles) is dated at 50,000 to 70,000 years ago. The evidence is so extensive and complex that archaeologists group the breadth of this development of early tool use into categorized technocomplexes.

Until about 40,000 to 50,000 years ago, sophistication of stone tools seems to have developed incrementally, with each group (*H. habilis*, *H. ergaster*, *H. neanderthalensis*) seeming to begin at a level higher than the previous, but with little further development within each group. However, after about 40,000 years ago, *Homo sapiens* manifested change at a much greater speed. This is consistent with the view that full behavioral modernity for humankind dates to about 50,000 years ago. It also furnishes hints as to the superiority of *Homo sapiens*. While tool innovation rapidly diversified in modern humans, we have seen that adjacent surviving populations of *Homo neanderthalensis* manifested little variation in their primitive technologies.

Use of fire also indicates a recognition of the connection between cause and effect. To no longer fear fire, as do nearly all animals, is a big step, enabling humans to find fire in one setting and harness it for another, along with deliberately making fire.

Hearths and other evidence of fire usage are found for each of *Homo erectus*, *Homo heidelbergensis*, and *Homo sapiens*, with passive use of natural fire sometimes dated to 1.5 million years ago and clear evidence of deliberately made fire dated as early as 300,000 years ago. By 70,000 years ago, fire was also used to prepare stones for toolmaking.

The connection of fire to the preparation of food is far more crucial than might be imagined. Dated from as early as a million years ago to 250,000 years ago, cooked food extended both the variety of food that could be eaten and its nutritional value—a dynamic linked to increased physical robustness, including brain size.

Cooking food implies conscious choice. Also, the cultural importance of cooking can't be underestimated, with the advent of cooking not only stimulating creativity and innovation but also introducing the matter of preference, both as to the kind of food and the method of preparation.

Consciousness and Language: the Pivotal Connection

Many investigators consider the development of language as key to understanding the arising of consciousness—perhaps initially as reflexive or more animal-like mind, which is less calculating and reflective, and then as more and more conscious (calculating, reflective, and introspective).

Anthropologists and cognitive researchers date the origin of language from about 50,000–35,000 years ago. They then see the transition from mind to more spacious consciousness as arising differentially across various cultural circumstances and timelines. Though many of us assume the inhabitants of all those eras possessed the same mental and conscious faculties we do, they assert that this isn't the case. Human mind and human behavior, being in constant development, have been quite varied at different times. If this is true, how and why circumstances have changed across the history of the world's cultures has also varied in different times and cultures.

This perspective helps us understand the dynamism of the world's cultures as we move toward globalization. Today we see dramatic differences in current world cultures. There are open societies with democratic systems and some understanding of universal human rights, and closed societies controlled by dictators or by shared cultural views that are restrictive and fear-based. Often these cultural views are connected to fixed religious beliefs and behavior dominated by concepts of ultimate reward or punishment.

The general view is that language began as grunt-like speech and gestures, used at first more for communicating orders and direction, as even occurs in some of the apes, then complexified into a more and more differentiated symbolic system. Perhaps the original seed was the recognition of individuality, of either a person or a thing, followed by the signal that denotes that person or thing—in other words, its name.

In primates, the Broca's and Wernike's areas of the brain control the facial, mouth, and throat muscles connected to sound making. Apes make calls using these parts of the body, and ape responses to such calls show that individuals and their kin are separately identified within the group. Similarly, laboratory chimpanzees readily associate distinctive sounds with distinctive objects.

Some scientists suggest primitive proto-language (sounds indicating commands, especially from the clan leader) must have been a part of the social structure apparent in *Homo habilis*, dated to at least 2.3 million years ago. Others suggest symbolic communication arose in *Homo erectus* and *Homo heidelbergensis* 1.8 to 1.6 million years ago. In contrast to eventual language, the primitiveness of speech at this point seems further indicated by the fact that *Homo neanderthalensis*, contemporary with early *Homo sapiens*, didn't evidence a sufficient anatomical structure for fully developed language.

True language is usually attributed only to modern humans, beginning earlier than 100,000 years ago, timed with the emergence of our species from Africa following the population bottleneck related to the Toba volcanic catastrophe. The drastic reduction of the human population at that time, followed by expansion of the population thereafter with an accompanying suite of skills, may explain the general uniformity of primitive language worldwide.

Extremely primitive languages consist of mostly nouns, verbs, and adjectives, with few complex elements such as articles, prepositions, conjunctions, or auxiliary verbs. Grammar is often quite fixed, and words aren't enunciated with inflection. Nevertheless, such languages complexify in short order, even as little as a single generation. When they do, they show remarkable similarity in their innovation, even if there has been little contact between the groups developing them.

This startling fact, which confused anthropologists for many years, suggests an intrinsic unity in humankind's inherited psyche—an important element in the vision of an unfolding Interspiritual Age.

Language is innately related to the development of wider consciousness. When language moves toward a complexified metaphorical structure, it reflects the growth—as a result of ongoing brain development—of a more spacious grounding of self-awareness, reflective consciousness, and complex trains of thought. It involves past and future, preferences, likes and dislikes, understanding cause and effect, calculation regarding these, high level reference systems such as numbers and counting, and even the projection of mental images whereby the individual imagines themselves doing a particular thing.

Scientists who have followed this developmental pattern in the time period from 50,000 years ago until the dawn of what we call historical time—where it can be studied by diverse remains and artifacts, and eventually written language—believe there was a gradual complexification of this originally more reflexive animal-like mind.

Especially important is the relationship of language and the development of metaphorical thought. For our consideration of spirituality, it's the development of complex and metaphorical thought, the language of storytelling, and the purveying of primordial ideas of who we are, where we came from, and where we are going, that comprise the spiritual landscape.

Early Evidence for Spirituality

One of the earliest spiritual activities, reflecting awareness of the individual as an identity, involved the ritualistic disposition of the human body following an individual's death. Evidence of burial of the dead in early humans goes back further than might be imagined. It has important implications for how to date the origin of self-recognition, individuality, and the sense of essence or soul. The earliness of human burials in the anthropological record suggests that spiritual awareness may have existed even prior to fully developed language.

There is debatable evidence that Neanderthals may have buried their dead with ritual. Remains of *Homo heidelbergensis* have also been found in specially constructed pits. Bodies were placed in shallow graves, accompanied not only by tools but also animals. Often the corpses were arranged in particular postures, even including facing prominent landmarks. What is known as "the provision of grave goods" suggests an emotional connection to the deceased and possible belief in a hereafter. Such burials extend back some 100,000 years. Universally, archaeologists and anthropologists consider such burial ritual as evidence of religious activity.

Prehistoric art offers another line of inquiry into the kind of consciousness that was arising in early humans. It shouldn't surprise us that the more sophisticated forms of this art date to about 50,000 years ago. These include both figurines and ornaments, along with the famous European cave paintings that date from 10,000–40,000 years ago.

As with other skill sets that were arising in early humans, precursors suggesting artistic use can be traced as far back as 300,000 years. The mix across time ranges from utilitarian creations such as pottery and stone vessels to objects that bear obvious motifs. Most interesting to the understanding of consciousness are objects that imply religious devotion, which can be traced to as early at 70,000 years ago in carvings, paintings, and figures (from which developed totemism) indicating animal worship and shamanic activity.

Far beyond a conscious sense of individuality and permanence of identity, such art and the ceremonial practices connected to it—attributed to both Neanderthal man and early *Homo sapiens*—link these early humans with mystical experiences. Such experiences include the attribution of power to imagined or envisioned entities, the possibility of spirit helpers, and the attribution of spirit to food prey. Also implied is the inevitable linkage of the object to the thing it represents, foreshadowing the religious role of idols.

The existence of individual and collective totems, together with practices in which the individual or the clan identifies itself through the totem, suggests linkage of early religious identity with social organization, involving God-Kings and religious hierarchies. The interactive nature of such practices—for instance, the ceremonial relationship of the hunter and the depicted prey—implies a relationship between collective entities, both real and projected. It also implies a collective field of subjective experience, again real or imagined.

Given all the other aspects of early human behavior at this horizon of 100,000-50,000 years ago, it shouldn't surprise us that evidence of religion also surfaces as modern humans step out onto the world stage as "the last man standing." At each crossroads after the advent of modern humans, we'll see that each new adaptation in evolution is also often a revolution.

7

Evolution and Revolution

"Those who cannot learn from history are doomed to repeat it"

Attributed to philosopher George Santayana

EVERYONE IS FAMILIAR WITH THE APHORISM THAT IF WE DON'T LEARN from history, we are bound to repeat it. This and its several variants appear to trace to comments by philosopher George Santayana in his volume *Reason in Common Sense* (1905). Such words have become perennial wisdom. The integrative era suggests we may be able to jump a step ahead, avoiding the fate of repeating history!

Polls indicate nearly 80% of people believe that patterns are discernable in history. Utilizing a transcultural, world-centric approach, teasing out these historical patterns has been the pursuit of academics from as early as the 19th century. Known as developmentalists or structuralists, their work evolved into those of modern integralists such as Ken Wilber, Don Beck, and Chris Cowan.

Remember the colloquialism, "It's just a phase"? Just as it's common for each of us to recognize stages or phases in a person's life because we observe the patterns, the developmentalists and integralists see patterns in history and suggest what they may mean, especially with regard to the future.

From Cosmology to the Challenge of Human History

Whether one subscribes to a belief in biological evolution or theistic creation, the process after the emergence of human beings has clearly involved adaptation, as all recognize. Success at developing skill sets has been and continues to be crucial for our survival.

The sweep of history has fascinated humankind, forming the basis of interpretations of history that are both secular and religious. These have come and gone among us for centuries, ranging from elaborate approaches like that of the materialist Karl Marx—proceeding from primitive communism to slave-based society, feudalism, capitalism, socialism, and perfected communism—to the more audacious beliefs of various doomsday sects. Organized religions support their own purposeful views of history, and courses like "The Goal of Redemptive History" or "Summing Up All Things in Christ" abound on the Western internet, with similar courses for Islam in the Near East. Academics have aimed at global syntheses, such as psychiatrist-philosopher Karl Jaspers' *The Origin and Goal of History* (1953), which brought us recognition of the Axial Age.

All of this illustrates the compulsion of our species to seek a deeper meaning in history, born out by a poll showing 77% of respondents believe in a purpose to history.[27] It's not surprising that developmental and even supposedly providential views of history are recognized by the interspiritual movement as evidence of humanity's interest in the patterns of our history.

Literature that points to a developmental view of history includes the basic teachings of Buddhism and India's Vedic tradition, which in the West has been prominent in the writings and influence of philosophers and theologians such as Pierre Teilhard de Chardin, Henri Bergson, Alfred North Whitehead, and the German idealist philosophers. It's these views that, since the late 19th century, have coalesced into the body of scholarship known as structuralist or developmentalist, proponents of which have included such philosophers and

---

[27] Yahoo Answers (UK), 2009.

psychologists as Jean Gebser, Clare Graves, Jane Loevinger, Abraham Maslow, Lawrence Kohlberg, Jean Piaget, and Susanne Cook-Greuter.

The audience for this approach has been broadened by those futurists already mentioned, with the work of Ken Wilber, along with Don Beck and Chris Cowan, now available in some 40 languages. However, although there is an urgent need to make the general public aware of these views and their implications for our future, most educational institutions are so entrenched in specialization—an addiction encouraged by our current society—that holistic or futurist views often filter out to the wider world only through the commercial book and periodical trade. Even then, there is pushback, especially by the corporate and financial establishments that have so much to lose from change. To understand the forces arrayed against the advancement of our species in its present crisis, we need only remind ourselves of the multimillion-dollar opposition to pollution control, tobacco reform, and alternative energy.

In our era of inevitable globalization, the transdisciplinary and transcultural search for informative historical patterns, which is a focus of significance for both the religious and secular dimensions, cannot be ignored. If, as Brother Teasdale predicted, interspirituality is the most likely direction of religion in the Third Millennium, we need to identify those elements that point to an emerging Interspiritual Age.

The Crossover Between Scientific and Religious Insight

The activities and skill sets of what scientists call "The Great Leap Forward"—including tools, weapons, clothing, fire making, the complexification of language, the creation of art, and burial of the dead—imply the presence of an analytic, reflective, and introspective mind, or what we call "consciousness."

Such internal qualities engendered an explosive external development involving the dramatic expansion of the geographic range of this intelligent creature. This beginning of our collective narrative brings us face to face with the crossover of scientific and religious insight.

Here it's possible to make a connection with the creation story of Adam and Eve leaving the Garden of Eden. There are more parallels with this story than may at first be obvious.

In a discussion on gotquestions.org, which addresses biblical questions, readers were asked what Adam and Eve were like.[28] Responses included comments such as Adam and Eve were primitive but not cavemen. A survey of the responses indicates that most of the characteristics of humankind that integralists date to about 50,000 years ago, and that developmentalists identify as humanity's "Magical-Animistic" epoch, are quite similar to some creationist ideas of Adam and Eve. They also mention such traits as the sense of good and evil, holding grudges, jealousy and revenge killings, along with clan and tribal beliefs and rituals, including deference to elders and magical spirits. The Genesis stories have all of these, from the snake in the Garden of Eden to the killing of Abel by Cain.

The sense of good and evil, and the holding of grudges, certainly fits the Genesis narrative, as well as the kind of social and religious activity it recounts. All of these traits typify primitive "animist" cultures (the academic term for primal cultures steeped in spirit-world beliefs). The integral writers also identify the vestigial elements of this epoch that remain with us today. Magical-Animistic behavior still occurs in primitive Third World cultures.

This culture of honor codes, curses, revenge, secret rituals, and celebration of brute strength is also found in more-developed societies, in the form of gang tattoo culture, mafia code culture, and even certain qualities of some military, athletic, and corporate subcultures. One need only watch advertising for the military to see how these codes are couched in these cultures: lines such as "the secret handshake," "the badge of the elite," "to take him out before he takes you out," and "to shoot things, to blow things up, is a man's dream." Athletic, corporate, club, and college hazing are further examples. Integralists suggest such behavior is still operative in about 10% of our modern world.

---

[28] www.gotquestions.org.

Although scientists and creationists agree on the general attributes of early modern humans, we're not so lucky when we rewind the tape a little further. The epoch prior to the Magical-Animistic period is called the "Archaic-Instinctive" period and refers to the era before *Homo sapiens* became "the last man standing," dated about 100,000 years ago. The scientific, and especially brain-mind, data from this period is important. This is humankind before the skills of the Great Leap Forward and prior to moving out from their point of origin into the rest of the world. These are the characteristics of the "last *few* men standing," including Neanderthal, Flores, Denisova man, and early-modern humans—often also called "Cro-Magnon man," the creature that outsmarted all others and went on to inherit the earth.

The Origin of Spirituality—
the Experience of "the Gods"

Characteristic of these ancient creatures was a more instinctive, reflexive, automatic, and survivalist kind of behavior—quite animal-like, actually. The early human mind was less analytic, reflective, and introspective, with a lesser sense of an individual self. This parallels the insight of Princeton psychologist Dr Julian Jaynes, put forward in 1976 in a bestselling study entitled *The Origin of Consciousness in the Breakdown of the Bicameral Mind*. Jaynes presented compelling evidence from ancient stories and early artifacts that the primitive reflexive human mind, which he dubbed the "bicameral mind," functioned by certain parts of the brain directly telling other parts of the brain what to do. His analysis of ancient texts in the context of what we know of brain pathology today prompted him to conclude that ancient peoples likely received this brain direction internally as voices and visual images. He suggested these directions became identified by early humans first as nature spirits and ancestors, then eventually as "the gods" of which we read in early texts. Evidence of this internal dialogue of the brain is reflected not only in stories of these gods, but also in the countless idols created to represent them.

As a result of the use of increasingly complex language, the brain developed in the direction of greater spaciousness, allowing the mind to debate with itself concerning what action the individual should take, instead of waiting to be told by the gods. From this development steadily emerged all the aspects of analytic and computational abilities, introspection, reflection, and creativity that reflect our modern conscious mind.

Jaynes showed that this development occurred at different rates in different cultures, since the pace of learning new skill sets was correlated with social conditions such as degrees of freedom and leisure. He also showed that the gradual replacement of the more reflexive animal-like bicameral mind by the increasingly conscious mind was reflected in tumultuous social change. Early societies that required little civil authority and law enforcement were, within a century or two of this change in the brain, in need of totalitarian rule to maintain order. Such previously unexplained ancient social transformations make sense if the minds of ordinary citizens had become diverse and discordant.

Jaynes' view is supported by the current understanding of anthropology that humans differ from all the primates in their unparalleled ability to teach and learn. If this trait set us apart originally, how easy then to understand the rate of skill set attainment that occurred as human culture complexified.

There is no need to interpret Jaynes' ideas just as a materialist matter of physical brain and emergent mind. In the context of the new physics, a continuum is understood to exist between relative formlessness and form, which enables us to consider Jaynes' bicameral model in a more holistic light. We can ask what's implied by further ongoing development of brain-mind spaciousness and what it says to us in the context of the current integrative and holistic age. Also, we can ask what it means in terms of the unfolding of creative spirituality in the coming Interspiritual Age.

Jaynes' proposal that the early bicameral mind has been gradually replaced by the more complex, calculating, reflective, and introspective conscious mind is reflected in the developmental idea of history championed by the developmentalists and integralists. It allows us to see early human origins, brain development, emerging consciousness, and the flow of history from a single perspective.

Whereas the vestiges remaining with us from the Magic-Animist epoch included a plethora of behaviors based on clan loyalty, competition, jealousy, grudges, and revenge, fortunately the vestiges of the earlier Archaic-Instinctive epoch seem to appear today in only a small number, perhaps as low as 1%, of our species worldwide. They can be observed in a variety of impaired behaviors, including infantile behavior, senility, and various kinds of mental or neurological impairment, whether natural or induced.

Julian Jaynes' views of cognitive development clearly suggest that in the primitive, more animal-like brain of early humans, the messages of one part of the brain to another were experienced as either inner voices or urges, or displayed as visual experiences. Ancient literature abounds with narratives of these experiences, though it's been hard for modern humans to understand what such experiences meant. Often they were dismissed as simply "mythology." However, it's now clear that early humans experienced a direct, and often urgent, relationship to this inner environment.

The overwhelmingly compelling nature of these experiences is apparent not only in references to them in ancient literature and art, but also in other behavior from early history that would otherwise seem peculiar. Understanding that early humans experienced such voices and visions directing them helps explain otherwise inexplicable behavior like belief in idols, oracles, and divination (drawing lots, throwing bones, etc.), which pervaded earth's early cultures. Whereas the modern mind would consider drawing lots or throwing bones an appeal to chance, study of the ancient religions shows these activities weren't related to a sense of chance, but to a search for direction. This makes sense of ancient civilizations such as Greece and Rome, which on the one hand had amazing technological skills and on the other consulted oracles or cast lots (threw bones) when making strategic civil and military decisions.

Paralleling these observations, analysis of dreams in primitive peoples reveals that far more of their dreams involve direct commands from dreamed personages than are experienced by those in modern societies. This makes sense of such phenomena as massive human sacrifice in the early Mayan culture of Mexico, deriving from a dream recorded by their king in which he recounted being commanded to offer such sacrifices by the Sun God.

Research clearly suggests that the spiritual acumen of humankind has been gradually developing from a primitive array of experiences to a more complex and sophisticated assortment of skill sets. Such research helps us understand why the magic-mythic lens has been so compelling to our species. Even hundreds of years after the arising of the human rational lens, subjective inner urges still persist as one of the great arbiters of what human beings believe about reality, motivating how they live their lives.

It's relevant to link our knowledge of brain development to what appears to be the ongoing expansion of spaciousness in mind and consciousness, including the worldwide trend that interspirituality identifies as an emerging unity consciousness. Much of the research on human cognition and consciousness has generally been in the context of the scientific view of consciousness, which limits it to the experience of individual body-minds—a view that differs from the wider shared collective consciousness held by the world's religions and spiritual traditions.

An Integrated View

Science by nature employs purely rational approaches. It views early humans as having gone through a pre-rational period that over thousands of years developed into the current rational and ultimately scientific epoch. Even as science characterizes the pre-rational period as one of immaterial superstition, it identifies much of modern religion and spirituality as part of an irrelevant pre-rational experience.

The world's religions and spiritual traditions have a different view. While acknowledging an early pre-rational period and the subsequent periods dominated by rationalism and materialism, they suggest that both ways of knowing are important to our future and advise the need for a post-rational discussion that will develop such a synthesis. Interspirituality and the integralists identify the current era as precisely the time for a more holistic and integrative approach.

The question is whether science and spirituality can agree on the need for such a post-rational discussion. The pervasiveness of this divide is illustrated by a television interview with the co-discoverer of DNA, Dr James Watson, who stated that the next frontier for humanity is the understanding of consciousness, while also asserting that the world's religions have nothing to contribute to this conversation. Integral philosopher Ken Wilber's statement that this view is "the gold standard of ignorance" highlights the fundamental disagreement.

We propose that the pre-rational period acknowledged by both science and religions was a primitive non-dual experience. It was replaced by the dualism of the rational epoch and in turn is being replaced by a trend toward a more advanced non-dual experience. We think this reflects the ongoing march of brain and cognitive development. It would suggest that what's propelling the current trend toward unity consciousness is extremely fundamental—the same ongoing trend in brain and cognitive development that has been propelling human development through history all along.

8

The Great Advances in Human History

"Tomorrow is not a movement in time. Tomorrow is a movement in consciousness"

Rafael Nasser

THE PERIOD OF SIMPLE AND TRADITIONAL CULTURES, BUILT AROUND CLANS and tribes, continued across the period from at least 50,000 to 10,000 years ago. This is a significant length of time and includes the Magical-Animist epochs. We call it the First Great Advance because it's character-ized by the movement out of Africa and into the adjacent Middle East, the Mediterranean region, and Europe—and eventually on through Asia.

This extended period saw marked oscillation in regional climates, influenced by the vast ice sheets to the north, a circumstance that appears to have aided human dispersion because ability to adapt to fluctuating warmth or cold opened up new land. Foodstuffs were ini-tially mainly based on hunting and foraging, again reinforcing the need to wander in search of suitable areas where they could subsist for extended periods. It's estimated that at about 25,000 years ago, the population of modern humans on earth was around 300,000.

Modern humans expanded into the southern Mediterranean and Middle East some 60,000 years ago, India and Australia 50,000 years ago, Europe and northern Asia 45,000 years ago, and East Asia and China 40,000 years ago. Also 40,000 years ago, a second wave expanded into Australia, Mongolia and Siberia 30,000 years ago, North America from Siberia by land and sea 15,000 years ago, and South America 13,000 years ago.

In this time period, areas in the Middle East such as the Fertile Crescent, which is the watershed and surrounding vicinity of the Tigris and Euphrates rivers, afforded lush and climatically comfortable regions. This was the result of an interplay between heat from the south and glacial melt from the north. Particularly from 13,000 years ago, this confluence of warm temperatures, abundant water, and rich soils resulting from glacial oscillations and runoff likely accounts for the abundant "Eden-type" stories in the cultural memory of this region, which have been handed down through oral and written traditions. A similar link has been found in ancient Egypt, where oral tradition recalls the Nile before its flow began toward the south, as incredible as this may seem.

Homo sapiens' expansion of their distribution across the Old World during this period resulted in marked divergences in physical appearances, such as features, hair, and skin color. This was itself significant, since before *Homo sapiens* became the "last man standing," we were one of a number of very different-looking humanlike creatures. By the epoch of the First Great Advance, we had become a diverse-looking creature, while remaining a single interbreeding population.

Let's Eat: Farming Is Invented

The widening distribution of early humans had a profound effect on further diversification of our skills and innovations, as did the rising sea levels that accompanied the end of the last Ice Age some 13,000 years ago. Because of these sea level changes, many groups of humans became isolated in ecologically diverse regions, which led to specialization in food production and the beginning of agriculture, particularly in southwestern Asia.

Understanding that crops could be raised from seeds was so compelling to everyone who heard about it that it triggered a revolution, with the innovations of agriculture spreading rapidly. The swift advances in all areas of food production across the planet, the result of our ability to teach and learn, are astounding. In Mesopotamia, these advances included foraged wild grains 19,000 years ago, the invention of the bow and arrow 15,000 years ago, development of millage and storage 14,000 years ago, the domestication of goats, sheep, and dogs 12,000 years ago, the annual harvesting of seeds 11,000 years ago, common use of wheat, barley, peas, and swine 10,500 years ago, common use of rye and cattle 10,000 years ago, and the common use of flax 9,000 years ago.

Added to these developments in Mesopotamia, the Jordan Valley saw the common use of figs 11,500 years ago, while in China the common use of rice occurred 9,000 years ago.

Farming spread to southern Europe, Egypt, and India by 6000 BCE, Northern China by 5000 BCE, all of continental Europe by 5500 BCE, and the British Isles by 5000 BCE. Also in 5000 BCE, cotton farming was begun in India, with farming spreading to Sudan by 3500 BCE and corn being grown in Mexico by 2800 BCE. Peru saw the introduction of farming in 2500 BCE, North America by 2200 BCE, and West Africa and the Saharan region by 2000 BCE. Corn was being cultivated throughout the New World by 1500 BCE.

Domestication of animals began with goats because they could feed themselves, followed by the introduction of other livestock as early humans learned to cultivate crops. The relationship of humans and the domestic dog, which appears to have expanded in a very short period after arising in northeast Asia, was of particular importance. Because there were no fences at the time, humans relied on their dogs to prevent livestock from wandering away. Larger animals like oxen were put to work for heavier and more complex tasks such as building, hauling goods, and irrigation.

These advances further aided a human population explosion. It's estimated that by 15,000 years ago, world population had grown to 700,000. During the next 7,000 years, as a result of the agricultural revolution, the emergence of larger villages and towns, and the ecological stability of new lands released by the receding ice, population surpassed 5 million. During this period we also see specialization within local societies, including construction of dwellings, the provision of water and irrigation systems, the building of roads, construction of implements, the development of defenses and military skills, storage of foodstuff to protect against famine, and even long-term planning. All this would lead to the coming era of cities and city-states, a second revolution.

Our Heritage from these Early Eras

Positive and negative elements remain with us from the earliest eras of humankind.

On the positive side is the inherent relationship most humans feel to nature. For instance, why does almost every household and business have pictures on the wall, many of which are of flowers, mountains, oceans, and other scenes of nature? This connection is a part of our nature.

The question is, how skilled are we in living out the implications of this connection? How many of us have pictures of nature on our walls, yet do nothing to protect the environment? Just because we have an inherent awareness of something doesn't mean we will act on it. As soon as complexification of societies began, humans began to feel separate from nature. As history moves forward, the implications of this sense of separation obviously become more and more complex. This problem traces to these early epochs.

An even more crucial heritage from this period is our inherent connection to the magic-mythic lens. In our rational, scientific era, it may be hard for us to understand that the majority of the world's population adheres to fundamentalist religious beliefs, embracing concepts that to many in the modern world seem preposterous. Despite this, the developed world's bestsellers in literature and film feature superheroes and purveyors of magical powers. A sense of the magical is deeply ingrained in humanity. The question is whether we can balance this inherent connection to the magical with critical thinking and the gifts the rational revolution of later centuries has brought us. The danger is to fall into the trap of believing in magical solutions or apocalyptic fates that are simply untrue.

We mustn't underestimate the implications of the fact that science and spirituality, which are our two most compelling ways of knowing about reality, coexist as cultures that have little to do with each other. Reflecting the current integrative age, all of the basic books of interspirituality—from the writings of Brother Teasdale to his mentor Father Bede Griffiths—include copious pages discussing the science-spirituality interface and the advances in both that point to a more dynamic, shared reality. This element was one of the major shifts in awareness that Brother Teasdale said would characterize the emerging Interspiritual Age.

The Second Great Advance: from Towns to Cities and Empires

Around 10,000-7,000 years ago—8000-5000 BCE—towns, followed by cities, and eventually empires, sprang up around the Old World as humanity entered the Early Bronze Age technologically. In the march of developmental epochs recognized by integral writers, and thus significant to the unfolding Interspiritual Age, this is the "Power Gods, Egocentric, Dominionist" period, dated from about 7000 BCE.

The explosive social growth of this epoch was possible because of several factors, not least of which was the development of a tiered citizenry that constituted a class system. This led to a division of labor for such work as food production, which was accompanied by regional distribution of goods and wider trade and barter. This allowed humans to diversify into two main groupings. The first of these was rural agricultural communities. The second was towns, followed by cities, that fostered specialty living.

European sociologist Jacque Ellul has focused on how revolutionary the development of city life was. However, like all revolutions, it was a double-edged sword. The movement of large numbers into towns and cities, supported by the surrounding rural areas and in turn giving back more sophisticated goods, created a better life for many. It also made possible leisure, which fostered interest in mathematics, art, and invention. Simultaneously, it created fixed class systems, authoritarian hierarchies, and knotty new concepts such as land and property ownership, not to mention land and property value. Perhaps even more challenging, it marked the beginning of a class of citizens who considered themselves separate from nature—a shift that would eventually have huge consequences.

The Emergence of the God-Kings

The greatest significance of this period was the rise of what are known as the "God Kings." Their coming on the scene was the foundation for church-state empires that would dominate the world for thousands of years, especially in this and the subsequent Totalitarian epoch.

For this social structure to arise required the convergence of two major developmental trends: the power of the magic-mythic lens, coupled with the ongoing complexification of human social structure and technological capabilities. The God-King signified the transference of magic-mythic authority from the clan leader of the Archaic epoch to the tribal leader of the Magic-Animist epoch, and then to this new cosmopolitan monarch of the town, city, or empire. There was no real change in the magic-mythic lens itself, only its transference to the monolithic and hierarchical social structures of the new order. Not only did the God-King hold this exalted social position, but he or she was also the titular voice of "the gods."

In modern times it's nearly impossible for us to imagine the monolithic social structures and mindset that accounted for these kinds of civilizations. The claim of the God-King to sacrosanct status was unchallengeable. Its untouchability is all that can account for the ancients' tolerance of despot after despot, just so long as they represented "the lineage." Fortunately this kind of mindset is easier to understand in the context of the gradual advance humans were making from the early more animal-like, reflexive mind to the critically thinking reflective conscious mind. In the early monolithic city-states and empires, especially before any of these states interacted with each other, the ruling spell of the God-King was far from easy to break.

This is the era of some of the first great civilizations we think of from our history books, such as Sumer and early Mesopotamia. The area of the Fertile Crescent was witness to the emergence of these city-states and empires. Some of the most intriguing specimens, such as Gobekli Tepe in southern Turkey—which seems to have arisen while many of the population around it were still living in the stone age—have only recently been discovered.

Town and city-states of the God-King period from the Pre-Bronze Age include Gobekli Tepe in southern Turkey (9000 BCE), and from the Early Bronze Age Jericho in Palestine (4500 BCE), Ali Kosh in southern Iran (4000 BCE), and Sumer in Uruk (Iraq, 3500 BCE).

The significance of the arising of the God-Kings and the empires that would dominate the world for millennia can't be grasped without appreciating the technological advances humans were making at the time. Even in our modern era, we comment that our technological abilities eclipse our moral and ethical skills. This perennial problem of humankind is one of the great challenges of the present time. Some of the great advances of the era of the God-Kings may seem commonplace today, but a little reflection shows how revolutionary they were for the time.

Gold and copper were introduced by 5000 BCE, the plough by 4000 BCE, the wheel by 3700 BCE, writing from 3200 BCE—and thereafter independently in many places—and the smelting of bronze by 3200 BCE.

One advance of the God-King period, writing, had profound implications for spirituality, since it reflects a radical development of symbolic thinking and consciousness. First known from the Sumerian (Sumer) empire around 3000 BCE, the method involved making marks on clay tablets. Known as cuneiform, it likely arose from more primitive practices evident in the same region from about 4000 BCE. Testifying once again to how quickly humans learn, the addition of written language to the spoken word soon spread throughout the early world.

The historical study of writing is the realm of the complex and intriguing field of linguistics. The evolution of increasingly more symbolic, abstract, and metaphorical language capabilities, along with the relationship of pictorial to alphabetical styles of writing, reflects how human mind and consciousness were unfolding. As a further illustration of the narrowness of the early, more primitive mechanical mind, writing wasn't used for any kind of complex communication or thinking, but primarily for accounting purposes to keep track of food storage and taxes. Early examples also lack abstract or metaphorical thinking, further evidence that the more complex conscious mind was still only gradually developing.

The era of the God-King reflects the terms the integral and developmental writers have used to describe this period: "Egocentric," "Dominionist," and "Power Gods." This was an era when the king was believed by his subjects to be linked to the eternal spirit world, which bequeathed to him his God-King identity. This time of unabashed ego is reflected not only in the king, but also in heroic personages and their exalted sagas, sung by the bards of the era and eventually written down in epic literature, as well as in myths of powerful magical spirits, spells, dragons, and the like. The older biblical stories likewise reveal that this was a rough and tumble era. Heroes lived life lustfully, with little concern for the collateral damage of their actions. Vestiges of this mindset still mark much of human behavior today.

The Transition from God-Kings to Totalitarian Empires

The 4,000-year epoch of the God-King civilizations was gradually replaced by a different kind of empire across the entire Old World, a system requiring strict totalitarian rule to maintain law and order. Though the demarcation of this change, which occurred around 3000 BCE, is well known, the reason for it has often mystified historians.

Civilizations of the God-King period appear to have been social

structures of tight monolithic conformism built around general recognition of, and natural loyalty to, the God-King and his or her royal family.
While there were magnificent public works projects during this period,
including both city building and monument construction, there's little
evidence of a need for strict law enforcement and social coercion.

The opposite becomes true as empires from North Africa to central
Asia arise and thrive in the Middle and Late Bronze ages. Not only are
the new kingdoms of this later period far more totalitarian, but even
the fabric of the early God-King empires appears to decay into increasing social chaos, which had to be offset by stricter authoritarian rule.

The reasons for a greater need for social control seem to lie in pivotal
changes occurring in mind and consciousness. Societies were adjust-
ing to the freer and more expansive, analytical, and reflective mind and
societal complexification of the period, to which an abundance of religious, social, artistic, and linguistic evidence points. This becomes all the
more clear if we posit that during the period of the God-Kings, the less
complexified, non-analytic, non-reflective mind—a continuation of the
Archaic epoch—was still dominant.

As situations arose to drive the development of the mind into a
more questioning mode, the monolithic social fabric broke down.
We are thinking of situations such as different peoples and languages
meeting each other, leading to arguing, fighting over gods and worldviews, and exchanging goods and slave populations. It's one thing to
expect natural allegiance to one God-King or set of gods, and quite
another when there are competing options. The confusion inherent
in such social uncertainty would likely be answered with oppression.

Evidence of a naturally monolithic social order in civilizations of
the God-King period is pervasive, ranging from the use of writing
for the enumeration of goods and conveying of orders from superiors
to the permanent positioning in all dwellings of effigies of the gods
and the God-Kings. Art in the form of publically displayed murals,
freezes, and mosaics from the period regularly depicts the God-King
listening to the gods, and the people worshiping the God-King—an
unmistakable illustration of social positioning and hierarchy.

Contrary to how our modern mind might view this, citizens of these kingdoms weren't robots, but there was an inherent unity built around a shared zeitgeist[29] that was constantly reinforced by the social structure. At least at the beginning, there would have been little contact with any contrary or competing worldview except in times of war.

A striking illustration of the divide between the cultures of the God-Kings and the later totalitarian empires is the meeting of the Spanish Conquistadors with the South American Inca tribes. History has found it hard to understand how a few hundred Europeans, thousands of miles from home, could conquer hundreds of thousands of Inca warriors who themselves had conquered and enslaved most of western South America. However, if the medieval European mentality represented a more calculating, analytical, even treacherous mind, while the Inca psyche followed the mode of the more simplistic, monolithic, follow-the-leader God-King states, it isn't difficult to understand. If the God-King could be quickly kidnapped and killed by these visiting foreigners, either the myth was shattered or the foreigners seen as representing more powerful gods.

The Epoch of Totalitarian Empires

There's no doubt that as the Bronze Age matured and the isolated city-state cultures began to mix, trade, fight, argue about their gods, and exchange large slave populations, a new kind of empire proliferated from North Africa across the Middle East and into Asia. With the monolithic social structures of the God-Kings no longer possible, the regional empires that arose and flourished survived not by the mythic power of a God-King, but by brute force. This period is often referred to as the Era of Regional Civilizations.

Six regional civilizations are usually recognized: Tigris-Euphrates River civilizations in Mesopotamia originating around 3500 BCE, Nile River civilizations in Egypt from 3100 BCE, the Minoan civilization on the island of Crete from 2800 BCE, the Indus River civilizations in India from 2500 BCE, and the Yellow River civilizations

---

[29] The defining spirit or mood of a period in history, reflected in the beliefs of the time.

in China from 2000 BCE. This was the high-tide of the epoch of Old World empires. Empires also flourished in the New World, although their isolation leaves them out of our discussion.

As empire building in the Old World reached the time of about 3000 BCE, we find more and more evidence of the gradual breakdown of social order and the arising of repressive social structures to counter it. Even in the rare civilizations such as Assyria that bridge both the God-King and later Totalitarian eras, this loss of social order is evident. It is paralleled by writings and art of the time that depict the local monarchs as unsure of their relationship with the gods and in search of new ways to obtain divine guidance. Assyrian freezes that once depicted the king standing in front of the image of the god listening intently now often depicted the king in front of an empty throne with no god apparent, often assisted by others trying to listen for guidance. In Julian Jaynes' work, this is emphasized as representing the gradual breakdown of the primitive monolithic mind to which the voice of the gods was clear. It signals the beginning of eras in which the developing conscious mind, not quite sure what to listen to, or listening more to its own individual analysis, sowed the ancient world with a kind of psychic chaos. Whose gods did you heed, and who represented them?

The potential for social upheaval resulted in political suppression, which plunged the world into four millennia of dictatorial social rule. For the integral writers, this is the era of Absolutist-Obedience Mythic Order and Purposeful Authoritarianism.

This era can be divided into roughly three periods. First came the middle and late Bronze Ages, followed by the Iron Age—both ages defined by the general kind of technology that dominated during these periods. Last came the Axial Age, unique in that this is the period in which most of the world's currently active religions arose. Given the social uncertainty and instability that typified the Totalitarian Age, this should come as no surprise. If the old gods had failed, or were no longer accessible, it was perfectly natural for the magic-mythic desires of humanity to search for a new slate of gods—or to begin to imagine that there might be but one God.

Patriotism Is Born

In the context of 40 centuries of totalitarian rule, it's not surprising that of the eight paradigm shifts delineated by Brother Wayne Teasdale for the designation of a new age, six have to do with undoing the bonds of loyalty to clan, nation, religion, and skin color, along with abstaining from violence to solve problems, coupled with the dream of moving toward holistic, heartistic, trans-traditional, trans-cultural, and transnational perspectives. The heritage of humanity's loyalty to leaders and flags, nations and names, anthems and patriotic stories—resulting in the death of countless millions in war—has been ingrained in all of us, reflecting the power of this epoch that endured for some 40 centuries!

We all identify with the list of empires from the Totalitarian epoch, be it from the movies, books, or even Sunday school, spanning 3000 BCE to 1000 CE, the period of the Bronze and Iron Ages. Early Old World empires include successive dynasties of Egypt, the late Minoan civilization of Crete, the Achaean and Mycenaean empires of the Greek peninsula, the later Indus River valley civilizations of India, the Majiayao and Shang cultures of China, the Dong Son culture of Vietnam, the later Assyrian and Babylonian empires, and the Middle Eastern cultures of Canaan, Ugarit, Kadesh, Megiddo, the Kingdom of Israel, the Hittites, Troy, Hekla, Urartu, and Phrygia. Late Old World empires were Phoenicia, Greece, Persia, Rome, Macedonia, the Selucids, Bactria, Maurya, Parthia, the Sassanids, and the Byzantium. New World empires encompass the Olmec, Teotihuacan, Maya, Zapotec, Mixtec, Huastec, Purepecha, Toltec, and Aztec civilizations.

In contrast to the homogenous cultural patterns of the God-King epoch, during this era social intermixing, trade, war, and the slave system reveal one empire and its gods and cultural styles vying against another. Not only were worldviews mixing and constantly being challenged, but new ideas were also spreading. The seeds of these new ideas then sprang new roots in far-flung societies where the wealthy leisure class had time for art, mathematics, and invention (or the cultivation of it in others through patronage). Odd as it may seem, the totalitarian structures that propped up these systems also generated the structures for revolutionary change within—as long as this was done carefully and didn't overly rue the local dictator, emperor, or king.

It's difficult, perhaps impossible, for us to imagine the confusion that resulted from contact, conflict, and absorption among peoples with different, singular understandings of reality. We perhaps gained some sense of it from the great era of world immigration of the 19th century, but even this awareness has faded for many.

The ironies of the Totalitarian epoch are many. While tyrants of the old order continued to rule, western philosophy arose and advanced. Even as this new thought sowed the seeds of scientific inquiry and early invention in some, others were seeking out oracles and divination to recapture the ancient voices of the gods. Historians emphasize that the voices of the oracles were never doubted—a testimony to how immovable humanity had become with regard to its early experiences of the voices of the gods.

Voices of the old gods are particularly associated with the Greek Oracles, spanning from 560 BCE to 390 CE. These included Pythia at Delphi, Dione and Zeus at Dondona, and Apollo at Didyma, Corinth, Bassae, Delos, and Aegina. Meanwhile, voices of the new thought arising with Western philosophy included, listed chronologically, the Greek philosophers Aesop around 600 BCE, Pythagoras, Aeschylus, Sophocles, Euripides, Herodotus, Socrates, Hippocrates, Democritus, Plato, and Aristotle circa 350 BCE.

The Great Religions Arise

Ironically, history shows that within these rigid states, the effect of specialization and the creation of leisure (for some) led to pivotal advances in human thinking and technology. The existential angst that affected the masses led others to seek fresh answers in reflection and introspection, resulting in the birth of the great religions and philosophies that still compel much of the world today. Thus the epoch of Totalitarianism became the Axial Age, which birthed the bases of many of the world's current philosophies and religions.

Early texts include the Epic of Gilgamesh from Persia around 2700 BCE, the Vedic texts in Hinduism around 1500 BCE, texts of monotheism in Egypt under Pharaoh Amenhotep IV around 1300 BCE, texts of monotheism in Persia through Zoroaster around 1200 BCE, and Torah texts in Judaism beginning around 960 BCE.

Founders of the world's religions were Lao Tzu in China and Zoroaster in Persia circa 600 BCE, Confucius in China born 551 BCE, Buddha in India born 542 BCE, Jesus in Palestine born around 5 BCE, and Mohammed in Arabia born 570 CE.

Some of the more pivotal events in the history of the world's religions include the fact that Judaic texts continued to be composed from 900 to 100 BCE, while the Upanishads in Hinduism arose circa 500 BCE. Around 300 BCE Buddhism diversified in Ceylon, Burma, and Tibet, with early Buddhist texts being composed circa 100 BCE. Moving into the Common Era (formerly referred to as "AD"), Paul of Tarsus expanded the Jewish sect of Christianity to the Gentiles, with the movement growing so fast that by 313 Emperor Constantine recognized it as the official religion of the Empire. In 622 Mohammed moved to Medina, becoming leader of the new Islamic faith. Around 600 CE the Brahman priesthood was established in Hinduism, while Moslem expansion in Europe peaked 732 CE.

Prolific as the explosion of thought and religion of the Axial Age was, it still reflected the rigid authoritarianism of the time. New beliefs that gave life fresh direction often resorted to enforcement in the form of new authoritarian structures, many of which endure today on the cusp of the Interspiritual Age. Absolute codes of conduct shaped right and wrong into commands of allegiance reinforced by the concept of eternal reward or punishment in an afterlife. Most often, new beliefs were projected in the form of exclusive priesthoods, conflicting and contradictory end-time scenarios, and adherence to sacred texts, all of which established immovable obstacles to dialogue.

As the cultures of emerging religions became enmeshed with the authoritarian structures of the day, they led to authoritarian European and Asian forms of state religion. Deciding not to share the subjective gifts their new paths offered, the different religions went the way of exclusivism, which led to centuries of war and cruelty as religion allied itself with the state. The tragic consequences can perhaps only be remedied by an unfolding Interspiritual Age.

Within the rigid structures of newly emerging religions and the societies they engendered, there was still the possibility for something fundamentally different and of immeasurable importance to emerge. Where spirituality and free inquiry could be pursued, from philosophical inquiry to the mystical and awakening pursuits of new Eastern paths and Western contemplative experimentation, something else was afoot. Even as the Axial philosophies show the conscious mind evolving into complex dualistic thought, the spiritual paths of the Axial Age evidence the emergence of nonduality.

All at once we had the birth of the Western philosophies and, flying in the face of the old religion of the Eastern and Western oracles, the birth of sophisticated mysticism of the world's new religions, East and West. In these were new gifts of perception and understanding by which the religions might claim their other label, the Great Wisdom Traditions.

Advances in Thinking Foreshadow a New Epoch

Just as peculiar as its effects on religion and thought, the crucible of the Totalitarian Age was also the wellspring for literary, mathematical, and scientific advances, reflecting the paradox of rigid social structures that bequeathed to some the climate for reflection and innovation. The astounding results set the stage for the advancement of science and technology.

The variety of advances in science, technology, and the arts is surprising. For instance, silk—so prized for its high quality and luxurious feel—was first used in China around 2700 BCE, reaching Egypt by trade around 1000 BCE. Written versions of the Iliad and Odyssey epics were extant in Greece by 850 BCE. By 520 BCE, Pythagoras in Greece had determined the earth is round. Geometry was invented in Egypt by Euclid around 300 BCE. The Hindu innovate numbers 1–9 emerged in India between 300 and 200 BCE. Around 260 BCE

Archimedes in Greece had invented the lever and calculated Pi. Just 20 years later in 240 BCE Eratosthenes, also in Greece, calculated earth's circumference. Forty years later, circa 200 BCE, silk production extended beyond China. Amazingly, Hipparchus in Greece measured the distance to the moon in 130 BCE. With the growing sophistication of astronomy, the Julian Calendar devised in Rome added the leap year in 46 BCE. Making labor considerably easier, the wheelbarrow was invented in China in 5 BCE, while a short time later in 1 CE the silk trade reached Rome and Greece. It would however be another half millennium before silk production reached Europe in 500 CE—the same year the Hindus developed the zero. By 825 CE Indian numbers had been popularized worldwide. By 850 CE Angkor had become the world's largest city, with a population of 250,000.

Thus closes the riddle of the epoch of Absolutist-Obedience mythic order, the era of purposeful authoritarianism. It added a full 40 centuries to the already prevailing 40 centuries of the God-King period—eight millennia of dictatorial cities, city-states, and empires. Yet from this rigid, egoic, and ethnocentric epoch came the rise of the world's currently reigning philosophies, religions, and precursors of much of modern mathematics and technology.

Regrettable behaviors and social structures from these earlier epochs still dominate much of humanity's existence in the form of fixed worldviews, aggressive allegiances to nations and religions, veneration of violence, glorification of patriotism and war, dictatorship, and oppression—indeed, every form of conflictive behavior imaginable.

Consider the following lines from the Greek epic The Iliad:

For our country 'tis a bliss to die (book 15);

We shall be better able to wear our armor, which never grows weary, and to fight our enemies forever and ever (book 19);

And all those left alive, after the hateful carnage, remember food and drink—so all the more fiercely we can fight our enemies, nonstop, no mercy, durable as the bronze that wraps our bodies (book 19).

Compare these to the words of Nazi SS commander Heinrich Himmler, the architect of the holocaust, explaining to his officers in 1943 how it was possible to perform their extermination duties and still be good, upstanding people:

> It is in our program—elimination of the Jews, extermination, a small matter... to [do] this and at the same time to have remained a decent person—with exceptions due to human weaknesses—has made us tough, and is a glorious chapter.... Let us thank God that we had within us enough self-evident fortitude never to discuss it among us, and we never talked about it. Every one of us was horrified, and yet everyone clearly understood that we would do it next time, when the order is given and when it becomes necessary.[30]

The combination of a fixed worldview with the condoning of violent behavior is how all terrorism is justified, as with Himmler actually believing the violence was justified by a correct religious view.

Integral writers see similar vestiges of our past in the structures of street, motorcycle, and organized crime gangs, the veneration of bad-boy/ bad-girl rock star behavior, reckless sexual behavior by celebrities and politicians, the excesses of mercenary soldiers and contractors in overseas wars, and even overly egocentric and dynastic business leadership. Integralists identify such behaviors in some 20% of our modern population, including those holding 5% of world power.

The authoritarian epoch similarly survives in behaviors that are even more common, such as literalistic and fundamentalist beliefs, guilt-based behavioral controls on the part of religious authorities, blind patriotic and militaristic loyalties to ethnocentric or nationalist identities, condoning of state-sponsored violence in the name of law and order, authoritarian "moral majorities," and corporal and capital

---

[30] Himmler's October 4, 1943 "Poznan speech," from The Holocaust History Project, used by permission of the Holocaust History Project (http://www.holocaust-history.org/himmler-poznan/).

punishment. Such authoritarian behaviors are still active in 40% of the world's population, including those who hold 30% of world power. All of these are vestiges of humanity's 80 centuries of authoritarian and totalitarian structures.

9

The Dawn of the Rational Epoch

"I think, therefore I am"

Descartes

AROUND 1000 CE, THE SOCIAL FABRIC OF THE AUTHORITARIAN EMPIRES began to unravel, propelled ironically by the cumulative result of subcultures and social opportunities their own success had created—niches for art, creative thought, and a growing sense of individuality. Perhaps most momentously, unanticipated natural calamities would also require the Old World populations to explore new ways by which they could survive and thrive.

Thus began what the integral writers call the Multiplistic-Achievist/ Scientific and Strategic period. In this period, the magic-mythic views of the world were challenged by new rationalist worldviews, which is why it's often referred to as the Pre-modern Era.

Encounter and clash between magical and rational worldviews were ongoing, of course, continuing to the present. Indeed, a major challenge for the coming Interspiritual Age will be to skillfully balance our experiences from the subjective internal realm with our knowledge from the objective external realms such as science and technology. From 1000 CE, the next millennium was to experience a seesawing—and at times more of a roller coaster ride—between these extremes.

Authoritarianism Breaks Down

As humanity moved into the Second Millennium CE, a fragmentation began in both religion and the religion-state structures of the time. This fragmentation was based not only on parochial rivalries and struggles for power, but also on the effect of growing private wealth. The rise of wealthy families, clans, and merchant guilds created alternate fulcrums of power. Whereas the feudal nobilities had exploited those below them based on authoritarian power, once these classes came to hold wealth through business, commerce, and banking, the nobility soon needed them to remain in power. The result across much of Europe was a new kind of civil structure consisting of small city-states or merchant republics.

The citizenry of these prosperous local and regional states also had increasing access to education—a result of the revolution triggered by the invention of the printing press, together with the exchange of knowledge, technology, and materials as commercial representatives of families and clans traveled widely and intermingled. In this new cosmopolitan environment nothing could be kept parochial for long.

This new civil structure emerged even as the unity of the Roman Catholic Church, enfranchised since the late Roman authoritarian period, weakened. As it split East and West, corruption abounded, compounded by the heinous excesses of the Inquisition—conducted from the 12th century—and nine economically and socially disastrous military crusades against Islam (1095-1291). Such behavior evidenced vestiges of the authoritarian magic-mythic mentality.

As Catholicism fractured, the seeds of the Protestant Reformation were sown, beginning with the Waldensians in the 1100s and culminating four centuries later with Luther's Ninety-Five Theses (1517) and the Treaty of Westphalia (1648). In this Reformation context, there occurred an equally powerful surge of rationalist and humanist thought, propelled not only by the expanding educational landscape of the time—universities abounded by the 12th century—but also by the central issue of free will championed by the Reformation. Both of these were aided by the rapid growth of technological invention generated by the new freedom of open inquiry. Fracturing of the church meant access to new literature, including the original Greek translations of the New Testament, which were championed by the new intellectual elite and eventually made available to the public.

In the world of education, the movement of rationalism got underway across Europe through the expanding university systems, bringing back the great Greek and Arabic scholars, the writings of the Romans Cicero, Livy, and Seneca, and the great Roman physician Galen. Embracing all aspects of intellectual inquiry and art, this movement was observational and investigative, foreshadowing the scientific method. From it would emerge the historically pivotal "representational" or "mapping" paradigm.

The implications of this new scholastic paradigm were simple yet profound. Instead of looking to the stories of subjective knowing in the narrative of religion, why not look outward and study the world around us? This would lead to a revolution. From a world that had relied on the "say" of the religious priesthood, the new scholastic order emphasized empirical evidence, reason, and the study and comparison of original texts of many languages.

This representational paradigm was to remain dominant until, in the 20th century, it became apparent that its capacities, based mostly on external objective knowing, may be inadequate for upholding a world that's once again teetering.

A Global Plague Spurs a Renaissance in Consciousness

As these conditions were unfolding from the 11th and 12th centuries, the growing cosmopolitanism of the era precipitated a calamity across the European continent. Pandemic illness spread from China through the Crimean and Mediterranean trade routes. By 1350, between 30% and 60% of the European population had perished. The Black Death, which is today regarded as a confluence of bubonic, hemorrhagic, and pneumonic infections accompanied by anthrax and typhus, depleted Europe for the next 150 years.

As with all great extinctions, this plague also opened up fresh opportunity. The civil climate of the era, which had begun to pit the magic-mythic lens of religion against the emergent rationalist thought, raised the question of whether this horrific catastrophe was a punishment from God or whether there were other explanations that are compelling to the inquiring rational mind.

The answer was to spring from the economic and social consequences of the plague. As the dramatic loss in population increased the power of the commercial and working classes, land and food prices declined as much as 30-40%, triggering a new social mobility. This further ascent of workers and tradesmen sealed the success of the emerging city-state and merchant republic social structure. A new social leveling had occurred. Intermingling the aspects of civil society, the arts, education, science, and invention, this rebirth—*la rinascita,* the Renaissance—flourished for a further two centuries.

Some of the highlights in terms of achievements during the Renaissance include the invention of the printing press in Gutenberg in 1450, with over 10 million books in print by 1500. Also circa 1500, Michelangelo, Leonardo da Vinci, and 80 other historic artists and architects thrived. Shakespeare and 12 other major authors appeared circa 1600, along with Thomas Tallis and 20 other famous composers. To these we can add Christopher Columbus and 12 other historic explorers, followed by Kepler and Galileo circa 1610, plus 12 other major astronomers, geographers, and alchemists.

From Renaissance to European Enlightenment

Historians differ on when the Renaissance merged into the wider rise of the European nation-states, the Holy Roman Empire (proclaimed in 1512), and the subsequent European Enlightenment. For obvious reasons, integral writers treat the two as parts of the emerging Rationalist Period. Usually, however, the transition is dated to the decline of Italy and the rise of the other European powers—typically around 1550, based on the sacking of Rome by the army of The Holy Roman Emperor Charles V. After this time, Italy's dominance gave way to stronger nations to its west.

This period of western European domination is generally considered to have matured by 1650, with the close of the rationalist epoch of the Third Great Advance around 1850 as development in the United States and the rest of the New World brought about a planetary political and commercial landscape. However, the contribution of the Renaissance and European Enlightenment to world history is preeminent, establishing most of the norms for world society.

By this time world population had attained 500 million. Political and scientific benchmarks of the European Enlightenment include the end of 30 years of religious war in Europe with the signing of the Treaty of Westphalia in 1648, and the stopping of Muslim invasions at Vienna in 1683—the same year the croissant was invented. By 1689 the British Empire had secured large parts of India. In 1756 there were wars between England and France in Europe, America, and India, with the American independence movement and Revolutionary War following in 1776. Hot on the heels of American independence was the French Revolution in 1789, with Napoleon coming to power in France in 1798. Soon after, in 1807, Britain banned the oceanic slave trade; the same year, the United States banned slave imports, effective January 1, 1808. Napoleon's ill-fated invasion of Russia occurred in 1812, and in 1813 Simon Bolivar fought Spain to liberate Latin America. That same year the British took control of all India, defeating the French at Waterloo in 1815.

Monumental strides were being taken in science and industry during this period. In 1687 Newton published his *Principia Mathematica*. In 1764 the invention of the Spinning Jenny automated spinning, while James Watt invented the steam engine just five years later in 1769. The same year as the American Declaration of Independence, Adam Smith published his capitalist manifesto in *Wealth of Nations*. By 1795 the French had adopted the metric system, with the smallpox vaccine being tested just a year later in 1796. The era of instant communication was also inaugurated during this period with the invention of the telegraph by both Morse and Wheatstone in 1837.

This was a prolific era for the humanities, with major figures of the European Enlightenment making their mark between 1630 and 1840. In religion, science, and philosophy, prominent individuals included Descartes, Hegel, Hume, Kant, Leibniz, Locke, Spinoza, and Linnaeus. In literature the most famous names were Balzac, Byron, Cervantes, Dickens, Goethe, Hugo, Keats, Milton, Moliere, Poe, Pushkin, Racine, Rousseau, Schiller, Scott, and Voltaire. In music there appeared Bach, Beethoven, Berlioz, Chopin, Handel, Haydn, Liszt, Mendelssohn, Monteverdi, Mozart, Schubert, Schumann, Verdi, and Wagner. In art, Bernini, Caravaggio, Delacroix, Goya, Rembrandt, and Velazquez were notable. Finally, in mathematics there were great names the likes of Abel, Bernoulli, Descartes, Euler, Fermat, Fourier, Galois, Gauss, Lagrange, Legendre, Leibniz, Lobachevsky, Newton, Pascal, and Wallis.

Consciousness in the Renaissance and European Enlightenment

Typical of the flow of history when viewed through the developmental lens, the worst of an epoch tends to shelter within it the slow expansion of dimensions of much higher value. Hence the Greek and Roman classical periods of philosophy and the humanities flourished even as civil structures languished in totalitarianism. Similarly, the distinctive mark of consciousness in the Renaissance and European Enlightenment is that these periods weren't simply a return to the classical Greek and Roman eras, but took on a creative and innovative life of their own, propelling the entire range of human activity—political, scientific, technological, and the humanities—to yet new levels of development.

As in the study of natural history, only in hindsight do we see the multilayered dimensions of what was unfolding in humanity's continued maturing. The new experience of rationalism was challenging the older magic-mythic lens—a challenge that continues to this day. Was the evolving human mind still responding mostly to messages from within, from its "gods"? Or was the brain's own dialogue now dominant? Had the Black Death taught us about God's wrath or triggered further discovery of our own human potential?

The juxtaposition of these questions in the psyche of this epoch reverberates through the biographies of its famous personages. Think of Leonardo financially supporting his wider genius by a career in the military crafts, Michelangelo painting for the papacy by day and secretly a member of the free thought movement by night, or the church subsidizing Renaissance art and literature even though the same art and literature formed part of a movement toward new freedoms.

Money was a powerful arbiter. New wealth, concentrated in trading, commerce, and politically independent city-states, allowed some revolutionaries such as Luther and Florence's freethinkers to be protected and supported, while only a few hundred miles away such wealth fell into the hands of individuals like Machiavelli and the corrupt Borgia popes. All represented this dramatic swing away from the magic-mythic lens to the emerging rational mind, which explains one of the characteristics attributed by the integral thinkers to the foundational figures of this Achievist-Strategic era: Achieve your goals, but without raising the suspicions or incurring the wrath of the entrenched establishment. In other words, your own survival might also mean the survival of your vision.

This era of development was largely a European phenomenon because only in Europe were the political and civil structures varied enough to foster the freedoms required for a movement away from the authoritarian mind. The rest of the world made other choices, from Kublai Khan and Genghis Khan in Mongolia and China to the Muslim empires to the east. India found itself struggling between its Muslim, Buddhist, and Hindu influences. The Toltecs, Aztecs, and Incas were isolated in the New World.

Today's Heritage from the Rational Epoch

The rational paradigm can be credited with ushering humanity into the modern age. However, for all its revolutionary benefits for humankind, a powerful heritage of this epoch that still influences world direction is the nearly unyielding nature of the rational paradigm.

Although the rational paradigm produced a bounty for our species, the restriction of inquiry to that which is seeable, touchable, and testable severely limited our ability to understand far more dynamic aspects of reality. This is the root of the lament, "We have so much advanced technology, yet we can't get along with each other." A chasm developed between the rational lens and the spiritual lens that remains today, prompting the question of whether a later integrative epoch can break the stalemate. A CNN report as recent as 2011 recounted how science and religion run on parallel tracks with only infrequent intersections.[31]

Another vestige of the rational epoch is the veneration of competition, with its emphasis on getting ahead at any cost, coupled with turning a blind eye to the collateral damage caused by the exploitation of both nature and our fellow humans. It would be left to future epochs to add the balance of sensitivity and ethics.

The initial insensitivity of technological development to natural consequence was a culmination of the mistaken idea that humans and nature were separate—a symptom seen as early in history as when humans began to exodus the landscape in favor of towns and cities. Such is the dynamic nature of evolution and revolution that every step results in new bounty as well as new shadow.

---

[31] "God No Longer in the Whirlwind," August 29, 2011.

10

The Coming of Worldwide Civilization

"We who have been born Buddhist, Hindu, Christian, Muslim, or any other faith can be very comfortable in each other's temples"

Ari Ariyaratne

IN CHARTING THE COURSE OF HISTORY, DEVELOPMENTALIST AND INTEGRAL thinkers often divide their epochs of development into two tiers. The first represents epochs still invested primarily in human subsistence, bequeathing to humanity a reasonably comfortable lifestyle on a worldwide scale. This has been a characteristic of all the epochs thus far.

The second tier acknowledges the emergence of a standard of living on a worldwide scale sufficiently comfortable to allow for the cultivation of the kind of humane values and vision that herald the Interspiritual Age.

Around 1850, there began to emerge a global civilization linked by communication, travel, and trade. The run-up to this globalized landscape was peppered with unparalleled international changes and upheavals. In 1848 the worker revolts in Paris spread to Italy and Germany. Two years later in 1850, the European countries carved

Africa into colonies. By 1854 Russia was fighting Turkey, England, and France in the Crimean War.

Meanwhile, in the United States, the southern states (the Confederacy) attempted to leave the Union in the years from 1860 to 1865, during which period Lincoln issued the Emancipation Proclamation, freeing the slaves in 1863.

Four years later in 1867, Karl Marx published *Das Kapital*, envisioning the Communist system. In 1870 Prussia defeated France and the united German states. Japan emerged as a world power in the Russian-Japanese war of 1905, while in China a republic replaced the Qing Dynasty in 1912, ending 2,000 years of empire.

There followed the First World War, spanning the years 1914 to 1918. During this war, in 1917, the Russian Czar was overthrown, with initial democratic elections held that same year, followed by the Communist overthrow of the democratic government in Russia under Lenin before the year was out. There followed three years of civil war in Russia, from 1918 to 1921, during which Lenin consolidated power for the Communists.

Also during this period, in the year 1919, the Ottoman and Austro-Hungarian Empires were dissolved. Further east in India, 1920 saw the start of Gandhi's nonviolent revolt against Britain, and in 1921 Britain granted independence to southern Ireland. The following year, 1922, the Soviet Union (USSR) formed from nations of the previous Russian Empire.

When Japan invaded China in 1931, it led to conflict with the United States. A year later in 1932, Hitler was elected in Germany and appointed as chancellor, dissolving democracy. In 1937 Nazi Germany began persecution of Jews, eventually killing 5-7 million. That same year, Japan occupied Beijing, inaugurating its conquest of China. Two years later in 1939, World War II was under way in Europe, spreading to Africa and Asia. By 1940 the world had divided into warring Axis and Allied powers. Finally in 1945 Germany surrendered, and the United States used atomic bombs in Japan to end the war in the Pacific. That same year, Germany and Japan adopted democratic constitutions.

The Beginning of Modernism

By 1850, world population had reached almost a billion and a quarter. In the Americas, the United States' Civil War (often called the world's first "modern war") marked a watershed in the applicability of democratic values to all peoples, involvement of Old World nations in a New World war, and the power of war to foster rapid industrial and technological development. For the first time, the world was interconnected through major technological innovations, commerce, and open migration. Science fueled developments in technology, such as the harnessing of electricity (Edison and Tesla), the emergence of an evolutionary worldview in the form of Darwin's theory of the origin of species, and Pasteur's work in immunology.

Economically, capitalism appeared to overwhelm and thus render obsolete the old European feudal order, producing new wealth not just for city-state and market centers, but also for larger and larger numbers of citizens. Central heating, indoor plumbing, electricity, trains, automobiles, airplanes, telegraph and telephone, movies, recorded music, pharmaceuticals, hospitals, and vaccination served to revolutionize daily life for some world citizens. Agriculture became mechanized, migration and travel commonplace, allowing a shift from 95% engaged in agricultural pursuits to more than 50% living in cities.

A spate of economic and technological developments transformed life worldwide. In 1840 railroad building began in Europe and North America; safe elevators were invented, making skyscrapers practical in 1854; and Alfred Nobel invented dynamite, establishing the Nobel Prize in 1866.

The year 1869 saw the Suez Canal and American transcontinental railroad completed. In 1876 both Alexander Graham Bell and Elisha Gray patented telephones, while Thomas Edison invented a practical light bulb 1879. By 1905 Henry Ford had invented the assembly line, mass producing inexpensive automobiles, while that same year the Wright brothers flew their first successful airplane.

In 1923 the United States stopped unlimited immigration. The first public sound movie success came with the release of The Jazz

Singer in 1927. The same year, a Washington to New York transmission inaugurated television, which began commercial broadcasting in 1930—the year, ironically, that saw the start of the Great Depression. By 1931 European hyperinflation had brought the Nazis to power in Germany. In 1937 E. I. DuPont invented and patented nylon.

Such was life in the First World. Meanwhile, nations with navies dominated the world. From India to Africa and the Americas, people faced the implementation of colonialism—world dominance by those who controlled these social and technological advances. England, France, Belgium, Germany, the Netherlands, and to some extent the United States, divided up the world.

In the arts and architecture, Picasso and others introduced abstract art. Structural steel and elevators birthed the era of large bridges and skyscrapers. New discoveries and inventions changed the worldview and lifestyle of world citizens on nearly an annual basis.

Scientific and artistic achievement during this period took off when scientist Louis Agassiz explained the world's geologic history in 1840, Hermann Von Helmholtz delineated the law of conservation of energy in 1847, and Florence Nightingale introduced modern hospitals in 1854. Four years later in 1858, Charles Darwin and Alfred Russell Wallace described evolution, and Darwin published his theory of evolution in 1859.

By 1862 Louis Pasteur had proposed germ theory and invented pasteurization. James Maxwell's equations united electrical and magnetic theory in 1865. The following year, 1866, Gregor Mendel discovered genetic inheritance, while in 1869 Dmitri Mendeleyev proposed the periodic table of elements.

In 1896 Pablo Picasso pioneered modern art. The same year, Marie and Pierre Curie discovered radioactivity. The following year, 1897, J. J. Thompson described the electron, and by 1900 Max Planck had proposed the existence of quanta, leading to quantum physics. In 1901 Frank Lloyd Wright innovated in open housing design. In 1902 William James published his classic *Varieties of Religious Experience*, followed by the publication of Albert Einstein's special theory of relativity in 1905 and his general theory of relativity in 1915. Then in 1917 solar eclipse measurements proved Einstein's theory of relativity. In 1919 Edwin Hubble discovered that the universe is populated with galaxies. Werner Heisenberg developed quantum mechanics and the uncertainty principle 1927. The following year, 1928, Hubble discovered that the universe is expanding. Also that year, subatomic particles were discovered, with Paul Dirac discovering the positron, Wolfgang Pauli the neutrino. In 1931 Kurt Gödel pioneered the new mathematics, and in 1933 Guglielmo Marconi discovered microwaves.

Thus the stage for a worldwide civilization was set. A new epoch began unfolding, characterized by the phrases Relativistic-Personalistic—Communitarian-Egalitarian. Its hallmarks would be a growing pluralism, relativism, group harmony, dialogue and diplomacy, give and take, open society, and goodwill. However, as with the pattern of all evolution and revolution, it would only emerge in the wake of catastrophe, in the form of the world wars.

Competition Leads to Calamity: the World Wars

The darker underbelly of the emergent cosmopolitan world involved competition for power and resources directly related to the ethos of the epoch of reason that preceded it.

During this period, marked by the latent violent behavior of the era of the local and regional God-King and the authoritarian era of towns and cities, humanity reaped the whirlwind in global competition for political power and economic dominance, as there emerged another historic face-off in the evolving human consciousness—the question of what comprises political, economic, and social greatness.

Does greatness arise through the democratic capitalistic model, as in the West with its contrary plutocratic economic doctrines of exploitation and fiscal authoritarianism? Or does greatness arise through totalitarian systems inclined to enforced conformity and social and economic planning, as in Communism and National Socialism (the Nazis)?

World War I, waged between 1914 and 1918, saw the German, Austrian, and Ottoman empires arrayed against the English, French, and Russian empires. Both sides freely drew military assets from their colonies, making the war multinational and multiracial. Because the sides were evenly balanced economically and technologically, some 10 million died. The nightmare only ended when the balance of power was tipped by America's entry into the fray in 1917. The same year, the Russian Empire fell from within to Communist revolutionaries.

World War II, spanning the six years from 1939 through 1945, erupted almost as a consequence of unsettled disputes from the First World War, as the ensuing global economic depression led to tumultuous social upheaval across Russia, resulting in 50 million deaths, paralleled by the rise of Hitler in Germany, the emergence of Mussolini as a strongman in Italy, and the galvanizing of the Imperial forces under Emperor Hirohito in Japan. Meanwhile, the Western powers, too economically weak to respond, stood by until it was too late to prevent the world from being engulfed in conflict. When the military goals of Germany finally precipitated war, it pitted these three dictatorships, known as the Axis powers, against the Allied powers, comprised of most of the remaining Western republics and capitalist nations, together with Soviet Russia. The use of the world's first nuclear weapons in 1945 marked not only the end of this war but also the emergence of a new technological age.

The advent of the atomic bomb also signaled the collapse of the colonial networks of the European powers, followed by the emergence of the United States and the Soviet Union as superpowers. The colonial nations had all contributed too much to the world war not to insist on their own independence. With the United States and the Soviet Union now the titular world powers, the interests of the European colonial powers waned. By 1950 they were giving up their overseas empires.

A World Pluralism Emerges

The cruel lessons of World War II taught much of the world there had to be a better way of competing and settling scores. The result was a new world culture of treaties and agreements. The United Nations formed in 1945, followed by world courts and organizations equipped to deal with matters ranging from trade to human rights. These signaled a consciousness of world pluralism and the desire for peaceful coexistence among nations, allowing for progress and development uninterrupted by war, other than limited regional wars. Though many nations were still ruled by authoritarian regimes, a new diplomatic and pluralistic landscape had emerged.

The world of the post-war era reflected the cultural ethos of the era, centered on personalism, relativism, communalism, and egalitarianism. The attitudes of this era became pivotal in the ongoing discussion of the world's future. However, while the period spawned an ethos with qualities critical to a positive world future, it also stimulated flaws that, if not identified and addressed, could stall or even kill global progress. This is because while the pluralistic and relativistic values of this era are of obvious value, they can also engender the pathology often called "the tyranny of mediocrity."

A major problem with listening to everyone is that it can be difficult to discern, let alone carry out, the best course of action. Compromises that inevitably accompany pluralistic diplomacy may fall far short of addressing crucial issues. While the ethos of the era aimed to balance flaws in the preceding eras, a lack of balance, wisdom, and vision resulted in a naïve suppression of all structure and hierarchy, thereby limiting healthy competitive growth. This, in fact, was the downfall of the experiment with socialism. "Great Society" dreams were dashed by the emergence of welfare mentalities. It's always a fine line.

Revolutions that don't successfully navigate this fine line often fall prey to disastrous returns to the earlier God-King type of mentality, turning to an authority that offers simplistic solutions to problems—a catastrophic example of which was the Pol Pot debacle in Cambodia. In the name of creating an agricultural peasant utopia, all social structures of any complexity were purposefully destroyed, including schools, hospitals, libraries, transportation, and government service departments. As the baby was thrown out with the bathwater, fully 25% of the nation's citizens perished. Only in retrospect did it become clear that the dream of an integrated society had been hijacked by God-King authoritarian behavior. Are we surprised?

Spirituality too was transformed by the shift toward a worldwide pluralism. On the one hand it resulted in a profound mixing among the traditions, making varied spiritual teachings and practices available on a worldwide basis and leading to ecumenical, interfaith, and interspiritual dialogues on which the movement toward an Interspiritual Age is based. On the other hand, it resulted in a hijacking of deeper spiritual experience either by naïve New Age superstition or the misinterpretation of deeper service-based values as permission to simply serve our own needs with a "just do your thing" mentality.

No one doubts the value of all that's good about the move toward pluralism. However, when pluralism is held as a static view, it restricts our vision of the world's future. Comfortable pluralistic nations can become blind to the world's challenges, which is one reason we see some American politicians preaching that a life like Christian America in the 1950s should be how the whole world lives. Others assert that America's participation in world affairs isn't needed, or that world environmental threats aren't real. Anti-American backlash to these views worldwide is apparent, with a 2011 study[32] indicating 63% of people polled outside the United States fear that globalization means Americanization. The blessings and curses of the shift toward pluralism are destined to be in play for a long time.

Beginning of the Integrative Epoch

Beginning with the end of the era of pluralism, developmentalists and integral thinkers identify a dramatic acceleration of world events, cultural changes, and paradigm shifts. Humans appear to be racing toward either meeting the implications of a newly integrative age, including interspirituality, or dooming ourselves to calamitous consequences.

Unprecedented change is inevitable as an overpopulated, resource-scarce planet seeks to integrate a multibillion cosmopolitan populace of myriad races, colors, creeds, and languages. As with the realities of natural history, from this point on we will either achieve successful

---

[32] Conducted by worldpublicopinion.org.

adaptive strategies or, steeped in blindness and unpreparedness, this new cosmopolitan world will fall into incoherence and chaos.

As noted earlier, three extinction scenarios confront the world as the present epoch draws to a close: worldwide war with weapons of mass destruction based on religious allegiances; war with weapons of mass destruction based on nationalistic identities; destruction of the planet through environmental degradation. Paul Ray, author of *The Cultural Creatives*, describes what he calls "hockey stick" change. The shape of a hockey stick is straight until it suddenly bends—and then it bends dramatically. Depending on how the stick is held, this bend can be dramatically upward or calamitously downward.

The era after World War II is often called The Era of Good Feeling. Wars were over and, for the most part, the world's citizenry could concentrate on "creating the good life" wherever the opportunity might be possible. Education, jobs, rising economies, ample goods and services, household appliances, and a variety of forms of transport all contributed to this time to "feel good." Even the music and art of the era—from expressionist art to the "beat" poets, and music, film, and television celebrating the new "family" and the "good life"—reflected this seeking of an existence oriented to "being." Only in exploited and politically closed societies did this era not offer the elevating promise of goodwill and a better life.

The positive aspect of this emerging world society lay in the hope of a new future in the "pursuit of happiness." Its stumbling block, however, would be near-complete investment in a new materialism and consumerism, with its irresponsible fiscal and commercial visioning, accompanied by unparalleled environmental destruction.

Cold War, Space Race, and Culture War

While the West and the Soviet Union faced off in what would become a 50-year Cold War, the space race between the two superpowers propelled technology to higher and higher levels of advancement. The Soviets launched the first satellite, Sputnik, in 1957, and by 1969 America had landed astronauts successfully on the moon. The term "culture war" emerged as the democratic West and the authoritarian East vied to prove which model of civilization best addressed the world's huge challenges.

Science was inextricably caught up in this juxtaposition. The same year James Watson and Francis Crick elaborated DNA, precipitating a new epoch in biological understanding, the Great Smog of London killed 4,000 citizens and incapacitated another 100,000. Following this 1953 catastrophe, Rachel Carson's 1962 book *Silent Spring* inaugurated a responsible pushback against rampant pollution. Despite this, the specter of a world unraveling was becoming more and more vivid.

In 1968, the wildly popular book *The Population Bomb* by P. R. Ehrlich announced "population control or race to oblivion?" There followed a bevy of world catastrophe books, from *Our Plundered Planet* to *Famine 1975!* These "roars the likes of Old Testament prophets," as a writer of the time called them, were a mixed blessing. While books like *The Limits to Growth* inaugurated responsible new paradigms for evaluating the runaway consumer economy, the world was spared imminent calamity by the ensuing, largely unanticipated Green Revolution—initiatives in agriculture that centered on high-yield varieties, expansive irrigation projects, modernization of agricultural equipment and management, and application of fertilizers and pesticides. This revolution spared the world for a time. As with all hockey stick change, still waiting in the wings are the consequences of the sheer enormity of this application of genetic and chemical engineering to the biosphere.

East-West Spiritual Cross-Pollination

Other paradigmatic shifts were sweeping the world. Interspiritual pioneer Father Thomas Merton's autobiography *The Seven Storey Mountain* appeared in 1946 and *Seeds of Contemplation*, *The Tears of Blind Lions*, and *The Waters of Siloe* soon after in 1949. India's pioneer evolutionary theologian Sri Aurobindo's works first appeared in American editions in 1949 and 1950. Roman Catholic evolutionary theologian

Pierre Teilhard de Chardin's long-banned book *The Phenomenon of Man* (*Le Phénomène Humain*) was made public in 1955.

Adding to the tide of East-West cross-pollination, hidden within the British rock invasion of the 1960s (from the Beatles to Ravi Shankar and psychedelic rock) was the popularization of what had been several decades of infiltration of Eastern philosophical and spiritual ideas into the West. Beginning with visits to the West by Swamis Vivekananda and Yogananda in the earlier 20th century, a new era began, as proclaimed by American Dr Wendell Thomas in his book *Hinduism Invades America*.

Paramhansa Yogananda's wildly popular *Autobiography of a Yogi* (1946) further nurtured this seed, uniting a literary genre from America's own Transcendentalist Movement that included Emerson, Thoreau, and Whitman, to name only a classic few, with modern writers such as Germany's Hermann Hesse, Argentina's Jorge Luis Borges, and America's J. D. Salinger and Father Thomas Merton. This genre subtly instilled Eastern spirituality in the West. Combined with the flower children and drug culture of the 1960s, which brought sweeping changes in attitudes toward sexuality, this seeding of Eastern ideas had undeniable effects on a culture steeped in the desire for integrative pluralism.

This Integrative-Systemic era transitioned into the calamitous 1970s. Iconic of the so-called Second Tier of human consciousness reaching out to the development of individual being and potential, the 1950s and 1960s initiated a worldwide emergence of the ethic of radical self-expression and inner searching. This entailed a coming together of potential consumerism and hedonism with inner journeying and an expression of the overall pluralistic ideal of non-harm.

Of course, there was pushback from ingrained and inherited violent authoritarian behavior patterns, along with the tendency to create a flatland of peaceful mediocrity devoid of the ability to discern a creative edge. The violence of the Vietnam War years, both in Indochina and on American streets, which reached an apex in the 1968 assassinations of Martin Luther King and Robert Kennedy, along with the violence at that year's political conventions, starkly portrays this dynamic.

The integrative epoch, ensuing around 1950, and the subsequent holistic epoch, unfolding around 1970, were interrelated—not only because of the short time periods involved, but also because the questions and challenges recognized in the earlier period would hopefully be addressed in the subsequent era. In a recent magazine interview, the founder of Spiral Dynamics, Dr Don Beck, explained that the integrative era involved the analytical left brain seeking to include feelings, while the subsequent holistic era involved the feeling right brain trying to use data skillfully.

The greatest challenge for the upheaval and uncertainty that typifies the integrative period is to not mistake problem identification for problem solving. As with a frenetic person who can never settle down enough to actually problem solve, a world caught up in upheaval is likely either to revert to solutions from earlier levels, which won't work, or be unable to envision and initiate new structures that can remedy problems. This becomes particularly challenging in complex social and political situations, since the identifiers of problems may not be the same people as those able to create solutions through new structures. In an intense or frenzied atmosphere, those with these two skill sets may not be able to locate or listen to each other.

The integrative period was more a time of individuals and small collectives identifying problems and seeking answers, while the subsequent holistic period was a time for actual collectives to function in a holistic manner.

An example of this tension today is the world's continuing addiction to growth-related values and blind consumerism, even as a sense of sustainability rather than constant growth is arising in the international consciousness. Recognition of the necessity of a sustainable future is futile if the powers that be are unable to rein in the constant emphasis on linear growth and consumer economies based only on creating new wants.

Another example is the danger that the desire to identify problems and solve them will be limited to its inherent predilection for purely analytical solutions. Many working in the arena of world dialogue, such as the United Nations, remark that the problem is "talk, talk,

talk," with little awareness that purely intellectual solutions for our global problems probably don't exist.

Fifth Great Advance: Automation and the Emerging Dream of Holism

The currently unfolding holistic epoch, which began around 1970, sees a world that continues to teeter between the implications of dramatic technological achievement and potential civil and environmental peril. Review of a dozen or more critical events from the period highlights this dangerous climate. There are glaring civil and political gulfs between stricter, more closed, magic-mythic cultures and liberal rationalistic cultures, which are often materialistic and corrupt. Freedoms in the liberal West teeter between the idealism of expanding populist social and political movements and the reality of the transfer of monetary and commercial wealth to just a few. East Asian societies create robust economies mixing capitalism and autocracy. Old autocratic empires that still survive see grassroots social upheavals demanding basic social and economic freedoms. The world appears poised between emerging desire, especially at the grassroots, for a new world-centric holism and retrenchment into older patterns that hope they won't need to change in order to survive an uncertain future.

It's worth highlighting some of the highly contrasted events and benchmarks of the period from 1968 through 2001. As mentioned previously, the year 1968 saw the tragic assassination of both Martin Luther King, Jr and Senator Robert Kennedy. With population growth influenced by diverse factors including a slowdown in human fertility, by 1970 the human population stood at 3.7 billion. That same year Father Thomas Berry launched the eco-spirituality (earth scholar) movement. In 1974 the Search for Extraterrestrial Intelligence (SETI) project got underway. The following year, 1975, the world biodiversity crisis was clearly identified. In 1977 the debut of the Apple II launched the personal computer era. By 1980 the worldwide sustainability movement had identified itself. In 1981 IBM began mass-producing the PC. This was also the year Microsoft software made its debut and the Intel microchip was born.

The period from 1984 through 1991 witnessed ongoing episodes of Hindu–Moslem sectarian violence in India and Sri Lanka. The death of the last major Soviet dictator, Konstantin Chernenko, occurred in 1985, which was also the year Mikhail Gorbachev initiated reforms. The Berlin Wall, built in 1962, came down in 1989, marking the end of the Cold War.

In 1990 human population topped 5.1 billion, as the Hubble space telescope revolutionized our understanding of the universe. The internet and worldwide web, developed from the late 1980s on, became fully commercialized in 1995 with the international NSFNET agreement. By the new millennium, three decades of mobile phone development had brought cell phones and other hand-held devices into nearly five billion households worldwide. The first animals were cloned in 1997. In 1999 Brother Wayne Teasdale coined the term interspirituality. A year later, in 2000, global warming and global climate change were clearly identified. The human genome was sequenced in 2001.

Ongoing episodes of Jewish–Islamic sectarian violence were prevalent in the Middle East between 1993 and 2001, with the United States intervening in Islamic regions beginning with Somalia in 1993, Afghanistan in 2001, and Iraq in 2003, following the Islamic extremist attack on the World Trade Center in 2001.

Holism and Interspirituality

It was with the dawn of the holistic era that the interspiritual movement came alive.[33] For the integral writers, summarizing the views of the world's developmentalist thinkers, this is the era in which humanity must begin to develop skill sets that balance self-interest with the

---

[33] The holistic era has included the heights of Paul Hawken's 2007 dramatic outlining of the worldwide grassroots progressive movement in *Blessed Unrest: How the Largest Movement in the World Came into Being and Why No One Saw It Coming*, publication of the major works on developmental history (Ken Wilber's *Integral Spirituality 2007*, of his 30-some books on his Integral theory), and Don Beck's and Chris Cowan's *Spiral Dynamics: Mastering Values, Leadership and Change* (1996). See these citations in the Bibliography.

interests of the whole. Such skills must include an ability to steer a rapidly evolving and unpredictable future, the evaluation of multiple sources of creative problem solving and critical feedback, and the ability to move information to where decision-making happens.

The development of interspirituality is critical to our ability to step out of the relative immobility of the relativistic-pluralistic epoch so we can engage in dynamic steering of the future. It epitomizes the dream of humanity's creative interior dimension stepping up to the imploding exterior dimensions created so blindly through the former epochs.

Will we reach the next stage, the integral thinkers' epoch of Global Mind? Or will we slide into global cataclysm, possibly ending in our extinction? If the latter, will this extinction be the result of nature or human activity on the planet?

At least we can breathe a sigh of relief that the *inevitable* natural disasters that will befall our planet are far off. All the continents should reunite again in about 250 million years. In about 5 billion years, our sun should go the way of supernovas, obliterating our solar system in its explosion. In any event, in 3–5 billion years, our Milky Way galaxy will collide with the Andromeda Galaxy. These are most likely the limits of our solar system's survival. Cosmologist Stephen Hawking envisions humans moving elsewhere in the cosmos before this event. If so, the universe should last at least another trillion years. Or it may never end.

11

The Field

"Out beyond...there is a field. I'll meet you there"

Jalal al-Din Rumi

APPEARING TOGETHER A FEW YEARS AGO ON THE TELEVISION TALK SHOW Charlie Rose, the co-discoverer of DNA, Dr James Watson, and the father of sociobiology, Harvard's Dr E. O. Wilson, were asked the following question: If the discovery of DNA defined the current scientific era, what would define the next era? They both agreed it would be an understanding of consciousness.

The same prediction has been made by Britain's pioneer of the new physics, Roger Penrose, along with one of the founders of string theory, Nobel laureate David Gross. Such views, relatively new for science—and refreshing, to say the least—reflect the emergence since the 1970s of the currently unfolding Integrative and Holistic period of history.

Disagreement about Consciousness

Since at least the Renaissance, the rational lens of science and the magic-mythic lens that underpins most of religion and spirituality have been on separate paths. Worldwide, they have developed into two coexisting but fundamentally different cultures of knowledge. As CNN and

NPR theological commentator Rev Dr Stephen Prothero of Boston University notes, these parallel paths seldom crossed in the past.

This divide has not only been reflected in the hard sciences (physics and chemistry), but also in the soft sciences (the more subjective realms of biology and psychology). Science is sure about evolution. Since most First World citizens have gone at least to high school, with 30% of Americans holding college degrees and 99% of Americans literate, it's startling that only 13% of Americans believe in biological evolution.

The divide has also been reflected in psychology. It isn't that conventional psychology hasn't known about the experience of unity consciousness. Sigmund Freud referred to the feeling of unity with everything as the "oceanic experience." However, the psychology of modernism opted out of investigating it, noting (as did Freud) that there was probably no physical basis for it that could be tested. Only in the last decade have books about the relationship of brain and mind become commonplace. Even those scientists who have helped us understand our development from a primitive, somewhat animal-like reflexive mind, to a more conscious, analytic, and reflective mind, have called this development consciousness itself or not quite known what to do with the word "consciousness."

Two Different Ideas

The emerging idea of a quantum reality, with a continuum between the infinitesimally large and the infinitesimally small, has changed the context of the discussion. The world's spiritual traditions have assumed for centuries that consciousness is a collective field, including living and non-living things, whereas from a traditional scientific point of view consciousness isn't a collective phenomenon and has a questionable, if any, interrelationship with the wider reality around it. As far as science is generally concerned, consciousness is an emergent quality of individual physical bodies.

Exciting proposals are being made in science, so that the field of brain, mind, and consciousness is in a state of flux. New views from the cutting edge of science have usually taken years to trickle down to the average scientist working in a laboratory or teaching in a university, let alone onto the street. The difference a few years can make is startling. In the interview with Charlie Rose in 2005, neither Watson nor Wilson distinguished religion from spirituality. Neither considered that spirituality might be about consciousness, reflecting a remarkable lack of awareness of the entire history of Eastern spirituality.

Watson further stated that understanding consciousness was pivotal, but doubted whether the world religions or spirituality had much to contribute to the discussion. Wilson didn't disagree—although Wilson, understanding the gravitas that subjective experience still holds for humanity, has written eloquently about the mutuality of science and religion in recent years.[34] The Charlie Rose episode is well known in the media of science and religion, yet we were surprised to see that at YouTube, where the video has been posted for a long time, there were less than a thousand views. In contrast, most celebrities, professional wrestlers, or NASCAR drivers receive tens of thousands of hits, if not hundreds of thousands.

These exchanges reflect both the gulf between scientific and spiritual understanding and the superficiality with which the subject is often treated.

The difficulty for science and religion, then, has been twofold: lack of common ground about consciousness, and fundamentally different starting positions about what consciousness might be. The discussion of consciousness by philosophers is another distinct camp. Moreover, scientists often don't talk to each other across disciplines, which means everyone is in their own groove. Any mutual discussion has occurred only in relatively recent years.

The Great "Pass Around"

It's almost a cliché in the emerging field of scientific consciousness studies to refer to the history of science and the question of

---

[34] *Consilience* and *The Future of Life*, for which Wilson was blacklisted by celebatheists.com for supposedly pro-religious comments.

consciousness as "the great pass around." Certainly this has been the tendency, historically, and no one denies it. For decades scientists considered the subject of consciousness out of their domain, in the realm of philosophy or theology. This was because of an inherent belief that something that appeared purely subjective probably wasn't approachable by objective experimental techniques. This was why Freud and early psychologists "passed" on studying the oceanic experience— unity consciousness—and said as much. They had to search for contexts in which something subjective might actually be measurable, and did come up with some angles—such as studying subjectivity in the context of measuring attention. But such starts were initially slow.

The idea that consciousness studies can't be objective is still the main argument used by scientists who don't believe the study of consciousness can be pursued scientifically. In making this point, they argue that half the methods used by scientists doing modern scientific consciousness studies rely simply on what people report. The other approaches are physiological studies of the apparatus of the human body, such as neurological and somatic—approaches which they say aren't unique.

The current field of scientific consciousness studies emerged in the 1980s, made up mostly of psychologists, neuroscientists, and behavioral biologists who dared to venture into this new territory. Many were young and intent on finding a way to make their unique mark on the march of scientific discovery. They founded new institutes and journals. The academic journal *Consciousness and Cognition* began in 1992, and the *Journal of Consciousness Studies* in 1994. By 1997, there was an Association for the Scientific Study of Consciousness.

These developments followed an earlier period in the 1970s of pioneer brain-mind studies. Most of this work emerged from the field of neuroscience. The Society for Neuroscience was formed in 1969. In 1970, 1973, 1977, and 1981, multiple Nobel prizes were awarded to brain-mind and neuroscience pioneers for breakthroughs in brain chemistry, brain neural networks, the roles of brain hemispheres in behavior, and new technologies for studying the brain. Detailed scanning of brain activity by Nuclear Magnetic Resonance machines became available in 1974, winning another Nobel Prize. In six more years up to the year 2000, more Nobel prizes were awarded for brain-mind related research.

Between 1973 and 1979, an entirely new field, "MBE" (Mind-brain-education science), emerged in the cognitive sciences. One well-known pioneer, neuropsychologist Michael Posner, contributed some 300 books and articles. In this surge of interest in brain-mind and consciousness, three pioneering neuroscience societies were also formalized in the late 1970s.

The Philosophical Debate

The philosophical discussion of consciousness is an old one, going back to famous names such as René Descartes (b. 1596), John Locke (b. 1632) and Immanuel Kant (b. 1724). As in the early scientific debate, the major philosophical issue concerned whether consciousness was a valid subject. This issue has been highly contentious. Even today factions disagree on whether subjectivity is real (the "realists" say no) and whether, if it is, its information is allowable (the "idealists"). Descartes felt there was no hope of understanding consciousness scientifically.

Locke and Kant relegated consciousness to what in philosophy are called "qualia," a pivotal Latin term meaning "raw feel." The philosophical problems with qualia, then and today, are huge. Is "raw feel" measurable in any way? If so, does it mean anything? The conversation is complicated by philosophy's own disagreements about knowing—the schools of objectivism (that reality outside of us can actually be known), positivism (that we can only know from sense experience combined with what we have been taught), and constructivism (that knowing is always a purely human construction).

As we would suspect, the modern philosophical discussion about consciousness is highly intellectual.[35] The debates boil down to subjectivity. When a leading realist philosopher synthesized the non-subjective view in a book entitled *Consciousness Explained*, his detractors among the idealists referred to it as "consciousness explained away."

---

[35] With elaborate ideas like the Higher Order Perception theory, Higher Order Thought theory, Self-Representation theory, Functionalism theory, Biological Naturalism theory, and many more.

The developments in both science and philosophy parallel not only the Integrative and Holistic eras, but also the change in "global mind" referred to by Willis Harman in his best-selling book *Global Mind Change*. Studies of the brain-mind reflect what Harman called the dual or dialectic advance of science—realizing brain and mind aren't the same, and searching for a language in which the relationship of the two could be studied and discussed. By the time scientific consciousness studies emerged in the 1980s, they reflected Harman's prediction that science would move from a dualistic or dialectic approach to complex problems, to one more in line with the new physics, involving a continuum.

What is Consciousness?

Surprising as it might seem, the question of what consciousness is shares much with the question of what space is. A leading scientist pioneering consciousness work, David Chalmers of Australia's Centre for Consciousness, has pointed out that humanity might be smart to treat both in the same way. What he means is space (at least science's conventional "vacuous space") is simply space—there's nothing there. So, with space and science, there has been little to directly test about space. Despite this, physics, cosmology, astronomy, and other disciplines have said "yes" to the reality of space and "yes" to the self-evident fact that matter and energy (which we now know are a continuum) occur in space. Yet as Dr Chalmers has pointed out, science has been reluctant to grant the same assumption to consciousness.

In the Great Wisdom Traditions of the world's spirituals paths, it has long been assumed such phenomena as thoughts, emotions, and feelings arise in consciousness, and that consciousness is distinct from them—just as space is distinct from matter and energy. As David Chalmers has stated, we even understand this in the realm of everyday common sense.[36] We talk about losing our mind, having our mind "blown," or "being out of our mind," but none of these require a loss

---

[36] In a telephone interview aired on livescience.com.

of consciousness. Similarly, when we lose consciousness, go to sleep, or are under anesthesia, we don't equate this with losing our mind.

This obvious distinction ends up mediating much of the challenge today when it comes to exploring the question of consciousness. As Chalmers has said, it creates realms of inquiry about consciousness that are relatively easy and other realms that are extremely difficult. The easy ones are those associated with the physical body and what can be observed and measured directly in physiology and neurology. This is also what the early psychologists said they needed as a reference point for examining the oceanic experience of unity consciousness.

The difficult problem is subjectivity itself—what goes on in those deeper, more enigmatic realms of experience that critically motivate human reaction and behavior, yet appear to leave few traces that can be touched or measured. It has been as difficult for scientists to get at this as it has for them to study behavior and emotion in other animals. The problem with science investigating these things is they aren't readily divided into identifiable or approachable components.

Approaching consciousness like approaching space isn't an easy sell for many conventional scientists. Integral philosopher Ken Wilber takes I, We, It, and Its, and places each of these viewpoints as one of four boxes in a quadrant. When one arranges these boxes of experience in a sequence ranging from more internal to more external, and more singular to more plural, science ends up in the 3rd quadrant (the upper right box of the four). As Wilber comments, although scientists live in a world that contains all four quadrants (the personal, the collective, and the institutional singular and plural), scientists are so used to doing their science only in the 3rd quadrant (where everything is touchable, seeable, and measurable) that anything not readily available for study in this manner is generally ignored.

Wilber refers to this as "the Quadrant 3 fixation," which simply dismisses anything outside this quadrant as probably irrelevant. This seems to be the basis for James Watson's assumption on the Charlie Rose show (though he might, in that moment, have been uncritically flip) that spirituality and religion don't have much to add to our understanding of what consciousness might be.

Changes in Scientific Thinking

The field of scientific consciousness studies has only been around since the 1980s. The two major players have been a revolution in scientific philosophy in the 1970s and 80s, arising primarily from the work of scientific philosopher Sir Karl Popper, and the gradual paradigm shift in science away form pure materialism. Popper was instrumental in getting science to move from inductive fact gathering to the deductive process of fielding a visionary idea, then testing to see if it was true.

Science made rapid leaps once it gave itself permission to think "big and long," then test to see if an idea could be confirmed. Much of what we know in physics and cosmology comes from this method. First we had the theories, then built the nuclear colliders and orbiting telescopes to test them.

As Willis Harman made clear in 1998 in his pivotal book *Global Mind Change*, what the world was changing its mind about was whether all phenomena were based only on physical causes. Harman's view, which has become universally accepted, was that since the new physics sees reality as a continuum from the infinitesimally small to the infinitely large, science was now moving to an understanding of how relatively formless things could be causal. This is, of course, absolutely relevant to the understanding of consciousness.

The Qualities of Consciousness

It's safe to say that even if science and spirituality don't seem to agree on how the study of consciousness should be approached—objectively, subjectively, or some combination of the two—they at least agree about the pattern they see. The disagreement is about what it means.

Everyone seems to agree that, whatever consciousness is, it's experienced by all humans, unless there is a brain abnormality, and seems to involve general awareness, subjective experience, the ability to have feelings, a sense of self, and the capacity to exercise control over the mind. Another way to look at it is to list active attributes consciousness seems to have: subjectivity, the ability to change, continuity, and intention.

Even with this agreement, consciousness remains an enigma because it's at once utterly familiar to us and yet unceasingly mysterious. Invariably the question arises whether consciousness is about anything. Is it about anything any more than space is? The universality of this question of "aboutness" is poignant when we recall that polls indicate 77% of people believe life has a purpose, while only 6% state they see no need for life to be about anything.[37]

Definitions of Consciousness

Most definitions of consciousness reflect the realm of experience represented: spiritual, scientific, or philosophical. However, a universal contribution of the philosophical debate has been to provide a functional definition of consciousness.

A mind is conscious when that mind is aware of another state of mind, such as thought. Obviously it's this kind of mind that has the ability to consider options. This conscious state of mind allows the mind to decide: Do I do this or that? Do I remember this or that? Do I foresee this result or that? Do I see myself as this or that?

This view fits the definition used by Dr Julian Jaynes in his book *The Origin of Consciousness in the Breakdown of the Bicameral Mind*, which accounted for early humans' transition out of the primitive reflexive mind and into a gradually more conscious rational mind. It also fits the historical pattern of emerging consciousness in spirituality. To understand its appropriateness to spirituality, one must extend the model beyond the rational era, which is where Jaynes stops. If there is ongoing development of increasingly more spacious mind, and the ethical and cognitive skill sets that accompany it, this fits the traits often associated by spirituality with persons of higher consciousness.

Another reason we were drawn to Jayne's view is that the lack of this kind of consciousness in early humans explains puzzling early spiritual and religious behaviors. For instance, the lack of an awareness of chance clarifies why the Greeks and Romans began drawing

---

[37] adherents.com, 2011.

lots and consulting oracles when making major political and military decisions in Greek and Roman times. The results were considered explicit direction from the gods. Blind obedience to authority, especially inner directions considered to be the gods, explains the simplistic conformity of citizens in the early God-King empires, together with the breakdown of civil authority in subsequent periods when these citizens, exposed to other ideas of reality, began to question the authorities and rebel.

An extension of Jaynes' view is consistent with basic views of consciousness and human brain development. Most scientists agree that ever-increasing conscious capacity in humans obviously had fitness value with regard to surviving and thriving. Nobel Laureate Sir John Eccles, in his pioneering work on the brain-mind, suggested that distinctive developments, both anatomical and physiological, in the cerebral cortex of humans led to the arising of consciousness. The noted American neuroscientist Dr Bernard Baars suggested that these developments account for the additional functions and skills that human consciousness provides. He called this combination of anatomical and physiological development with expanding functional skill sets "integration consensus."

12

Taking Spiritual Experiences Seriously

"Things seen are things as seen"

Wallace Stevens

IN TIMES PAST, IT DIDN'T MATTER WHAT WAS TRUE. WHAT MATTERED WAS what people thought was true. But is it really that different today?

We often assume the truths science has discovered and the tenets taught by specific religions dominate the view of the earth's 7 billion humans. The facts are quite the opposite. We have seen that some 70% of the earth's population has a non-scientific worldview. While 85% are at least culturally associated with a particular religion, only 35% say they are active in the religions of their culture, while 65% claim they don't believe in any religion at all.[38] This suggests the vast majority of the world's 7 billion people really have no specific view of reality.

Science has spent at least two decades gradually moving toward a focused scientific study of consciousness. The major difficulty of science in moving forward with studies of consciousness has revolved around methodology—especially if the methods rely, as some skeptical scientists say, "just on what people report." Is what people report

---

[38] Gallup Millennium Poll, 2011.

important? Certainly the opinion poll information we've presented indicates it matters. What people believe seems to be the platform on which our world is broadly built.

For instance, even if evolution is true, if only 13% of Americans believe in biological evolution, small wonder so many Americans vote for political candidates who support the teaching of religious views in public schools, oppose various forms of medical research, and advocate other public policies that reflect America's ranking as 18th in the world when it comes to having an informed citizenry.[39]

Why People Believe What They Believe

While science has only recently turned its attention to the phenomenon of consciousness, for at least two centuries libraries of the world have abounded with accounts of the experiential history of human beings, nearly all of which reflect the Great Wisdom Traditions' view of consciousness—a view far more in accord with what people claim to experience in their day-to-day lives.

This isn't to say people can't be mistaken. An entire field of psychiatry studies how our brain can be tricked into seeing something that didn't happen. Commercial magicians rely on this, and their results are sometimes astonishing.

People tend to report things in the context of the culture of their time. Before people began reporting night visits and abductions by space aliens in modern times, they described extremely similar occurrences in medieval times, except the culprits back then were malevolent spirits bearing the common names of their time. No matter how many people report seeing UFOs, we are all familiar with the controversy of whether UFOs can be considered credible. This topic provides interesting statistical data on the question of what people say they experience, be they spiritually or scientifically inclined. As with all seemingly nonnormal phenomena, the polls are divided between believers, skeptics, and those who consider such phenomena on the order of hallucinations.

---

[39] Reuters, 2011.

In terms of Americans, some 56% believe in UFOs, with 48% saying such UFOs are from other planets, while 72% of these believe there's been a cover-up of UFOs, and 68% believe there's also been a cover-up of extraterrestrial life.[40] The breakdown regarding "what did you really see" is equally interesting: 48% said they were alien spacecraft, 12% secret government programs, 9% hallucinations, 19% hoaxes, and 7% travelers from another dimension.[41]

At issue in reports of UFOs is the question of "what really happened." We are familiar with the debate over "what really happened" during jury trials. Witnesses are called who have experienced an event and are asked to give their account. People may remember events quite differently, or even remember nothing at all. As we say, "Things seen are things as seen." It's for this reason the jury votes. It literally votes on what's true! We take this so for granted that probably few of us have considered what this really says about the credibility of what people report.

The validity of direct experience also perplexes mainstream science. In 2005, when a scientist reported seeing and tape-recording a supposedly extinct Ivory Billed Woodpecker in a southeastern American swamp, money poured in for further research. When other scientists fielded a video of an extremely large unidentified bird and asked for money, there was none to be found. Why? According to cognitive scientists, it was because everyone agreed the Ivory Billed Woodpecker had once existed, as testified by many in the distant past—and hence someone reporting it again struck a chord. With the other bird, the evidence wasn't compelling because it didn't reference anything already known. Given previous experience, its large size suggested, even if subliminally, that it might be a hoax.

Of course, underlying this entire predicament is the fact that all reports of human experience, no matter whether the phenomena reported turns out to be "real" or not, are ultimately an experience in consciousness and, at the bottom line, someone's brain. From this fact comes the oft-cited brainteaser, "If there's no one somewhere to

---

[40] Roper Poll, 2002.
[41] Roper Poll, 1999.

experience something directly, or experience it secondhand through a third party recorder such as a camera or other sensor, does it really exist?" Ultimately, at least on this planet, all "knowing" is filtered through the human brain.

What People Say They Have Experienced

Regarding consciousness, here are polls reflecting what people say they have experienced. We include categories that might be considered "normal," and also ones more likely to be considered "non-normal."

Polls on Normal Consciousness Activities

Believe in and Practice Prayer (United States: 49%, NBC, *Time*)

Believe in Miracles (U.S.: 69% *Time*, 79% NBC)

Practice Meditation (Worldwide: 14% of world (Hindus), 6% of world (Buddhists), 10% of Americans, independent of tradition, Yahoo.answers 2011)

Practice Yoga (U.S.: 7%, *yogajournal* 2008)

Polls on "Non-Normal" Consciousness Experiences Americans Say They Have Experienced (Gallup Poll, 2011)

Extrasensory perception, or ESP (41%)

Hauntings (37%)

Ghosts (people returning from the dead) (32%)

Telepathy (mind to mind communication) (31%)

Clairvoyance (unique knowledge of the past or future) (26%)

Astrology (25%)

Communication (of any kind) with the dead (21%)

People with supernatural powers (21%)

Reincarnation (rebirth in a new body after death) (20%)

Channeling (spirit entity speaking through a person) (9%)

Healing powers of spirit or mind (55%)

Combined results of the above: 22% believe in five or more categories, 32% believe in at least four categories, 57% believe in at least two paranormal categories, and 1% believe in all categories.

What People Believe In (Gallup Poll, 2011)

Any one of the above listed experiences (73%)
[same question 10 years ago (76%)]

Believe in none of the above listed experiences (27%)

Spirit possession may be a part of mental illness (42%)

These polls don't show any significant differences related to background. Religious people tend to report only slightly more non-normal experiences than the non-religious (75% versus 66%, which is statistically insignificant compared to the sizeable majority reporting such experiences).

Another factor in the contentious debate about consciousness is the question of what is pre-rational (that is, non-rational, as in the thinking process of early humans), rational (as gradually developed through human history and prevalent in modern thinking), and post-rational (if it exists at all, a current and future combination including the fruits of both spiritual and scientific knowing). While the world's spiritual traditions, and particularly interspirituality and the integral thinkers, insist that a post-rational paradigm is both real and necessary, much of the purely rationalist community identifies the post-rational as the pre-rational or non-rational.

This divide explains the programs often seen on mainstream television in which someone reports a non-normal experience, and someone from the international Skeptics Society then proceeds to debunk it. Such confrontations are rarely a dialogue. The person reporting their experience—some of whom are pilots, former high ranking military or civilian officers, or even governors of states—tell their story and present their evidence, if they have photos or other evidence. The guest from the Skeptics Society then basically says none of this can be true, since such things don't exist, adding in a kind manner that it's unfortunate this person or group of people suffered such a hallucination.

It took nearly ten years for over 10,000 reputed sufferers of Morgellons Disease (a strange skin condition that, among other debilitating symptoms, produces multicolored fibers under the skin) to have the syndrome studied by the US Center for Disease Control and Prevention and several major universities. Previously the syndrome had been dismissed by the medical establishment as a mental problem called "delusional parasitosis," with the fibers explained as "artifacts planted by seriously disturbed psychosomatic individuals." Today the syndrome has been traced back to early reports from the Middle Ages. There is a worldwide registry for sufferers, though we are yet to understand what the syndrome is or why it occurs.

Religion and Spirituality's Common Ground on Consciousness

Nearly all the world's contemplative and mystical traditions acknowledge that phenomena such as thoughts, feelings, and emotions arise in consciousness yet are distinct from it. This is what leads to narratives about the everlasting and imperishable nature of "soul," often identified as consciousness itself. This view of consciousness is what accounts for the overriding historical spiritual view that consciousness is a shared collective field involving all things, within which some things, such as fully conscious intelligent life, are more actively involved in sentient interactions.

Each of the world's religious or spiritual traditions has emphasized particular elemental aspects of consciousness, which has given the appearance that their views differ. In reality the different traditions have simply spotlighted particular aspects—much like the millennial story of the blindfolded men touching an elephant and each trying to describe it.

Three coessential aspects of consciousness have ended up being differently emphasized by the various world traditions, leading to historical confusion and the division of religions into traditions and sects. The first aspect has been the overriding one: that consciousness is the overarching, inherent, imperishable, *transcendent* nature of all things, circumscribing and containing all things, so that differences are merely a matter of temporary appearance. This is the core of unity consciousness and consistent with science's view of an all-inclusive quantum reality in which everything is made of the same thing. In spirituality, this emphasis is mostly associated with Eastern paths such as Buddhism and Hinduism, even though in their truest form they don't stress one emphasis above another.

The second aspect of consciousness is that the absolute uniqueness of everything is also a part of the mystery bundled in all statements about the transcendent. This would in some ways parallel science's view of relativity. In science, it's simultaneously true that on earth the basic laws of classical Newtonian physics and Euclidian geometry govern, while in the wider universe they are replaced by other laws and principles such as quantum physics and spherical geometry.

The emphasis on the absolutely unique nature of the individual, though not absent at all from the Eastern traditions, has been more a feature of Western traditions including Christianity, Judaism, and Islam. The difference in emphasis probably explains why belief in reincarnation is more associated with Eastern paths, and the uniqueness of the individual soul with Western paths. The big picture transcendent view is also absolutely unique, not just the sum of its parts. This, of course, is why so many traditions personify an idea of "God."

The third aspect is that all things are relational. While the transcendent big picture is true, and the immanent unique individual little picture is also true, they are mutually dependent. For example, in the human body, all our organs are unique and perform specific functions, though they are brought together to form a multicellular organism.

The Source of Division

When particular religions or spiritual traditions have emphasized either transcendence or immanence, schisms have tended to result, subdividing the world's religions into myriad traditions and sects. This is the underlying problem that interspirituality seeks to address. The same divisions have occurred in philosophy and science when discussions have emphasized subjective versus objective views, with proponents becoming in historical terms either "idealists" or "realists" (otherwise known as "reductionists"). It's as if physicists were to divide into conflicting factions, arguing over whether light is a wave or a particle, when quantum theory allows it to be both.

The message of interspirituality is the unity consciousness that returns these three aspects to their inherent oneness. As Brother Teasdale said concerning the dynamic of unity consciousness, "All relative truths are the product of dualistic perceiving and thinking, while all absolute truths are the fruit of nondual perception and thought."[42]

The most significant nondual element of the body is "the heart." Even the use of this, which is really a metaphor, reveals the subtle interactions of the three interrelated aspects we have described. What is "the heart"? When we use the word, people know what we mean. They know we aren't referring just to the body's physical organ. There are other inherent elements immediately in play—love, kindness, compassion, understanding, unanimity, and so on.

The Spiritual Experience of Consciousness

Why does the spiritual view of consciousness continue to arise even in a world where most of science insists such a view is primitive superstition? Why do humans continue to read their *qualia*—their "raw feel"—in ways that are often more compelling to them than the objective information science has offered?

As is often said, there is nothing like a "true believer" to scare others away from an inquiring conversation. Just as we have clarified

---

[42] MH, p 58.

the difference between religion and spirituality, we need to distinguish the experiential spiritual literature of the world's Great Wisdom Traditions from the holy books, theologies, and more dogmatic literature of the world's religions. We are speaking of the thousands of volumes of the classical spiritual literature by the sages and saints across the world's myriad spiritual traditions—literature that's superbly crafted, eloquent, and deeply compelling.

The difficulty is that much of this literature hasn't always been understood. In fact it has been terribly misunderstood, frequently interpreted through the eyes of strict religious belief rather than the experiential reality that underlies it. Misinterpretations often come from dumbing down, which results from viewing the insights through an overly romantic or magic-mythic perspective. Many religious interpretations of ancient wisdom do damage on the same scale as when this wisdom is examined through a purely rational lens.

The result is that, with regard to non-normal phenomena, one can have useful and credible conversations about such happenings, and one can also be engaged by entirely useless discussions conducted by well-meaning but hopelessly misinformed individuals. In most cases, it's a problem of the overly romantic or magic-mythic lens.

A simple example serves. One could suggest that it was brilliant of Heinrich Schliemann to consider the legends of Troy to be true and, indeed, in 1871-72 discover the ruins of the legendary city. At the same time, it's highly unlikely all the individuals, past and present, in search of the ancient city made of gold—Eldorado—will be equally lucky. Why? Because it's easy to identify the element of greed-related psychological projection in the legends of Eldorado. What greedy medieval adventurer would not have been attracted by, or be motivated to further embellish, the promise of a city made entirely of gold? There was no such unrealistic incentive with regard to searching for Troy. Similarly, it's this tendency to embellish or exaggerate that has given much of the New Age movement a bad name.

In his many writings on Eastern wisdom, Ken Wilber has been an eloquent clarifier of the damage done to ancient wisdom by the Western ego-based and consumer-driven mind. As he put it, it has made "mush" of what could be many potentially useful conversations, especially between the arenas of science and spirituality.

The Genie in the Icebox

When the philosophy of science is taught in colleges and graduate schools, a metaphor is employed to express science's frustration with trying to take spiritual experiences seriously—especially non-normal experiences. The metaphor is referred to as "the genie in the icebox."

This is what science says spiritual people claim: "There is a genie in the icebox. He is really there, believe me. But the nature of the genie is that when you open the door, you don't see him." This is the argument used to convince people they should pay no attention to that realm of experience.

Everyone agrees that all mental experiences happen within the neural apparatus of human beings. We then share our experiences, talking about them. Every aspect of reality we take for granted comes from this kind of collective reporting.

However, many experiences—especially visual, auditory, touch, and smell—are experienced as arising outside the individual. Sounds, actions, or smells come from another person or object. The same is true when someone experiences a non-normal experience such as a mystical experience or hallucination. The scientific data from brain imaging shows that the same area of the brain is used when something is seen outside the body as when it's experienced in a dream. Likewise, the same part of the brain is involved in thinking of someone and reporting that their presence was felt.

The point is made because it sums up the dilemma of science as it attempts to investigate consciousness and cognition. The only methods available depend on human reporting, ranging from something as subjective as asking for a description of what was experienced, to narrowing it down to something like "do you notice anything when I do this?"

Much of consciousness-related study comes down to what humans report. The reality of the presence of the genie in the icebox appears to teeter on this fulcrum. If it can't be photographed, recorded, or in some other way verified, belief in its existence is dependent on whether the "raw feel" of the experience is compelling.

Experience Always Seems to Rule

In the enigma of the genie in the icebox, there's a further rub. From statistics on reports by real people, individuals who end up departing from the view that consciousness resides only in our physical apparatus do so because of something that has happened in their individual experience. This is particularly the case when the individual is a scientist.

The relationship of belief and experience is intriguing. Some of the materialist organizations committed to debunking non-normal spiritual experiences suggest that belief in such things is related to education. For example, when an individual of documented high education or intelligence believes in non-normal experiences, it's believed to be the result of some other kind of flaw such as their personality or emotional makeup. While there may be some truth to these views, let's also be clear that to hold predetermined purely materialist views is a bias.

Nearly all of the materialist groups consider belief in God or spiritual experience as either "impossible to corroborate" or "logically impossible."[43] Such views often equate that which is either not directly measurable or not mentally logical with being false. Also, these groups publicly acknowledge spending huge amounts of money to spread this view, which can hardly be called objective science.

As philosopher Ken Wilber notes, the risk to science lies in the predetermined generalities of both sides. Citing the example of people who assume visible light is all that exists, he points out that their opinion changes instantly when they don goggles that can see infrared or ultraviolet! Science can only speak of what it observes. However, historically, what science has been able to observe in one century or another, or in one decade or another, has changed dramatically.

---

[43] See the website of The Skeptics Society.

The best of science today prefers the maxim "never say never." Science of the 1960s laughed at the hippie notion of "vibes," yet today M-theory has elaborated a vibratory universe. Continental drift, today's field of plate tectonics, was scorned for generations. Being an expert on how birds came from dinosaurs will get you a prestigious job these days, whereas a few decades ago it meant ruin for a scientific career.

We live today in a universe acknowledged as a continuum from the most infinitesimally large to infinitesimally small. It's no longer a world in which normal and paranormal are seen as strict dualities. So when scientists venture into proclamations about God, they veer from doing science. Having said this, we can never be quite sure what real science will be able to tackle next. This realization should inform our ongoing debate about what is actually real or not real.

Another problem is with statistics about belief. That an experience may be interpreted through the lens of a belief or cultural narrative doesn't alter whether one has the experience. The earlier Gallup Poll cited didn't find significant correlation. Other studies, such as UFO and ghost-related polls, show that direct experience motivates some 90% of people's views, whereas general belief accounts only for the other 10%.[44]

The public might hope for a useful dialogue between individuals who have had such experiences and those who seek to debunk this kind of experience. But fruitful dialogue doesn't occur because, as we've seen often on television, the scientist, pilot, astronaut, high-level military official, or even former governor recounting such an experience is politely dismissed as having hallucinated.

The real problem is such experiences seem to be unrepeatable under controlled conditions. Despite this, those who have had such experiences mostly continue to believe in the "raw feel," and thus the validity, of their experiences. Even as recently as 30 years ago there was no field of scientific consciousness studies, so it's likely these matters will be elucidated to a far greater degree in the future—especially as the integrative and holistic epochs unfold. For the time being, because the

---

[44] Associated Press/Ipsos poll, 2007.

science-spirituality divide has been entrenched so long, most media attention begins with the assumption that the two arenas exclude each other.

13

Scientific Consciousness Studies

"String theory requires all these extra dimensions"

Sir Roger Penrose

THE SCIENTIFIC STUDY OF CONSCIOUSNESS BEGINS WITH THE INSIGHT THAT the brain is made up of myriads of neurological elements and pathways, which appear somehow to be brought into a coordinated unity. Interference with these elements or pathways by means of chemicals or physical intrusion, particularly into certain parts of the brain, blanks out or accentuates certain elements of the system and can also disturb the unity of the coordination.

This rather physical approach to consciousness through manipulating aspects of the brain is relevant since a specific part of the brain controls our sense of the difference between ourselves and our world. We are speaking of the top rear areas of the brain, which science calls the superior parietal lobe. When this brain area is blanked out, as studies show it is in prayer or meditation, the result is a sense of holism and connectedness.

The basic experience of consciousness correlates with networks in the brain that involve the common day-to-day experiences we share. Whether waking or dreaming, consciousness is experienced by all as phenomena that arise in the brain—in the form of thoughts, sensing, messages, pictures, emotions, and so on—then fade into the background only to be replaced by other phenomena. This day-to-day, common sense landscape of consciousness parallels the simplest concept of consciousness in the Wisdom Traditions—as for instance in India's classical Vedanta, where the regular states experienced by everyone are noted as waking, dreaming, dreamless deep sleep, and that which is aware of all of these at once (*moksha* in Sanskrit).

It's remarkable that this landscape of the coming and going of phenomena is at once so simple yet so complex. How does the "raw feel" of all this happen, and what's its significance, if any? Obviously, "raw feel" attends learning, a fundamental part of any human development. But what purpose does "raw feel" serve? This dilemma has left numerous students of consciousness mystified, asking questions such as, "What does the wetness of water tell us?" Yet many find the ultimate satisfaction in this mystery and say it will never be, nor was it meant to be, otherwise. What would become of wonder without wonder? Can it be okay for everyone to be a little right and a little wrong? This is the kind of satisfaction an interspiritual world might instill among all beings.

Quantum Ideas of Consciousness

The important frontier opened by the scientific study of consciousness is the relationship of consciousness to the understanding of quantum fields and electromagnetic fields from the point of view of the new physics. Quantum theory is a dynamic view that allows paradoxical phenomena to be in interplay, in a sense like a sun shower in which rain and sun are both present. Similarly, electromagnetic fields involve an interplay between both electrical and magnetic elements. Such paradoxes parallel paradoxical statements in the world's wisdom literature, such as "form is formlessness, and formlessness is form."[45]

---

[45] The Heart Sutra, a classic from Buddhism.

The difficulty has been finding a synthesis between how consciousness might be explained as quantum fields and how it might work as electromagnetic fields. However, advocates of both groups agree that classical physics has been unable to offer an explanation of consciousness.

The theories take on some fancy names, but this is typical of science. The most well-known physicists who propose explanations of consciousness based on electromagnetic fields are Susan Pockett and Johnjoe McFadden with their "EM Field Theory." Two other teams have proposed views combining electromagnetism with quantum theory: Mari Jibu, Kunio Yasue, and Giuseppe Vitiello with "Quantum Brain Dynamics" and E. Roy John and identical twins Andrew and Alexander Fingelkurts with "Operational Architectronics."

In this view, when nerves in the brain called "neurons" fire, they create tiny electromagnetic fields. These fields become exponentially larger and take on various configurations depending on how many myriad networks of neurons are firing and which they happen to be. The varying levels or frequencies in the fields hold digital information (akin to notes on a staff of sheet music), and the modulations of the levels (like the lines on the staff of sheet music) correspond to experiences sensed in the "raw feel" as objective, subjective, choosing options, simple recognitions, and complex recognitions. A chief proponent of consciousness as electromagnetic fields, consistent with the scientific view of consciousness, believes such fields occur only locally—that is, in each individual. The other, consistent with the spiritual view of consciousness, believes there's a collective field shared by all.

The most well-known physicists to propose ideas of consciousness related to quantum theory are Karl H. Pribram and David Bohm (the Holonic Brain theory of quantum mind), along with Stuart Hameroff and Roger Penrose (the Orch-OR theory of quantum mind). Another prominent scientist, Gustav Bernroider, did work expanding the concepts of Bohm. These views are much more difficult to describe to the non-scientist than those involving electromagnetism.

The word "quantum" comes from Latin meaning "how much?" This is because quantum theory involves explaining the extremely peculiar and paradoxical behavior of the infinitesimally small elements of energy and matter that form our reality. It's the peculiar oddness of this behavior that caused science to struggle for decades before being able to understand the world of the infinitesimally small and finally atomic energy.

A factor that renders this quantum realm even more difficult to understand is that the conventional rules and relations of time and space don't necessarily apply when one is speaking of this mysterious and enigmatic realm at the intersection of matter and energy. Highly advanced mathematics are necessary to understand this realm at all, which explains why pioneers such as Einstein, Heisenberg, and Gross lived most of their lives in the domain of math. To even enter the field of quantum theory, one must know mathematical systems such as advanced calculus, differential equations, differential geometry, probability theory, and statistical mechanics. The electronic technology that peppers our daily lives—such as integrated circuits, fiber optics, computer memory, lasers, CDs, DVDs, and GPS "Garmin" systems—depends on this new insight into how the world of the infinitely small operates.

In the heart of this quantum realm are what might best be called waves of information—actually waves of mathematical probability, referring to the chances that this might happen or that might happen. For instance, if you jotted in a notebook all the things that might happen to you when you leave your house each morning, it might help you understand such a matrix of possibility. Such a list could include almost endless scenarios. Imagine that some of these possibilities might arise, while others won't. Then imagine these scenarios happening, subsiding, or not happening at all—like waves arising and collapsing. This continual arising and collapsing of waves of information could allow myriads of thoughts, emotions, feelings, analyses, points of view, and possible options to arise in the mind, be resolved, fade away, then arise again. This is a loose metaphor, but it gives us some idea of how this world, described in such fancily named quantum brain theories as Quantum Brain Dynamics, Operational Architectonics, Holonomic Brain theory, and Orch-OR theory, might work.

A great deal of supportive work is required to convince the wider scientific community that either electromagnetic field concepts of consciousness, or those involving quantum fields, have perhaps unraveled the mystery of how consciousness works.

The Future of Consciousness

Two decades ago, probably no one would have imagined scientists would agree that understanding consciousness would define the next scientific era. However, this understanding parallels the unfolding of the Integrative and Holistic eras of history, as well as the predictions by philosophers of science that science would adopt a view consistent with reality as a unified whole.

Our species' unique ability to teach and learn is unparalleled in any of the primates. When adult chimpanzees are given the same tests for teaching and learning as very young human children, chimps only occasionally pass new skills on—and usually only short-term within their family or clan. In contrast, when young humans learn something new, they are inherently proactive about passing it along. This is not to ignore recent scientific evidence that intelligence and emotions in many animals is far more advanced and complex than once suspected—higher apes, dolphins, and elephants among them—but what we are talking about with regard to cognitive skills in humans is of another magnitude.

History shows that new skill sets, once innovated, spread through humanity with breathtaking speed. When early humans developed farming, the earliest methods spread continentally within 500 years, with additional significant innovations occurring within a millennium. In an archaic epoch that itself lasted 7,000 years, this is extremely fast. Similarly, when writing developed, it spread nearly everywhere within a millennium. In fact the notion was so compelling that the skill appears to have arisen independently across numbers of cultures as soon as people got the idea.

Escalating energy from this relationship between new knowledge and the rapid spread of new skill sets drives our modern world at a dizzying pace. Students in Second and Third World universities master the same skills as those in the First World and compete for the same high-tech careers. Myriads learn computers, texting, and networking, then innovate and become entrepreneurs, developing new goods and services.

Modern worldviews change with remarkable speed. The academic field of "discourse studies," otherwise known as "discursive theory," developed only since the 1990s, explains how, when information and narratives about reality enter the public dialogue, behavior changes accordingly and rapidly. It's as if they establish what Dr Rupert Sheldrake calls a "morphic field," which in turn changes people's views of reality and tacitly changes reality itself.

For example, when global warming first entered world awareness in the mid-1990s, nearly 70% of Americans were unaware of it as an issue. Not until 1997 did it become a subject of regular polling.[46] By 2007 the numbers had reversed, with 87% aware of the warming phenomenon.[47] Of those, 75% considered it a danger, a number unidentified with particular political affiliations.[48] When it became a political issue and a subject of media propaganda, the numbers changed again, so that by 2011, 76% of Democrats believed the phenomenon to be real, whereas only 41% of Republicans believed it. Meanwhile, 90% of Europeans believed in it.

The point is that human skill sets related to cognitive skills and human worldviews populate at a far faster pace than purely physical evolution. The factors that drive them also fluctuate wildly. Yet, as clearly seen in the Integral and Spiral Dynamics views of history, together with psychologist Julian Jaynes' tracking of the gradual development of the conscious mind, the long-term trends always remain consistent.

Our view is that consciousness will continue to expand as it has in the past, but at a faster pace. This will be particularly driven by the relationship of new knowledge and attendant skill sets, with a trend toward a more-spacious and creative mind, along with the skills that

---

[46] Gallup, 1997.
[47] Neilsen, 2007–2009.
[48] Stanford, 2007.

accompany such an expansion. The direction of this development will parallel the unfolding from the Integrative to the Holistic Age, and a part of this emerging holism will be a skilled understanding and synergy between our interior and exterior, subjective and objective ways of knowing and working. The nature of this growth in spaciousness and skills will be precisely the unity consciousness and movement toward a holistic world transformation spoken of in the vision of Interspirituality and across the entire international spectrum of integral and evolutionary consciousness movements.

This trend is universally reflected, not just through those leading scientists, philosophers, and spiritual leaders detailed here. Asked whether they believed in a universal spirit or unifying universal power, 92% answered in the affirmative, including 21% who claim to be atheists.[49] In the New Age community, 52% worldwide were found to believe in a shared quantum field that includes the whole of reality.[50]

Sociologist Dr Paul Ray, in his famous work *The Cultural Creatives*— those distributed throughout the world's population who support progressive and transformative world change—suggested that in the year 2000 there were more than 50 million cultural creatives in the United States (about 25% of the adult population), with a further 80-90 million in Europe. Originally, Ray suggested that cultural creatives could dominate western populations as early as 2020. The website Enlightened Economic believes a case could now be made that this will occur much earlier. If true, this may account for the rapid explosion of the world's Occupy movement, which grew to international prominence within a month of its inception in the fall of 2011. A Reuters' poll a month into the Occupy Wall Street movement in New York City indicated that 67% of New Yorkers supported its general vision, while 87% supported the movement's right to live in and protest from New York City's Zuccotti Park.

The prevailing worldview that the subjective realm of the humanities and the objective realm of science would remain separate, championed in C. P. Snow's famous 1959 lecture and subsequent book *The*

---

[49] *Washington Post* poll, 2008.
[50] A survey by DMT-nexus Forum.

Two Cultures,[51] has seen the arising of a predicted third culture. In *The Third Culture*,[52] John Brockman, scientific literature historian and founder of The Edge Foundation, seems to further support the rapid acceleration toward the global and holistic worldview predicted by the developmental view of history. This inevitable development was announced in the 1993 reprinting of Snow's own classic, in a new introduction by Cambridge University professor Stefan Collini.

This convergence is already apparent in many new research approaches, including both scientific and spiritual consciousness perspectives, especially since the discovery of nuclear magnetic resonance scanning (NMR). This cutting-edge technology, which won Nobel Prizes in 1943, 1944, 1952, 1991, 2002, and 2003, allows researchers to see both form and function simultaneously. Widely publicized work by cross-disciplinary researchers such as Dr Joseph Chilton Pearce and Dr Andrew Newberg at the University of Pennsylvania has utilized NMR to link neuroscience with spiritual experience and belief. Dr Newberg's work has been widely publicized in books such as *Why God Won't Go Away* and *Why We Believe What We Believe*.

Another pioneer is Dr Bruce Lipton, a developmental biologist whose books *The Biology of Belief* and *Spontaneous Evolution* have been widely influential.[53] In 2009, Lipton received the international Goi Peace Award. This interwoven understanding of the relationship of self, brain-mind, and our ongoing development toward a peaceful and harmonious world has also been echoed in recent books such as Dr Philip Sheperd's *New Self, New World*[54] and Dr James Olson's *The Whole-Brain Path to Peace*.[55] The relationship of spirituality to consciousness itself has become a prominent topic at the cutting edge of science and philosophy. A 1997 international study, *Nonduality*[56] by Dr David Loy, published by Yale University, has already been translated into three languages.

---

[51] See Snow, C.P. [1959] 2001 in Bibliography
[52] See Brockman, J. 1995 in Bibliography
[53] See Lipton, B.H. 2011 in Bibliography
[54] See Sheperd, P. 2010 in Bibliography
[55] See Olson, J. 2011 in Bibliography
[56] See Loy, D.L. 1997 in Bibliography

14

The Spiritual World

"Enter through the narrow door"

Jesus of Nazareth, Luke 13:24

WORLDWIDE, NEARLY 6 BILLION OF OUR PLANET'S MORE THAN 7 BILLION inhabitants believe in some kind of a spirit realm. The idea that this view is simply going to go away as we move into the Third Millennium is wishful thinking. So, what is the spirit world and what is the heritage it brings from our planet's history to an uncertain future?

Generally, the expression "spiritual world" refers to the entire dimension of consciousness, including the "spirit realm" or "astral realm" referred to in virtually every religious tradition. Stories of this dimension are recorded across humanity's entire collective narrative and contain all of the mysteries that accompany such an ethereal and elusive notion.

Is the spirit world real? How has it been reported as experienced down through the centuries? Are there common threads from this grand but elusive chapter of our human story that might actually inform modernity and further light the way toward a positive future? Or is it all just "bunkum" that ought not to concern modern humans?

What are the challenges, even the *pathologies*, that have confronted our species when we have ventured into this realm of reported experience? Question and enigma, subtlety and nuance have historically pervaded discussion of the spirit realm. It's no easy discussion for our species, especially in the modern era, dominated as it is by the rational lens.

The Historical Breadth of Spirit World Experience

Virtually every modern culture is underpinned by enigmatic narratives of the spirit realm. To the tens of thousands of indigenous tribes that preceded the modern world and that in some cases persist today, the spirit world was the realm of ancestors and nature spirits. Ancient words from these cultures translate as "the animal fathers" and "the forms of the land." Shamans, or medicine men and women, mediated between the human world and the surrounding spirit realm. The position of shaman was reserved not just for those of special training, but for instruction at the edge of what many of us would consider reality. Adepts who wished to be a shaman had to enter the subtlest dimensions of reality and learn how to "work" there.

With ongoing development of human civilization, the notion of spirit realms only increased in complexity. Ancient Egypt, which was typical of many early cultures of the God-King period of history, saw humans as an amalgam of essences carried over into an afterlife as "*Akh* essence," characterized in their hieroglyphs as a flying bird.

Each of the world's empires in the historical epoch of the God-Kings had their own highly developed idiosyncratic views of the spirit realms, which seeded the vaster array of cultural narratives about these dimensions when the totalitarian empires spread across the populated world in the succeeding centuries. All these narratives carried this element of the ultimately mysterious, the rarified edges of the unknown.

To the forefathers our own historians record as the seed of our eventual modern world—ancient Greece—this spirit realm was the *aether* (heavens), home to *pneuma* (spirit). Plato wrote of the shamanic roots of such beliefs, recalling ancient traditions of "listening to and learning from the plants" embedded in the oral traditions that had predated even ancient Greece. In the nearby kingdoms of the Near

East, Persia and India, the terms used were *akasha/atman* (life principle as formlessness and form) or *prana* (the vital nature). To early wandering Germanic and Scandinavian tribes to the west, this realm was identified with a myriad of words pointing to breath or wind. In the cradle of monotheism, ancient Judaea and adjacent Arabia, a host of words all pointed toward a world above, an astral realm.

The notion of astral realms characterized consciousness both East and West, from mystery religions and sects that followed after the classical philosophers of Greece, to the Koran's narratives of the Prophet's ascent of the "seven heavens" and the narrative of *Yetzirah* (the formative realm) in Jewish mysticism. For early Christians who were certain of Jesus' immediate return, it was the heavenly *pleroma* (fullness), home of the divine in a region of light above to which they were destined to ascend.

The Spirit Realms Become Divided as Heaven and Hell

As the era of the ancient totalitarian empires arose, what better way to enforce the primacy of your social construct and religious beliefs than to make them matters of salvation or damnation? Thus did the message of ultimate reward and punishment enter humanity's understanding of the spirit realms.

There were nearly 30 major totalitarian cultures during the 40 centuries of this totalitarian epoch. The one most relevant and familiar to us was Rome. From Rome evolved not only the structures of early modern Europe but also the social and religious structures of most of today's First World. This First World, composed of Europe and its colonies to the west and the boundaries of Russia with China to the east, dominated the world stage until the recent pluralistic period that emerged after World War II.

The spirit realm message of the Church of Rome, as with its centuries long rival to the east, the Caliphates of Islam, was the divided spirit realms of heaven and hell—with, in some cases, intermediate realms such as the purgatory of orthodox Rome or the *Barazkh, olam mithal* of some of the Islamic traditions. At least in the religion of Rome, as defined by the biblical texts chosen for Emperor Constantine by Eusebius, the primacy of heaven versus hell contained the whole host of heaven. Therein were to be found not only the souls of those departed from earth, but also angels and demons—and ultimately, in that masculine dominated world, "God *him*self."

The coexistence of these church-based views with the culturally entrenched popularity of astrology and the persistence of the more complex beliefs of various mystery schools was fragile. Astrology, quite different from esoteria concerning the spirit worlds, enjoyed an easier place within the medieval church. Having been a part of European culture since ancient times, its codices were consulted even by church officials. The non-orthodox notions of spirit realms of the post-Greek, Jewish, and early Christian esoteric schools were another matter. Depending on where one practiced these arts from the 12th through 16th centuries, the Church's inquisitors might not be far behind. The same was true of alchemy.

Despite this, the landscape of European politics was diverse enough that the major resources of the esoteric schools survived. With the arising of greater religious, philosophic, and scientific freedom, the long-hidden resources of the mystery schools not only surfaced again but also gained prominence in public thought, resurging particularly with the Renaissance and the new thought's melding of approaches to the spiritual and healing arts, mystery religions, gnostic sects, and healing cults.

One influential group, the medieval Hermetists—whose symbol became the familiar winged staff and snakes logo of modern medicine, the *caduceus*—arose from ancient writings attributed to a Hermes Trismegistus, portrayed as a combination of the Greek god Hermes and the Egyptian god Thoth. Hermetic views, combining mysticism and medicine, held great sway because they were believed to represent the wisdom of the early intellectual center of the Mediterranean civilization, Alexandria. Two other influential mystical healing schools originated with 15th century doctor-occultists—the Swiss-born Paracelsus and the German-born Christian Rosenkreuz. Each of these schools would see their spirit world cosmologies survive into the modern day. From these roots also arose the famous 18th century work of Sweden's renowned mystic, medium, and clairvoyant Emanuel Swedenborg.

Around the cusp of the 19th century, during its period of peak popularity, spiritualism actually emerged as a religion. Its activities involved some of the most prestigious political and cultural leaders of the world, a fact often forgotten by the rationalism of today. The spiritualism of that era was frequently integrated with and greatly influenced by 19th century science, particularly its western dualistic ideas of reality. Spiritualists spoke of myriad levels or spheres of the spirit realms, each complex and each differing drastically from one another depending on the nature of the souls or spirits inhabiting them. Descriptions of these levels often involved all the arcane details of life on the earthly planet—including places and surroundings, habits and occupations, and the nature of relationships and personality traits.

Ancient Notions Persist into the Modern Day

By the 19th and 20th centuries, the vast literature of Theosophy had emerged, seeking to meld the mystical notions of the Great Wisdom Traditions (particularly those of the East) with 19th century science. Famous Theosophists such as H. P. Blavatsky and C. W. Leadbeater described the spirit spheres and zones in great detail.

From this socially influential movement, the spirit worldviews of the Paracelsians (traced to Paracelsus) and Rosicrucianism (traced to Christian Rosenkreuz, whose narratives hadn't been published for two centuries) arose. From these groups, which still have followings today, arise the roots of the view of the spirit realms that pervades a vast literature of esoteria across many languages. In this literature, ancient Eastern and Western views are nearly seamless, particularly because most of the Western schools find their roots in the East. All these descriptions of the spirit realms experienced a resurgence with the coming of the free presses of Europe and America in the last two centuries. The revival reached millions worldwide.

In the East, the landscape of the spirit realms was portrayed by Sri

Aurobindo, whose body of less esoteric writings (on the arts, politics, and sociology) formed part of the cornerstone of India's emerging nationhood and served as a key resource for Western developmental thinkers. In the West, depictions were included in the popular books of Alice Bailey (whose Ageless Wisdom School seeded much of today's New Age Movement) and the Fourth Way writings of G. I. Gurdjieff and P. D. Ouspensky, still followed by many as the Gurdjieff Work.

In perhaps the most runaway spiritual bestseller of all times, Paramahansa Yogananda's *Autobiography of a Yogi*, Yogananda described in detail the astral realms and discussed their relevance to the millennial views of life and death. In the psychedelic era, Timothy Leary and his associates Ralph Metzner and Richard Alpert guided psychedelic drug adepts through the dimensions of the ancient *Tibetan Book of the Dead* in their manual *The Psychedelic Experience*. Also, few of us can forget the late 1960s–70s era of the bookstore hits by Carlos Castaneda telling the semi-fictional accounts of his studies with a northern Mexican shaman Don Juan.

Modern Settings and Modern Academic Study

Even if we don't personally ascribe to the notion of a spirit world, or perhaps consider the idea of a spirit world either irrelevant or "wacko" (in the language of DNA co-discoverer Dr James Watson), we are surrounded by a world firmly entrenched in these heritages. To see the imposing variety of narratives belonging to this heritage, one need only examine the use of the word "spirit" across cultures.

Our planet's languages abound with ephemeral, finely nuanced, multi-dimensional usages of the word "spirit," each full of complex multiple meanings and allusions: *Geist* in German, *l'esprit* in French, *ruach* (wind as spirit) in Hebrew, *gi* (breath as spirit) in Chinese, and so on. *Geist* in German is enigmatic in its meaning. To translate it into English, it's either compared with words like mind, spirit, or ghost, or used in word combinations such as "spirit/mind" or "spirit (mind)" to express the complex meaning. In French, *l'esprit* is equally elusive. Always combined with other words to provide nuanced meanings, the word *esprit* itself derives from Latin for spirit. On the darker side, words for spirit have given us our modern slang terms such as "bogey man" or "humbug"—from *húm* or *ium*, meaning "breath" in the Germanic and Scandinavian languages, joined with their word for ghost or goblin, *bug*.

In American daily life, the word "spirit" is everywhere and carries multiple meanings. For instance, we use the familiar phrases "the spirit of the age" and "the spirit, not the letter, of the law." In sports, the cheer "you've got the spirit, let's hear it," is used, while we also speak of a "spirited" horse. Then there's the common everyday RSVP, "I'm tied up and can't attend, but I'll be there in spirit." Given that worldwide over 50%[57] of citizens participate in the religions of their culture, these concepts of the spirit realm still permeate modern culture.

Particularly elaborate explanations of the spirit realms occur in mystical Hinduism (Vedanta, Advaita Vedanta), many varieties of mystical Buddhism, mystical Christianity (Gnosticism and the Christian Mystery Schools), Jewish mysticism (Kabbalah), Sufi and non-Sufi Islam, and modern-day indigenous Shamanism. Other detailed views occur across the academic study of religion, or with the adherents of smaller sects: the Greek mystical schools (Hermeticism and Neoplatonism), esoteric disciplines such as Kashmir Shaivism in north India or the Druze Near Eastern mystical school, specialized schools of yoga (such as Sant Mat/Surat Shabd), the resurgent Rosicrucian and Paracelsian followings, the literature of Theosophy (Blavatsky and Leadbeater) and Anthroposophy (Rudolf Steiner), and more current offerings such as Eckankar (the Light and Sound of God school) and the various Ascended Master schools of the New Age movement.

If we conduct a headcount of how many currently participate in such views, the number includes virtually six-sevenths of world population.[58] The fact of this influence simply can't be ignored by the world's remaining one billion people.

---

[57] In America 83%, according to the American Religious Identification Survey, 2008.
[58] adherents.com, 2011.

Mainstreaming of Esoteric and Mystical Studies in World Academia

One list of major academic resources in English[59], from the University of South Florida, identifies just short of 400 compendiums or sourcebooks on academic studies of mysticism, including the spirit realms. A *Who's Who in Mysticism* published by that same university and encompassing only Western subjects of interest before the year 1700 includes nearly 100 mystics or mystic schools and some 40 academic sourcebooks. The American Academy of Religion (whose motto is "fostering excellence in the study of religion") has a Mystical Studies Group and Western Esoteric Studies Group, and lists nearly 150 additional academic source groups for their studies and activities. A survey of studies of Islamic mysticism in America published by Loyola University, The Academic Study of Sufism at American Universities, lists nearly 20 academic programs and 80 reference sources. In Judaism, the association called "Israel: Society, Culture and History" represents scholars at seven universities in the United States, United Kingdom, and Israel, and has as of 2010 devoted a volume to the study of mysticism in 20th century Hebrew literature.

This records only some of the most recent activity in English. It's probably impossible to estimate the amount of academic study of our planet's mystical notions across the world's other languages. The implication is when Dr Watson stated that anyone interested in religion today is most likely "wacko," he was simply unaware of the body of this work worldwide.

It Takes Big Minds to See Big Pictures

Some of the most famous investigators who have made important contributions to today's more-evolutionary approach to the world's millennia of spiritual experience often earn the tag of "polymath." These are scholars who have mastered multiple areas of expertise and

---

[59] Published by the University of South Florida under the title "Mysticism and Modernity" (http://pegasus.cc.ucf.edu/~janzb/mysticism/).

understanding. It's worth mentioning because it takes these kinds of minds to comprehend the complex landscape of today's world. They are an important breed, differing from proponents of just one or two sectarian points of view.

The perspective of a polymath naturally embraces multiple sources of information and multiple sources of feedback and analysis. Along with Ken Wilber's voluminous work on the history of spiritual phenomena, two outstanding historical examples who have greatly influenced current understanding of our planet's millennial spiritual narrative are Romanian/French polymath Dr Mircea Eliade and America's Dr Michael Harner.

Eliade, who was fluent in five languages and could read three others, is generally credited as the founder of what is known as the Patternist school of comparative religion. This world-centric approach seeks to recognize general patterns and collective meaning from the planet's myriad mythologies. France's Claude Lévi-Strauss, often referred to as the "father of modern anthropology," and America's Joseph Campbell, author of the influential book on myth *The Hero with a Thousand Faces*, are also world-famous for their similar approach to these ancient stories.

Eliade and Harner also stand out because they were influenced little by their allegiance to organized religion. Both could be considered interspiritual pioneers. Eliade himself was outspoken in his desire to deconstruct the inherent behavioral dangers of organized religion and its dogmas. These were perils he had experienced firsthand, when as a Romanian he had to decide who to align with in World War II and could only settle on "a lesser of evils." His most famous theory, "hierophanies," explained how religious experience is directly related to resulting social behavior and structures that inevitably propel history toward more or less ethical results. He emphasized that the nature of religious narrative and activity creates structures that actually serve to tear down our species' ethical potential.

Harner's views, stemming from his studies of ancient religious experience and modern-day shamanism, paralleled this sensitivity. He also warned that ignoring the heritage of collective wisdom in our ancient myths and spiritual practice is at our own peril. Wilber has been more direct, calling the denigration or denial of this collective heritage "the gold standard of ignorance."

What People Actually Believe about the Spirit World

The nature of a discussion about the spirit world is different when people are familiar with either the ancient or esoteric notions of the spirit realms than when they have only been exposed to the narrative of heaven versus hell. If Islamic and Hindu nations are omitted, the United States ranks number three in belief in heaven (87.5%), led only by the Philippines (96.5%) and South Africa (90.7%).[60] Ireland and Canada rank high (80%). Some ten countries—including Japan and Korea, Australasian and Latin American countries, plus countries from Europe such as Italy—are in the 60-70% range. A number of core European Union countries have numbers down in the 30-50% range, such as the United Kingdom at 55%. The lowest numbers (10-20%) come from Eastern European and Scandinavian nations. In terms of the Islamic and Hindu nations, several score at near 100%, such as Saudi Arabia, Egypt, Indonesia, and Bangladesh. Hindu India comes in at 72%.

Questions specifically about hell bring a different response. Whereas in the Islamic and Hindu nations about as many believe in hell as believe in heaven, in the West the numbers drop dramatically. Across Europe and Australasian nations, 20-30% less people believe in hell than believe in heaven, including nearly all the core countries of the European Union. In the United States, the number is 13% less. Curiously, five countries have more people who believe in hell than heaven—make of it what you will. These are Mexico, Greece, Germany, Iceland, and Italy (the difference being some 10% more).

If 30% more people in Europe and Australasian nations believe in heaven than in hell, what does this mean in terms of their view of the spiritual realm? In other surveys, 87.5% of Americans believe

---

[60] The World Values Survey, 2007.

in heaven, whereas only 34-56% believe in spirits. So who inhabits heaven? According to a Fox News poll, 92% of Americans believe in God, whereas only 71% believe in the devil (the devil's numbers have gone up 10% in the last few years). Young people are more likely to believe as much in heaven as in hell and God or the devil, with women usually believing 10% more than men in both and Republicans 10-20% more than Democrats.[61]

As far as inhabitants of the astral realms, people of religious belief included God (92%), angels (78%), the devil (71%), and other kinds of spirits (34%).[62] Belief in heavenly spirits went up to 78% or even 85% depending on how the question was asked.[63]

A study by Pew in 2008 indicated 74% of American Christians believe heaven is the place where good souls go after death, with only 64% believing in hell as the destination of bad souls. Many believe heaven is interactive with earth's affairs, with 75% convinced that God intervenes in day-to-day life and 34% that God or other mediators answers their prayers. For Jews and Hindus the numbers are similar, though in each case about 10% less than reported by Christians.

A similar poll by the *Christian Post* in 2009 indicated 78% of those interviewed believe souls migrate to heaven or hell after death, while a 2003 Harris Poll put this number at 84%. Gallup[64] also revealed 21-38% believe in interactive communication with dead spirits, 9-15% in channeling spirit entities, 41% in demons and demon possession, and 25% in the reincarnation of spirits (in 2003 Harris put this number at 40%). A surprising 2006 study by Monash University in Australia indicated 70% of those interviewed said their life had been influenced by intervention from other realms. Perhaps reflecting our ancient shamanic roots, a survey for fur companies[65] learned that 32% of those interviewed believed in animal spirits in the spirit world, while a 2011 poll by ABC News indicated 47% of pet owners believe their pets will go to heaven.

---

[61] Opinion Dynamics Corp., 2003.
[62] Fox News, 2004.
[63] ABC News, 2005.
[64] 2001, 2005.
[65] FoxyCreations, 2011.

Similar statistics indicate how strong the influence of the magic-mythic lens remains. A 2001 study by America's National Science Foundation noted that 32% of Americans and 46% of Europeans believe lucky numbers influence reality. On the more humorous side of the magic-mythic paradigm, a 2011 CBS poll indicated that across all ethnic groups and religious affiliations, 43% of those polled believe the spirit realms help athletes win games, especially when the athletes are "believers." This figure ranges from 59-80% among some religious affiliations and ethnic groups. Although the conventional idea of God would allow "Him" to watch all the games at once, it would be interesting to know how the favorites are chosen! The magic-mythic paradigm is also still strong even in supposedly non-religious people, as a 2003 Harris Poll indicated when it reported 27% who say they aren't Christians still claim to believe in the virgin birth and the resurrection.

Who Goes to Whose Heaven or Whose Hell?

For those who believe the simplified, popular view of the spirit realms as just heaven and hell, further interesting questions arise. Who will go to whose heaven and whose hell? This may seem humorous at first glance, but it becomes a serious issue in the context of cross-tradition marriages and situations in everyday life in which adherents of the various religions are friends concerned for each other's destiny. Among Christians, only the most rigid sectarian groups, numbering 21% of Christians, believe that only their adherents will go to heaven.[66] Among denominations whose members represent demographically wide cross sections, the numbers of those who believe in such exclusion range only from 50% to as low as 40%.[67] However, the importance of "right belief" is still strong, with 30% believing eternal life depends on belief and 29% that it depends on behavior.[68]

A Century Landscape poll in 2007 indicated upward of 70% of

---

[66] Pew, 2008.
[67] ABC News, 2005; Pew, 2008.
[68] Pew, 2007.

Christians consider the possibility that non-Christians might go to heaven. Learning of this, a prominent Buddhist teacher, the Venerable Thich Tam-Thien, joked that he surmised a pretty good Buddhist might go to heaven, whereas a really good Buddhist would go to Nirvana.

The major religions differ in their views of this heavenly "what," "where," and "who," but much of the difference results from the over-simplification of the discussion. Beliefnet.com provides a useful outline of what the main religions teach about the afterlife. The survey includes what Christianity (divided into Catholicism and Protestantism), Judaism, Islam, Hinduism, and Buddhism believe about the spirit realm. Generally, the Western religions teach the dichotomy of heaven and hell, while only some of their mystical traditions consider reincarnation. Both Hinduism and Buddhism emphasize spiritual attainment in this lifetime, the return of reincarnated souls, and spirit realms designed to handle this celestial back-and-forth traffic.

Better than Heaven and Hell

The millennially deeper mystical teachings of all the world's religions are far more complex than simply the notion of heaven and hell, and it's here that the real bounty of wisdom lies when it comes to modern humankind. With six-sevenths of our world population believing in some form of the magic-mythic paradigm, it's extremely unlikely the way forward will be to discard them. Rather, there will need to be further integration of these understandings with those of modern science and psychology.

We'll need to differentiate the content in these beliefs that's negative for the planet—such as exclusive claims one or another of these views are right—from that which is positive for the planet. This involves identifying the real *wisdom* in these ancient teachings in terms of what they have to say to us concerning the way we live life and face death. We need to glean from these ancient narratives insight that can lead to new skill sets for our species.

Planet-wide, we need skill sets that will give us a deeper mastery of our lives—a sensitivity to values, quality, meaningful work, cultivation of leisure, care of our environment, and the nurturing of a healthy multiculturalism. We also need skill in understanding the subtle realms of reality. These are the elements Brother Teasdale identified in the realm of the heart. Imagining a planetary citizenry with a confident sense not only of its collective identity but also of its role in the cosmos is a powerful vision.

15

The Spirit Realms In Everyday Experience

"Some enchanted evening you may see a stranger across a crowded room"

Rogers and Hammerstein

IT MAY BE HELPFUL TO PROVIDE AN *EXPERIENTIAL* UNDERSTANDING OF THE spirit world that just might make sense.

Perhaps the best way to understand how the spirit world may work is to look at your experience of your mind. To inquire within your mind, you bring up or remember an old event, feeling, or emotion, which then appears as if it's popping into your consciousness. Sometimes you have to search a little for that event, feeling, or emotion. You may initially receive glimpses, which you are perhaps able to enhance either by concentration, relaxation, or hypnosis. At times stuff pops up without any real inquiry. Often an *array* of phenomena pops up simultaneously.

When you access your own mind, you appear to be inquiring *internally*, whereas in accessing the rest of reality you seem to be inquiring *externally*. That is, you seem to be inquiring into the larger realm of what's around you, beyond the confines of your own body. Experientially, then, we "reach into" our own mind and "reach out to" the wider realm of the spiritual world. But the process is much the same.

From an experiential point of view, it also appears information is stored in the wider matrix around us in much the same way as we store it in our mind. Take a look "inside" your mind, then take a look "outside." Are not both occurring in your brain? This is why so many of the millennial wisdom traditions refer to the entire phenomenon, both interior and exterior, as "the dream." They see the workings of our brain's mental world of waking and dreaming as paralleling the larger spiritual world around us. To come up with a scientific explanation for this phenomenon will be one of the tasks of the forthcoming integrative and Interspiritual Age.

The Levels of Experience We Have Every Day

In addition to our physical experience of the world, most modern spiritual and self-help teachings speak of "subtle realms." These include thoughts, feelings, and emotions, together with reflection, introspection, and intuition. At a deeper level, the spiritual traditions speak of spiritual, mystical, and paranormal experiences.

The traditions also take into account the interaction of these levels and speak of a "causal realm" or "causal nexus" where the worlds of form and formlessness appear to work together, causing things to happen. An experience of this synergy can be as simple as when you decide what meal to pick from a menu in a restaurant, mulling an array of internal and external criteria. Or it can involve far more poignant "peak" or "life-changing" experiences. We have all experienced events in which combinations of circumstances influence our entire makeup, causing us to make a sudden shift, such as meeting and falling in love with one's spouse. Changing one's life after "hitting bottom" is another classic example of this phenomenon.

A variety of language is used to describe what people are experiencing. For instance, such phenomena are often spoken of as occurring in our consciousness. Or people may refer to them as held in a "field" of experience. The spectrum of these levels of daily experience is well known to us from our experience of falling asleep, as we move from waking awareness to the world of light sleep, then into the world of dreams, and finally into deep sleep in which dreams cease and there's no sense of identity. This movement from the obvious physical realms into the deeper subtle realms is something we do every day.

Some Enchanted Evening

These three levels—physical, subtle, and causal—resonate for us from the song "Some Enchanted Evening," popularized by the Rogers and Hammerstein musical South Pacific. Say the lyrics, on an enchanted evening you may see someone across a crowded room (the physical realm), and somehow will know (the subtle realm) that somewhere you will see that person many times again (the causal realm).

We not only understand the message of this song, but we sense the interplay between the realms, which is a part of the beauty and often causes us to shed a tear. A song about romance and the world of the heart such as this can be called "magical," which is the reason it's at once personal and has profound universal appeal. No wonder it sold millions of copies.

No doubt we all remember poignant sacred events in our lives, such as when we first met a lover or said goodbye to a loved one at the moment of death. When those who aren't religious recall such moments, they touch the same ground as religious people. Most of us go to movies, read books, dance or observe dance, listen to music, or fashion art of all kinds in order to touch upon these moments we all consider precious. No matter whether we are religious or not, the word "sacred" doesn't sound out of place when attached to such moments of common experience.

A Collective View

The religious traditions all teach that there's a shared collective field of consciousness that encompasses the earthbound and the spiritual realms. The physicist Roger Penrose aptly calls this wider collective the "quantum plenum" (as in a plenary session at a conference where all the attendees gather), contrasting it to the world of an individual phenomenon. This collective hosts the interplay of the most cosmically large and the most cosmically small—a grand stage indeed.

There's interaction involving communication in the form of reaching in and reaching out and, reportedly, coming and going.

The reasons humans believe in this wider collective consciousness vary. Sometimes their belief derives from the religious beliefs they have been taught from childhood. Other times their belief is rooted in a tradition they felt drawn to and adopted later in life. It's important to pay attention to the literally thousands of cases of individuals who initially doubted the existence of the spiritual realm, or the so-called "paranormal," who come to take these matters seriously after personal experiences of their own. Of particular interest are many who are mainstream scientists who have moved from purely materialistic worldviews to more holistic or integrative worldviews because of personal experiences. Often these aren't just single experiences, which might be dismissed, but series of experiences that end up capturing the individual's attention.

Two experiences are particularly common. The first entails multiple experiences, usually diverse, that indicate to the subject that consciousness involves a shared collective field. The second kind of experience is considered scientifically verifiable by the individual, though probably not repeatable, most often involving either telepathy and remote viewing (inexplicable thought, image, or information transmission, which they then checked out) or clairvoyance (seeing something in the future and then having it happen). Less common are experiences of communicating with deceased individuals (either by voice, image, or both) while awake, and also near-death experiences. In all cases, because such individuals were trained scientists, they were stunned. The cumulative result of such experiences is usually voiced as "needing to factor into my view of reality what I couldn't question I had experienced." In such cases it becomes hard for these individuals to dismiss these experiences.

One of the outstanding examples of a highly educated materialist changing his view occurred with the near-death experience recounted by British-born New Zealander Dr John Wren Lewis, a mainstream scientist-psychologist whose story is recounted by Wikipedia and in *What is Enlightenment* magazine, among other sources, many from academia. In the 1970s, Lewis was president of the British Association for Humanistic Psychology. An outspoken skeptic on the matter of spirituality, the spiritual realms, and non-normal phenomena, he experienced a dramatic shift after a near-death experience in 1983. Following this event, Lewis reported that he consistently experienced the kinds of states of consciousness and spiritual realms referred to in the literature of the Great Wisdom Traditions, which he had spoken out against in previous years, becoming convinced that the shared consciousness field isn't a matter of spirituality but of reality.

Since that time, Lewis has authored and coauthored scholarly articles, together with a book, with prominent dream psychologist Ann Faraday. Lewis—and others, such as psychologist Dr Imants Barušs, who have written about the implications of Lewis' reports—suggests that his experiences point not only to the traditional accounts of the Great Wisdom Traditions but also to quantum field realities such as David Bohm's and Basil Hiley's notion of implicate order.

Barušs himself, associated with Kings University College, Canada, has authored several important books straddling science and spirituality. As did Brother Teasdale, he has suggested that for individual scientists to experience compelling episodes involving these realms is probably the most effective way to hasten a more holistic investigative approach.

A prominent example of scientists studying such phenomena is summarized in the work of Dr Dean Radin, who became Senior Scientist at California's Institute for Noetic Sciences in 2001 on the heels of a prolific career at conventional scientific institutions. Across a vast range of popular and academic publications, Radin has advocated for a more open mind among materialist scientists concerning subtle phenomena.

Honest Skepticism from Both Sides

There's a wide spectrum of resistance to more holistic contexts for such inquiry. This resistance is particularly strong in what has come to be called the "skeptic's community." Many such skeptics land somewhere between actual skepticism concerning the paranormal and outright strident claims that such phenomena simply can't be true.

It has to be said that this community does a great service in exposing fraud and insisting on the highest standards of scientific rigor while investigating claims of the paranormal. One result has been a helpful literature in psychology and psychiatry documenting how firsthand experience or eyewitness accounts can be truly misleading in the reporting of phenomena, especially those from subjective experience. However, some of the "debunking" groups haven't always been honest. Among others, Dr Dean Radin has documented outright misrepresentations of his work by such groups.

There are several popular jokes that reveal the spectrum of this debate. One holds that while everyone should have an open mind, it shouldn't be so open that one's brain falls out. Another makes fun of the tendency for committed skeptics to dismiss all non-conventional experiences outright, which they may do either because of their academic training or for perhaps deeply rooted psychological reasons. In this joke a skeptic at a skeptics' convention greets another skeptic with the words, "I don't believe we've met," only to be answered with the reply, "I don't believe that you don't believe we've not met."

In practice, scientists like James Watson and the British scientist Richard Dawkins come to the discussion with preconceived notions of what can or can't be true. Usually these are based on the scientific presupposition that the modern discussion of spirituality is the same pre-rational superstition of primitive humanity and thus irrelevant. What's odd about this viewpoint is that it's strangely non-evolutionary! Fortunately, most people are simply asking for some open-mindedness and an even-handed investigation into these phenomena.

If Real, How Is the Spirit World Structured?

Given all the metaphors we have been using for this discussion, the question of "structure" may seem quite out of place. But we think you know what we mean.

The question contains the same paradoxes encountered when we ask how our mind is structured. Such questions carry all the enigma of how a quantum field might work or the layer upon layer vibratory world predicted by string theory. M-theory, which has grown out of string theory, also predicts a multiverse built on eleven dimensions, with universes that might all be close to us, even in the room in which you are reading this book. These universes wouldn't usually touch each other because of the way the strings are attached. Science is only at the initial stage of proposing how such a multiverse might work.

Whether we are speaking of the arising and subsiding of waves in a quantum field, which are experienced by an observer as objects, or talking of mystical matters, we are again touching on what we have referred to as the "nondual reality," meaning "not two." Everyone understands this "not-twoness" to some degree, as illustrated by the common sense we all seem to have of the yin-yang symbol, where if the white of yin and the black of yang are spun, we get the dynamic interactive world of grey. Remember when, as a kid, you tried to explain your way out of something that wasn't exactly your fault? You made a case that it wasn't just black and white, taking refuge in the gray. This also comes up in arguments about "nature" or "nurture." Are we born with certain traits, or do they develop over time? We tend to agree that it's a bit of both.

In terms of a spiritual world, we suggest a simultaneity of being, in that things are both a multiplicity and at the same time a unity. It's similar to the fact that light can be understood as a wave and a particle. Black and white, yin and yang, waves and particles, "still love them but also want a divorce," oneness and multiplicity—we're familiar with all of these.

Is it Actual Structures or Just Our Lens?

In providing an account of the levels, planes, realms, or whatever you want to call them, of the spiritual world, are these actual structures or just our way of looking at them?

When a film is projected on a screen, the lens can dramatically alter the image. Depending on the machine doing the projection, we can have conventional to wide-angle or fish-eye projection. We can also show higher or lower resolution, or even create a completely scattered unintelligible image. Similarly, it may be that when it comes to describing complex phenomena, the limitations of language cause us to think we are experiencing things that are "out there" or experiencing things as a result of our own lens. We know when we think we see a car coming down the street, we are really seeing it in our own brain.

Are the spirit realms objective, so people's experiences truly are "out there" in such a manner that everyone who experiences them agrees on them? Or does what is reported vary so much because each recollection has been called up by the individual consciousness of an experiencer?

There's an important mystical element here, because we must also acknowledge that, in both scenarios, if an experiencer were completely one with an event, there would be no experiencer and no experience—as is reported in the Great Wisdom Traditions. Modern physics similarly speaks of an undifferentiated singularity that existed before the Big Bang.

The suggestion that a good way to understand how the spirit realms might work is to reference our own day-to-day experience of phenomena arising and subsiding in our own minds certainly solves the problem of who goes to whose heaven or whose hell. The souls from the world's different traditions would simply go where they think they go, just like we do in our own dreams or reveries. In such a view, the spirit realm would be like the thought-forms that come and go in our dreams. This solution is captured in the joke about the religion that thinks its people are the only ones going to heaven. We could tell this joke on all such religions!

Narratives of Spiritual, Astral, and Subtle Bodies Aren't Going Away

All you have to do is go to a Hollywood movie to see a depiction of spirit bodies, astral bodies, auras, and so on. For the sake of the movie, such phenomena have to be portrayed objectively, which might range from a special effects "light body" to someone swathed in tinfoil. With the use of music and other techniques, the movie industry even has ways to portray vibrations from such a body, such as when a person is walking down a street at night and decides either to walk past someone or go the other way.

In nearly all esoteric, mystical, or occult teachings, there's a recognition of a "soul" or "spirit"—some kind of body in the subtle realms—that underlies the physical body. In many traditions, this body continues on into the spiritual realms after death of the physical body. All the indigenous shamanic traditions understand this, and often characterize this spirit body with metaphors related to nature. As we have seen, words derived from ancient terms for breath or wind are the most common. Both the world of the spirit and its actions are similarly portrayed in nature symbols: sun and moon, rivers and oceans, and even fire. Characterized as the immutable primordial stuff each of us *is*, the spirit or soul is considered the seat of the sacred and is referred to as such in nearly all the world's religions. Think of "the most sacred body" in Islam, the "immortal nature" in mystical Christianity, the "diamond" and "body of light" in Taoism and Buddhism, and the "seat of inherent bliss" in many Hindu Yogic traditions.

Nearly all views of the spirit realms as interactive are based on these notions of countless spirits or souls. It's this soul or spirit body with which the shaman or medium communicates, and there exists a vast literature about work in the spirit realms, full of fantastic accounts of astral traveling and celestial happenings. They are the accounts of individual adepts from across the world's many spiritual traditions, often reflecting and paralleling the larger sagas of those peoples, and including descriptions of the gods and spirit entities of their sacred texts.

These are not just narratives of individual souls and their exploits, but also portray each sacred tradition's ideas of the human subtle body, its structure and its energies. Some of the most well-known of these are the descriptions of the energy body, with its centers and meridians associated with the ancient healing arts of acupuncture and hot stone placement. Anthropologists now propose that acupuncture-related modalities that use stones or needles may date back as far as the Ice Age, far earlier than later drawings and renderings of the centers and meridians that emerged as the world entered its God-King epoch. Accounts emerged 5,000 years ago in the Ayurveda healing arts in India and 4,000 years ago in the Shang Dynasty of China. A frozen mountain man, carbon dated to perhaps 10,000 years ago on the cusp of the last Ice Age, was found to have a satchel of the special stones reflective of this ancient art. Today acupuncture is used as a legal medical modality in virtually every country of the world, often in the context of the world's religions.

Descriptions of the Spirit Body

If we consider the esoteric and mystery schools, details of the human subtle, spirit, or energy body have been described by nearly every spiritual tradition. Sometimes these depictions are as complex and meticulous as medical descriptions of the physical body's sensory systems. The New Age movement has made the notion of energy centers, or "chakras," known to millions worldwide. The word "chakra" comes from Sanskrit and is associated with ancient Hinduism and Buddhism. The idea was also known in the Greek notion of "energy loci."

In addition to acupuncture, the popularity of these concepts has linked the idea of energy centers in the body to a variety of other modern activities such as Reiki and other forms of hands-on healing, aromatherapy and sound, and color and light therapies. Like acupuncture, Reiki has found a place in the medical establishment. Meaning "mysterious atmosphere" in Japanese, it was developed in the early 20th century by a Buddhist mystic who drew from the ancient notions of the chakras and meridians. Reiki presumes the existence of the spirit or subtle body and the notion that energies can be transferred from one body to another. The Catholic Church is one of the few major religious branches to suggest that Reiki is inappropriate for its members.

The idea of the spirit, subtle, energy, or astral body was also a staple of the teachings of the widely popular Theosophical Society of the 18th and 19th century spiritualist movements. People were drawn to these teachings because they seemed to make some sense of what so many experienced in their daily lives, such as intuition, instinct, and the proverbial "hunch." These experiences led to our wide use of the term "sixth sense."

Spirit Body, East and West

In Eastern traditions, the subtle body is generally seen as any number of etheric coverings, layers, sheaths, or energy levels. The emphasis in these traditions is on using these energy levels or sheaths in the work of unconditional love and service, thus manifesting the traits that typify the divine nature in these traditions.

This concept is paralleled in modern Western esoteric understanding, mostly because pioneers in those traditions either drew their syntheses from Eastern sources or because, as with some of the ancient Greek mystery schools, they independently derived understandings quite similar to those in the East. The era of the God-Kings in which so many of these teachings originated was located around a Middle Eastern axis. Few of the great kingdoms of that epoch—Egypt, Persia, Assyria, Mesopotamia, Judaea, India—were located far from that Middle Eastern epicenter. Archaeologists now acknowledge trade routes from this epicenter east to China and Java and west to the Mediterranean region as early as 800–500 BCE.

These shared geographic confluences in many ways account for the common notion of spirit with which most of our planet's 7 billion people are familiar—the idea that the spirit is a kind of etheric double of the physical body. In various languages this is called everything from soul, spirit, ghost, astral body, etheric body, and energy body to the bioplasmic body of the Theosophists. Compared to the perishable physical body, the independence, separate life, and ultimate immortality of this double was also a common understanding. It was the *vardoger* or *etiainin* in Scandinavia (meaning "first comer") and the *ka* (the spirit double that maintained all the memories of the physical body's life) in Egypt.

The German word for spirit double—*doppelgänger*—has taken on particular significance from scientific studies of "out of body experiences." Used in several languages by renowned writers ranging from Germany's Johann Wolfgang von Goethe to Russia's Fyodor Dostoyevsky and England's Charles Dickens, it became standard in journalism with the dizzying number of famous people reporting the experience. These have included Abraham Lincoln and the legendary authors John Donne, Percy Shelley, and Goethe himself. The term was also adopted by the medical profession for studies on the effects of stimulating the brain with electromagnetism. A prominent study of the scientific inducement of the *doppelgänger* phenomenon in Swiss hospitals was published in the prestigious scientific journal *Nature* in 2005. Little wonder that this phenomenon has also found its way into the popular media in characters like The Invisible Man, The Incredible Hulk, and Spiderman.

A particularly modern upsurge of interest in the spirit double arose with the rage concerning Kirlian photography in the 1970s. Using ideas pioneered earlier by the Russian electrical inventor Semyon Kirlian in the 1930s, electrical currents were applied to objects on a photographic plate, a process that created mysterious aura–like images when the plates were developed. Publications in scientific journals in Russia and also by America's Smithsonian Institution called worldwide attention to the phenomena. Subsequent studies suggest the physics behind this phenomenon is that of the "voltage corona effect." It's debatable whether the effect represents an actual aura or is an artifact of the process itself. In any event, the method has been developed for medical use in Russia, where it has been shown in numerous studies to effectively diagnose stress. Russian studies have also claimed to link Kirlian evidence to the centers and meridians of acupuncture. Several other possible medical uses of Kirlian photography have been pursued elsewhere in the world.

Proponents of the validity of Kirlian images of the aura recall earlier research by the 19th century British physician Walter Kilner, whose work gained prominent support for a time across English medicine. Kilner produced images of the supposed "etheric double" through specially prepared goggles. Using such visualizations, Kilner appeared to make verifiable strides in medical diagnosis. The difficulty was that the goggles, which apparently allowed visualizing of more subtle wavelengths of light, varied in results when used by different individuals. Since diagnosticians tended to produce widely different results, the method fell out of favor after Kilner's death.

The similarity of the etheric or spirit double of Kirlian photograpy and Kilner's images to the reports of the spirit or soul from time immemorial cannot escape notice. The concepts seem to arise from quite different heritages and assumptions. Kilner viewed his images as scientific data and was outspokenly against their use as metaphysical evidence by the Theosophists of his time.

Whatever their objective meaning, there's no doubt the idea of the spirit or soul as astral body, etheric double, or spirit person also parallels the various spiritual traditions' views of what falls away at death and what continues on into the spirit realms. It also parallels nearly every tradition's view of personal development. Not only is the goal to unite with the "higher" and that which is "eternal," but in some traditions even to nurture the powers and energies of that higher body in preparation for what's to come.

These ideas are so widespread they dominate our popular notions of souls, spirits, and ghosts. While the higher self is called to merge with all that's good in heaven—"let earth and heaven combine, angels and men agree" (Charles Wesley)—the lower elements bound to lust and passion remain earthbound as the common ghost or spook, as witnessed in such television programs as *Moonlight* in Europe and *True Blood* or *The Vampire Diaries* in the United States.

16

Stories of Spirit Levels, Planes, and Realms

"Every spirit makes its house"

Ralph Waldo Emerson

MOVING BEYOND THE INDIVIDUAL, WHAT DOES THE SPIRIT REALM LOOK like in the collective? If they still exist in some form, where are all these celestial places and all these people who have come and gone from the earth since our history began?

Nearly all the narratives from our religious, spiritual, and esoteric traditions address this mystery by referring to multiple levels, planes, or realms within the spirit world. The number of these planes is most often seven—though it depends on how you count. If you consider sublevels, the number of niches in the spirit world can range from six to 70!

Just as modern physics distinguishes the actions of the quantum field as simultaneously involving "all of it" (the "quantum plenum") *and* each individual phenomenon, most of the world's spiritual traditions claim their spiritual planes are contained in that nondual dimension of oneness that scientists say held the entire universe in a singularity prior to the Big Bang. Some spiritual teachers combine the languages of spirituality and science to suggest each of us holds within us, as center or soul, this same singularly that preceded the Big Bang, seeing this as what allows us to experience the sense of oneness—unity consciousness—so naturally. Scientific terminology is often also used to refer to the spiritual centers of the body, the so-called chakras, suggesting they are our hard drives to which are connected all the various software of our neurological apparatus.

Nondual Plane and Archetypal or Shamanic Plane

Consciousness and the spiritual realms are divided between a so-called "nondual" realm in which all is one and the realms in which things are experienced as happening, often referred to as shamanic or archetypal realms. In the singularity of science or the oneness of a nondual realm (in which Westerners would consider everything united with "God"), nothing is actually experienced as happening, since there's no separation or differentiation of any kind—no separate observer to observe.

This state is also reported in the deepest spiritual experience or highest spiritual states recorded in the world's spiritual traditions, though it's difficult to use many of the terms and labels from those traditions since some refer to the experience itself while others refer to the location in the celestial realms of those who are having this experience. Suffice it to say that the Western world speaks mostly of complete union with God, to the point of absorption and consequent nullification of the independent experiencer. In the Eastern Hindu, Buddhist, Jain, and Sikh traditions, the Sanskrit word *Samadhi* (loosely meaning "to be held together") is often used, frequently in combination with modifiers. Again, it implies a unity that's complete. While the state of unity occurs simultaneously, all these traditions acknowledge that it contains within it the whole multiverse of experience.

We've noted that during sleep each night, we traverse from the world of dreams, in which things are happening, to the realm of deep sleep, in which there's no awareness of our separate existence, and therefore no identity. The difference between dreamless sleep and the ultimate experience of unity in the mystical traditions is that something is reported about the latter, or we wouldn't even know about it! Some who report such states note only occasional glimpses of their individuality, enabling them to realize they are fully absorbed. Others report that, somehow in the simultaneity, there is no experiencer, whereas there is awareness of the totality of what's occurring. Fortunately, researchers interested in the implications of such reports and modern scientific ideas of quantum consciousness are now investigating these phenomena. Yale University (Dr Judson Brewer) and New York University (Dr Zoran Josipovic) are hosts to two of these exciting programs. It's possible it's a heightened sense of awareness in which one is aware of the "all," rather than the obliteration of awareness that occurs in deep sleep.

The Problem of Experience Chasing

Those who experience only the dimensions in which things appear to be happening often think this is all there is. Thus a drama develops around spiritual experiences that lacks a simultaneous understanding of that which is eternally resting in unity and peace at the same time. How many times have we attended some kind of religious event and felt something was missing? On the other hand, few of us fail to detect profound peace in the presence of a calm, centered individual—which is why the Dalai Lama has such widespread appeal. Who wouldn't want the Dalai Lama as their wise old grandfather?

Isn't one of the things that gives spirituality a bad name all the people who dwell on every kind of phantasmagoric experience imaginable? Little wonder a famous scientist like James Watson considers the issue "wacko." This world of spirit drama is highlighted in literature such as the Book of Revelation (The Apocalyse of St John the Divine) in Christianity, the great spiritual battles of Hinduism's Mahabharata (of which its more famous *Bhagavad Gita* is a part), and the sagas of Milton's *Paradise Lost* and Dante's *Divine Comedy*. We also see it illustrated in Dutch painter Hieronymus Bosche's "Garden of Earthly Delights" and the etchings and engravings of England's famous mystic artist William Blake.

These depictions of the realms of spirit interaction, featuring epic legacies among the celestial cast of heavenly characters, vary only in the times they reflect—be they the narratives of indigenous peoples and their shamans, the epic narratives of the many sacred texts, the artistic images of many periods, and even current popular narratives such as Star Wars, Lord of the Rings, Narnia, and Harry Potter. We view these as archetypal, a term that's apt because the archetypal realm is a realm of heroes, heroines, and villains.

Loosely, "archetype" means symbolic representation or a term that's readily and universally understood and, when used metaphorically, usually portrayed as a personality or behavioral type. The problem with the archetypal realm of experience is that it's addictive and can interfere with actual personal growth toward the fruits of authentic spirituality such as love, compassion, service, and depth of discernment. As India's famous sage Ramana Maharshi remarked, if all one is looking for is a more fantastic experience, that frustrating pursuit can go on, literally, forever.

Ken Wilber and the integralists have gifted us with one of the most pertinent insights in modern time with regard to direct spiritual experience. They simply note that the habit in humanity to date is for each person or group to assume their direct experience is normative or true, whereas that of others isn't. This pernicious tendency is referred to as the "myth of the given" and has led to much religious conflict throughout history.

In his Omega Vision, Brother Teasdale provides us with a putative spiritual law, that what is true will always exceed all experiences of it or reports about it. You will remember in our introduction to interspirituality we discussed the history of the world's religious experiences as a *single* collective experience unfolding toward humankind's full potential in the world of consciousness and heart. The need is for humanity to set its bar far higher than what has so far occurred. We all need to recognize that it's perfectly natural for each of us to imagine our religious experience is the true one. If we take this as a given, we can think about how to proceed skillfully together beyond this predicament.

Spirit Realms in the Great Traditions

The language surrounding the stories of realms of the spirit world varies widely among the world's religious traditions, although there are common threads. Part of the problem of distilling this aspect of the traditions is that so many of the terms have been used, reused, translated, and transposed across the traditions, in large part occasioned by the influence of early Mediterranean culture on Judaism, Islam, and Christianity. Early schools of esoteric healing, such as the ancient Hermetists who claimed to hold the wisdom of Alexandria's lost library, saw their views creep into nearly every Middle Eastern religion. With these ancient mixings and the widespread popular literature of the West after the 18th century, the history of many of these ideas and concepts can become confusing. However, there are some major categories and descriptions that will make sense for most people.

Narratives about the adventures of supposed spirits has made for tantalizing reading, sold a lot of books, and created some sensational spiritual careers. Quality control has been a problem. How do you compare Gurdjieff's classic *Meetings with Remarkable Men* to some of the less substantive books all of us have seen on the popular bookstore shelves?

Closely related to the astral realm among notions of the subtle realms is the so-called "mental plane." Narratives about the mental plane are important because they involve understanding how communication is reported to work in the spirit world. In his deeper conversations with friends, Brother Teasdale spoke of this and called this realm the "symbolic element" of reality.

We're familiar with the general storyline from the accounts of psychics helping locate missing people, having seen it on *Unsolved Mysteries* and other shows. Notice that the psychic needs a photograph, an article of clothing, or some other reference item for the missing person. In the story, this item allows the psychic to make contact. Why? Brother Teasdale used to say that in the subtler quantum realm such items "carry information." We see the same phenomenon in books and movies in which holy water or a crucifix has an extraordinary effect on a demon or other kind of spiritual villain. We have also heard of how a poltergeist entered a house via an old piece of furniture bought at a yard sale. In the wildly popular Harry Potter and Narnia novels, we encounter totems, charms, wands, and peculiar word combinations that cast spells. In other words, there's an ancient narrative about how information is carried in the so-called spirit realm.

Brother Teasdale explained that it's easy to understand the notion of this ethereal communication by comparing how images appear in two schools of art: impressionism and symbolism. If you look at an impressionist painting, especially up close, there isn't anything that stands out as a precise physical object. But if you stand back about 20 feet, suddenly the haystacks in Claude Monet's "Haystacks at Giverny" appear, as do the flowers in the window boxes in Camille Pissaro's street scenes. If you look at a symbolist painting (or even some expressionist paintings), such as C. R. Mackintosh's "Harvest Moon," subtle but clearly recognizable forms stand out. This is how Brother Teasdale described the workings of this symbolic or mental plane. The elements of communication emerge in subtle and ethereal ways. As with the paintings, if the eye and mind of discernment are sharp, the images and messages can be read.

Because of the connection with communication, some traditions also call this the "causal plane." Other examples are many of the professional psychics who make the rounds in the media. You'll notice they often refer to various "symbols" or "keys" they "see" in or around someone that help them make predictions. For example, if they "see" a suitcase, they discern the person is about to take a trip. The entire field of reputed clairvoyance, second sight, telepathy, remote viewing, and the like refers to this realm of the supposed spirit world. If you strike up a conversation with anyone who is adept at spirit interaction, you'll certainly be told some interesting stories. It's up to you to decide what to make of them.

Higher Realms, East and West

In the East, a common thread is the existence of a plane of pure consciousness unrelated to individuation or ego-identity, which we have referred to as the nondual. Not all descriptions are the same, but in Buddhism the idea of a "buddhic plane," or in Hinduism Sri Aurobindo's concept of the "Supermind," refers to the unity consciousness associated with this plane.

It has been common for the Eastern traditions to jump directly from the astral and mental planes, where things are still seen as happening, to the nondual planes of pure unity consciousness. In the West there has been greater fixation on the spirit drama, resulting in additional levels between the astral and mental planes and those of pure awareness. In Christian esoteric traditions, the spiritual plane is a further level of spirit drama before reaching the realm of unity, the divine plane. In Judaism, the divine plane is called the "I Am" or "logoic" realm.

Important to this heritage also are The Seven Levels of Heaven in Islam and the recognition of seven levels in certain esoteric Jewish and Hindu mystic schools. Of all the traditions, Islam has been more coherent in its concept of spirit levels across its many cultures.

The idea of seven crops up in so many traditions because it's anchored in early astrology, which influenced all of these traditions. The number seven is related to the number of primary objects in the sky known to early astrology—the seven classic planets, often called "the wandering stars," before science discovered more about our solar system. The number seven crept into Christian mystical views from the Hebrew Scriptures. In Judaism, the Talmud also refers to seven levels of heaven, while in Hinduism there are seven "higher heavens," the Vyahritis (although the number may vary). The number seven has also been attached to hell, as in the seven levels of hell (Naraka) in Jainism or the seven hells of Inanna in ancient Sumerian myth.

In the mystical traditions, the realms are understood more ethereally—for instance, as different space and time—in relation to levels of consciousness, while their more mundane popular traditions simply people the different levels with a variety of casts of celestial characters. Christianity, Judaism, Islam, and Zoroastrianism (the religion of Alexander the Great's kingdom) all speak of a hierarchy of angels connected with such realms. Some scholars have noted that such concepts are even part of Mormonism, which otherwise seems to have such a unique mid-American origin—further testimony to the universality of the concept.

The Spirit World Is Probably Already Interspiritual

When we consider modern views of consciousness from both religious and scientific viewpoints and meld these with the perennial reports of the spirit realms, we arrive at some evocative insights. For instance, it's helpful to view the shared collective consciousness in the way we view our own experience of our mind. It suggests that phenomena appear from "in" and "out" of the collective field of the spirit realms in the same fashion we seem to experience them arising from "in" and "out" of the mind.

We can surmise that whatever reservoir feeds this phenomenon acts in a manner analogous to the seemingly endless reservoir from which thoughts and sensations arise in our minds. As already noted, some scientists posit that these may be waves of quanta arising and subsiding in a quantum field, which are recognized by the senses as phenomena. Or they may be electromagnetic fields or vibratory string phenomena. Whatever the mechanism may prove to be, it produces an image or message, then subsides into the larger ocean of that field just like waves on the ocean.

This view helps us understand how nothing that enters our mind is ever lost. Barring injury or impairment, every memory appears to be recoverable either via normal reflection or with the aid of concentration or hypnosis. Similarly, as Brother Teasdale said of his view of the symbolic element of reality, no event or person would ever be lost in the spirit realms but would always be fully retrievable. This is consistent with the millennial tales of these realms in which departed souls show up. Brother Teasdale suggested this is what Jesus meant when he asserted that "every hair on your head is counted." This is an evocative suggestion and may make some sense of how a wider quantum field or vibratory string field might support the common experience individuals have of their own minds and the Wisdom Traditions' depictions of the spirit realms.

All of this suggests the spirit realms are already interspiritual. In their accounts, all of the traditions have to some extent been correct. Each tradition has a part of the story; each sees a part of the landscape. In which case, all of the realms—made up of the thought forms that create and sustain them, just as occurs in our dreams—would be present in the collective reservoir. In the esoteric traditions, this notion has often been called the "Akashic Record" (from *akasha* in Sanskrit, meaning "written in the sky"). This record is viewed as a library in which is recorded every phenomenon that has ever arisen, a concept originating in one of the schools of ancient Hinduism known as the *Samkhya*. This is the record that in popular parlance can reputedly be "read" by psychics and clairvoyants.

Such a holistic view, including the realm of mind and a wider collective field of the spirit realms, allows all the traditions' depictions of the spirit worlds to be understood as somewhat correct and simply reflective of the current state of evolution at which humanity finds itself. It also allows that the realms themselves could be real, sustained by the thought-forms creating them from within and without. Their ongoing reality may be similar to what sustains the reservoirs of our dream world in our minds. Our dreams are full of precise details, past memories, and even the exact voice inflections of old friends. We also have recurring dreams—storylines that appear to have some kind of permanent nexus in our mind's reservoir. Thus all the persons and places depicted in the spirit realms would be available in the same way our memories are available.

An example is the husband of a departed member of a sect that believes only their group goes to heaven. The husband, who is well known in that sect for his apparent psychic acumen, reported that his wife, who preceded him in death, contacts him frequently from the spirit realm and tells him that the teachings of the sect are incorrect. She was surprised to find that the spirit world is diverse and stratified, much like living in a city. All kinds of ideas of reality and beliefs are found there just as on earth. More often people are clustered by temperament than by belief or religious denomination, although the latter occurs with groups who are stuck in a certain view of reality. Some even have their little gated enclaves where they can carry on much as their religious traditions promised them. Overall, just like on earth, everyone is continuing to learn and work things out. The point is that there is room for everyone's experiences.

The precise way in which a quantum or vibratory string reality might work with regard to our minds and the idea of an encompassing collective spiritual world that connects us all is a frontier for both science and religion to examine. We need to remember that through the centuries science has frequently changed its fundamental paradigms. What seemed out of the question in one century has often become plausible in the next, especially as fundamental elements of reality are discovered and factored into the larger equation. New supercolliders are allowing us to peer into the dimensions predicted by string theory and M-theory. A deeper understanding of how a vibratory reality may operate, layer upon layer, may be available sooner than we may imagine.

Where the Rubber Meets the Road

In his classic work on religious experience, William James noted four commonalities to all spiritual experiences: they intrude into one's consciousness, and then one seems to return to normal; they are very difficult to describe; there's a sense of deep knowing that comes with them; and they seem to come out of nowhere.

In light of human history, perhaps the last characteristic is the most tantalizing. We find ourselves, 10,000 years into civilization, surrounded by stories and narratives that are deeply entrenched in who and what we are. Since spiritual experience is out of the realm of ordinary experience, in a sense it's in the same general category as mental illness. In fact, brain research shows that many of the same areas of the brain are activated by both of these abnormal experiences! What then accounts for the fact that spiritual experience can be profoundly life changing and produce individuals of exceptional ethical and behavioral acumen, while mental illness can lead to total breakdown and incapacity? The stark contrast of these two results raises deep questions about our human experience of the subtle realms.

Can we believe the myriad narratives that record experiences of the spirit world? The philosopher Richard Swinburne of Oxford University applies a common sense test, typical of that which would apply to a witness in court. Witnesses are brought to court to testify about what they say they experienced. Generally, only in the context of an opposite story by another witness does the court question the first witness' validity. Another philosopher, Rudolf Otto, says what's compelling about the reporting of spiritual experience is that it appears deeply compelling to *others*, a quality he calls "numinous."

What makes stories like that of the children at Fatima, which was declared "worthy of belief" by the Catholic Church, different from a child claiming to see Mickey Mouse? And how is an experience of Mickey Mouse different from an experience of a burning bush? There are differences, particularly regarding numinosity—the ability of such reports to be compelling, even life changing. The experience of the Virgin Mary by the children at Fatima is classed by scholars as a "religious mystical experience" because it has a context in a particular religion. It's suggested if the children had been in China, they would more likely have reported seeing Tara, a feminine manifestation of Buddha nature.

In contrast, a burning bush is considered a "natural mystical experience," in that it doesn't directly relate to a particular religion and yet could be transformative. These are not small matters historically. Human sacrifice within the Latin American Aztec culture, which may have taken upward of 250,000 lives per year, was initiated after a God-King was "told" by the sun to begin such practices. Whatever these experiences are, they have changed not only individuals but also history.

What Validates the Claims of Mystical Experience?

The relationship between religious experience and ethics and behavior has been a perennial point of controversy. It's fair to say that from the advent of modern science in the 18th century, which began to question the validity of religious experience, the argument for the validity of religious experience was its life-changing power. A host of philosophers, such as the famous Immanuel Kant, held this view, which dominated the cultural understanding of religion until the 20th century. But just as world history changed dramatically with the world wars, so did this moral justification of religious experience. It then appeared that religious-like experiences could turn matters quite dramatically toward the sacred *or* the profane.

Humanism, based in part on the writing of ethical philosopher Felix Adler, had pointed this out ever since the degrading social excesses of the 19th century's industrial revolution, though it took two world wars to truly challenge this view and for it to become obvious that religious mystical experience could have a pernicious result. Witness the right wing religious cults that lined up within Christendom to support the Nazi regime and its allies. Meanwhile, natural religious experience was turning others into pacifists, conscientious objectors, and even martyrs for causes of peace—as with the famous episodes involving Buddhist monks protesting the Indochina wars.

Little wonder that science, particularly psychology, has weighed in on the issue of the unquestionable validity of religious mystical experience. The entire fields of transpersonal psychology and psychology of religion study this phenomenon. Dr Andrew Newberg of the University of Pennsylvania School of Medicine has been an initiator of neurotheology, a discipline that melds neuroscience and anthropology. Similar to our view that new awareness results in new skill sets due simply to how evolutionary selection unfolds, Newberg and his associates also hold that it's inevitable that thoughts lead to actions. When this is considered in the context of human myth over the centuries-long process of civilization building, religious people and religious-based societies don't seem accidental but actually scientifically predictable.

Spirituality and Our
Current Evolutionary Threshold

With the advent of advanced imaging and neuro-measurement apparatus in recent decades, the neuroscientific community began to study the relationship of mind to observed religious experience. From this work has emerged the seminal field of the Cognitive Science of Religion. The study of religious experience as a cognitive phenomenon took shape in the 1970s when several fields of inquiry collided: sociobiology (which investigates biological bases for social behaviors), sociology of religion (how religions evolved in societies), anthropology of religion (how religions evolved through history), and transpersonal and evolutionary psychology. The literature produced on this subject by these fields of research since the dawn of the new millennium is enormous. An International Association for the Cognitive Science of Religion was formed in 2006, just two years after the passing of Brother Wayne Teasdale.

The science the Cognitive Science of Religion brings to the study of spirituality has important implications for the question of whether the narratives concerning the spirit world are real or not. It's a quandary because one of the cardinal principles of the Cognitive Science of Religion is that it may not matter. This new science tends to emphasize the social import of what people take to be true, as opposed to what might be true—a realistic approach. If, contrary to all science, religious views are adopted by the masses of humanity—as the statistics we have cited indicate—there may be very different implications for our future world.

According to the Cognitive Science of Religion, spirituality arises as one kind of experience, but is then turned into another. In other words, spirituality arises from the compelling mystical experiences of individuals fueled by the self-authentication typical of all such experiences. Then society co-opts and transforms the experience into religion as a device to ensure socially acceptable behavior according to a norm decided by other social agencies. The secret of religious experience as a currency for such a hijacking is that religious notions appear to be both easy to remember and easy to use—perfect for the control of humankind.

For both religion and science, there is a disconcerting possibility that our species may, as they say, "not be playing with a full deck." Consequently, the Cognitive Science of Religion ends up asking the same question as interspirituality: Can a new threshold in consciousness be achieved and this historical hijacking cease? It's one of the evocative questions of the new millennium and the integrative and Interspiritual Age. If a spiritual inclination is part of the fundamental wiring of human beings, it's even more imperative the world turn toward spirituality itself as its religion—as Brother Teasdale recommended. As he made clear, "The necessary shifts in consciousness require a new approach to spirituality that transcends past religious cultures of fragmentation and isolation."[69]

Such a spirituality would need to be grounded in a profound understanding of the natural diversity of the individual mystical experience. In Brother Teasdale's own words, "This new paradigm must be able to accommodate all human experience, knowledge and capacities." He added that it must be "built both on intellectual integration and direct experience" and "make available to everyone all the forms the spiritual journey assumes."[70]

As echoed in Brother Teasdale's Omega Vision and Ken Wilber's credo of myth of the given, this spirituality would understand that everyone will naturally consider their unique experience as a guide. Further, only an immature spirituality would seek to prove who's right and who's wrong. This is Brother Teasdale's prescription for our species entering the world of the heart—a tall order for countless religious people. But as Brother Teasdale recognized, "This revolution will be the task of the Interspiritual Age."

---

[69] MH, p 12.
[70] MH, p 65, 26, 35.

17

Early Pioneers of Interspirituality

"A leader is best when people barely know he exists. When his work is done, his aim fulfilled, they will say: we did it ourselves"

Lao Tzu

THE EMERGING INTERSPIRITUAL AGE IS A CULMINATION OF THE VISIONS OF many throughout the world's spiritual traditions *and* a new threshold in the development of the world's spiritual paths, which are converging toward what Brother Teasdale called the possibility of a civilization based on the heart. Every tradition and path has played a part in this development.

Throughout history, even as great teachers, leaders, sages, and saints of the world's religions were paving the paths of their traditions, another breed of visionary was already grasping the unity consciousness of a single path that's inherent in them all.

We have seen that in the biological history of the earth, as the dinosaurs reached their apex, running around often unnoticed among them were the smaller mammals that would write the next chapter. So too while the histories of the world's religious and spiritual traditions were still being written from parochial points of view, the *interspiritual* visionaries whose time has now come were overlooked, misunderstood, ignored, and even maligned. Many were dismissed from their churches, synagogues, mosques, ashrams, monasteries, and convents. Eventually nearly every one of them has come to be revered as a pioneer of both their own tradition *and* the future contribution their tradition would make to a global world culture and the interspirituality such a world requires.

Early Pioneers

A recent compilation of pioneer figures in the world's interspiritual heritage included 42 pivotal individuals.[71] In many cases these are individuals who wouldn't have come to prominence were interspirituality not gaining visibility as part of the wider phenomena of globalization and multiculturalism. Even in a book dedicated to the interspiritual paradigm, it would be impossible to write about each of the 42 pioneers. We can treat in detail only some of the most outstanding, and those whose legacies embraced broad areas of the human endeavor in realms that transcend the boundaries of spirituality and religion. However, the variety of their names alone, reflecting the languages of many cultures, impresses us with the breadth of this legacy.

It's no accident that the majority of these figures come from the 19th and 20th centuries, which were the beginning of the age of pluralism. By the mid-19th century, the world's cultures were beginning to collide with each other as a result of expanding world commerce and the consequences of the otherwise unfortunate colonial era. The cosmopolitan colonial powers were also colliding with the great indigenous traditions of the world.

If one remembers the lessons of earlier cross-cultural collisions that divided the world's Second Great Advance into the early *monolithic* period and later *totalitarian* period, the result was a profound confusion

---

[71] Interspiritual Multiplex, 2011, at http://multiplex.isdna.org/classica.htm#Photo%20Archive.

of identity and a tumultuous challenging of long-held worldviews. As the planet's Third Great Advance ended and its Fourth Great Advance, the movement toward pluralism, unfolded, we see the same dynamic, but moving more rapidly in a positive direction. Characteristic of these pivotal shifts is global interaction and intermixing among religious and spiritual traditions—the same kind of blending that characterizes the mid-19th century and its flowering in the 20th century in the integrative epoch, leading to the current movement toward a global holism.

Early Eastern Interspiritual Pioneers

In the East, early interspiritual giants spanned the cusp of the 19th and 20th centuries: Baha'u'llah (the founder of the trans-traditional Baha'i tradition), Baba Virsa Singh (the Sikh founder of the interreligious Gobind Sadan movement), and writers of international influence such as Paramahansa Yogananda (whose *Autobiography of a Yogi* was read by millions, as mentioned earlier). There were also great pioneers of cross-traditional dialogue and discovery, such as India's Swami Vivekananda (who wowed the crowds at the Chicago Exposition and the first Parliament of the World's Religions in 1893), Hazrat Inayat Khan (pioneer of Universal Sufism within the Islamic cultures), and India's Sri Ramakrishna (who eloquently embraced Hinduism, Christianity, and Islam).

Then there were great religious political figures: in India Sri Aurobindo and his companion "The Mother," Frenchwoman Mirra Alfassa. They were giants in the Indian independence movement, the birth of progressive science, and the unifying of traditional Yoga practices. Of course, there was also Mohandas Gandhi, the "Mahatma" (great soul) or "Father" of modern India.

Names that are famous to many, though perhaps less known and seemingly unpronounceable to Westerners, include Brahmabandhah Upadhyah (a pioneer Hindu Christian renowned in India), Pandurang Shastri Athavale (founder of the pan-religious Self-knowledge Movement), and leaders instrumental in early East-West dialogues such as

Swami Atmananda Udasin (a beloved leader of the influential Monastic Interreligious Dialogue movement—an association comprised of monastic contemplatives East and West, of which Brother Teasdale was later a part—from which emerged a Hindu-Christian dialogue rooted in Christian missionary contemplatives who had turned their attention Eastward and Hindu swamis and teachers who had turned theirs toward the West).

Early in this movement's emergence, as the 20th century unfolded, were influential figures like Swami Abhishiktananda (the Hindu name taken by French Christian Benedictine monk Henri le Saux), his beloved Indian associate Swami Chidananda, and another Frenchman Marc Chaduc (who studied with le Saux and then took the name Swami Ajatananda). René Guénon was another prominent French writer who contributed to the melding of Western and Hindu understandings. In June of 1973 at Rishikesh on the banks of the Ganges, a pivotal ceremony took place in which these Westerners officially joined with the indigenous *sannyasi* (renunciant) religious orders of Hinduism. This was an important culmination of what had become known worldwide as the Christian Ashram movement. It had become firmly rooted when Benedictine Father Bede Griffiths permanently joined le Saux and his associates in 1968 at their ashram called Shantivanam ("Forest of Peace") in Tamil Nadu, India. Le Saux, who had founded Shantivanam in 1950, desired to retire to a hermitage there. With the arrival of Griffiths and other Christian-Hindu monks, the venture took on an even more influential role in the melding of East and West. From this second era of Shantivanam emerged influential voices including Brother Teasdale, scholar and mystic Andrew Harvey, and yogi and famed musician Russill Paul.

These interspiritual meldings were further infused by the number of Westerners who journeyed East, particularly in the 1960s and 1970s, creating a plethora of teachers, writers, and pundits who, either staying in the East or returning to the West, were part of the "Eastern spiritual invasion" so well-known from that period.[72] As the 20th century

---

[72] Philip Goldberg has chronicled this era eloquently in a recent book, *American Veda* (2010).

moved into the 21st, there are names of near-celebrity status from this infusion: Ram Das (icon of the 60s and the era of the Beatles) and Amma, or Ammachi, the famous "hugging guru" known for her philanthropic work around the world.

Early Western Interspiritual Pioneers

The number of interspiritual pioneers in the West is no less substantial, ranging from the work of Madame Blavatsky and Carl Jung on the spiritual side, to religious and secular humanists such as Felix Adler (ethical philosopher and founder of America's Ethical Culture movement) and A. C. Grayling (the British chronicler of humanism, wherein you didn't need religion or spirituality to recognize a universal ethic of benevolence and service).

To these we can add trans-traditional rabbis such as Leon Klenecki and Joseph Gelberman (doing what Felix Adler, also originally a rabbi, had hoped to do before he was dismissed from the Jewish clergy), along with Quaker Alison Davis (founder of the International Third Order, a lay association exploring the wide-ranging gifts of all the world's spiritual traditions). There were major students of the indigenous traditions, such as Frithjof Schuon (who synthesized wisdom and art from the world's native traditions) and Michael Harner (who pioneered the academic study of nontraditional religions).

There were also outspoken interreligious Protestants such as Korean-American interfaith seminary founder David S. C. Kim and comparative religionist Huston Smith, whose book *The World's Religions* (originally entitled *The Religions of Man*) remains a popular introduction to world religions. Huston Smith is equally well known for The Great Chain of Being model that graces almost every understanding of the inherent unity of the world's religions. This unfolding was truly a cosmopolitan affair.

Roman Catholic champions of interspirituality are perhaps among the most well known in the West. The most famous is the French Jesuit priest, paleontologist, and pioneer cosmic theologian Father Teilhard de Chardin. Also pivotal in their interspiritual roles have been Father Francis Archarya Orsos of Belgium (a Cistercian monk who pioneered dialogue with Hinduism), American Sister Pascaline Coff (a Benedictine nun who helped bring the Monastic Interreligious Dialogue movement to the West), Spain's Father Raimon Panikkar (pioneer Hindu–Christian scholar and author of the popular bestseller *The Unknown Christ of Hinduism*), Chiara Lubich of Italy (Catholic activist and founder of the Focolare and New Humanity Movement of lay volunteers), German Willigis Jaeger (expelled Catholic priest who pioneered Western Zen), and America's Matthew Fox (priest and pioneer of interreligious thought in the West). Each of these were pivotal interspiritual trailblazers, some whom were able to remain in the Church and others who were expelled.

Perhaps the most well known of these pioneers in the West was Father Thomas Merton, the noted American writer who entered contemplative monasticism and became an eloquent spokesperson for the fusion of Western mystical spirituality with Zen Buddhism. Not far behind is Father Thomas Keating, founder of what has become known as the Centering Prayer Movement. All these pioneers represent a significant aspect of the interspiritual legacy, and each is already the subject of books and biographies.

Celebrities Light the Way

In recent decades, the world has been blessed with a body of popular media that, without many realizing it, widely disseminates the elements of the interspiritual vision. Today's most read popular poet worldwide is the interspiritual Sufi known as "Rumi" (Jalal al-Din Muhammad Balkhi). And who isn't familiar with His Holiness the Dalai Lama, who was such a close friend of Brother Teasdale, along with Vietnamese-born spiritual leader and writer Thich Naht Hahn and South Africa's Archbishop Desmond Tutu? These well-known public figures not only appear on television but also counsel many of the world's most powerful politicians and financial leaders.

Although the Dalai Lama, Thich Naht Hahn, and Archbishop Tutu may be the most familiar to a majority of the world's citizens, other interspiritual spokespersons frequent the circuit of public speaking, television shows, and international gatherings.[73] Good examples are pioneers of the Christian Muslim dialogue, such as Harold Vogelaar and Neil Douglas-Klotz, along with chroniclers of the Eastern religious experience such as Donald W. Mitchell.

The interspiritual message also permeates the arts and the cutting edge of philosophy. South American artist, playwright, and film-maker Alejandro Jodorowsky weaves modern and ancient spiritual themes and images into an avant-garde paradigm of near-cult status. Loosely known as "psycho-art," the genre's well-known films have included *El Topo* and *The Holy Mountain* (the latter financed by John Lennon). On the philosophy front, there are the leaders of the well-published developmental and Integral movements, such as writers Ken Wilber, Don Beck, and Eckhart Tolle, who have reached millions in the general public with blockbuster books. After Tolle's appearances on television with Oprah Winfrey, few don't know of his books *The Power of Now* and *A New Earth*.

The overall penetration into world culture by such trailblazers shouldn't be underestimated. Through them has developed most of the progressive understanding that today characterizes the United States and much of the rest of the world. Such spiritual undercurrents shape many of our general cultural inclinations such as love of the underdog, outpourings of grassroots aid in times of natural or political disaster, our sense of fair play (even in sports), and clichés and phrases such as "it is what it is," "being in the zone," "it's cool," "doing the do," "I'm OK, you're OK, it's OK," "live and let live," and "this too shall pass."

All of these contributions flow from a wellspring of profound understanding regarding the potential for humanity and the planet. It perhaps hasn't been said better than by Sri Aurobindo's companion, The Mother:

> ...we are in a very special situation, extremely special, without precedent. We are now witnessing the birth of a new world; it is very young, very weak—not in its essence

---

[73] A visit to YouTube garners a host of interviews and special programs to watch.

but in its outer manifestation—not yet recognized, not even felt, denied by the majority. But it is here. It is here, making an effort to grow, absolutely *sure* of the result. But the road to it is a completely new road which has never before been traced out—nobody has gone there, nobody has done that! It is a beginning, a *universal beginning*. So, it is an absolutely unexpected and unpredictable adventure.

There are people who love adventure. It is these I call, and I tell them this: "I invite you to the great adventure."

It is not a question of repeating spiritually what others have done before us, for our adventure begins beyond that. It is a question of a new creation, entirely new, with all the unforeseen events, the risks, the hazards it entails—a *real adventure*, whose goal is certain victory, but the road to which is unknown and must be traced out step by step in the unexplored. Something that has never been in this present universe and that will *never* be again in the same way. If that interests you... well, let us embark.[74]

Iconic Figures of East and West Usher in the Interspiritual Age

Certain iconic figures can help us further understand the breadth and depth of the planet's emerging unity consciousness. From nearly 200 years of a developing evolutionary world vision, and perhaps as many as 2,000 important books, we can pick out several men, women, and movements to give us a clearer sense of the qualities of this emerging vision.

The word "icon," which is Greek for "image," offers nuanced meanings to guide our selections. In the simplest sense, icon means

---

[74] The Mother, from "The Mother, Questions and Answers" 1957-1958, *Collected Works of The Mother* Vol.9, p.151-152; see Mother [The], [Mirra Alfassa] 1978 in Bibliography; see also Aurobindo Gosse [Sri Aurobindo], 1972, *Collected Works of Sri Aurobindo* in Bibliography. Quotations reprinted with permission of Sri Aurobindo Ashram Trust.

"representation," referring to what we select to represent something in a manner that aptly summarizes what it's about. More mystically, icon means "window." Such windows are a way to understand not only the breadth and depth of something but also what qualities are required to represent it. In art, it's often said that icons aren't just two- or three-dimensional like a painting or statue, but evoke a further dimension of insight, showing us something deeper about the substance of the matter or the breadth of what's involved in carrying the representation itself—something that explains why the icon is looked to.

By nature, such examples bridge east and west, north and south, while also clearly portraying both the awareness of interspirituality and the skill sets that must be attached to it for it to become the initiator of profound change.

An Icon of the West: Scientist and Priest Teilhard de Chardin

In the West, no one more exemplifies the diversity inherent in the interspiritual journey than French Jesuit priest and scientist Teilhard de Chardin. This is true not only because of his vision and the depth of his academic qualifications, but also because of the courage and fortitude with which he pursued his world-centric vision. At once fiercely loyal to his calling as a priest and his own eclectic mystical and scientific vision, his now famous books didn't appear in print during his own lifetime. Ultimately he became a cult figure in both his own church and across the world's religions, long before there was any official acceptance of his visionary views within the Roman Catholic Church itself.

Today the Roman Catholic Church still considers Teilhard's theological views, which include a cosmic and universal view of The Christ, as out of their mainstream. However, Catholicism has embraced much of Teilhard's developmental view of the history of life on earth and its connection with the origin of human consciousness. Reflecting this, the Roman Catholic Church's published views on evolution are among the most balanced and truly scientific in the world, carefully distinguishing the realm and method of science from the domain of religion and spirituality. The Vatican Observatory has been at the cutting edge of recent studies of cosmology and extraterrestrial life.

Today such views are commonplace among Roman Catholics, but for Teilhard, like others who envisioned such views early on, it was a long and arduous road toward acceptance. In line with our comment that with every catastrophe a new birth is taking place, Teilhard's own life mirrors defeat turning into opportunity.

Nature Mystic and Scientist. Brother Teasdale said in *The Mystic Heart* that nearly every mystic begins with a profound sense of connection to nature. Teilhard, born in 1881, felt this connection from the time he was a child. His fascination became a spiritual one, but the curiosity of his intellect also followed a scientific path. It was perhaps natural for his temperament to take the route of a highly academic religious order like The Society of Jesus. As a Jesuit, Teilhard received copious training in theology and philosophy, but also could pursue professional training in geology and paleontology. Priests were part of the academic establishment in France, so the young Teilhard became a fixture at the French museum of natural history in Paris, with some of Europe's most astute scientists as his mentors. This seemingly peculiar path served him well because, when his unorthodox theological views endangered his career, his prowess in science allowed him to carry on with his overall work.

By curious twist and turn, Teilhard's frequent exiles from Europe, handed down as disciplines by his superiors for doctrinal infractions, led to some of his most important scientific discoveries. He was also able to find access to books in other lands that were banned by the Roman Catholic Church in Europe. One that was particularly influential in his life and work was Henri Bergson's *Creative Evolution*, which had been banned by Pope Pius X. Bergson's views weren't compatible with some of the mainstream of science, though they allowed Teilhard to consider a more holistic view of biological development that could also contain the spiritual.

Often relieved of priestly duties and therefore with time on his hands, Teilhard was able to join the original English expedition of famous paleontologists Arthur Smith Woodward and Charles Dawson, which by chance uncovered the famous artifacts of the Piltdown Man—bone fragments collected from a gravel pit at Piltdown, East Sussex, in England. Unfortunately for all involved, the Piltdown fossils turned out not to represent an early human. Nonetheless, Teilhard's association with these famous British scientists furthered his career, and he was soon able to join expeditions to study the famous ancient cave paintings of Europe, together with a chance to travel to China in 1919 to work with the famous paleontologist Emile Licent. Teilhard's and Licent's different personalities and talents led to a remarkably productive research partnership.

It was during this period that, based on their discovery of early human fossils and tools, Teilhard began developing his views, much like those of the later Julian Jaynes, that linked toolmaking, fire-making, and other skills with the arising of human consciousness. This was the birth of Teilhard's views of evolving cosmology, moving from geosphere to biosphere, and finally the wholly different emergent world of human consciousness—a layer of existence Teilhard came to call the "noosphere."

Relating this to his own mysticism, Teilhard was able to imagine that the entire story of planet earth and humanity had been a grand ascent toward higher and higher capabilities—even a reaching toward a God-like nature, a future destiny he came to call the "Omega Point." He also believed this ascension through evolution meant humans are inherently "one," and he called this vision of unity consciousness "unanimization." His vision of evolution followed a spiral model of unfolding, foreshadowing the views put forward today by Integral theory and Spiral Dynamics.

Controversy and Exile. When Teilhard returned to Europe after working with Licent, he used his academic appointments to develop, write about, and teach his theories. This soon led to a resurgence of discipline from his superiors. In 1925 he was asked to either sign an agreement to be silent about his ideological views or leave the Jesuit order. This crisis caused controversy among his friends and colleagues. Because of his dedication to the Church, and most likely his inner trust in his own spiritual experience of God, he agreed to the terms of this restriction. Lacking any way to formally teach or work academically in the West, he had no choice but to return to China and, by 1928, was on his way east to what would become the most productive years of his scientific career. When he arrived in China, he was immediately asked to join the most prestigious community of Western scientists, located in Peking.

Teilhard's new discoveries came as part of an expedition that uncovered Peking Man, a pivotal element in our knowledge of human development. He then joined the American Museum of Natural History's Central Mongolian Expedition, which was soon made famous via the popular books of Roy Chapman Andrews, an iconic figure of the early 20th century's explorer-adventurer writers who later became Director of the American Museum. Toting a six-gun, Andrews is often cited as the historical person behind the fictional character Indiana Jones. As an author of children's book as well as scholarly treatises, he was also one of the founders of the Boy Scouts. Although Teilhard didn't seek fame, his connections helped bring it to him—so much so that he is considered the historical personage behind characters in at least six novels or films, the most well known being the character of Jean Telemond in Morris West's bestseller *The Shoes of the Fisherman*.

Posthumous Publication of His Famous Works. Banned from theological activity, Teilhard's goal was to complete his now classic work *Le Phénomène Humain* (*The Phenomenon of Man*) so it would be available in the event of his death. It was perhaps fortuitous the destiny of this book lay with the twists and turns of Teilhard's uncertain relationship with the Church. During visits to Europe, he attempted to submit revised versions of his work that might pass the religious censors. None of these efforts bore fruit. In a state of exhaustion, in 1947 he suffered a serious heart attack right when he was hoping to re-establish himself in European academia in response to prestigious offers brought to him by his scientific fame, including one by France's most prestigious university—the Sorbonne. Though he had been awarded France's highest academic and intellectual award, the Legion of Honor, Church authorities didn't allow him to accept any of these offers. Instead he was advised to move to the United States, where academic freedoms within the Church were somewhat more relaxed.

Teilhard's superiors agreed to his transfer to the United States, where he lived in relative obscurity in a Jesuit community in Manhattan and was able to finalize *The Phenomenon of Man,* and other works, unimpeded by the revisions that might have been required had he succeeded in other versions through the Church censors. He was able to visit France one more time, in 1954, and died on Easter Sunday, 1955.

The Phenomenon of Man was published in French in 1955, in English in 1959, and subsequently in 15 other languages. As a visionary treatise on geological, biological, and human development—including both a scientific and spiritual worldview—it's a classic to holists but remains controversial with the conservative mainstream of both scientific biology and theology. Typical of books that position themselves between the orthodoxies of different cultural realms, *The Phenomenon of Man* is either scorned as "anti-scientific," as in the case of Nobel Prize-winning biologist Peter Medawar, or lauded as groundbreaking in the case of leading scientists and thinkers who formed a committee to ensure the timely publication of Teilhard's work after his passing. This committee included famous names like Dr Arnold Toynbee, Sir Julian Huxley, and M. Andre Malraux.

After his death, the works of Teilhard de Chardin became foundational for entire movements, organizations, federations, and institutes dedicated to his and similar integrative and holistic views of biological and human development. Painters and sculptors dedicated works to him, and even a symphony was written in his honor. Following in his footsteps, noted scientists and futurists have further developed aspects of his far-reaching works. Notable among those who credit Teilhard's work as their inspiration are the famous architect and futurist Paolo Soleri, and within mainstream biology Dr Robert Wright, author of the influential books *The Moral Animal* and *Nonzero: The Logic of Human Destiny.* Wright's work in its own right is worthy of mention in connection with what today is called the Evolutionary Consciousness movement.

Perhaps most fitting in summarizing the legacy of Pierre Teilhard de Chardin is the title of a short story collection recalling his memory by Flannery O'Connor, *Everything that Rises Must Converge.*

Icons of the East: India's Sri Aurobindo and The Mother

Not many of us could occupy the role of guru, sage, scholar, pivotal political figure for an entire nation, and futurist, but Sri Aurobindo— born Aurobindo Ghose in 1872 in India—did just that. Few of us could meet and combine our talents with an equally dynamic and pivotal person of the opposite gender, bringing together the masculine and feminine energies, but Aurobindo did this, too, in his nearly 40-year spiritual and amazingly productive relationship with Frenchwoman Mira Alfassa (1878-1973), who became known in India and through-out the world as "The Mother."

Today Auroville, India's experimental community based on global-istic and holistic views, is a beacon for the developing global holistic message. But there's more to the story. People still living who knew them say Aurobindo and The Mother paid special attention to bring-ing East and West together. For many years, Aurobindo left the daily operations of his spiritual community to his companion and mem-bers of the community as he labored hour upon hour on his spiri-tual and sociological treatises. He knew that with the convergence of the world's cultures, a time would come when the Western mind, so dominant in the 19th century, would prove inadequate to the chal-lenge of a new future for our species, which would require the contri-bution of the Eastern mind. Sensing that, eventually, the development movements of the West—those who inaugurated the syntheses that have become Integral theory and Spiral Dynamics—would discover him, Aurobindo became a developmental writer and thinker, so much so that his writings are now central to the global syntheses put forward by futurists and integralists.

In his voluminous works, one of Aurobindo's gems was his com-mentaries on the natural differences between Eastern and Western minds. One compelling metaphor he offered was that if we look at the structure of reality as a necklace, the Western mind offers expertise on every detail of each bead, while the Eastern mind sees the string that binds them. Aurobindo saw the Eastern and Western minds as complementary aspects of the kind of holistic mind that would be needed for a successful planetary civilization. His most famous works are the philosophical writing of *The Life Divine* and his understanding of the Indian spiritual traditions in *The Synthesis of Yoga*. He also authored one of the most famous poetic works in the English language, the multi-volume *Savitri*.

Meeting of East and West. Aurobindo was educated in the West, sent as a child to study in England—initially at St Paul's, London, then at King's College, Cambridge. An outstanding scholar, he became an acknowledged expert on not only the classics but also English literature. While he was at Cambridge, events in colonial India positioned him as a potential leader of the Indian people. From an early time he had seen that England couldn't long maintain control over India and that India itself would need to take on the responsibility of creating a modern civilization grounded in its own culture, which included playing a prominent role in the world. Consequently, at the age of 21 Aurobindo returned to India to support the independence movement.

Uncertain of the best way for India to pursue its independence, Aurobindo toyed with outright activism, and even rebellion, but felt drawn to India's spiritual heritage for empowerment in both his personal and national transformation. Becoming an ardent student of the yogic disciplines, he came under the tutelage of a well-known Indian Yogi, Vishnu Bhaskar Lele, and soon began having experiences of great spiritual depth—a fact that served him well, given that his political activities placed him in the hands of the police. During his incarceration in the central jail in Calcutta, his yogi arranged for him to be visited by the venerated Indian Sage, Vivekananda, who was also famous in the West. Consequently, he underwent some of his most profound breakthroughs in universal spiritual understanding during this period, revolving around a higher unity consciousness that he referred to as "supermind," a potential he believed to be latent in all humans—and the way our species would be able to build a transformed world.

At his trial in 1908, fortunately for world history Aurobindo was acquitted. The trial, coupled with his public reports of his experiences, propelled him to national prominence. But his writings on spirituality and India's political future became so popular that he again became embroiled in political controversy—to the point that, in 1909, the British Viceroy and Governor General of India labeled him the most dangerous man in India, forcing him to flee. Fortunately, India also had colonial areas controlled by the French, which enabled him to take refuge in Pondicherry, arriving there in the spring of 1910.

Working from this independent French colonial area, during the next decade Aurobindo not only established a burgeoning influential spiritual community but also completed the bulk of his voluminous works on literature, sociology, politics, and spirituality, for which he is world-renowned. Along with these dozens of volumes, thousands of collected letters shared with hundreds of Aurobindo's students—many of whom became prominent figures in spirituality, politics, and the Indian independence movement in their own right—account for his fame.

Collaboration with His Spiritual Companion, "The Mother." Aurobindo also figures in spiritual history for his early realization of the centrality of the feminine message and the role of the divine feminine in the transformative history of our planet. In 1914, he was visited by the well-known French writer, artist, and spiritualist, Mirra Alfassa. Born of Turkish and Egyptian parents in Paris in 1879, Mirra became a major figure in the cultural and spiritual life of Paris, counting among her friends many of the elite of French society and intellectual and artistic circles. Aurobindo and Mirra immediately recognized a spiritual bond, one which both intuited as having historical implications.

Aurobindo came to recognize Mirra as a spiritual equal and companion in his visionary work. In 1920 she began living in Pondicherry, and by 1924 Aurobindo had delegated management of nearly all the matters of the spiritual community to her so he could concentrate on the writings he was sure would become so indispensable to the coming globalization he envisioned. Recognizing the role of the divine feminine for the unitary era, Aurobindo began referring to Mirra as "The Mother," and made the role she embodied prominent in his writings. The name "The Mother" became the name Mirra was then to be known by in India and around the world. India's independence was announced on August 15, 1947, which happened to be Aurobindo's 75th birthday. Sri Aurobindo transitioned in 1950.

After Aurobindo's transition, The Mother continued pioneer innovations she had conceived with him at his Ashram and in their vision of a multinational community that would express their world-centric concept of the planet's future. This vision, which became the Indian experimental city of Auroville, gained worldwide recognition, especially through United Nations and UNESCO publications, throughout the mid 20th century. Auroville's inauguration in 1968 was attended by representatives from over 100 nations. Its work as a guiding international institution has continued ever since, with prominent members of the community like Aster Patel and Sraddhalu Ranade travelling the world.

In her last years before her transition in 1973, The Mother also published a number of major spiritual works, further elaborating her understanding of the world's spiritual heritage, the potential of humanity, and particularly the future of the human body as the container for a being that's carrying consciousness to higher and higher levels of physical, spiritual, and ethical perfection.

As with Teilhard de Chardin, the central themes of Aurobindo and The Mother were the visioning of a matured humankind sharing a unity consciousness and building a world that reflects those ideals. For Teilhard, it was reaching the Omega Point pointed to by the Christ Consciousness taught by Jesus of Nazareth. For Aurobindo and The Mother, it was the manifestation of the divine or Supermind in all humanity.

As Aurobindo had predicted, his writings were discovered by the 20th century developmentalists and have taken their place in creating the vision and heritage that has been unfolding through the

Integrative, Holistic, and coming Global Age. The Mother's writings elaborate the implications of this potential for the spiritual life and aspirations of all who wish to be a part of the world's growth into its Global Age.

Brother Teasdale and Interspirituality's Early Roots. Just as Charles Darwin authored the synthesis of evolution from the work of a large number of historical forerunners, Brother Wayne Teasdale's *The Mystic Heart* seems to have filled this role for the emerging interspiritual paradigm. Living and writing as official hermit for the Roman Catholic diocese of Chicago, Teasdale had both the time and the knowledge to produce this synthesis. He spent time in contemplative monastic communities and the Eastern Christian ashram movement, knew most of the spiritual celebrities of his time, and completed a doctorate in theology at New York's Fordham University, writing on the interspiritual thought of his mentor Father Bede Griffiths. Teasdale considered both Griffiths and Father Thomas Keating his spiritual "fathers."

The roots of the interspiritual movement go back to when English and French missionaries went to India in colonial times and discovered the profound wisdom that underpinned this Asian culture. It began with the French Jesuit priest Father Roberto de Nobili in the 16th century. The Catholic religious orders of the colonial era were explorers and also scholars, with some more open-minded than others. Exploration led to scholarship, and scholarship led to increased understanding. Entire ancient texts had to be translated into English, then comprehended by the Western mind. By the 19th century, there emerged prominent Catholics who also appreciated the universal spiritual roots of the Indian culture. A sequence of such individuals led to what became known by the late 19th century as the Christian Ashram movement—the ashram being the place in which spiritual wisdom could be pursued.

Following the late 19th century Catholic convert and Hindu holy man Brahmabandhab Upadhyay, a number of Christian priests also became recognized as Hindu gurus. The most famous of these were early 20th century pioneers Father Jules Monchanin (also known as Swami Parah Arubi Ananda), Father Henri le Saux (also called Swami

Abhishiktananda), Swami Ajatananda (a successor of Abhishiktananda), and Father Bede Griffiths (also known as Swami Dayananda). Their combined work culminated in the founding of the interspiritual Shantivanum community in Tannirpalli, in Tamil Nadu at the southern tip of India. From that ashram came not only Brother Teasdale but also other early interspiritual voices such as Andrew Harvey (the modern voice of Sacred Activism) and Russill Paul (teacher, musician, and pioneer of the Yoga of Sound).

18

Toward Unity Consciousness

"Together we stand, divided we fall"

Pink Floyd

THE LEAP FROM A FEW HISTORICAL GIANTS TO AN EVOLVING IDEA THAT'S destined to reach its own high tide reflects nature's own pyramid of development. As in nature, with time the numbers and diversity of any community can rise exponentially. So it is with the evolutionary consciousness movement, the sum total of this great coming together over centuries that's trying to define humanity's potential.

There's an elegance to the fact that the evolution of consciousness is essentially the same process Darwin recognized in nature a century and a half ago. Process is eternal, its progression full of emerging results at each twist and turn. How curious that this reality, so self-evident in our daily lives, was somehow lost on modern humanity. The inherent hope and promise of the simple fact of the movement's emergence has eluded our sense of destiny for some time, frozen in flatland by dogmas that emerge from culture.

While spirituality is dynamic, religion has claimed fixed outcomes. Such outcomes appeal to humanity's still developing ape-like mind because they are easy to remember and thus easy to perpetuate. We see such manipulation in politics every day.

Currently there are over 4,000 religious traditions. Historically the number has probably exceeded 60,000.[75] Nearly all of these feature some kind of static worldview—who we are, where we came from, and where we're going—mostly at loggerheads with each other. The interspiritual view that all this has been one flow, one experience, now moving into fruition in a globalized and multicultural era, offers a different perspective that blows the lid off static worldviews—just like Darwin's theory did in the 1860s.

200 Years and 2,000 Books

Names like Deepak Chopra, Barbara Marx Hubbard, Lynne McTaggert, Ken Wilber, Don Beck, and Andrew Cohen are well known. But there are a significant number of recognizable leaders who are involved in this high tide of the evolutionary consciousness movement. A group calling themselves the Evolutionary Leaders lists 60.[76] However, the phenomenon is far more complex.

Just as eons ago there were as many kinds and sizes of flying dinosaurs as there are birds today—not just the showy giants that populate our books about dinosaurs—there are at least two centuries of authors and pioneers, and at least 2,000 major books, that articulate this progression. If we look back, we can date the roots of this globalizing realization to the earliest straddling between the world's Great Wisdom Traditions and the implications of modern science. This puts us squarely in the mid-to-latter 19th century when Darwin published his *On the Origin of Species*—right when our species was embarking on the epoch we have called The Fourth Great Advance.

Origins of the Evolutionary Consciousness Movement

By the mid 19th century, we began to see clear evidence of dialogues and syntheses between the spiritual and the scientific. As the 19th

---

[75] adherents.com.
[76] evolutionaryleaders.net.

century closed, there had already been one Parliament of the World's Religions (held in Chicago in 1893), inquiry between spiritualism and 19th century science in the founding of Theosophy, and the appearance of pivotal texts on the relationship of objective and subjective knowing by such researchers as Williams James, Sigmund Freud, and C. J. Jung.

With the onset of the 20th century, there was a vibrant mixing of Eastern and Western understanding, prominent in the literature of the First World, featuring names known to nearly every avid reader: D. T. Suzuki, Evelyn Underhill, P. D. Ouspensky, and Rudolf Steiner, each of whom attempted to bridge the scientific-spiritual gap—as in the internationally influential *Creative Evolution* by Henri Bergson, together with further emergence of the developmental vision in writers like James Mark Baldwin and Jean Piaget.

As the 20th century progressed, Western cultures dominated by Christianity were swept by a similar transcultural dynamism in the religious writings of Joseph Campbell, Martin Buber's *I and Thou*,[77] Alfred North Whitehead in philosophy, Arnold Toynbee's histories of the rise and fall of cultures, and Arthur Lovejoy's classic *The Great Chain of Being*,[78] known to nearly every student of religion if they have stepped for a moment outside the tradition of their birth.

All these works reflect our characterization of the Fourth Great Advance, which continued until after the Second World War. As the Second World War was about to plunge the world into uncertainty, the discovery of LSD and the popularization of other psychedelics, natural and synthesized, introduced a precarious path for the human subjective search. Theosophy's J. Krishamurti emphasized the enigmatic "pathless land," while Paramahansa Yogananda's book *Autobiography of a Yogi* was a runaway bestseller.

As we passed beyond the world wars and entered the integrative epoch, integrative texts began to abound. In Europe, Fritjof Schuon wrote on *The Transcendent Unity of all Religions* in 1948. The same year, Thomas Merton entered contemplative monasticism from where he

---

[77] German 1923, English 1937.
[78] See Lovejoy, A. O. 1936 in Bibliography; hereafter, all book titles of the evolutionary consciousness movement not specifically footnoted appear in the Bibliography.

would popularize the subjective journey for millions of readers. In this post-War period, western psychology reached a clinical high tide, with works emerging on love, sex, learning, and the clinical definitions of psychological illness. We have already referred to Aurobindo's work and that of Teilhard de Chardin, both from this period. The syntheses of Karl Jaspers recounted the rise of the world's religions in the Axial Age and introduced the lexicon of Eastern philosophers to the philosophies of the West.

The phenomena of the 1960s are, of course, legendary in this culmination, including an international countercultural wave that embraced every aspect of culture from music, art, and pop-spirituality, to recognition of the perils that might face our species in the future—pollution, overpopulation, resource competition, corporate greed and corruption, and war. In the United States this was the era of the Civil Rights movement and the work of Dr Martin Luther King, Jr.

Evolutionary Consciousness in Popular Culture

This cusp between the 1950s and 1960s was also the era of the "Beat" poets or "Beat Generation," remembered by many readers from a clutch of New Yorkers: Allen Ginsberg (*Howl*, 1956), William S. Burroughs (*Naked Lunch*, 1959), and Jack Kerouac (*On the Road*, 1957). "Beat" has multiple meanings, initially meaning "beaten down"—a reference to the revolutionary tone of the era. But when the Beat generation merged nearly seamlessly into the hippie and peacenik movements of the 60s, the meaning took a turn. Consistent with the paradoxical language of the Eastern spirituality manifesting throughout the West, "beat" came to mean "with the beat" of change or evolution. The message of this 50s and 60s radicalism was already consistent with what became the implicit principles of both the evolutionary consciousness movement and Brother Teasdale's view of the emerging Interspiritual Age: peace and tolerance, rejection of materialism and militant nationalism, and an embracing of the heartistic and mystical elements of our humanity.

Many readers will readily recognize their own special experiences of this era. If you read fiction, you'll remember the wildly popular messages of J. D. Salinger (*Franny and Zooey, The Catcher in the Rye*), Hermann Hesse (*Steppenwolf* and *Siddhartha*), and William Golding (*Lord of the Flies*). If you read spirituality, you'll remember Shunryu Suzuki (*Zen Mind, Beginners Mind*), Alan Watts (*This Is It* and *Psychotherapy East and West*), the American tours of Maharishi Mahesh Yogi, and Harvard Divinity School's Harvey Cox's influential cultural overview *Religion in the Secular City*. Aldous Huxley's elaboration of his "Perennial Philosophy" and his *Brave New World* are also famous from this time.

Students of science will recall Rachel Carson's pivotal book on pollution *Silent Spring*, the Club of Rome's compilation *The Limits to Growth,* and Paul Ehrlich's *The Population Bomb*. Sociologists often refer to these as the modern era's apocalyptic literature. Followers of psychology will never forget their reading of R. D. Laing's *The Divided Self* and *The Politics of Experience*, along with Thomas Szasz's *The Myth of Mental Illness*. In the genre of holism, nearly everyone knows Abraham Maslow's *Toward a Psychology of Being* and Thomas Kuhn's *The Structure of Scientific Revolutions,* which helped us comprehend the phenomenon of paradigms.

Few will not know of *The Beatles* and their flirtation with Eastern spirituality or the wider phenomenon of "psychedelic rock" (witness hundreds of thousands of hits at YouTube even today). In this era of collision between transformative vision and pop culture, rockers *The Doors* took their name from the prolific pen of a famous visionary contemporary, writer Aldous Huxley, whose *The Doors of Perception* and *Brave New World* have been blockbuster literary successes. Equally remembered are other icons of this flamboyant era: the psychedelic experiments at Harvard University by Timothy Leary and Richard Alpert, and the controversies that swirled around the "hip" pop artists Andy Warhol and Roy Lichtenstein. Each well portrays Marshall McLuhan's memorable mantra of the time: "The medium is the message."

Such popular phenomena sunk the roots of the evolutionary consciousness message further into the substrata of world culture than we often realize. Except for the fundamentalist sectors of the world, which are information proof, the myriad characters and movements left not only an indelible mark of a more holistic vision on the world but also momentum in that direction.

Coming of Age in the Holistic Era

It ought not to surprise us that the cresting of the emerging evolutionary consciousness movement, of which interspirituality is a part, began around the year 1970 with the Fifth Great Advance, The Dream of Holism. Much of this demarcation results from the influence of the new physics, and with it a recognition of deep synchronicity between humanity's interior and exterior ways of knowing. It was at this time the first literature about the earth as an integrated organism (the eventual "GAIA" of James Lovelock) began to emerge. From 1969, now classic books began to appear, melding these formerly divided cultures of knowing: Charles Tart's compilation *Altered States of Consciousness*, the work of Elizabeth Kübler-Ross *On Death and Dying*, and Fritz Perls' gestalt therapy.

In 1976, the implications of the new physics were popularized widely in Fritjof Capra's bestseller *The Tao of Physics*. The same message was brought to the world's contemplative and monastic communities throughout the 1980s by interspirituality's own Father Bede Griffiths in a series of speaking tours and articles in prominent periodicals. In 1970, Gary Zukav's bestseller *The Dancing Wu Li Masters* furthered this conversation on the worldwide stage, winning the American Book Award for Science.

The sheer variety and number of developments in academic fields around the world, more and more finely grained, elaborated the meaning and implications of a world propelling itself toward multiple perspectives and holistic integration.

Selected Developments During the Emerging Holistic Epoch

Institutions and Organizations: The founding of nearly a dozen interfaith seminaries, the California Institute of Integral Studies, Sofia University (formerly the Institute for Transpersonal Psychology), The Claritas Institute, Sophia Institute, Hoffman Institute, The Association for Global New Thought, World Wisdom Council, World Wisdom Alliance, World Commission on Global Consciousness, Alliance for a New Humanity, EnlightenNext, Conflict Transformation Collaborative, United Religions Initiative, The Foundation for Conscious Evolution, General Evolution Research Group, International Society for Systems Sciences, The Social Healing Project, The Oneness Project, the Institute of Noetic Sciences, the organizations built around *A Course in Miracles* and EST.

Centers and Associations: Esalen and Tassajara Hot Springs in California, California Institute of Asian Studies, Naropa Institute in Colorado, the Snowmass Initiatives group, Omega Institute for Holistic Studies in New York, Blue Spirit Costa Rica, Edinburgh International Center for Spirituality and Peace, Integral Institute and Integral Multiplex (virtual), Interspiritual Dialogue in Action, Interspiritual Multiplex (virtual), Spiritual Paths Institute, Evolutionary Leaders, Agape International Spiritual Center, the Contemplative Alliance, The Charter for Compassion, the Occupy movement.

Publications and Media: Shambhala Publications, *Journal of Transpersonal Psychology, Journal of the Scientific Study of Religion, The Yoga Journal, What is Enlightenment?* magazine, New Dimension Radio, Namaste Radio, the journals *ReVision, Parabola, Somatics, Kosmos,* and *Consciousness and Culture,* the State University of New York's book series on a holistic postmodernism.

Seminal World Conferences: Revival of the Parliaments of the World's Religions, world religious summits of the Temple of Understanding, various issue-based global summits of the United Nations, first Conference on Voluntary Control of Internal States, first Association of Humanistic Psychology conference on the transpersonal, the international Transpersonal Conferences, the international conferences on A Unity of the Sciences, the Esalen conferences on Ecopsychology, the Kyoto World Conference on Religion and Peace, the Science and Nonduality Conference.

The Integral Paradigm Emerges: The 1970s also saw the publication of syntheses establishing pivotal paradigms of thinking for the holistic age, from Julian Jaynes' *The Origin of Consciousness in the Breakdown of the Bicameral Mind* to the massively influential Integral theory beginning in 1977 with Ken Wilber's *Psychologia Perennis: The Spectrum of Consciousness* and continuing on through over 20 books by Wilber now available in nearly 40 languages. From Integral also grew the understanding of Spiral Dynamics, developed by Don Beck and Chris Cowan, and other views of reality rooted to a great degree in the work of Arthur Koestler, a British polymath renowned for both his works in fiction and nonfiction who coined the term *holon* in 1967 to refer to the well-known phenomenon of things that constitute a whole and a part at the same time, like organs in the body or the interconnected elements of the ecosystem. As Koestler recognized, the implications of the hierarchies and holarchies comprised of holons was barely beginning to be understood as the integrative and holistic eras unfolded.

Holistic Health and Healing: With holistic awareness also emerged new understanding of nutrition and alternate modalities in medicine and the healing arts. Who isn't familiar with the works of popular writers like Drs Andrew Weil, Deepak Chopra, and Kenneth Pelletier? Chopra's 1989 publication of *Quantum Healing* is often considered a game changer in understanding the relationship of health, wellbeing, and consciousness.

Also emerging from this emphasis was new literature on the healing modalities of feminine spirituality, as in the works of Marija Gimbutas, Anica Mander, Anne Kent Rush, June Singer, Carol Christ, Judith Plaskow, Jean Shinoda Bolen, and Tsultrim Allione. The diversity of these testifies to the global nature of this unfolding.

The Evolutionary Consciousness Movement Today

Exponential growth of the world's consciousness movement continued through the next two decades, bringing with the new millennium a diverse landscape of authors, speakers, pundits, and spokespersons. Most of us are familiar with *What is Enlightenment?* magazine founded by Andrew Cohen. Many may have attended the annual conference on Science and Nonduality.[79] In a way that wasn't possible even a few decades ago, leaders can now be brought together across great distances to meet personally, discuss diverse issues, and propose mutual and synergistic solutions. In recent years, gatherings such as Integral Institute, The Contemplative Alliance, and Evolutionary Leaders have allowed prominent authors and spokespersons to meet personally and regularly.

Most of us need no reminder of the names of these frequently seen celebrities and near-celebrities who spread the message of humanity's developmental transformation. The catchiest names that come to mind in an arbitrary scan across the media landscape include Ken Wilber, Don Beck, Deepak Chopra, Eckhart Tolle, Marianne Williamson, Barbara Marx Hubbard, Lynne McTaggert, Andew Cohen, Dean Radin, Duane Elgin, Brian Swimme, Michael Dowd and Connie Barlow, Matthew Fox, Robert Wright, Yasuhiko Kimura, Llewellyn and Anat Vaughan-Lee, Bruce Lipton, Jean Houston, Michael Beckwith, and Michael Brown, to name just a few.

In addition to individuals we know from our day-to-day media, there are a host of lesser known but immensely important scientists and religious scholars whose contributions have further grounded this holistic message of our world's potential. Among these, Russian-Belgian Nobel Laureate Dr Ilya Prigogine pioneered study of reality's structures and makeup. Austrian-American Dr Erich Jantsch elaborated concepts of self-organizing principles. The title of his most famous book, *The Self-Organizing Universe: Scientific and Human Implications of the Emerging Paradigm of Evolution,* illumines the overall vision of evolutionary consciousness. Drs Francisco Varela and Humberto Maturana pioneered studies of how organisms actually co-create their environments, setting a prescription for how our species might succeed in the future with global problem solving. Their work seeded the field now known as "autopoiesis," coined by them in 1972.

---

[79] www.scienceandnonduality.com.

American-born British physicist Dr David Bohm in a now famous book, *Wholeness and the Implicate Order,* suggested a synthesis of the new physics, consciousness, and the human brain. Bohn had been hounded out of the United States, his patriotism questioned by the fanatics of the McCarthy era. Hungarian-born scientific philosopher and systems theorist Dr Ervin Laszlo, who was also instrumental in bringing Eric Jantsch's work to the world, authored over 70 books, extending his pioneering work in systems theory to a comprehensive view of evolution.

In 1979, Princeton University scientists formed the influential Princeton Engineering Anomalies Research (PEAR) program to investigate paranormal phenomena. In one of their most well known announcements, they published evidence of non-random field effects surrounding the half-billion people watching the 1995 O.J. Simpson verdict. After 28 years of work and over ten million tests, PEAR concluded that scientific evidence exists for consciousness affecting or interacting with surrounding phenomena.

Even more startling ideas of how reality may work have also emerged from the current integrative and holistic periods. Most well known of these are the writings of Britain's Rupert Sheldrake and America's Michael Murphy, Willis Harman, and Margaret Wheatley. Each of these thinkers, like Ken Wilber and the integralists, crosses the murky line of scientific objectivity and human subjectivity. While conventional science argues that its implicit rules of what can and can't be considered scientific data protect the integrity of the scientific enterprise, holists and integralists argue (more and more successfully it seems) that restricting the conversation and ruling out certain kinds of information is simply unrealistic in the complexly layered reality now known by our modern world. Harman echoes the tension surrounding this faceoff in the title of his most well known book *Global Mind Change.*

As already mentioned, Sheldrake is well known for his theory of morphic fields—the view that there are collective subjective effects on reality that influence the actual direction of development and events. An academic discipline, modern discursive theory, suggests this in the simplest of ways. When humans project ideas in writing or other media, these can become game changers for the behavior of entire cultures. We need only think of Adolf Hitler's *Mein Kampf* or Thomas Paines' *Common Sense*. Murphy, a founder of Esalen Institute, has written profoundly on evidence documenting metanormal capacities in human beings, including such phenomena as clairvoyance, hypnosis, healing, telepathy, and "trained states" as often seen in the martial arts. Wheatley has been influential because her similar penchant for bringing the subjective or seemingly magical element into motivational and organizational work has proven fruitful to many in the business world. Similarly, Ken Wilber's polymathic abilities have allowed the influence of his holistic models to reach into multiple fields, culminating in his celebrated *Sex, Ecology, Spirituality: The Spirit of Evolution*.[80] There have also been innovators who concentrated on the relationship of the unfolding evolutionary consciousness and the domain of religion and spirituality itself—an outstanding example being the work of philosopher and cross-cultural spiritual pioneer Ashok Gangadean, with his Awakening Mind, Awakening the New Consciousness and Global Dialogue Institute initiatives.

The integrative and holistic eras have understood the significance of mythology in reflecting the deepest urgings of human beings, with two centuries of study to draw on. Our modern media are full of epic stories of superheroes, imagined perfect worlds, and the struggle to attain these. We often fail to recognize why such books, movies, and even video games capture our fascination. We simply enjoy them, though the roots of these inner identifications run deep. They do much to maintain the magic-mythic lens in the most modern of times.

Our missions to space, our knowledge of the extreme diversity of life on earth, and astronomy's growing knowledge of planets other than ours have tweaked our hope of finding life, even intelligent life, elsewhere in the universe. Television shows recount stories of UFO encounters and extraterrestrial visitations, while astronomers on talk shows suggest there must be someone else out there—and perhaps civilizations thousands or even millions of years ahead of us.

---

[80] See Wilber, K. 1995 [2001] in Bibliography.

The European Space Organization's High Accuracy Radial Velocity Planet Searcher, which observes stars light years away, indicates that rocky planets not much larger than our earth are common in these stars' habitable zones. In the Milky Way galaxy alone, planets that could sustain life are suggested to number in the tens of billions, with over 100 in our own neighborhood.

Equally tantalizing is science's deeper investigation of the roots of civilization. The ages for early civilizations keep getting pushed farther back. Even the horizon cited by us for the rise of the earliest civilizations, around 7000 BCE, may soon be pushed back by recent archaeological findings such as those in southern Turkey (Gobekli Tepe) and western India (Gulf of Khambhat), which may date as early as 10,000 BCE.

Given the mammoth monuments and public works some of these early civilization display, what did the ancients actually know of sophisticated technology and engineering? How did they develop those skills, and how much of this early knowledge was lost in subsequent darker ages, only to be rediscovered recently? Did extraordinary things occur that modern humans dismiss as myth? Are ancient notions part of our holistic comprehension of our own future—for instance, sacred geometry, cosmic harmonics, and celestial resonance? Is there an echo from the blessing of an Egyptian pharaoh upon his city, laid out according to the geometries of stars and other celestial objects? "As above, so below" reminds us of modern science's understanding of fractal geometry: "The same from near as from far."

The sense of a sacred geometry permeates the world's religious traditions, from the finely crafted geometries of Islamic and Hindu architecture—based on sacred concepts of space, alignment, and complementarity—to the more esoteric notions of magical numerology. It permeated the thought of Greece's philosophers Pythagoras and Plato, from whom it became part of the medieval German astronomer Johannes Kepler's grand geometric scheme, the *Mysterium Cosmosgraphicum* ("Cosmic Mystery" or "Secret of the World"). The concept was lost for a few centuries with the upwelling of the subsequent rational lens.

Today the new science speaks of fractal geometry and fractal technology, structures that repeat in patterns from the most microscopic to the most cosmically large. The mathematics of the repeating sine wave permeates the structures of ecosystems. Plato's "five solid forms" dominate crystalline structures. Logarithmic spirals form objects ranging from microscopic seashells to the universe's colossal spiral galaxies. Tetrahedrons and pyramid-shaped structures dominate cosmic construction from the elemental particles of compounds to the geometries of giant planets like Jupiter. Varieties of pyramidal structures compose nature's myriad crystalline structures, reflecting in macrocosm the shape of the molecular bonds that make up their superstructures.

The ancients recognized the significance of these shapes. They built great square pyramids, with four sides at the base, not only in the famous Egyptian complexes at Giza but also in at least 40 other ancient sites around the world. In Egypt, these shapes were further identified with icons of good health and wellbeing—mystical forms depicting sacred balance. The popular deity Hathor, goddess of both successful childbirth and good health, was represented as a cow, depicting not only motherhood and nurturing but also the sacred geometry of being sustained by four legs. In sacred healing traditions tracing their roots to Egypt, even today the square pyramid shape is called the "the icon of balance." Not surprisingly, Hathor was also the goddess of miners, who observed such crystalline structure on a day-to-day basis.

Why was Hathor also the goddess of music? Philosopher and archaeologist J. J. Hurtak believes these synchronies point to something deeper that the ancient Egyptians were trying to express, reflecting modern physics' understanding of our multidimensional universe. If you make pyramidal shapes into more complex structures, called polyhedra, you get the multiple dimensions spoken of in string theory.

Hurtak has been studying the subtle acoustic and vibratory phenomena of pyramids around the world, directly listening for that whisper from the ancients. In the early 1990s, with permission of the Egyptian authorities, he and his associates brought hi-tech acoustical equipment and computer software into the Great Pyramid to examine the spectrum of sound within the walls of the Grand Gallery and in the King's and Queen's Chambers. They found repeating patterns of sound that suggested the structures were generating not only non-random configurations but also patterns closely correlated with human physiological activity, such as the human heartbeat and subtle respiratory rhythms. The suggestion is that this data points to original ritual purposes for the chambers—that they were built to induce mystical or creative states. If the sound patterns are a product of the architecture itself, this would explain why they are still detectable after thousands of years.

In later studies with musicologists, assisted by his wife Desiree and using more-advanced equipment, Hurtak was able to identify recognizable musical elements in the sound patterns, specifically configurations of F sharp and A sharp. These might have been harmonic initiation points similar to the modes used today by sound-assisted meditators to trigger and sustain mystical states or by sound therapists to induce states of relaxation and wellbeing. In constructing their sacred chambers the ancients may have discovered methods for initiating mystical states. If so, consistent with their cosmologies, it's suggested these reflected not only the natural vibrations of their Mother Earth but clues to the dimensions that were yet to come.

From Shamans to Scientists

Just as the whisper of the ancients echoes through modern studies of the geometry of our cosmos, so echoes the holistic understanding of the ancient native shaman in modern ecology and medicine.

As the new millennium dawned, American Passionist Father Thomas Berry, a student of both Teilhard de Chardin and native shamanism, articulated a succinct statement of eco-spirituality, the now famous "Twelve Principles." Motivated by an urgent sense that the planet's commercialism might soon destroy the biosphere, Berry made his entire ministry about the ecological message.

Berry's call for a new unity with nature reached millions worldwide, not the least of which was former senator and United States Vice President Al Gore. In 2007, Gore and the Intergovernmental Panel on Climate Change received the Nobel Peace Prize for their work informing the world about the human role in climate change. Just three years before, the Peace Prize had gone to Kenya's Wangari Maathai, founder of Africa's Green Belt Movement, which was initially a women's movement that advocated massive grassroots action as the only sure route to world change.

The public success of Berry, Gore, and Maathai paralleled the predictions of sociologist Paul Ray, published in 2000. Ray identified nearly 150 million Americans and Europeans who share a progressive worldview centered on the issues of spiritual development, ecological advocacy, and the transformative political role of women. Eco-spirituality would eventually find even more fruition in its merging with advancing studies of planetary ecology and the new Integral methods. In 2001 the Declaration of Amsterdam joined thousands of scientists in designating the earth an interconnected organism of geosphere, biosphere, and noosphere. By later in the same decade, the founders of the GAIA hypothesis (now the GAIA theory being tested in numerous scientific forms) even received honors from major scientific societies. The jury was still out on how much of the big picture view ("strong" GAIA) is good science compared to solidly supported smaller elements of the theory ("weak GAIA," the parts easier to prove).

Entire new scientific disciplines owed their genesis to this new holistic view—palaeoecology, ecophysics, earth systems sciences, and biogeochemistry. All of these became important in our measures to determine how real and how immanent is the danger of global climate disruption. Ecology also joined with Integral. In 2011, the voluminous *Integral Ecology* joined guiding ecological texts on scientists' and university students' bookshelves, doing exactly what its subtitles indicate—uniting multiple perspectives on the natural world.

Shamanic practice has also joined with progress in the healing arts as holistic and alternative medical approaches have become more and more welcome in the integrative and holistic epoch. One African shaman has been featured in an important South African movie *Voice of Africa*, released by the Academy for Future Science. Zulu practitioner Credo Visamazulu Mutwa uses vibratory healing modalities that reflect his tradition's ancient understanding of profane space and sacred space. Much like the context imputed to the sacred Egyptian pyramid chambers, this practice utilizes enclosed ceremonial spaces and vibratory energies such as prayers, chanting, and dancing.

Recalling Julian Jaynes' account of how the ancients apparently observed palpable results in their oracular and ritual practices, Credo also employs methods similar to those cited by Jaynes: the throwing of bones and touching of the body with sacred stones. These objects are believed by the practitioner and patient to hold healing vibratory energy generated by the ritual practice—energy that can be transferred to the patient by touch. The shaman is also believed to kindle energy through the body of the subject by quick movements of his hands in addition to body contact with the stones. As the ritual continues, the shaman and patient join in a semi-trance state of music and secret language. Jaynes also recorded the universality of trance states in the oracles believed in by so many of the ancients. In the Zulu practice, the patient is believed to receive subtle realm energies from the ritual, the stones, and the actions of the shaman.

This kind of practice isn't that far afield from the assumptions about energy transfer associated with practices now accepted in the West, such as Reiki and therapeutic touch—or even the use of microwave devices in conventional Western physiotherapy.

Studies of musical healing methods like those of Credo Visamazulu Mutwa demonstrate how shamans still use mystical methods based on bringing subjects into non-normal states of awareness. In the Zulu language, a shaman with these abilities is called *Mabona*, "one who sees energy." Further insight into such practices is also found in recent Western studies of a modern-day Hawaiian shaman Opuni, whose healings are well known across those islands.

An interview with Opuni about how his methods work recalls the views of Credo put forward in the film *Voice of Africa*. Opuni says his methods work *only when the shaman and the patient truly join in the same understanding of reality*. Tantalizing in these accounts is the parallel with modern physics' demonstration that it's possible to create localized situations that have their own identity with regard to the mechanics of time and space.

19

The Great Coming Together

"Man is a transitional being, he is not final...
The step from man towards superman is the next
approaching achievement in the earth's evolution...
inevitable because it is at once the intention of the
inner Spirit and the logic of Nature's process"

Sri Aurobindo

THE VIEW THAT ANY TEACHING THAT WOULD DIVIDE US CAN'T BE TRUE might be considered a credo of modern interspirituality and the evolutionary consciousness movement. Self-evident, it emerges from nearly all the recent literature of interreligious discussion.

Brother Teasdale said the true interspiritual discussion via the unconditional lens of the heart could underpin a new era in interreligious discussion. He himself was a part of such seminal efforts, including his role on the Council of the Parliament of the World's Religions, his participation in the seminal Snowmass Initiatives, and intimate interreligious dialogues hosted by himself and colleagues including Father Thomas Keating and His Holiness the Dalai Lama.

With numerous colleagues, he cofounded the Interspiritual Dialogue, which became Interspiritual Dialogue in Action following his transition in 2004.

In 1993, Teasdale had been involved with the refounding of the Parliament of the World's Religions in his home city of Chicago. This tradition was revived following increased interest in interfaith dialogue promoted especially through organizations associated with the United Nations and interfaith associations such as The Temple of Understanding, which through the 1960s and 1970s promoted various spiritual summits on three continents. The founder of the Temple of Understanding, Juliet Hollister, is an example of what one person's commitment can bring to the world stage. Seeing the desperate need for the world's religions to step up to global challenges, Hollister worked with Eleanor Roosevelt, Albert Schweitzer, The Very Reverend James Parks Morton, His Holiness the Dalai Lama, and others to revive an activist platform for the interfaith community, founding the Temple in 1960. Interspiritual pioneer Fr Thomas Keating became its first president. Also, the American interfaith movement gathered steam in the civil rights era with the galvanizing of faith groups around the cause of social justice.

In 1965, the Roman Catholic Church's Vatican II conclave issued the *Nostra Aetate*, a new vision of the role of interfaith cooperation in the world. This now iconic event was a testament to Pope John XXIII's historical legacy. In New York City, the leadership of the Episcopal Cathedral of St John the Divine founded a multifaceted Interfaith Center of New York, combining interfaith dialogue with social service visions across denominations. In 2007, a broad world coalition of Muslim scholars issued a statement on interfaith harmony. King Abdullah of Saudi Arabia followed with sponsorship of a world interfaith conference hosted by the King of Spain. His Holiness the Dalai Lama, who had received the Nobel Peace Prize in 1989, hosted world interfaith leaders gathering in India.

Contemplatives were also gathering worldwide, not only through the Snowmass Initiatives with their Nine Guidelines for Inter-religious

Understanding,[81] but also through the Monastic Interreligious Dialogue movement and other far-flung associations.[82] Regular international symposia on contemplative living were sponsored by Mind and Life Institute, along with annual conferences on contemplative outreach by the Center for Contemplative Living.

Beginning in 2008 groups such as the Contemplative Alliance regularly brought together some of the world's most well-known contemplatives and mystics for face-to-face dialogue. As Teasdale had predicted, the effect of one-on-one meetings among respected spiritual leaders was becoming a powerful leaven for understanding and recognition around the globe. Among the contemplative leaders and well-known mystics who participated in joint statements from these gatherings were, from Islam, Imam Dr Amir al-Islam, Imam Mohamed Bashar Arafat, Shaikh Kabir Helminski, Shaikah Camille Helminski, and Llewellyn Vaughan-Lee; from Buddhism, Ven. Bhikkhu Bodhi, Ven. Thubten Chodron, Acharya Sam Bercholz, and Lama Surya Das; from Christianity, Father Thomas Keating, Rev Cynthia Bourgeault, Rev Joan Brown Campbell, Dr Thomas P. Coburn, Sister Joan Chittister, Rev Matthew Fox, and Rev James Parks Morton; from Hinduism, Dr Amit Goswami, Aster Patel, Swami Ramananda, Swami Atmarupananda, Sraddhalu Ranade; and from Judaism, Rabbi Schachter-Shalomi Zalman, Rabbi Shefa Gold, and Rabbi Naomi Levy.

In 2010 the Temple of Understanding assembled and honored a broad cross section of interfaith visionaries in a well-publicized event in New York City. The centuries-long convergence of the evolutionary conscious, integral, and interspiritual movements was well on its way.

Does this convergence now enter an even deeper mainstream in the globalization conversation, or does it continue to evolve nuances not quite yet suspected or anticipated? We will likely see a little of both. However, there are some challenges looming that likely haven't been considered by most people.

---

[81] See Miles-Yepez, N. [Ed.] 2006 in Bibliography.
[82] The Contemplative Alliance, The Center for Contemplative Mind in Society, The Mystics and Scientists Conference, The Center for Action and Contemplation, the Lighthouse Trails Research Project, the Leadership Conference of Women Religious, The Chaudhuri Center For Contemplative Practice, the Center for Consciousness and Transformation, the Center for Contemplative Inquiry, and many more.

Where Does the Great Coming Together Take Us?

Hoping for a culmination of this Great Coming Together, we may think something is possible. But when we look more carefully, it simply might not be. Philosophers have been onto this for a long time, and the flaw in the original formulation gives the predicament its name: the "double standard fallacy" or "double-speak dilemma."

Religion and science both face this dilemma. The new physics has had to confront it for several decades as it formulated its theories of the elusive quantum realms. A *shared* solution to this dilemma is part of the anthropological leap forward being asked of *Homo sapiens* at this moment in our evolution.

Here is the problem for religion. If it is religious tolerance or, even better, religious pluralism that we propose as our answer to whether religions will be an asset or liability for our earth's future, is religious tolerance or religious pluralism actually possible? Is there a contradiction in envisioning a pluralism of religions when religion by nature isn't pluralistic but exclusive? In street language, is this a classic catch-22 or double-speak? If so, what of spirituality? If spirituality is by nature different from religion, is there a way by which spirituality—which Brother Teasdale suggested could be the "religion" of the third millennium—might resolve this impasse? Could unity consciousness prevent the usual hijacking of spirituality by religion that the Cognitive Science of Religion predicts as our downfall?

Originally world religions based their exclusive viewpoints on a philosophical view called "foundationalism," which simply meant that once you lay down beliefs, all future beliefs are validated by those older, assumed beliefs. This is much like the world's legal system, which operates largely on precedent. As ecumenists and religious pluralists began to exert their influence on the world's religions, the meaning of "foundationalism" changed, becoming a buzzword for the search for a universal meaning or message in all the traditions.

Long before Brother Teasdale coined the word "interspiritual," a little-known group of "religious foundationalists" were getting their message out. Their medium was mostly theological journals, so the message didn't reach the wider public and enter the popular literature of the evolutionary consciousness movement. Nonetheless there were three kinds of foundationalist messages, and Brother Teasdale utilized all three—although, like Darwin in making evolution popular, he developed some more-compelling arguments and added new elements.

The three bases for a foundationalist view of world religions that might allow for religious pluralism have been basic teachings held in common (such as the Golden Rule, which occurs in at least 21 world religions), the common ethical foundations taught by all (the message of Humanism since the 19th century!), and the possibility of a common mystical experience.

Although there weren't a large number of theologians who directly supported the early foundationalist approach, the number of major theologians who were attracted to the discussion about the possibility of common principles was significant. It included such famous names as Wilfred Cantwell Smith, Harvey Cox, John Cobb, Langdon Gilkey, Juan Luis Segundo, Karl Rahner, Jeremy Bernstein, Raimon Panikkar, and Hans Küng.

In 1974 Thomas Merton addressed the possibility of a common mystical experience, calling it a "communion of mystical-contemplative experience." The Liberation Theologians of the 1950s to 1980s (who waned after official admonishment from the Vatican) added a further uniting principle—the responsibility all religions share in creating economic and social justice.

A major problem for foundationalist perception was that it wasn't yet a global discussion. Most were Christian theologians trying to find a possible way forward with the other world religions, especially after Vatican II. There was no worldwide dialogue as has been possible since the new millennium. For the early foundational discussions, the stumbling block was, again, the apparent contradiction between religions and pluralism, coupled with the lack of any universal agreement on what uniting principles might clear the way forward. The foundationalists were ahead of their time. But there is more to the matter:

the stumbling block that they had run into was universal, being faced by the search for a unity of the sciences as well. The question of what constituted unity within multiplicity—and how this might look for a globalized earth—was actually facing every field and every aspect of culture.

One of the most influential books of recent years in the field of science is *Time's Arrow and Archimedes' Point: New Direction for the Physics of Time,* by Huw Price, Bertrand Russell Professor of Philosophy at Britain's Cambridge University. In a nutshell, it lays out the dilemma for a unity of the sciences with regard to the "double standard fallacy"—the double-speak dilemma. In a particular challenge to modern physics, quantum mechanics' search for an understanding of the elusive quantum reality also faces this question of how something can apparently be two things at the same time—much like the contradiction suggested by the term "religious pluralism."

The dilemma was summarized in a now famous riddle proposed by Austrian scientist Erwin Schrödinger. The purpose of the riddle was to point out the difference between how physicists say reality actually works in the dynamic quantum reality, and what we in day-to-day reality observe. A cat, a flask of poison, a potential source of radioactivity, and a Geiger counter are all sealed in a box. There's a random chance the potential source of radioactivity will emit radiation. If any atoms begin to decay and the Geiger counter detects an alpha particle, a hammer in the box is rigged to strike the flask, release poison, and kill the cat. The problem lies in ascertaining what the result will be for the poor cat, given that we don't know whether radioactivity has occurred. When viewed through the lens of quantum reality, the cat would have to be simultaneously dead and alive. This is because the fate of the cat reflects a wave function in the quantum reality, which is comprised of simultaneously decayed and undecayed states. However, in the everyday world, we know if we break into the box we will find the cat either dead or alive. When we break into the box we create a freeze-frame moment. Our imposition at that moment collapses the quantum wave into a moment when we can observe the cat in a black-or-white manner.

The cat riddle has perpetually fascinated the scientific community with regard to how reality appears in our day-to-day world when the physics underlying this reality is doing something quite different. It has become what's known as Bell's Theorem, the contribution of Ireland's Dr John Stewart Bell to modern physics. According to this theorem, no theory in our everyday physical reality can reflect all the elements of the wider quantum world, which is simply a more dynamic realm. It is similar to Brother Teasdale's Omega vision that no understanding or experience of the ultimate can truly inculcate all of its dimensions, and thus be claimed as ultimately true by any world religion. Bell's Theorem holds that in the quantum world, the cat must be able to be simultaneously dead and alive because, in that world, any viewpoint in any moment necessarily contradicts the opposite option. This has regularly been observed in the subatomic world. In quantum reality you can't simultaneously measure pairs of properties. This is physics' famous Uncertainty Principle. As Huw Price points out, the enigma of the Schrödinger's Cat and Bell's Theorem results because we humans live within the framework of time. The underlying quantum world is quite different.

How does this relate to whether it would be possible to have religious pluralism in an Interspiritual Age? From the cat and Bell's Theorem, it's clear that it has something to do with *simultaneity*, which in turn is connected with unity consciousness.

Responding to the riddle of Schrödinger's Cat, Sir Roger Penrose has said what most mystics of the Great Wisdom Traditions would say. We recognize that everyday consciousness allows us to have simultaneous perceptions of an alive or dead cat. Similarly, Brother Teasdale and interspirituality suggest we can all recognize a state of consciousness in which our spirituality can honor a particular religious view—even an apparently exclusive one—and yet act from a universal heart and unity consciousness. Interspirituality goes on to suggest that as this practice matures, it's less likely the exclusive religious view itself will continue to be seen as useful.

The Solution: a Challenge as Old as Archimedes

When science approaches enigmas in the quantum world, it looks to something suggested by the Greek mathematician Archimedes some 2,300 years ago. The concept carries Archimedes' name, "The Archimedean Point." According to legend, Archimedes claimed he would be able to lift the earth itself if he could find a unique point to stand on and a strong enough lever.

The philosopher Rene Descartes refined Archimedes' principal in his views of certainty, suggesting that a unifying principle is precisely this immovable point. Modern physicists suggest the dynamic quantum worldview allows for such a "one size fits all" universal point of view. Theologians have also used Archimedes' term. When they debate whether pluralism among the world's religions is actually possible, they refer to the Archimedean Point as "God's point of view."

Huw Price suggests that the Archimedean Point is located in the deeper timeless reality of the quantum realm, not within our time-bound reality. This suggests the realm of consciousness and raises the question of what it may be as a quantum reality. It's in this dimension that unity consciousness lies. Just as Sir Roger Penrose noted our everyday consciousness can simultaneously perceive both an alive and dead cat, Brother Teasdale noted that simultaneously holding a traditional and a universal religious view is simply "being rooted but not stuck." Teasdale was convinced, as are all who share the interspiritual experience, that the common realization of all contemplatives and mystics is the unity consciousness in which the other is seen as an aspect of oneself. For interspirituality, this is the Archimedean Point, the unifying principle that makes an Interspiritual Age truly possible.

The Wiener in the Warp Drive

A number of years ago a spoof on the television series Star Trek featured a debacle in which the Starship Enterprise's warp drive—its forward speed toward its ultimate destiny "to go where no other had gone before"—had been compromised by sabotage. When Captain

Kirk inquired of engineer "Snotty" concerning the nature of the malady, he was informed someone had thrown a wiener into the apparatus powering the Lightspeed Drive.

The wiener in the warp drive of today's natural evolution toward higher ethos for our advancing species may well be the world's financial and banking communities. Why this is the case is something most people are unaware of.

For instance, many imagine the Federal Reserve is a branch of the United States government, when in reality it's a syndicate of private banks that prescribe fiscal policy in their own interest. They print money at a cost to us and run a system by which they reap the lion's share of the advantages of controlling the investment industries and setting interest rates. They hope the average citizen doesn't realize that while that paper money may be a large percent less in value several years from now, if one had bought an ingot of silver a decade ago for, say, $2000, it would be worth more than $17,000 today.

Many don't realize that in 1792, less than 20 years after the Declaration of Independence, the first nationwide financial bailout took place at the expense of the American taxpayer. It stemmed from the unethical activity of a group of Washington officials and bankers—the so-called "6% Club"—who, among other things, defrauded the soldiers who had fought our revolutionary war out of the IOUs that had been given for their services and walked away rich. A banking panic ensued, with a crash of the then-fledgling Wall Street markets, and the government stepped in to reimburse the banking and trading houses to keep them afloat—much to the publicly voiced consternation of a few of our founding fathers such as Hamilton, Monroe, Madison, and Jefferson.

From this emerged the precedent that "whoever holds the paper" (in this case the IOUs) gets the payoff, no matter who they might have defrauded in the process. Back then there were no laws. Since then, every time there's been a banking fiasco, due usually to the out-of-control greed of the system, a bailout has resulted, in effect allowing the financial barons to "double dip"—that is, take their fraudulently gained profits and also be reimbursed by the public for their losses. In the 2008 world financial fiasco, the holders of the paper—the banks and other financial houses—got their bailout money and, once again, no one was held accountable for the mortgage market's evident fraudulent activities.

Critics suggest the system is still rigged to explode periodically so the "double dip" can recur as part of the financial ethos of "survival of the fittest." The problem is that "survival of the fittest" isn't even good evolutionary science anymore. If everything in the ecosystem were actually devouring everything else—with no sense of balance, feedback loops, or homeostasis—the entire ecosystem would come crashing down. This is the danger of a financial and business system that falsely believes its activities are insulated from any other aspects of human reality.

From main street to Occupy Wall Street, this characterization is presented with some hyped metaphor, but the general message has been clear to segments of both the right and the left in the United States since the 2008 fiscal meltdown, as amply reflected in public opinion polls. While 97% of Americans believe the financial system should be fair and customer friendly, 61% believe the system is rigged in favor of the wealthy and privileged. Further, 55% believe this inequity endangers the future of the United States and the world.[83]

World Public Opinion organization reported in 2011 that 87% of Americans believe their government is corrupted by financial special interests. A 2011 survey by the Center for American Progress Action Fund and Greenberg Quinlan Rosner Research showed even more startling results: 81% of Americans believe the average American now works harder for less. Some 75% say the system exists to enrich Wall Street and break down the viability of the middle class, while 72% think that only the wealthy are benefiting from the fiscal and political direction of the nation. A 2011 Gallup Survey showed that only 13% of Americans think the financial system of the United States is prudent. According to another Gallup poll, a whopping 87% of Americans believe that 1% of Americans controls 42% of America's wealth.

These views aren't unknown worldwide. The Arab media outlet Aljazeera runs regular stories on the meltdown of Americans'

---

83 Pew, 2011.

confidence in their financial system. European statistics are similar. In 2011, public opinion polls in the United Kingdom's *Daily Mail* indicated some 60% of British citizens consider the financial system rigged, while statistics from the University of Pennsylvania showed that in 14 of the 17 nations in the European Union, more than 50% of their populations believe the financial systems are manipulated to the advantage of just a few. A Google search of news stories concerning what opinion polls show about American negativity toward the financial system brings up over two million entries. With the 2012 LIBOR interest rate manipulation scandal unfolding around the world's fifteen largest banks, it appeared certain that ordinary world citizens would soon learn they have been systematically fleeced by their banks for years.

This problem creates more than just a significant backdrop to the planet's ongoing process of globalization and the context in which significant percentages of world citizens are moving toward a sense of unity consciousness, equanimity, and higher ethical ideals. The profile of a sector of world society bucking the wider worldwide trend fits the clinical definition of cancer, wherein a group of cells in the body attends only to its own needs, inevitably killing the host. This is a quite realistic possibility for our world's future.

All this said, an upwelling literature on economic and financial reform has brought to bear a significant amount of progressive thinking on addressing the potential cancer of a runaway financial and banking industry. Widely read books such as *Sacred Economics, Conscious Capitalism, Conversations with Wall Street, Right Relationship,* and *The Great Turning* have brought to light alternative views of how financial and banking systems might serve the world in more equitable ways.

As one African speaker suggested at a world conference on equitable directions, we must all ask who created the assumptions that have allowed tiny percentages of the world's population to control the financial destiny of everyone else. If we are to renegotiate these assumptions into actual working agreements that not only benefit everyone but ensure an ongoing positive evolution for our planet, we must identify where the fulcrums of power lie.

Let's Not Be Naïve

Although it's helpful, perhaps even an epiphany, to understand the kind of leap required of the human heart and consciousness to build a better world in an Interspiritual Age, we can't be naïve about the realities that daily confront us on the planet. For all the hope we can point to, there's ample counterevidence in the ongoing crises that lack any sense of kindness, fairness, or even good judgment. We are still riding a runaway train.

In the world religions, the natural tension accompanying this challenge is reflected in the recent exchange between His Holiness the Dalai Lama and CNN's religious commentator Dr Stephen Prothero. In a response to an op-ed piece by His Holiness in *The New York Times* suggesting that universal kindness and compassion are the path forward for humanity, Prothero, author of *God Is Not One: The Eight Rival Religions That Run the World—and Why Their Differences Matter*, suggested the Dalai Lama's view is naïve and misconstrued. Recalling the view of the Cognitive Science of Religion (CSR) that spirituality is one experience and religion quite another, and that religion hijacks spirituality to different ends, the predicament for humankind is clear. CSR suggests that religious views—easy for primates to remember and easy for primates to use—may not ever be able to address the critical challenges that face us.

The future is an open question. What come to mind are words attributed to one-armed explorer John Wesley Powell during his first descent along the Grand Canyon's raging Colorado River. There are several versions of the legend, but perhaps this one speaks best to The Great Coming Together: "We have an unknown distance yet to run, an unknown river to explore. What falls there are, we know not; what rocks beset the channel, we know not; what walls rise over the river, we know not. We may conjecture many things, but not put off by vague rumors and senseless feelings, we simply press on."

20

Seeing What's Coming

*"After the game, the king and the
pawn go into the same box"*

Italian Proverb

THE CURRENT GLOBAL LANDSCAPE OF RELIGION AND SPIRITUALITY IS ONLY one of several spheres of human endeavor—science and technology, politics and governance, economics and finance—in which a unity consciousness conversation is occurring. All these realms are complex, but the religious and spiritual landscape is truly intricate.

Further complicating the matter, few of these domains proactively speak to each other, while others are at cross-purposes. This predicament raises the critical question of what it may take for humanity to problem-solve for the future from multiple perspectives. Is it possible that our species will exhaust its ability to problem-solve, thus far so central to our survival?

Even more troubling, if diverse domains of human endeavor are failing to communicate creatively, their momentum is monolithic *precisely* at a time when a veritable host of collective external threats and challenges confronts us. Facing such a predicament, our species could inadvertently be defeated—actually go extinct—as a result of a cosmic slight of hand, an ironic twist of "divide and conquer."

Like the divided Greeks facing Persian invaders 2,500 years ago, our planet's current peril may be met by a number of possible responses. The ideal response would be a shared sense of planetary vision. Another response might be piecemeal, group by group, which would probably not be enough.

An Ever-Evolving Landscape

We recognize today that we live in a developmental world, the heritage of two centuries of modern science. Has the phenomenon of religions on our planet been a static or dynamic affair? Do we see world religions as a contemporary flatland of competing world traditions that are largely inconsequential in terms of the world's future, or is there a dynamic content? When we consider the size and influence of religions worldwide, we will see that we can characterize 22 religions as major, another dozen as sources of world influence, and at least five that operate influentially on a global scale.

It seems to many that the paradigm shift now underway in our species is an inevitable result of evolution itself. If so, the process has been ongoing since the Big Bang some 14.7 billion years ago. For this reason, instead of looking at the world's current religions from a purely horizontal vantage, the modern evolutionary view sees the unfolding of subjective spiritual experience as an ever-expanding and ascending tree—a gradual but steady transformation of human experience into first intelligence, then higher and higher consciousness. In other words, the global awakening occurring presently is the culmination of history, resulting in a transformed planet.

The Yoruba have a saying, "The trees are God's great alphabet." All the world's religions and spiritual traditions can be seen as a single ever-growing and branching tree, ultimately reaching a height and breadth where its leaves—the planetary citizenship—can spread out in the sun. An unknown author long ago wrote, "This tree has seen so many suns rise and set, so many seasons come and go, and so many generations pass into silence, that we may well wonder what 'the story of the tree' would be to us if they had tongues to tell it, or we ears fine enough to understand."

In English there are few if any synonyms for "tree." This attests to the universality of the symbol, whose widespread use isn't accidental. The symbol of the Tree of Life occurs widely in mythology, philosophy, the world's religions, and science. In its metaphorical sense, it's a mystical and iconic image that suggests the interconnectedness of all things. Particularly in science and religion, it plays the role of a logo that depicts common descent (or ascent) in the evolutionary sense.

In mythology this iconic image is also known as the World Tree. In primal cultures that adhere to the principle "as above, so below," the tree connects the heavens to the underworld. In most indigenous societies, the mystically powered drum of the shaman is cut from the wood of a tree. In religions, the tree is central to cosmological stories of all five continents and is detailed in the cultures of New Zealand's Maoris, Africa's Yoruba, the Maya of Latin America, the Persians and Judeans of the Middle East, the Hindus and Buddhists of the Far East, together with the Slavs, Norse, Druids, and Celts of Europe, not to forget the indigenous tribes of North America. In many of these traditions it stands in the center of the world garden, symbolizing the arising of all things, most particularly humankind, and the culmination of all these things in the future. Thus in the Judeo-Christian scriptures the Tree of Life appears at the beginning in Genesis and at the end in the Revelation of St John.

In Hinduism the World Tree (depicted as the sacred Banyon, in which a single tree can encompass an entire forest with its expansive roots and branches) is rooted in the heavens but finds its fruition on earth. In Buddhism the World Tree is the cosmogenic tree, variously referred to as the Awakening Tree, Tree of Ambrosia, the Wise, or Perfection. It symbolizes the reaching to the heavens of the Buddha himself, whose enlightenment is said to have occurred at the foot of a Bodhi tree. In Christianity Jesus springs from "the root of Jesse" and consummates his ultimate legacy on a tree.

The tree icon is central to all the heroic stories of mythology. It signifies a rite of passage from primal to eternal, initiation to ultimate transformation. There is universal significance to the hero in the various mythologies. As Jesus is portrayed as the original logos made flesh,

Buddhist cosmology sees the birth of the Buddha and the birth of the universal root of transformation as synonymous. The icon is also seen as denoting spiritual practice itself, as hero or heroine sets out in quest of the World Tree or Sacred Mountain and ultimately achieves alignment with all that's universal and eternal. Sociologist and theologian Mircea Eliade referred to these common stories as "The Myth of Eternal Return."

In science the tree is just as central. It appears in the branching diagrams of developmental change, depicting both the arising of forms and functions *and* the collective ascent from shared ancestors reaching back at least 3 billion years. A global scientific attempt to record the actual evolutionary relationships of all living things is named The Tree of Life Project.

This coherence of the symbolism of the Tree of Life in world religions is astonishing. In all, the tree icon appears in over 30 specific ancient cultural legends. Common to all of these is the universal motif of mutually interdependent and interconnected growth, coupled with the centrality of humankind as the ultimate fruit of the tree itself. Its branches interweave and attend each other. Humanity not only honors but also nurses the tree. In some legends the tree further signifies the ongoing arising of civilizations, suggesting a coherence to history of ongoing advancement and betterment.

Tree legends also depict religion's understanding of humankind's knowledge of good and evil, together with the relationship of mortality and immortality, heaven and hell. Legends of the Tree of the Knowledge of Good and Evil originated later than the more central accounts of the Tree of Life. This likely reflects the need of the totalitarian regimes (from 3000 BCE) to strictly enforce their social structures. It was during this period of political need for social suppression that religious institutions also emphasized and further elaborated the fear-based narratives of heaven and hell. In some traditions the meaning of Tree of Life and Tree of the Knowledge of Good and Evil becomes somewhat blurred during this era.

The promise of ultimate transformation remains central, since the Tree of Life stories not only predate those of good and evil but also represent the spiritual high ground. In some of these stories, the leaves of the World Tree depict both people and coins, representing humanity as ultimate value, and the spreading of the leaves to the sun signifies the highest consciousness or enlightenment.

In Christianity the tree symbolizes at once the resurrection and ascension story, and in the Book of Revelation the final unity of the nations. In the ancient texts of India, the Upanishads, the cosmic tree Asvattha symbolizes the living universe itself as an aspect of Brahman. The action of the tree reverses the usual order of human limitations, allowing the transformation of humankind, which is the central shared message of all these narratives. At the core of the Messianic story, the Christ is the Tree of Life—humankind imagined at the beginning as the child of God, reclaimed as the fulfillment of history. Lakota Chief Crazy Horse envisioned the same end, asserting that in a divine recognition of each other, humans would live as one.

The narratives depict how world religions and spirituality see themselves as an indispensable part of humankind's destiny. Perhaps most poignantly, in the medieval mystical schools it was understood that the roots, trunk, and branches of the tree represent human knowing, while its leaves symbolize the immediate application of this knowledge to everyday life. It's as if the knowledge of our species' ability to problem-solve by linking cause and effect is embedded in the deepest reservoirs of our shared mythological heritage.

Although these synchronicities between the World Tree and Tree of Life across all the world's religions have been known for some time, it has taken the challenges of a globalizing world and an emerging interspirituality to compel us to inquire about their implications. If so many world religions are based on understanding of these myths of eternal return, what pathways are available to these religions to shed the exclusivity and reactivity that characterize so much of their political posturing in the world today?

Our common mythologies invite us to think of the world's religions and spiritual traditions as a single yet diverse experience of our entire species' history of asking and answering the perennial questions of who we are, where we came from, and where we're going. They also suggest it isn't only a shared heritage but a collective interior reservoir of wisdom from which we might successfully approach what appears to be a precarious future.

Brother Teasdale addressed the nature of the shift that would be necessary for religion and spirituality to become an evolutionary asset for our species instead of a reactive liability:

> We need to understand, to really grasp at an elemental level, that the definitive revolution is the spiritual awakening of humankind. The necessary shifts in consciousness require a new approach to spirituality that transcends past religious cultures of fragmentation and isolation. The paths are many but the goal is the same. The direct experience of interspirituality paves the way for a universal law of mysticism—that is the common heart of the world. It is difficult to predict the precise shape of this forthcoming breakthrough, but I think it will…. [be] a subtle refinement of what they [the Great Wisdom Traditions] have known.[84]

The Ascending Tree of World Religions

If you were asked to think of our planet's variety of plants, animals, nations, and cultures, would you think of just the animals and plants, nations and cultures that exist on the planet right now? Or would you think of all the animals and plants, nations and cultures that have come and gone? Polls show that most people (75%) will think of just our current world, not in the context of a longer history.[85]

The first is a horizontal view, a flatland. The second is a vertical view, dynamic, developmental, evolving, including every participant from time immemorial. This is the iconic World Tree, the Tree of Life in all our heritages, and is the motif we will use in delving into the world's traditions to discover their universal message.

A tree of world religions traces our species' subjective experience—its

[84] MH, p 12, 47, 79.
[85] University of Maryland, 2002.

inner raw feel. It's what we see when we view the world's religions in the vertical perspective of time. Branches reflect the East, the West, the North, and the South—as well as the old and the new. Every branch, no matter how large or where placed, has relevance to the entire tree. There are complex interactions among interwoven limbs, crossing over and crossing back. The branches reach ever upward and outward, spreading more and more leaflets in the sun—countless experiences, practices, and methods. The entire tree at once displays the freshest leaves—these first moments in our new millennium—*and* the legacy represented in the age of the tree.

Brother Teasdale himself utilized the image of a tree, writing at length of the efficacy of this natural iconography for comprehending both the spiritual and material dimensions of our reality. For Teasdale the tree was a theophany—a revelation of the divine—whether the Tree of Life story in creation accounts, the special place of trees in indigenous narratives, or the tree-symboled meditations of iconic monastic Saint Bernard of Clairvaux on the intertwined mystery of our divine nature.

Citing his love of such natural iconography in the language of his colleague eco-theologian Father Thomas Berry, Teasdale also coined his categories within interspirituality from the biological terms for forests—particularly apt, since the same mixing and crossing over is universal in the plant world. The mixing and hybridizing that Teasdale attributed to the histories of so many religions is known in science as "reticulate evolution." The word "reticulate" means weblike.

The world's religions have also developed in each other's company. In science such interactive sharing in co-development is called "co-evolution," a term that delineates an entire branch of science. In line with this, Teasdale observed that the interdependent relationships of the world's religions are both subtle and also fundamental.

In visualizing this tree, the base is a single large trunk. What does this represent? There are two aspects to the symbolism.

First, every religion had an origin, usually in a compelling individual who had a spiritual experience and shared it with others. If others found the narrative compelling, a tradition began to emerge, expanding like the branches of a tree. If circumstances didn't smile on a particular tradition, its growth became stunted or even truncated. In what science refers to as the "operational view," which is simply observing what actually happens, we aren't concerned with what might or might not be true in any particular tradition. Our interest is solely in observing how the tradition operates.

Second, the tree is planted in the earth. Not only did most religions originate from an individual sharing a compelling narrative, but virtually all of the ancient religions began as an indigenous experience of early peoples—a clan or tribe—in a particular landscape, usually with a close relationship between the people and the land that nourished them. Life was simple in such primal contexts: it was about survival, which in terms of both nourishment and healing depended entirely on their relationship with nature.

Brother Teasdale points out that nearly all the world's major religions started out as indigenous religions "somewhere, somewhen." There are still thousands of these indigenous religions on the planet. Some of them, over time, complexified with the development of their peoples and cultures.

World Religions by Popularity

Again without reference to what may be true or not, but taking into account that most faiths are based on some kind of sacred text, we can also trace the operational success of various traditions according to whether their religious narratives were at some time or other a "bestseller." We should bear in mind that many of the more ancient traditions were spoken, not written, which means we only have secondary accounts of their beliefs.

An estimated 600 works are considered by the currently existing world religions to be sacred texts.[86] These include texts attributed to some of the world's early religions. The diversity of these texts and their origins is astounding, dating in some form of publication from about 8000 BCE

---

[86] New York Public Library and *Encyclopedia Britannica*.

in both the Middle East and China, and being published in some form or another from about 2500 BCE. Currently about 50 "official" explanations are recognized by the 22 most prominent world religions. Looking beyond these traditions, there are about 90 sacred texts from the Asian region, 140 official statements of beliefs across Christianity, another 84 official statements or texts from the Middle Eastern regions (67 from Persia alone), and 63 from outside the Middle East.

Sacred Texts of Major World Religions

Generally: 47 "official" published explanations for the core 22 current major world religions (74 if broken down into subcategories within those religions)

Specifically: including and exceeding the 22 current major world regions

"Eastern" Religions as defined by Asian Region:	92 foundational sacred texts [NYPL]
Christianity:	140 foundational sacred texts for Christianity
Judaism:	10 foundational sacred texts
Other Regional Middle Eastern Religions:	84 foundational sacred texts, 67 for Persia alone
Regional Religions Outside the Middle East:	63 foundational sacred texts
Indigenous Religions:	7,000 worldwide indigenous religious narratives
Africa:	3,000 tribes, 20 major sacred texts
America:	3,000 tribes (1000 North America, 2000 Latin America), 100 major modern texts explaining these religions
Oceania:	1,000 tribes (700 in New Guinea alone), 20 major modern texts explaining these religions
New Age Religions:	5 foundational texts
Spiritism:	7 foundational texts
New Religions of the Last Decades:	6 foundational texts

Sources: *Encyclopedia Britannica* and New York Public Library [NYPL]

Rolling in the indigenous traditions, there are some 7,000 tribes—3,000 in Africa, 3,000 in America (1,000 in North America and 2,000 in Latin America), and 1,000 in Oceania. Some of these traditions didn't originally have sacred texts, but the number of authoritative texts that explain the beliefs of such traditions numbers, respectively, 20, 100, and 20. There are also about a half dozen foundational texts for New Age religions, seven for spiritism, and another six that represent new religions of the last decades.

Were we to make such a measurement today we would find the books that represent the world's major religions are our bestsellers, read literally by millions. Moreover, religious books have a major impact on world opinion. If we Google religious books, some 225 million entries are to be found, along with 26 million entries for religious book publishers. If we Google for sacred texts, some 6 million entries come up.

People read religious material for different reasons. Historically, many religious books were required reading—for instance, for children and youngsters growing up in any of the world's traditions. Others are popular among individuals who newly discover and identify with a tradition, or who read of a varied path of exploring diverse spiritual practices. Some religions have been forced on people through war or slavery. Even today those religions that control political systems ban the books of competing traditions.

If you walk into a bookstore in New York City you'll readily find a Bible as well as the Koran. You might have to look further to find the Tao Te Ching or the Tibetan Book of the Dead, and you might be really hard pressed to find a book of Mayan or Aztec scriptures. Would a bookstore in Hays, Kansas, or Tijuana, Mexico, offer up these same choices with equal availability? It's doubtful. What about the complete teachings of Zoroaster? Not so easy—and yet, at the time of Alexander the Great this was *the* planetary bestseller, Zoroastrianism being the global religion of the time, encompassing the known Mediterranean world. What of Quechnian scriptures? Probably not heard of.

Religions by What They Do

There are two basic ways in which religion has traditionally been done. These form major parts of our tree of the world's religions: those that have lived out beliefs in cosmic narratives of origins and destinies with their cast of characters; and others that seem to have simply explored consciousness, seeking what it is and how it works. The religions with magic-mythic scenarios—casts of celestial characters, prophets, messiahs, and end-time scenarios—are known as "revealed religions." Those that tend to explore consciousness we will simply call "consciousness religions."

In revealed religions, someone reported experiencing a celestial messenger—an angel, a prophet, ascended masters, or even God in person, who revealed a message, often leading to the writing of a sacred text that's understood as given from on high instead of as the product of a subjective experience or cultural influence. Another characteristic of revealed religions is their end-time scenarios, often involving apocalyptic stories about how the world will end. Most revealed religions are included by academics among the "theistic" religions, referring to the fact that they believe in a God.

Religions that simply explore consciousness are most common today in the East and often have historical (but not necessarily sacred) texts that aren't necessarily theistic. "God" may not be part of their message. Some feature various personifications of behavior or aspiration that have become represented in their lore as "gods," especially within their cultural trappings as organized religions. Though some of their ancient narratives are portrayed through the magic-mythic lens, usually the narrative is less about the "gods" than the qualities they represent or personify. Most of these religions don't have a celestial cast of characters and rarely include end-time scenarios.

Exploring the Branches

There is a Cherokee saying, "Between every tree is a new world." If we combine our perspective on the world's religious and spiritual traditions as an ever-growing tree with the fact that the stories and narratives of the tree's diverse branches have been variously popular with assorted people at different times, we get a sense of the grand panorama of our species' collective religious experience.

Because of our arising consciousness and its developing capacity to project ideas and visions, as well as tell stories, these early experiences were also allied with an experience of spirit realms. This is why we must acknowledge not only the vast diversity of nature-based religions, but also the legacy they bequeathed to all religions in terms of our collective sense of spirit and the spirit realms.

Those religions that are still close to their sense of the spirit realms are called by modern students of religion "animist" traditions. This term is most often associated with indigenous or nature-based religions and, as in the word "animated," refers to the intimacy such traditions have with their narrative's celestial cast of characters. In an animist experience, nearly every circumstance is seen to have special meaning, especially in relation to the spirit realms—from whether you walked left instead of right in the forest, missed a shot while hunting, or got on the wrong bus while travelling to the market. Such primal experiences date from the Archaic and Magic-Animist eras, between 100,000 and 50,000 years ago.

With this in mind, we can immediately acknowledge a huge branch coming off the base of our tree that consists of indigenous or native traditions—the "animist" or spirit world-oriented religions. There are some 7,000 worldwide today, and probably at least 55,000 historically.[87] As some of these traditions complexified, sometimes on a relatively local scale and at other times spreading even to empires, they became the first massive sub-trunks of our tree.

Another heritage comes from our indigenous experience. Humankind's mystical nature infuses every aspect of our tree, from the most primal to modern day religions. The specific energy-related experiences so strongly identified with our indigenous heritage are alive and well today in everything from energy-based healing traditions and magical

---

[87] According to people who try to project such numbers, for instance the *Encyclopedia Britannica*.

traditions (yes, even "black" or "white") to recognized medical modalities such as acupuncture, reiki, shiatsu, polarity therapy, therapeutic touch, and biofield energy therapy. Under the banners of complementary or alternative medicine, energy medicine, energy therapy, and energy healing, such modalities are well known and widely utilized throughout the world, having enjoyed a particular resurgence during our current integrative and holistic era, and are advanced enough today to distinguish between "veritable" and "putative" kinds of therapies. The former are based on scientifically verified forms of energy, the latter on hypothetical or speculative forms. The survival into modern times of such ancient and geographically diverse insight concerning our bodies, our nature, and our surrounding environment testifies to the convergence of history underpinning the emerging Interspiritual Age.

Just like extinct animals and plants, or countries and nations, most religions that have existed no longer exist. So at the base of our tree of world religions are not only the primeval indigenous traditions, but also the branches of religions now extinct. It behooves us to consider the peoples in their millions who died fighting for these religions that are now long gone. We might think in terms of "love's labors lost," especially when the views of some of these ancient religions today seem silly if not ridiculous. Yet people warred and died for these arcane worldviews.

Along with religions, deities have also come and gone—at least 2,500 major ones according to a recent *Encyclopedia of Gods*. These are just the big ones, the subjects of bestselling religions through time. Indigenous traditions and what are often called "primal traditions"— the early oral traditions prefiguring many of the world's religions—add thousands to this roster.

The Biggest Boughs

"To whom much is given, much will be required," Jesus tells us in Luke 12:48. The core of our tree of world religions has several major appendages, nearly all of which originated in the Axial Age. From these Axial religions, which form the axes of entire world cultures today, diversified the core religions of our planet. If we looked at size and current geographic influence of these alone, we might choose ten or twelve with major current or historical influence, further identifying five that are unquestionably large and influential, each transcontinental in scope. Interestingly, five are recognized whether named by geographic region of origin—China, India, Persia, Judea, and Greece—or by current names of religions that in the broadest of senses inculcate those heritages: Hinduism, Buddhism, Judaism, Christianity, and Islam.

22 Core World Religions

Christianity:	2.1 billion persons
Islam:	1.5 billion
Hinduism:	900 million
Chinese traditional religion	394 million
Buddhism	376 million
Native-indigenous	300 million
African traditional & diasporic	100 million
Sikhism	23 million
Juche	19 million
Spiritism	15 million
Judaism	14 million
Baha'i	7 million
Jainism	4.2 million
Shinto	4 million
Cao Dai	4 million
Zoroastrianism	2.6 million
Tenrikyo	2 million
Neo-paganism	1 million
Unitarian-Universalism	800,000
Rastafarianism	600,000
Scientology	500,000
Secular/Nonreligious/ Agnostic/Atheist	1.1 billion[88]

---

[88] Barrett's Religious Statistics (used by *Encyclopedia Britannica* and *World Christian Encyclopedia*) latest edition, 2001.

The Big Twelve Major Religions

Indigenous traditions, Baha'i, Zoroastrianism, Sikhism, Islam, Jainism, Judaism, Taoism, Shinto, Christianity, Buddhism, Hinduism[89]

The Global Big Five

These are often called the "Axial" religions—religions that are transcontinental and the axis of entire world cultures, listed by broadest definition and chronology: Hinduism, Buddhism, Judaism, Christianity, Islam.

Sources that elaborate the world's axial religions *and* philosophies often also include Greek philosophy as axial because of its nearly inseparable relationship with how Western revealed religions have understood their heritages. Modern interspiritual writers have pointed out that, in today's integrative and holistic epoch, the same is true for the relationship of Eastern philosophy to global understanding of all the world's traditions, especially the understanding of their mystical core.

---

[89] *The Major World Religions* (most influential classic religions, listed here in order of their *internal* diversity, from least to most), New York Public Library 2011.

21

How Religions Operate Today

"There are many paths to the treetop but the view is always the same"

Perennial aphorism

EACH OF THE WORLD'S AXIAL RELIGIONS AROSE WITHIN THE BEHAVIOR patterns of the ancient totalitarian epoch, representing the movement of human consciousness and heart within the still oppressive contexts of those nearly 40 centuries of tyranny. Their magic-mythic lens then evolved into the subsequent Rational Age, and it's this mix of the magic-mythic and the rational that's poised to attempt integration in the current integrative and holistic age. The question is whether they can outgrow the behavior typifying their origin and move into an integrative and holistic relationship that's supportive of the planet. To do so, world religions will have to avoid the fate predicted by the Cognitive Science of Religion—that because of the human "monkey mind," religious exclusivity will ultimately hijack deeper spiritual understanding.

Despite this prediction, expanding consciousness could instead embrace the simple truth proposed by physicist Sir Roger Penrose—that just as the human mind can comprehend the seemingly contradictory truths of the quantum reality, it could grow to simultaneously grasp the seeming contradiction of religious pluralism. Brother Teasdale was sure it could, which is the quintessence of his "interspirituality," along with his awareness that such awakening characterizes the contemplative core of every religious tradition on earth.

This convergence is possible not only because of inevitable globalization, but also because all five major religions—and indeed the wider 22 core religions—share the Archimedean points that could unite them. These points include:

- Their common mystical core—experiential unity consciousness

- Universal ethical teachings and behavior aspirations

- Mutual commitment to the self-evident truths of economic and social justice.

The ultimate potential of these points remains in question, which was the conundrum that ended up dividing the early explorers of this conversation—the Western post-Vatican II foundationalist theologians. When that debate was later admonished by the Vatican, some nevertheless continued the dialogue. These included the mystics Thomas Merton and Raimon Pannikkar, together with the liberation thinker Harvey Cox. It was the *experiential* position of the mystics that seeded the later eruption of the world's interspiritual conversation.

The structure of revealed religions tends to be archetypal, a fact that's mirrored in the most recently revealed religions. An example is the Latter Day Saints with their *Book of Mormon*, which they believe to have been revealed to their prophet Joseph Smith principally via the angel Moroni. Unification and its *Divine Principle* was similarly revealed through the Rev. Sun Myung Moon. We can also cite Scientology with its book *Dianetics*, which was revealed through its founder L. Ron Hubbard.

Each of these religions includes either elements of the standard Western lexicon of heavenly characters or their own unique

magic-mythic versions. The similarity of the mythological personages and elements contained across all revealed religions, no matter how ancient or recent, has caused scholars to suggest that subtle
cross-influences, primal and archetypal notions, and universal story
elements somehow pervade the deepest reaches of even our current
human psyche. It's either that or, if these religions have all been actually revealed from heavenly sources, heaven is quite diverse either in
its views or in its active messengers. Another possibility, typifying the
history of conflict among religions, would be that only one revealed
religion is true and the rest are false. Interestingly, the former two
views would be quite acceptable to interspirituality, whereas the latter
is the pathology that interspirituality is trying to address. Nonetheless,
revealed religions still share the same mystic core and mystic traditions
as all the world religions: a profound testimony to the oneness of our
human experience.

In contrast, consciousness religions can be practiced without any
reference to a theistic framework. This doesn't mean revealed religions
don't also have a mystic core and mystic traditions. Consciousness religions may also feature celestial characters in their ancient sacred narratives, though usually these are considered mythological. Because of
this, consciousness religions seldom have end-time scenarios.

In characterizing Buddhism and Hinduism in this way, we do so
sensu lato, a Latin buzzword meaning "in the largest sense." This is
because Buddhism and Hinduism include myriad historical sub-tra-
ditions. As noted earlier, Hinduism is the most internally diverse religion in the world with Buddhism a close second.

Sociologically, one of the advantages of consciousness religions
is they are less fixated on the question of who's ultimately right in
terms of theologies and creeds. Except in situations tied to cultural or
nationalistic identities, seldom do terrorists act in the name of consciousness religions.

An insightful reader may have already recognized the natural
complementarity—a yin and yang, so to speak—of revealed and consciousness religions. Both views are important, especially in light of
our historical tree. Historian Arnold Toynbee deemed the mutual

understanding of these two great spiritual paths as one of the most crucial thresholds our species must cross on its long journey. Teasdale said this view of Toynbee led, in great part, to his own exploration and definition of interspirituality.

A great Middle Eastern thinker, Seyyed Hossein Nasr, also emphasizes this in an important but little known book *Knowledge of the Sacred.* His work is another example of how the Eastern predisposition toward inherent unity would eventually be discovered by the Western developmentalists.

Theologian Stephen Prothero's popular 2011 book *God is Not One* singled out eight religions that are competing for control of our world and worldview, stressing *why their differences matter* by choosing precisely these words for his subtitle. The book raises the question of what the driving vector will be for the coming decades. Will it be the kindness, love, understanding, and equanimity predicted by interspirituality? Or will it be the reactivity we see in so much religious behavior? Prothero characterizes this predilection in the phrase of his subtitle *The Eight Religions that Rule the World.*

Prothero and His Holiness the Dalai Lama have themselves faced off on the level of evolutionary development possible for our species. The Dalai Lama has maintained that the route of kindness and compassion can transform our world. Writing in *The New York Times,* while not looking down on kindness and compassion, Prothero has considered the Dalai Lama's view unrealistic, even naïve. The same uncertainty is echoed in environmentalist Paul Hawken's declaration to the effect that if one still has hope for the human race, one hasn't seen the data; but if one doesn't have hope, one doesn't have a heart.

To the question of what may happen to the world at the hands of religion and spirituality can be added the other standard extinction scenarios: competition based on national or ethnic identities, and environmental degradation. These are long-term trends. Another serious and perhaps more acute trend is the behavior of the world's financial powers. A culture seemingly devoid of any sense of collective value or responsibility, they appear to condone or even advocate a survival of the fittest ethos taken from antiquated 19th century views of Darwinism. The banking and financial houses nearly crashed the world's economies in 2008 and very well may do so in the future.

The Top World Religions by Wealth

Nearly all world religions at the global level operate through multiple national and fiscal jurisdictions. For such global institutions, the number of jurisdictions could exceed 100, and the number of religious-based financial corporations could well exceed 1,000. Many of these jurisdictions are subject to laws that separate church and state. So, how are categories defined to measure the financial influence of religions worldwide?

If we're talking about the wealth of individuals in various religions, data from several sources in the West indicates the top three are Judaism, Catholicism, and Protestantism, in that order. However, such raw statistics are misleading. A detailed 2010 *New York Times* survey by columnist George Blow showed that the wealthiest nations are more nonreligious. Religious nations, especially religious states as in some Islamic theocracies, generate tremendous wealth. However, they may show high per capita incomes but wealth distribution is quite rich-poor. Some 25 countries show the most religiosity *and* the generally poorest wealth distribution. These nations are most often aligned with the big five global religions, indicating that rich-poor disjunctions are most common among the adherents of these religions. This startling fact may point to the relative ethical results of religion versus spirituality.

The United States is an interesting exception because of its religious diversity, particularly its independent protestant sects and alternative religions. However, high religiosity and more diverse wealth distribution are misleading. Though the nation has a strong middle class compared to much of the world, opulence is concentrated in a tiny percentage. High religiosity and better wealth distribution also characterize a few of the more secularized Catholic nations such as Italy, Greece, and Ireland. The same demographic is true of Israel. Interestingly, Russia (which might be considered a global superpower by military might) is found among the nations that show both low religiosity, low general wealth, and dominance of a rich-poor culture.

A 2012 study in *The Economist* showed similar results but factored in additional variables not necessarily tied just to religion, such as cycles of political unrest and degrees of industrialization. Long-term stability and national economic planning can change religious-based demographics substantially. Switzerland and South Korea are exemplary cases of per capita financial wellbeing. Both countries also have generally high but diverse religiosity. Singapore stands out in wealth—number one per capita in the world—as well as being religiously diverse, with Buddhism the most dominant, and Islam most prevalent in the Malay peninsula.

How does one define the parameters for gathering data on the financial wealth of religious institutions on a global scale, especially state-based religions? Though there are numerous studies of particular jurisdictions, the only numbers ventured about total assets appear at Yahoo Answers and seem to be divisible into three classes: multibillions (upward to and exceeding $100 billion), tens of billions ($10–50 billion), and multimillions (upward to 1 billion).

Of several studies pursuing this kind of data, all agree that the richest in the West is the Roman Catholic Church. However, it cannot be defined simply as the Vatican. The latter operates as a nominally independent state of which the Vatican Bank (or Istituto per le Opere di Religione) is only one institution across many jurisdictions. Estimates of the total assets of the Roman Catholic Church reach into the multibillions (although a good deal of that value is in art, real estate, and stock or commodity investments).

Also mentioned as significantly rich are the Anglican (Church of England) and Mormon communities, both with tens of billions. Similar studies show those two communities readily tied or exceeded by grand totals from televangelism and evangelical Christian megachurches. Various self-help gurus and even Free Masonry are also reported to be worth multimillions. Data from the East is more rare, although one Hindu community in Kerala, India, is estimated to be worth tens of billions, while numerous other Hindu communities are reported to have multimillions.[90]

Evaluation of the Arab and Persian oil states and their relations to state-related religious institutions is also enigmatic. Helpful is a 2011 study by *The Banker* of Islamic financial institutions subject to Islamic religious law (Sharia). There are over 500 of these in 47 nations, and a number are state based. Total assets subject to Sharia law are estimated at about 500 billion dollars. The order of these by country includes Iran, Saudi Arabia, Malaysia, Kuwait, United Arab Emirates, Bahrain, and Dubai. This figure represents only 7% of estimated total secular world banker assets.

In sum, the influence of religions worldwide comes from numerous diverse and complex vectors—historic, cultural, political, and financial. This, and the fact that 6.1 billion world citizens report a religious worldview, indicates the role of religions in the future of globalization is crucial. However, the variables involved in its ultimate effect are complex—a fact that highlights the importance of clarifying the general message of an emerging Interspiritual Age. This message would be spiritual, not just religious—a harkening back, as Brother Teasdale said, to the shared heart and love-related experiences of spirituality. This is the only route out of the choking boundaries of exclusivist religious custom.

Today's Challenge: the Tangled Web at the Top of the Tree

Four days before his assassination by American soldiers, Chief Crazy Horse of the Lakota was at a pipe ceremony with the legendary Lakota Chief Sitting Bull. Crazy Horse first advised that he had never fought an American soldier except in self-defense, and since the Indian defeat of the U.S. 7th Cavalry in 1876 had tried to live in peace but had been constantly dogged by the white man. It was said that he then remarked, "I see a time of Seven Generations when all the colors

---

[90] Nearly all of the above studies have been conducted by various world financial magazines or financial survey groups.

of mankind will gather under the Sacred Tree of Life and the whole Earth will become one circle again. I salute the light within your eyes where the whole Universe dwells. For when you are at that center within you and I am at that place within me, we shall be one." These words, coupled with Chief Crazy Horse's murder four days later, raise the paradox of the process of civilization.

It was said by the Mohawk Chief Thayendanegea, "In the government you call civilized, the happiness of the people is constantly sacrificed to the splendor of the empire. Hence the origin of your codes of criminal and civil laws; your dungeons and prisons. We have no prisons; no pompous parade of courts. We have among us no exalted villains above the control of laws. Daring wickedness is never allowed to triumph over helpless innocence. The estates of widows and orphans are never devoured by enterprising swindlers. We have no robbery under the pretext of law."

These two accounts portray the stark difference in values among the theatres of influence vying for control of our planet as we have entered this new millennium.

At the top of our Tree of the World Religions is a tangled web of beliefs, creeds, and end-time scenarios. As we ascend near the tree-top, we also see the two great boughs—one mostly West, one mostly East. They represent the two still primal kinds of religions—those that explore consciousness and those that believe they have a reality-binding revealed narrative. This was the divide that fascinated historian Arnold Toynbee when he called Brother Teasdale to join others already pioneering the uniting of East and West.

Among these many others were Father Bede Griffiths in Shantivanum, India, Father Thomas Keating of the Snowmass Inter-religious Initiatives, His Holiness the Dalai Lama, and Ken Wilber and the integral pioneers. Teasdale made this exploration the subject of his widely read books, and the vision of Father Bede his doctoral dissertation and further elaboration of interspirituality. The Dalai Lama, Wilber, and Bede wrote the forewords or prefaces—and this was just as the new millennium dawned.

Brother Teasdale envisioned the unity consciousness experience as the pivotal common ground. However, he didn't expect this experience to happen for everyone, but sensed it is an overall direction the entire species is taking as consciousness continues to become more spacious and the species gains more skill sets to accompany its expanding awareness.

Thus our tree incorporated major new branches as its boughs extended into the 19th and 20th centuries, foreshadowing the integrative and Interspiritual Age. These included:

- Attempts, no matter how idiosyncratic, at understanding science and religion together—from the theosophy, humanism, and new thought movements of the 19th century to the more recently and soundly scientific fusions of the 20th century, involving both spiritual thinkers and scientists. Such attempts encompassed evolutionary consciousness, Integral and Spiral Dynamics, global scaling, science/wisdom and sacred geometry/myth synergies, the implications of quantum, string and cosmological theory, changes in scientific philosophy and metaphysics, morphogenetics, and research on non-normal phenomena

- Ecumenism, interfaith movements, the founding of interfaith seminaries, the debates of the foundationalist theologians after Vatican II and the emergence of crossover syntheses such as those pioneered with Christianity and Buddhism by Thomas Merton and others, Christianity and Hinduism by Bede Griffiths and Brother Teadsale and others, the rising prominence of Sufi mysticism in global Islam, attempts at reconciling the central tradition of the Abrahamic faiths (Judaism, Christianity, and Islam), the interreligious Snowmass Initiatives and Inter-Monastic movements, Centering Prayer, Interspiritual Meditation, and other clearly cosmopolitan attempts at understanding the common wisdom core of world religions

- Emergence of new and more holistic religions, no matter how idiosyncratic, melding the magic mythic with the modern: the New Age movement, A Course in Miracles, Scientology, the new spiritism, the new Shamanic movements, the new God, Goddess, and Ascended Master teachings, the Energy-work disciplines, and the understanding of Integral as an emerging ministry.

The core trend in all 4,000 or more modern religious paths involves this manifesting of unity consciousness.

The tragedy is that brilliant works bridging the divide, from the foundationalist theologians to classics of East-West religious like Raimon Panikkar's *Christophany* and others from Aurobindo, Griffiths, Teilhard, Abhishiktananda, Nasr, Fox, Needleman, and so on, aren't widely known to the public. What better news would there be were the unnecessary divisions and divides among so many aspects of the world religions exposed as such to the wider public. Through the eyes of individuals like these just mentioned, each comprehensively understanding all the traditions, the differences are seen simply as illusions. The average person is well capable of understanding this, particularly through the eyes of the heart and unconditional love—again, core teaching of all the traditions.

This shared ethic of love, kindness, selfless service, and equanimity forms another of the great Archimedean points of the world religions. It is central to all the ethical writings of the Great Traditions, and particularly principal to the historical reform and revival movements that have characterized all the traditions. When forgotten by the traditions themselves, or made subservient by political or financial pathology, it has sprung up in independent movements. Humanism is perhaps the best example—the legacy of Ethical Culture and other humanist movements, which declared that this shared ethos was in fact the core of religious experience itself: deed over creed.

From Einstein to Schweitzer, the number of social heroes who have embraced and emanated from such movements is huge indeed. This sense of shared ethos spawned the liberation theologies in the turbulent times of social and political change that typified the birth of the Integrative Age in the 1970s. The unifying principle generally acknowledged as the fourth Archimedean point of the world's religions—the shared commitment to social and economic justice—is rooted in that era.

However, it is the unifying principal of the shared mystical core within all religious experience that appears key. It is a spirituality deeply rooted in the heart experience of oneness, accompanied by the conviction that any creed, belief, background, history, or other factor that could cause separation between human beings is secondary, if not irrelevant.

Before their admonishment by the Vatican, the foundationalist theologians were in a quandary about whether any of these unifying points could actually serve a global transformation for our species. All were acknowledged as real and promising, but none at the level of potential of the last one. If indeed the direction of our brain-mind evolution is toward the nondual—toward the natural understanding of profound interconnectedness and all that awareness implies—this potential may well be lifted out of the realm of spiritual hope or speculation into the palpable realm of the obviously true.

22

Embracing the
Tree as One

*"The message of love that is in the trees
is the whole leaf and our root tribe"*

Umatilla Saying

INTERSPIRITUALITY IS ALREADY HAPPENING. ACROSS THE TOP OF OUR TREE, the phenomenon of unity consciousness has happened and continues to happen in every spiritual and religious tradition—yes, even subjective modes of inquiry that might not identify themselves as religious or spiritual. The sense of profound interconnectedness, of the lack of real separation in any aspect of reality, and of all "others" as inextricably a part of ourselves, is universal. It's the implications of this that have to be emphasized as we push into the current holistic age.

In the now popular trans-traditional experience, individuals recognize, value, utilize, and even cherish practices, insights, and teachings from not just a single tradition, but two, three, and often more. The mixing of yogic practice among other religious activities worldwide is an example. In America alone, 30 million people utilize yoga along with their regular religious practice, most often Christianity or Judaism. Millions of others enjoy practices rooted in Shamanic traditions—be it energy work, vision quest, or journeying. Mixing the Eastern religions with Christian practice is also popular. Books on Eastern spirituality sell by the millions in the West. Fritjaf Capra's *Tao of Physics* saw the first edition of 20,000 copies sell out in less than a year, and it's now in 43 editions involving 23 languages. From such trans-traditional experience, people not only come to savor all the traditions but, sooner or later, many consider them indispensable.

The deeper movement of this experience is a profound understanding in the substrate of heart and consciousness that indeed this is *one* experience. This is true interspirituality. Because this is so comprehensive in connectedness, it's close to the phenomenon the perennial traditions have called "awakening"—the ultimate recognition of non-separateness or oneness.

Awakening: the Shared Heritage of Unity Consciousness

If we brush across the top of our tree of the world's religions, a major feature of every tradition is the common mystical experience of unity consciousness. At its core, this is a life-changing understanding of inter-connectedness that results in a person truly seeing all "others" as aspects of oneself. Recognizing there isn't an individual identity—what is conventionally called the "ego"—to protect is an unparalleled experience of freedom that creates unusually energetic and dynamic personalities.

This state of consciousness is spoken about in almost every living spiritual tradition, as well as in many of those no longer active, and also recognized by philosophy and psychology as the "nondual experience." Most simply, it's the circumstance in which discrete identities become blurred or even experienced as united. In ordinary everyday reality, identities are distinct—you and the person sitting across from you are easily distinguished. But in the underlying quantum reality, if you could shrink that small and experience reality at the subatomic level, the boundary between such identities wouldn't be clear at all. In the quantum realm, identities become indistinct, as happens in certain mystical experiences.

The new sense of reality encountered is often sustained. In the Great Wisdom Traditions, the term "enlightenment" is often used. Its scientific meaning, complete understanding of a situation, parallels its meaning in spirituality—that of profound comprehension of the way things are. This primal understanding, coupled with the sense of interconnectedness and lack of separation that accompanies it, connects the experience inextricably with unconditional love.

In the spiritual traditions, this state has many names. In the East, terms like *samadhi, nibbana, satori, kensho, prajna, nirvana,* Buddhahood, and realization of the Self are used. In Jainism, the experience is called *kevala jnana*, absolute knowledge. Hinduism adds the adjective describing ultimate freedom, *moksha*. In the mystical Islam of Sufism, the word *ma'arifat* is used, referring to ultimate knowledge. Elsewhere in Islam, the term *fana fi Allah* means annihilation. In Zoroastrianism, the world religion at the time of Alexander the Great, *vohu nanah* referred to ageless wisdom or good mind. In the Kabbalist mysticism of Judaism, the word *Ein Sof* is used, meaning oneness or unity consciousness. In Christianity, various terms are used: illumination, Christ-consciousness, God-Consciousness, or *gnosis*. These aren't all comparable terms, since there are subtle differences; but the general meaning is similar.

The nature of this knowing is so unique, so incomparable, that those who experience it often say of it, paradoxically, "There is no such thing" or, "It does not exist." In this light, the Dalai Lama said it's so clear that it can't be seen. Yet it's also said to be the ordinary nature of all things.

The 19th century German comparative religionist Rudolf Otto was one of the first to introduce the notion that the Archimedean point, or unifying principle, of enlightenment was the great leveler and ultimate conclusion of the consciousness process. He introduced the word "numinous" to the vocabulary, pointing to this experience that occurs irrespective of religious or cultural background. To be "numinous," something had to appear quite final with regard to all comprehension, compelling in the most extraordinary way—what Otto referred to with the now-famous Latin phrases *mysterium tremendum* and *mysterium fascinas*, referring to a level of significance that invokes fear and trembling.

Otto's use of "numinous" distinguished it from spiritual experience and even mystical experience, in the sense that these can still involve dualism—that is, oneness and our experience of everyday reality are two separate realms, at least until the former embraces the latter. Thus it's important to distinguish awakening and enlightenment from a variety of dualistic mystical phenomena such as near-death experiences, mystical and shamanic epiphanies, or being born again in relationship to a deity or Messiah. The latter experiences can be both important and life changing, but they are most momentous when they lead to the actual experience of unity consciousness. The difference between dualistic and nondualistic experience is often most clear by the behavior that results. A person feeling born again in relation to this or that deity or Messiah may be very loving but is apt to believe their way is "the only way." This dualism disappears in nondual experience, because the latter cannot feel separate from anything.

A tremendous amount of insight has been added to our understanding of the terms "awakening" and "enlightenment" as the interspiritual dialogue has unfolded. One of the most important is the recognition that the term "extraordinary" can be misleading when it comes to awakening. In the experience of actual enlightenment, the ordinary and extraordinary no longer appear separate. Accordingly, "awakening" is often used to refer to the initial experience of the nondual state, while "enlightenment" tends to refer to its more mature complexion after years of maintenance and cultivation.

A person in sustained nondual consciousness is a person of resonance, sharing a felt-sense with everything and everyone. This phenomenon is important in terms of human potential, in that it points to what all human beings can become—recalling Aurobindo's and the Mother's reference to this state as "supermind," and Teilhard's visioning of the character of humankind at the Omega Point. But it is important to understand this through a unified lens about what's ordinary and extraordinary. If one interprets the description above through a magic-mythic lens, one will expect something that's unrealistic—the perfect person, the perfect teacher. This is why so many of the awakening traditions are characterized by aphorisms such as "after enlightenment, the laundry" or remind all adepts "if you want to see how enlightened you are, go spend a week with your family."

Some proponents of interspirituality don't agree on whether there actually *is* a common experience underlying the universal mystical or contemplative process. Just as with the debate of the foundationalist theologians and contemplatives—Cox, Merton, Panikkar, and others—some say they experience this unity, while others say they still see only diversity.

On this score, the integralists have provided a great tool in what they call the Wilber Combs Lattice, which is a chart that represents shared spiritual experiences and various cultural lenses, depicted as vertical and horizontal axes. The lattice suggests that the core experience is the same (profound interconnectedness and loss of the sense of separation), but it's interpreted as different as a result of cultural lenses. Accordingly, individuals who experience a profound consciousness of unity don't have trouble recognizing a common core in the experience, whereas individuals who look through a culturally influenced intellectual framework often don't recognize the inherent unity and even argue against it.

Another important distinction is between the experience of awakening and truly awakened behavior. For many years mystical communities imagined that awakening matured the entire personality by some instantaneous, miraculous means. This was an unfortunate misunderstanding, involving the old magic-mythic lens. Although awakened states could be seen by all as real, they were often only temporary states that went away, leaving behind a normally flawed individual. Worse yet, some communities fell victim to the charisma of initial awakened states, only to venerate a member or leader and later discover that this same person created great harm socially, financially, or sexually. In the oddest of cases, some adepts would even display spiritual or paranormal powers and still not be such a loving, kind person.

It was a great contribution of the integral understanding of psychology and spirituality that all have strong and weak traits, which experiences of awakening don't automatically transform. The occasional "cataclysmic awakening" might create a suddenly quite mature and stable individual, but this is rare. Accordingly, if something in you insists that there should be some consistency between the high-minded words or even charisma of a spiritual teacher and their actual behavior, you have the right idea. The truly awakened individual will show a combination of clarity of consciousness, insight and discernment, and perhaps even some paranormal gift. But if it's "the real deal," the person will also embody authentic love and kindness.

One can learn about nonduality or awakening and be quite adept at a mental understanding of much of what it entails, yet not experience it directly in consciousness and heart. This is actually a good thing because, at least initially, far more people will understand a unified worldview intellectually than embody it in their heart and consciousness. In fact the mental understanding of profound interconnectedness or oneness is quite widespread, perhaps including up to one third of our planet's citizenship—something that a visit to internet book sites bears out. You'll find over 10,000 books on enlightenment or awakening, 1,000 on oneness and interconnectedness, 20,000 on transformation, 30,000 on the new physics and unified field theory, 5,000 on the unity of science, and 17,000 on globalization. In other words, millions all over the world aspire to some kind of a transformed life and worldview. Sociologist Paul Ray put the number at over 150 million in his studies of *The Cultural Creatives*. In his bestseller *Blessed Unrest*, environmentalist Paul Hawken identified over 100,000 not-for-profit organizations worldwide that are working for transformative change. If one adds the burgeoning self-help or self-improvement literature, another half-million books pertain.

Historical Ironies and Paradoxes of a World Awakening

As the world pushes toward transformation, there will be experiments in development that won't work, or only work partially. Some will even leave collateral damage in their wake. This is a natural byproduct of evolution. In looking at animals and plants, entire eco-logical communities disappeared because they didn't work anymore, given where things were going.

Even while developing in the right direction or experimenting with a new possibility, some enterprises may not work. This is a truth in nature and will also be true of experiments in human transformation and what it means and predicts. There will be many uncharted frontiers. This is why mature collective discussion from multiple perspectives is so important as the holistic age unfolds.

When an individual experiences awakening they feel liberated from normal circumstances, sensing a primordial and energizing freedom. This is why so many who have this experience evidence a palpable charisma, the result of dancing to a different drummer. Although ideally "waking up" combines this energizing experience with a profound movement of the heart, this isn't always the case. An awakening can be skewed with narcissistic or delusional tendencies. An example of such a skewed awakening can be seen in the character of Colonel Walter Kurtz in the movie *Apocalypse Now*. Colonel Kurtz had awakened into a world that had no rules other than those he himself created. A charismatic character, Kurtz decided to organize his own army so he could "pull out all the stops" and fight war the way he believed it ought to be fought: mercilessly. Martin Sheen's character, Captain Benjamin L. Willard, is then sent to kill him because "war has to have rules" or it may get out of control. If you find yourself comparing the pathological radical freedom of Colonel Kurtz with the likes of Adolf Hitler, Heinrich Himmler, Joseph Stalin, and others, you are getting the point. Their charisma came from their dancing to a different drummer, and the result was sad indeed.

Though perhaps 95% of people who operate from an experience of personal liberation are careful, we frequently read of the kind of indiscretion and abuse that can accompany such experiences even in spiritual leaders and teachers. We must simply be realistic about this. Thank goodness that the larger 95% are exemplary, with many of them embodying the lofty character the awakening phenomenon points to. Brother Teasdale himself was a remarkable example.

Although undeniably a charismatic leader with a profound message, he was also demure and humble, with a sense of humor and the quality of not taking himself too seriously.

This kind of experience, and the skill sets that come with it, represents the direction our development as a species is taking. Consistent with the trajectory of world history, we are developing a more spacious consciousness and the skill sets that arise with this increasing spaciousness, enabling us to move out of the rational and more dualistic period of our history and into a post-rational nondual worldview. If our species continues to reflect its successful patterns of development from the past, new skill sets will arise to make world transformation an actual possibility. This is the hope.

The Ultimate Meaning of the Tree

Said Albert Einstein, "All religions, arts and sciences are branches of the same tree. All these aspirations are directed toward ennobling man's life, lifting it from the sphere of mere physical existence and leading the individual towards freedom."

Teasdale recognized the transformational awakening potential within all spirituality as the revolutionary quality that identifies the emerging Interspiritual Age. Ken Wilber called it the "conveyor belt" for humanity to its next potential level. The modern Sufi mystic and leader Llewellyn Vaughan-Lee asserts that a transformational role for religion and spirituality still exists if, as a species, we decide to take up the challenge.

How can humanity break the historical pattern of religion hijacking spirituality into exclusivity and aggressive, even violent, behavior? What's the formula for linking humankind's interior and exterior senses and skills? Can the magic-mythic lens and the rational lens join in a progressive, transformative, integrated lens? Globally, what new awareness must arise, and what are the attendant skillsets that must accompany it, if humankind is to survive and thrive?

23

The Meaning of 2012

*"Oh my God, the world is ending and
I didn't know. How could this happen?"*

Respondent to a public opinion poll regarding 2012

NOTHING FRAMES THE PRESENT CACOPHONY BETTER THAN THE BUZZ concerning 2012. The debate about whether the year has some special significance has not only been a big attention getter but also a big moneymaker.

The fact that a number of ancient traditions appear to have pointed to this date as having some kind of cosmic significance has given both well-meaning and not-so-well-meaning individuals cause to create lots of hype: books, television shows, and even movies. The number of predictions and agendas is astounding. You have likely heard of some of them, but probably not all. The History Channel and Discovery Channel have both hosted specials billed as documentaries on the various theories. Then there's the movie *2012: We Were Warned*. Consequently the message has reached millions worldwide.

A 2011 poll by One World Many Answers indicated 26% of respondents are worried about the world ending in 2012 and 2% are convinced it will. Another 30% consider the whole matter a moneymaking scam. Nonetheless, the official NASA website established a question and answer outreach focused on 2012. Among the more than 5,000 inquiries were questions concerning whether suicide might be advisable. If you Google "2012 End of the World" you'll find 128 million entries. A search at Amazon will bring up 1,000 books on the topic, and many appear to be selling well.

All the hype aside, is there any significance to the date at all? This question also raises the matter of whether the date portends something apocalyptic or is some kind of benchmark in our earth's ongoing evolution.

The Source of the 2012 Scenarios

The aspect that has given 2012 newsworthiness has been the number of ancient traditions for which it can be claimed that 2012 has special significance. Those most commonly referenced reflect a mixed bag of legitimacy: the Mayan calendar, Aztec mythology, astrology, the *I Ching*, predictions of the Timewave Zero and Web Bot computers, various New Age galactic alignment scenarios, massive advertising of the French village Bugarach (nearby Mt. Bugarach) as the cataclysmic epicenter, and Nostradamus.

There are also non-apocalyptic voices that speak of 2012 along the lines of a benchmark in our evolution not much different from the other benchmarks we have set out in our discussion of the developmental view of history. These would include the popular Indian Guru Kalki Bhagavan, along with the European and American groups that support the Conscious Convergence view. We detail the sources of the 2012 concept in Appendix II.

The second issue is the most important, and why the matter is worth discussing. Just as our world religions reflect a wide variety of conflicting and exclusive views, so does the 2012 debate. Even as it's impossible for all of the conflicting views of religion to be correct, the same is true of the claims concerning 2012. The debate is a microcosm of the problem of the pathology of religious exclusivism.

The issue is typical of the usual disjunction of the magic-mythic and the rational—a disconnect with some five centuries of history behind it. Whereas 2012 magic-mythic apocalyptic views are dismissed by the rational lens, which brands the entire discussion as poppycock, the holistic integrated lens asks a different question: what can we learn from the 2012 debate that helps us understand why it's as compelling as it is?

The source of the 2012 scenarios appears to be the so-called Mayan Long Count calendar, for which December 21, 2012 is regarded by some scholars as the end-date of the last 5,125-year cycle. While there's little doubt that defining epochs of history is a strong theme in Mayan literature, the question is whether these ancient views hold any useful information for us today.

The end-time scenarios that arise from the Mayan theme are generated by joining the interpretations of the mathematics of the Mayan calendar with apocalyptic events and celestial characters in both Mayan and Aztec myth. Some experts question whether this merging is appropriate. December 2012 marks the conclusion of a *b'ak'tun* made up of 20 *katuns*, totaling about 400 years. According to the Long Count calendar, the classical Mayan period occurred during the 8th and 9th *b'ak'tuns* and the current 13th *b'ak'tun* will conclude on December 21, 2012, to be followed by the 14th. In many popularized versions of the calendar, the end of the 13th *b'ak'tun* is also associated with Mayan and Aztec hieroglyphs involving a god named Bolon Yokte (or Bolon Yokte' K'Uh). This god, also known as The Nine Lords of the Night and the Nine Strides, is always depicted in apocalyptic fashion, embellished with many obvious symbols of oblivion: funerals, execution, death, and perdition.

Whatever Bolon Yokte signfies, he appeared early in Meso-American myth, known not only from Mayan and Aztec narratives, but also from the accounts of three smaller regional civilizations. In all of these he is associated with conflict, war, and the demon world. For this image to be associated, even if not directly, with the various interpretations of the mathematics of the Mayan calendar has created a rich context for doomsday predictions.

December 21, 2012 isn't the only date associated with the combining of the end of the 13th *b'ak'tun* with Bolon Yokte. It had been previously attributed to other dates, including July 27, 615 (using the Gregorian calendar), March 24, 603 (by factoring in data from other gods), and May 2003 or October 2011 (based on calculations later revised when these dates passed). Another set of calculations pushes the meaning of the math well into the future—in one case 41 octillion years from now, which itself would be 3 quintillion times the current known age of the universe. Nevertheless, there is enough scholarship pointing to December 21, 2012 as meaning *something* in ancient Latin American math and myth to provide fertile ground for proponents, through their many lenses, to offer their interpretations.

The clincher for much of the popularity of the 2012 debate has been the association of the math and these myths with additional astronomical and astrological information. The rationale for this is twofold. First, if you are looking for an apocalyptic scenario for modern times, it certainly packages best when wrapped in modern data concerning the cosmos. Secondly, it just happens that Bolon Yokte, according to some interpretations, was a Star God. To many, especially the 56% of our world's population that believes in extraterrestrials, this has an uncompromising significance.

Even without UFOs or Bolon Yokte returning as an extraterrestrial, the overarching astronomical and astrological scenarios for 2012 concern what science calls "precession." Precession involves the effect on the spin and axis of our earth in relation to the gravitational pull of other heavenly bodies—not only that of the sun and its planets, but also the wider movement of our solar system within the arms of stars that comprise the Milky Way. Reports that galactic alignments in 2012 might have disastrous consequences for the stability of our planet only further the restlessness surrounding the debate, especially in the popular media.

The Magic-Mythic Lens Is Still Compelling for Our Species

Even if all the possible doomsday scenarios are baseless and portend no harm, the 2012 narrative still highlights one of the most pervasively compelling visions of our planet, which is that our humanity has steadily been evolving and is headed toward some kind of maturation. Given human history since Darwin and the developmental paradigm, it was all but inevitable that the 2012 question would emerge as a public debate. The phenomenon has generated over two-dozen well-publicized predictions of what may happen—all detailed in our Appendix II.

Examination of these predictions shows that the magic-mythic lens remains extremely compelling for our species. Popular books and the media thrive on it. As a result, there has arisen a culture of counter-fact. A major problem is many of the scenarios taken as fact by the wider public have resulted from two centuries that have elapsed in which academically-based data has been shaped in the popular media by interpretations, changes, additions, and outright distortions.

"Urban legend" is the phrase often used in common parlance for how fiction, or partial fiction, finds its way into the public mind. Urban legends become entrenched because it's often difficult for even discerning individuals to sort out when strains of untruth found their way into otherwise mostly true accounts. The public is also apt to believe some of the strangest ideas because, given the lack of confidence in government—not to mention outright censorship in some nations—a huge credibility gap exists with regard to "official lines" on matters.

Often the skeptical community only exacerbates the situation by claiming to debunk everything that can't be caught, touched, or measured. The relegation by skeptics of anything "spiritual" to the realm of pre-rational superstition hasn't been helpful.

The mix of credible and less-credible threads does little to boost the credibility of the idea that 2012 is special. The debate ends up being a litany of claim upon claim. Because of this, in addition to the NASA website, NOAA (the National Oceanic and Atmospheric Administration) has had to launch a website and establish a hotline to clarify facts about 2012. They have been joined worldwide by government agencies, cultural groups, and media watchdog agencies in trying to inform the public about the host of predictions and the credibility of their sources.

Officials of the Mayan tribes of Guatemala and other Latin American indigenous tribal organizations have stated there is no apocalyptic content in their understanding of their ancient calendars and mythology. The mayor of Bugarach, France, has asked the public not to believe the statements made about his village as the epicenter of an impending 2012 cataclysm. Although such statements may have some effect on public perception and reaction, they have done little to arrest doomsday predictions.

Every narrative is niched within certain subcultures of the world, which each see through drastically different lenses. Accordingly, the wildest of scenarios can be regionally popular and, being commercially successful, spread. This has particularly been a problem with Mayan and *I-Ching* interpretations, which have been widely debated by scholars. Such debates give the discussion credibility, while the version that emerges in the media is commercialized to capture public imagination.

There is perhaps no better example of the conundrum that subjective, spiritual, and religious experiences pose for a globalizing society than the scenarios predicted for 2012. The predicament challenges humanity to attain a higher level of consciousness when it comes to how we determine what's "true."

Why All the Fuss?
Non-apocalyptic Holistic Views of 2012

Though there's always a chance that some kind of disaster will strike the world on December 21, 2012, it's statistically unlikely. However, there's a more authentic way in which rich mythologies can inform our species. Ancient texts contain collective subjective truths about human nature, the human experience, and our hopes and dreams as a species.

When one looks deeper at all the source material concerning 2012, a compelling thread suggests an interpretation compatible with the modern mind. This is a developmental view, highlighting the perennial call to co-creation and to assuming responsibility for our world—not just hoping for apocalyptic events to rescue us. This approach involves going beyond the magic-mythic lens in which apocalypticism is embedded, instead seeing ancient narratives no differently from when a grade school teacher asks pupils to explore what they have *really* learned from Harry Potter, which isn't that witches exist and that you can fly on magic brooms.

In the 1960s and 1970s, just as the integrative era dawned, the seminaries of many of the world's Christian denominations began to teach the new criticism, treating the Holy Bible as a historical document. This was a huge step for a revealed religion that held its sacred text to be "the word of God." The developmental view of history predicts all the world's revealed religions will make this transition, essential to any future view of "truth" that could be universally compatible with globalization. Islam will most likely be the next major revealed religion to go through this transition. Judaism already has in most of its cultural contexts, as the result of decades of humanistic and intellectual influence on its religious beliefs.

The apocalyptic narratives of 2012 fail to pass the test of facticity not only because they can't all be true, but also because a different kind of message is embedded in them. In this view, 2012 represents a further benchmark in the evolution of human consciousness, another step in the direction of higher awareness and advanced skill sets that will affect our future. Just as in the developmental view of history we can look back to the year 1970 and see emergence of integrative visions, syntheses, and pivotal new insights, it's likely that 2012 will be similarly recognized in hindsight. Ironically, this will probably make sense of the doomsday predictions of 2012. It may be the point at which we finally abandon hopes for a "divine intervention from somewhere" and at last become serious about co-creating the future of our planet.

Worldwide, this non-apocalyptic view of 2012 is already the widely discussed understanding among the millions of well-educated clergy and scholars in the mainstream religions and secular academic institutions. They simply had no reason to hype the matter. The sad thing is their institutions could sorely use all the money that has been generated by the commercializing of 2012. One of the central misalignments of our confused era—a pathology to be addressed by the Interspiritual Age—is this misplacement of value on sensationalism, celebrity, and nonfactual hype.

The non-apocalyptic view also has its advocates, many of whom understand that some of the sensationalism around 2012 isn't simply from commercialism, but is a result of a natural tendency within so many of us to gravitate toward the magic-mythic lens. This same inclination makes millionaires of those who have brought us such blockbusters as Star Trek, Star Wars, Narnia, Lord of the Rings, and Harry Potter.

But this lens is shifting. In the East, the most outspoken and highly organized adherents of the co-creative view of 2012 have been those of Indian teacher Kalki Bhagavan, who has for some time been pointing to 2012 as a benchmark in the ongoing enlightenment process of our species. The message of his 15 million active followers is that 2012 is the end of a historical period known as the Kali Yuga, or degenerative period, to be replaced by a new historical period often called the "wind of unity consciousness." This is a view consistent with scientific and other Eastern yogic views of ongoing brain-mind evolution. It's also the vision forecast by Sri Aurobindo and The Mother, echoed today by their international community in India. It predicts acceleration of the trend toward recognition of the profound interconnectedness and oneness of all things—the quality Brother Teasdale marked as essential to shifting toward an actual Interspiritual Age.

In the West, Swedish Mayan calendar scholar Carl Johan Calleman, who founded the Conscious Convergence Movement, has spoken worldwide for December 21, 2012 as a benchmark in the world's ongoing conscious evolution—particularly after publication of his 1994 book in Swedish, *Mayahypotesen*. His view—and that of the somewhat similar Harmonic Convergence and Hopi Indian Sixth World Consciousness movements—basically reflects the developmentalist concept that, beginning with the Big Bang, the universe first experienced an evolution of matter, followed by an evolution of consciousness. In contrast to the developmentalists, these groups also chart some specific scenarios for human development, depicting earth's evolution as moving through series of waves, each series becoming exponentially shorter than previous series. With the developmentalists, they see human evolution trending toward higher and higher capacity.

Comprising so many hardcore and mainstream academicians, the developmentalists built their developmental history on extremely detailed data sets, whereas the Conscious Convergence adherents have relied more on metaphysics—and yet there are remarkable coincidences in their general scenarios, with the Conscious Convergence view seeing current human history as a "sixth wave," paralleling the post–World War II eras of the developmentalists. Their sixth wave remarkably—and independently—parallels our Sixth Great Advance, a further demarcation that we made among the more generalized epochs of the developmental view of history.

Just as we, along with most mainstream developmental scholars, believe December 21, 2012 symbolizes a benchmark in human consciousness history, Conscious Convergence adherents are of the same view. In fact this non-apocalyptic view is also the default setting for some of the New Age doomsday predictors as well—just in case every one wakes up on December 22, 2012 and everything seems okay!

One of the more popular authors on the "return of Quetzalcoatl" view, Daniel Pinchbeck, says he's also fine with that date if it amounts to a symbolic passing of an old age and its replacement with a new. He characterizes this as the end of strict materialism and the dominance of purely rational and empirical worldviews, seeing it as the beginning of a more integrated era that's able to skillfully embrace the intuitive and mystical capacities of our species.

Have a Party on December 21, 2012

In any case, the impending date of December 21, 2012 is a clear invitation for a party wherein everyone can eat, drink, hopefully be merry, and wait to actually see if anything happens. As with Y2K—the turn of the year 2000, around which so many predicted calamity—it's most likely that the next day will dawn just like any other. Yet even this will have nothing to do with whether 2012 ends up marking some kind of new epoch in our species' ongoing evolution. Such things are only recognized over much larger periods of time, as in the many clear benchmarks readily apparent today within the developmental view of history.

Of course, the skeptics and reductionists take the opportunity to spin the entire matter in a different way. For them, any special considerations regarding 2012 simply reflect irrelevant pre-rational superstition. There's a heavy sprinkling of political innuendo as well. Recently published skeptics' views about 2012 having anything to do with advancing human consciousness invited caricatures best paraphrased as indicating rebellion against mainstream Western culture, including efforts to instigate countercultural sympathies that can result in sociopolitical revolution.

Similarly, a psychologist opined that people interested in a significance to 2012 are people who are unable to find needed answers in their lives, who then turn toward imagined realities and make-believe hopes and dreams, at worst tinged with a paranoia concerning their possession of some kind of secret knowledge. Of course, these same caricatures are aimed at religion and spirituality by those who see through the purely rational lens. For them, any discussion of things outside what can be touched and measured in conventional reality amounts to pre-rational superstition.

An integral and interspiritual view is very different. It inquires into the interplay of our interior and external ways of knowing, seeking to understand the universe of discourse related to drastically different experiences within our wider reality. Further, it asks how these integrate into wellbeing, wholesomeness, and healthy behaviors in terms of acquiring skill sets that also address a higher ethos in the collective—the world of "We," including all that's transcultural, transnational, trans-traditional, and world-centric.

24

Moving Toward the World-Centric

"The Interspiritual Age will be birthed by a new set of historical circumstances. These are already being reflected in the shifts of consciousness taking place across our planet"

Brother Wayne Teasdale

WE NEED ONLY LOOK AT MAPS OF THE WORLD OVER TIME TO SEE HOW our history has moved from countless local and regional governments and states to continentally expansive or even transcontinental nations. The examples are many. For instance, China has gone from up to 15 medieval dynasties to the current People's Republic and Taiwan. A map of Europe in 1000 CE shows some 50 city-based or regional states, a far cry from today's single European Union with its 27 national components.

Of course, the process has also gone back and forth in fits and starts in some regions. The once transcontinental Soviet Union (the USSR) gathered some 20 original smaller states into its Soviet of four subdivisions, only to dismantle into the 15 independent nations of today. Nine nations became the single nation of Yugoslavia in the World

War II era, then returned to seven nations today. Reflecting the flux of these national identities over centuries, one of the seven current nations retains the original flag of none other than Alexander the Great.

The overall historical trend is clear since, even when national numbers have increased in some sectors of the world, it has usually been in the context of civil relationship, free trade, and sometimes even open borders. The sad legacy of this history is the millions upon millions who died in the civil conflicts and wars that accompanied these geopolitical transformations.

The prefix "trans" is Latin for "across" or "beyond," iconic of history's inevitable trend. During the tense years of the Berlin Wall, who would have imagined open borders within a united Germany? During and after World War II, who would have envisioned a European Union? Or when Napoleon and Wellington engaged at the Battle of Waterloo, who could have conceived of the Chunnel that now links the United Kingdom and France?

This overview illustrates not only the direction of globalization but also the fact that relationships between peoples have tended to improve. This observation is at the heart of the developmental view of history, and Integral and Spiral Dynamics, in current bestsellers like Harvard cognitive scientist Steven Pinker's *The Better Angels of Our Nature: Why Violence Has Declined*.

These trends are in stark contrast to the reality that our world faces possible extinction as a result of wars caused by conflicting national or religious identities. Were a benevolent extraterrestrial to visit and assess our planet, it would find our global society both confusing and scary. When the alien "phones home" to report, we would likely hear something like, "Can you believe these people? They continue to fight over different mythological views of their origins and destinies, over their national identities, flags and anthems, skin colors and ethnic identities, even differences about sexuality. Meanwhile they foul their planet with every kind of pollution, not to mention dividing their social structures into the very rich and the very poor. There seems little hope this stupidity won't end up in a cataclysm."

How then will religion, which is exclusive by its nature, respond to this challenge of globalization, be able to see things more holistically, and act accordingly?

What Kind of Globalization?

The People's Republic of China has a government department dedicated to influencing the course of world globalization. It's likely this is the case with many nations. Yet opinion polls show an overwhelming majority of humans worldwide desire a healthy multicultural environment.[91]

Similarly, in spite of decades of sectarian attacks on the goals of the United Nations, especially in the United States, polls show perhaps as many as 80% of people agree with its charter.[92] Also, we have found in our national and international discussions that when the overarching vision and values of interspirituality are aired within every mainstream religion, its aspirations and values are widely embraced. The only question that arises is how interspirituality would affect the current structures of organized religion. When acquainted with history, most people recognize that the exclusivity of religion reflects the behavior of an older planetary era. In place of this, they long for behavior that values cooperation, synergy, and mutuality. Some 78% support the vision of unifying principles, and up to 90% believe in the importance of a benevolent multiculturalism.[93]

The desire that multiculturalism might be reflected in healthy development has made the buzzwords "transnational," "trans-traditional," "transcultural," and "world-centric" prominent in the global discussion. The entire coterie of the evolutionary consciousness movement, futures scholars, integralists, and transformational activists stand in this unfolding tradition.

Eckhart Tolle's *A New Earth* advanced this discussion and sold millions of copies worldwide, as did Paul Hawken's *Blessed Unrest*. The

[91] Pew, Gallup, 2007.
[92] unausa.org., 2011.
[93] Pew, Gallup, 2007.

same message was in Paul Ray's *The Cultural Creatives,* which defined at least a third of our modern world as viewing reality through a more progressive lens. This trend grows ever stronger in the "circles of empathy" that are arising via the internet social media and blogosphere in reaction to world crises—from Tunisia to Egypt, Libya, and Syria. Photos and videos of human rights abuses, even genocides, are seen around the world nearly instantaneously.

A negative vote by the United Nations Security Council, where today five of the world's traditional old powers still retain a veto over actions in the interest of the rest of the world, can't stop a global public outcry on behalf of universal human values. The worldwide influence of such circles of empathy is undeniable and has also united the global backlash against the excesses of the banking and financial industries. These advances have taken trends already obvious in our developmental history and amped them up to a new level.

Brother Teasdale clearly saw the emergence of the "trans" phenomenon across multiple frontiers. However, Teasdale's own tradition, Roman Catholicism, repeatedly made headlines in 2012 when it publicly censured religious orders of nuns for their emphasis on social and economic justice issues over those of the Vatican's anti-abortion and anti-gay messages. Also in the news is Rome's silencing of priests on women's rights and the handling of the church's pedophile scandal. Blowback from Ireland's Association of Catholic Priests against these Vatican decisions, together with reaction to the reprimanding of American religious orders for their questioning of tradition, has suggested to many the beginnings of a "Catholic Spring."

These kinds of responses from the world's largest and wealthiest Christian denomination, along with the stoic sectarianism of so much of worldwide Islam, highlight the lack of a mature sense of global community, mutuality, and shared universal ethics, indicating that international progress toward transformation may be difficult indeed.

To be hurtling toward globalization without the benefit of the world religions' truest reservoir—that of the universal values of spirituality, a shared human ethos, and wisdom—is a sobering thought. Nevertheless, the relentlessness of evolution, as Teasdale observed even as he was writing *The Mystic Heart*, means if the world's religions don't take this more universal path, the mandate will be handed to others. This insight was echoed 10 years later when Paul Hawken's *Blessed Unrest: How the Largest Movement in the World Came into Being and Why No One Saw It Coming* announced that this shift was already happening. As has occurred so often in historical, biological, and social evolution, when something stands in the way of inevitable trends, it's simply bypassed and the direction realized through other means.

The Mystical Pursuit and Social Transformation

Following the success of *The Mystic Heart*, Teasdale advocated to his colleagues a "two-pronged approach," involving proactive and simultaneous attention to both transformation of individuals (the "I-space") *and* change aimed at altering the narrative of the institutional "It-space." Teasdale believed that, ultimately, the unity consciousness experience would become universal.

However, because he also knew the process would be slowed by politically closed societies and entrenched financial powers, he advised that the world's religions should turn not only to emphasizing their shared experiential mystical roots but also their shared universal ethical values. He saw the emerging interspiritual movement as a vanguard of this message to religions, with an emphasis on deed over creed.

In line with his mentor Bede Griffiths' emphasis that the two current cultures of knowing—spirit and science—must also find their common ground, Teasdale championed this melding as well. He wouldn't have been surprised by the emergence of atheist Richard Dawkins' bestseller *The God Delusion* and Rupert Sheldrake's 2012 bestseller *The Science Delusion: Freeing the Spirit of Enquiry*. Moreover, he would have understood in this context the 2011-2012 public debate between his friend His Holiness the Dalai Lama on the path of universal love and kindness, and the view of Steven Prothero's *God is Not One*, about the world religions' competition for global power, and why their differences matter. This innate understanding was reflected in Teasdale's own embrace of the pivotal value of the integral map and the developmental view of history.

For all its insistence on the magic-mythic view of reality, the New Age movement has expanded this more holistic message into a worldwide multibillion-dollar enterprise. There are paradoxes of course. While the recent New Age bestseller *The Secret* may allow someone familiar with the subtle realms of reality to manifest an intention or dream, the same methods can come up a complete dud when used formulaically or as a form of *hocus pocus*. Also, the yoga that's spreading worldwide is often taught as if it was nothing more than another form of going to the gym. Such teaching has little or nothing to do with the principles of deeper consciousness of authentic yoga—rendering it "unrecognizable," to borrow a term used by prominent spiritual leaders in India when they see what yoga has been turned into. At the same time, up to 70% of younger people hold progressive political and social views, as well as yearn for transformative understanding.[94]

However we look at it, the growing world of "trans" is inevitable. Though its growth has been gradual, it appears unstoppable. As bus and train placards read across modern South Africa: "The journey is never long when freedom is the destination."

The Collective World of "We"

The spiritual, consciousness, and integral discussions are all clear that history is moving into the epoch of "We." This is a crucial developmental stage because the selfish needs of "I" aren't able to create a sustainable world. Further, the runaway excesses of the impersonal institutional "It"-space must be met by a resurgence of a dynamic sense of "We."

The world is characterized today by a disconnect between what should be a seamless relationship of personal life and the institutional world. We know that in most of the workaday world, the concerns of

---

[94] People-Press.org, 2010.

the heart must be left at home. In fact we are advised explicitly in most places of employment not to bring such concerns to work.

The "I" and "We" who built today's institutional space now find that it most often takes control of *them*. Even Bill Gates has joked that he created Microsoft, but if he's not careful, it tells *him* what to do. Moreover, the institutional space seldom reflects the collective values, hopes, and dreams of the individual or family—unless one is part of the privileged elite. This massive disconnect between the hopes and dreams of "I" and the control structures of the world has brought on the Arab Spring, the Occupy Wall Street movement, and the rumors of a Catholic Spring.

The need for a humanizing of the controlling structures worldwide has been apparent for some time, though obviously they differ culture-to-culture and nation-to-nation. Until recently, upheavals occurred more often in cultures and nations with stark disjunctions between the enfranchised and disenfranchised, the free and the controlled. That was when the context was mostly political. But the economic context has become paramount in recent decades with the decline of what had been a strong middle class in many of the First World cultures. The apparent push of the financial and business sectors for greater profit and power has, many believe, accelerated this disenfranchisement enough across First World nations to foment rebellion there as well. Some semblance of a middle class, upward mobility, and access to "the good life" or "the American dream" seemed real, certainly for a decade or so after the Era of Good Feeling of the 1950s. But in this millennium, for many this sense of an even playing field and equal upward opportunity has disappeared.

The consolidation of wealth by a small percentage of individuals across the First World has been of particular consequence in the United States. Some 70–80% of Americans feel that, since the last decade, a family can no longer expect its children to live a better life than they did.[95] Healthcare has been nonexistent for 50 million people in the United States, while home ownership is also ceasing to be a

---

[95] CBS News, 2011.

realistic goal for many American families. A secure job with benefits and the opportunity for a fulfilling retirement has also disappeared for most Americans, except in the top tiers of wealth.

The financial debacle of 2008 resulted in major social blowback. Even a former Secretary of Labor, Robert Reich, has pointed out in a potential doomsday scenario for the United States that the middle class sustains the economic structures of the United States.[96] The wealthy may consolidate more and more wealth, but the bottom drops out when the economy, centered on the middle class, can't carry itself. With the election of 2004, there was a recognition of this lack of a sense of "We," which was echoed in the winning slogan of the election year, "Yes We Can." But 30-40% of Americans think little came of it.[97]

The Cognitive Science of Religion notes that a dangerous tendency of our species' monkey mind is its habit of liking simplistic sound bites that are easy to remember. For many, this describes what has happened to the word "freedom," which has been manipulated to argue for no government oversight of the private sector. Where this has permitted the business and financial sectors to perpetrate all kinds of abuses, the result is large numbers of Americans now unknowingly vote against their own best interests. Motivation by buzzwords, accompanied by little to no critical thinking, has become a fixture of First World politics—the subject of an insightful analysis by George Lakoff in his book *Metaphors We Live By*. Pushback against this kind of political manipulation has become global in the last decade. What many call a worldwide "outbreak of We" has ignited a transformative process in many regions of the world as the 21st century advances into its second decade.

"We" and the Advancing Consciousness

Much of the modern discussion about reality now centers on the implications of the simple two-letter word "We." Arthur Koestler's revolutionary insight about our inherent nature as "holons"—that everything is *both* a part and a whole—has gained global traction.

---

[96] Robert Reich at blogspot.com, 2012.
[97] *Newsweek*, CBS News, 2012.

Once only known from the world of toys—the ornamental and bejeweled "eggs within eggs" or "dolls within dolls" of Europe's 19th century wealthy royals, and later the "schmoos inside of schmoos" popularized across the post-war world by Lil' Abner cartoonist Al Capp—the seamless relationship of what's a whole and what's a part is today a standard aspect of our everyday understanding of life and exercising of common sense. This is "We" on a grand sliding scale—and it's full of challenges.

Many believe the disconnect between individuals and institutions resulted from when the world entered the phase of emphasizing the individual. This indispensable revolution, which swept the world in the last two centuries, occasioned a jump from individuals to institutions that somehow omitted "We." This revolution's emphasis on hierarchies and structures catering to self-interests at the expense of the wellbeing of the wider collective is seen by many as a blunder of historical proportions.

The lack of a skillful "We" led equally to the failure of the world's naïve socialistic experiments. These aimed to address collective needs but lacked the ethically mature individuals to execute their benevolent vision. A French classic lamenting this failure is entitled simply *L'espérance trahie* (*Hope Betrayed*).

Seeing the scope of these failures after the world's transition from monarchy to democracy has led many to view the current threshold of our evolution as an attempt to move from "I" to "We." This has implications for every aspect of human life, not least of which are the challenges facing our shift to globalization and multiculturalism. Moreover, such a change affects the structures of experience and consciousness that underpin our species' sense of the religious and the spiritual.

Central to an evolutionary view of the rise of "We" is the necessity that awareness of "We" be accompanied by new skill sets that can actually manifest a successful collective. Such a result would represent the integration consensus to which science attributes our ability to couple a need with a solution, linking a cause with an effect. At every stage of our historical development, humanity has either achieved these skills in "We" or not met its next threshold. A classic example is how, 100,000 years ago when the Ice Age descended upon both our ancestors and our cousins Neanderthal man, we found solutions whereas our cousins didn't. Consequently Neanderthals became extinct.

Interspirituality's central emphasis is humanity's ability to succeed in creating a world the ideals of all the great religious and spiritual traditions speak of. This emphasis on what Brother Teasdale called "will"—desire for, and thus the energy to create, a transformed world—is a value shared by seekers of transformation, both religious and secular. It's what allowed Brother Teasdale to paint the vision of interspirituality across both religious and non-religious worldviews.

Interspiritual and sacred activists alike portray the sense of the collective in mystical terms, saying it emerges almost as a new "sense" or "raw feel"—something nearly *visceral* and experienced as qualitatively different from anything encountered before. Individuals *and* collectives seem to first recognize it as "available," then begin to experience it as both "real" and accompanied by a skill set that makes possible new abilities among circles of people working together.

The Mother announced the availability of this emerging new energy of collective consciousness in 1956, just as the integrative era began, and predicted changes the world would begin to see. A decade ago, Ken Wilber began writing of the "miracle of We," and the integralists elucidated the long-unfolding patterns leading to the challenges of the new millennium.

In the past two decades, the Embodiment movement—seeing the transcendent message of the Great Wisdom Traditions as descending into every aspect of the physical world, including the human body— has swept through the world's spiritual and wisdom communities. It demanded something new for the individual and for the community—not to "wake up and detach," but "wake up and engage." This signaled a major shift away from the spiritual bypass that had characterized the often self-serving spiritual seekers of the late 20th century, to a new holistic breed of fully embodied spiritual activists for the 21st century. Soon after, the street movements that now characterize the tumultuous climate of the current era erupted worldwide.

Failure Always Came Down to the Lack of an Integral Approach

When ethical philosopher Felix Adler wrote some of the foundational documents of ethics and humanism near the end of the 19th century—*Reconstruction of the Spiritual Ideal* and *Life and Destiny*—he nailed the understanding of an ethos based on the ideals of religion but not needing the dogma of religion to put it into practice. He had all the ideas right, and many of them can be compared with those of Brother Teasdale and Ken Wilber. Adler called this new world "the ethical manifold," whereas Teasdale called it the emerging Interspiritual Age and Wilber called it the Integral Age.

The post-world war humanist era failed to achieve much beyond the establishment of basic international forums for arguing one intellectual formulation against another. Because they didn't recognize consciousness—and with it spirituality—they overlooked the great subjective reservoirs that serve our species. Following these precedents, whole sectors of our world, especially in science and academia in general, also continue to ignore these deeper aspects of human nature. Formalized religions, being themselves creatures of intellectualizations, creeds, and dogmas, make the same error, stripping from spirituality the deeper subjective gifts and leaving the same limited potential of arguing about concepts. Without an underlying subjective praxis of love and caring, such an endeavor soon turns into conflict.

Religions around the world motivate billions with simplistic, limited, and often patently false ideas about reality. Meanwhile humanism, which is the default setting of the secular world, embraces all the elegance of a sophisticated understanding of reality but can't seem to achieve an everyday practice that goes deeper than endless intellectual arguments over ideas. In other words, religion often lacks the sophistication of actual knowledge, while secular humanism lacks a compelling praxis. This disconnect is another frontier that will need to be addressed as the integrative and holistic age matures, especially in the context of an emerging interreligiosity and interspirituality.

The spiritual cores of Buddhism and Hinduism have done much to cement a relationship between sophisticated knowledge and compelling praxis. We need only witness the influence of Gandhi's methodology on the world, thereafter adopted by so many, not the least of whom was America's Martin Luther King, Jr. The same has been true of the influence of Buddhism in the last decade's political and economic transformations of Southeast Asia. When Toynbee speculated about the pivotal historical ramifications of the meeting of Eastern and Western thought, he obviously had in mind this integral marriage of the combined skill sets of sophisticated knowledge and heart-motivated praxis. Sri Aurobindo was pointing to the same with his use of the metaphor of a necklace.

You Have to Admit It's Getting Better

Many of us remember the phrase "You have to admit it's getting better" from a popular Beatles song. The phrase is often used to summarize the long-term historical analysis of Integral and Spiral Dynamics, which provide an optimistic vision of the world's progress to date. Looking back through our history, it's been a dicey past, with some long periods such as the Dark Ages appearing bleak indeed. Yet on many fronts, we can see that humankind has gradually become just a little better.

Perhaps most of the world's 7 billion citizens have never heard this positive view of where history appears to be going. Moreover, when the positive view is suggested, many doubt it. In his bestselling 2012 book *The Better Angels of Our Nature: Why Violence Has Declined*, Harvard's famed cognitive psychologist Steven Pinker has rendered the world a service by articulating this view with massive documentation. The credentials surrounding this book and author vaulted it into instant public attention.

In our long history, we have grown from the rough and tumble survival instincts of cave people up through the early advances of ethnocentric development—the world of clans, then tribes, and ultimately races. We then moved on through the eras of towns and cities to kingdoms and empires. We saw these evolve from totalitarian structures to the kinds of subcultures that lead to education and refinement, and ultimately the birth of religions, ethical structures, free thought, and the sense of the self-evident rights of individuals. Finally we moved from regional nations to continental and even transcontinental federations and unions, encompassing a pluralistic world-centric level of development that is today transcultural, trans-traditional, and transnational. With these directions, as assessed by external measures of structure and form, have come transformations of ethos and character.

Growth in Quality

Some truly horrific things go on in every era, but the institutions that mark our advance toward a world-centric society—international organizations for political mediation and trade, the role of international treaties and agreements, the intertwined networks for communication for everything from culture to commerce—mark our gradual ascension.

With this ascension has come the reduction, at least generally, of some of the greatest social scourges—slavery, lack of the rule of law, the oppression of women, the abuse of children, the mistreatment of the aged, cruelty to animals to some degree, and our emerging sense of the universal right to education and healthcare. It's often said the best thing both pessimists and optimists can do is to study developmental history and relax a little with a big smile from seeing that gradual upward ascension is in fact occurring.

In terms of human behavior, one of the clearest examples of this progress is seen in both individuals and societies simultaneously—the gradual growth from reactive to accommodating behavior, and from accommodating to transformative behavior. Individuals start out stormy in youth and adolescence, move onto a plateau known as "mellowing," and in later life shift into a truly transformative and creative period of adulthood.

The world has also moved through sequential stages. Our species moved from egocentric behavior, through ethnocentric behavior, and now into a sense of world-centric. The earlier stages were ripe with reactive behavior, especially wars. Yet somehow, especially after the world wars of the 20th century, there emerged a plateau of mellowing, as if humanity realized there had to be a better way than the global conflicts through which we had just passed. The result was more-accommodating political, cultural, and economic organizations.

Following this there emerged the world's own transformative era, the dream of how higher ideals might propel our globalizing species to a better life. We see this today in the spectacular rise of attention to people-based governance and management, edging toward replacement of the older models of strict hierarchical elite-based control. Although such transformative models are in their infancy, they are succeeding and being accepted. This acceptance isn't simply because of their lofty ideals, but also because they surpass the results of the old models.

Another example of change is highlighted in the popular book *Global Mind Change*, in which scientist Willis Harman notes that the world has gradually changed its mind about why and how things happen. After the Renaissance and the emergence of the rational era, humans were fascinated by strictly materialistic ideas of origin and cause. After all, it was the discoveries from the emerging discipline of modern science that had brought so many a better life. However, as our world complexified, we found these explanations didn't entirely satisfy us. We had moved toward a dualistic, dialectical view of origin and cause, in which we spoke in twosomes: brain and mind, nature and nurture, formlessness and form. As we began to realize that reality is a seamless interconnected whole, it became necessary to move yet again, this time toward an integrated lens that encompasses everything from the infinitesimally small to the infinitely large. This is a reality in which formless and form aren't separate, as also stated in the perennial wisdom of the East's classic *Heart Sutra*. This intrinsic relationship of spiritual and scientific knowing is discussed annually by scientists and spiritual adepts alike at the international conference on Science and Nonduality.

From the point of view of science, the evolutionary process will always pick "what works," selecting the adaptation that leads to fitness. Similarly, the spirituality associated with interspirituality and unity consciousness will always choose what serves the wellbeing of all because it sees the other as an aspect of itself.

25

Darker Visions Interrupted

"When we speak of the Divine Feminine, the gateway to our Wholeness, we are speaking about both receptivity and action, receptivity-in-action"

Kavita Byrd

WE CAN'T FORGET THAT SOME FUTURISTS PREDICT A MUCH DARKER scenario—a vision that comes either from not seeing the adaptive nature of the evolutionary process or from failing to catch the vision of the collective wellbeing through the lens of the heart.

The tenor of this darker scenario is a pseudo-Darwinian world of the "fittest," controlled by a wealthy and privileged few. In this scenario there is no longer a substantial middle class anywhere in the world. Neither is there social mobility nor safety nets of any kind, with an exploited working class enslaved by debt and their need for access to the fundamentals of life. This is a world no different from the world that already exists in many of the heinous dictatorships on the planet. Such a world could encompass the whole globe if our species makes unenlightened decisions.

Life in such a world would be run by the "casino"—the financial and banking machine that owns the politicians and the courts. Five years ago such a scenario might have been expected from only conspiracy theorists, but more recently it was brought into focus by none other than former Secretary of Labor and now professor at the University of California, Robert Reich.[98] It's reminiscent of a magazine cartoon in which a patient sitting with a psychiatrist says, "Doctor, what do we do now that we know all my paranoid fears were true?"

In this scenario the world's remaining open societies become closed. All basic freedoms are curtailed, initiated by politicians' real or concocted fears of terrorism of all kinds, coupled with the establishment of a world economic dictatorship centered on a privileged few. The path to this world dictatorship involves the gradual shutting down of the world's free presses and free access to information.

Supplementing this total control of information is the promotion of countless diversions to entertain our monkey mind, such as handheld devices of all kinds that engage and amuse with games and advertisements, replacing critical thinking and reflection with addictive motor skills. Advertising permeates every aspect of public media exposure, shaping lifestyle and guaranteeing perpetual debt. Short ads precede every news and information tidbit, along with constant bombardment of trends based on celebrities, sports, and gossip, divorcing the media from social and political awareness.

In such a society everyone is in debt and has been since childhood. All financial transactions, purchases, internet preferences, and media choices are tracked by computers monitored by government and corporations. Corporate personhood has expanded to corporate constitutional license. Rules governing relationship to an employer supersede constitutional rights, to the point that employers have their own police and militia. The employer can determine the individual's allowable personal habits; and if one doesn't conform, livelihood is lost. Any writing beyond short tweets and texting requires special permission, as does creative activity of any kind, all of which

---

[98] In his blog at salon.com.

is monitored. All resources have been privatized, including access to water and anything agricultural such as seeds or tools. Government and the corporation are indistinguishable. Of course, some of this is already true today; in this scenario it has simply been carried further.

This dark scenario stands in stark contrast to the progression seen over thousands of years. If nothing else, the contrast illustrates Paul Ray's notion of "hockey stick" change. The hockey stick is straight for much of its length, then suddenly bends. The direction of that bend depends on how you hold the stick. One good thing about recounting the doomsday scenarios of conspiracy theorists is it provokes us to greater vigilance.

The Crucial Emergence of the Feminine Voice

After something like 6,000 years of cultural patriarchy, the rise of women is now an undeniable trend. This cutting edge trend in the evolution of our species is a major source of hope in terms of interrupting those forces among us that would bequeath to our species a dark future.

Until recently, males were not only the external rulers of society, but the masculine psyche also structured the stories and myths that have framed our view of reality to the point that male experience became *the* human experience. This bias skewed our species' sense of what should be a complementary yin-yang relationship.

Masculinity and femininity arose in the era when, to protect the gene pool from the incessant thermodynamic tick down of time and the inevitability of death, the genomes of plants and animals segregated into two pools. The strategy of reproducing by the joining of these two pools supplied a genetic mix that guaranteed freshness and renewal—similar to shuffling a deck of cards between rounds in a card game. From this natural beginning, the story of sex and gender complexified as a result of social factors.

A fundamental problem is the generally masculine structure of myth and sacred story, in most of which the feminine is defined in relation to the masculine. In the ancient stories, the woman's role is attendant to the adventures of male heroes—be it as goddess, temptress, or ultimately the hero's prize. In all manner of nuance, the woman is defined as what can be known, and this takes on dimensions both cosmic and sexual. The woman is also mother, which means the womb that carries both male and female children takes on universal meaning.

Even in cultures in which initial creation myths depicted a measure of equality between masculine and feminine, this inherent equality rarely played out well in the culture itself. Neither did equality fare well in the stories that frame the identities and ethos of men and women.

This confusion in the human psyche has had pivotal consequences. As sociologists and psychologists have pointed out, it has led to a pathology in the male that he can't easily admit. On the one hand he is afraid of and subtly subservient to his mother, while on the other hand he must also subjugate himself to woman as wife in that, in normal circumstances, she can say "no" to sex. The masculine doesn't want to admit this subservience. Consequently the woman—indeed the goddess—is blamed as the temptress, to be both desired and held in revulsion. She is both the beauty of young life and the hag of death. In such a tug of war, the feminine in mythology often becomes the icon of everything that is both sought and yet sorely misunderstood. She is simultaneously the benign and the terrible. Only in recent years has an understanding of the feminine as bringing wholeness emerged.

The Arising of Patriarchy

Gender is a social construction, as the recent unraveling of typical stereotypes of sexuality and gender roles has revealed. But when you run it through the lenses of countless cultures and the substrata of the primal stories and myths, it emerges as complex indeed. Dr David Schnarch's landmark *Constructing the Sexual Crucible*[99] and the groundbreaking *Sex at Dawn*[100] (a *New York Times* bestseller and one of NPR's favorite books for 2010) show just how complex sexuality really is, and how tragically misunderstood.

---

[99] See Schnarch, D. M. 1991 in Bibliography.
[100] See Schnarch, D. M., C. Ryan, and C. Jetha 2010 in Bibliography.

Traditionally religion has been the major interpreter of male and female roles. For at least 6,000 years nearly all religions have been patriarchal. We say 6,000 years because there's ample evidence the male domination of religions was less a part of the most primal of ancient societies. When these were close to the land and formed of more intimate clans and tribes, women often had an equal or even a dominant role. Nearly all shamans among the primal indigenous traditions from which sprang our world religions were women. Globally, it's arguable that a majority still are.

Several factors now came into play to place males center stage. Societies moved out of the context of the intimate home—a move accompanied by the growth of languages, social structures, and collective narratives, each of which are products of civilization. Religions also expanded from clan to tribe. As hierarchy began to develop in the newly stratified structures that became towns, cities, and eventually empires, males became dominant.

We see this move to patriarchy in the division of the early boughs on our tree of world religions. The traditions in which women maintained their clerical or priestly roles were the nature-based religions, extending into more-developed societies that were still agricultural in emphasis. Women also remained central in the religions that particularly emphasized philosophy, where there was a value for wisdom and especially for oracles, wherein women were judged as more able to "hear the voices of the gods." These philosophical and oracular traditions made special places for women in their priesthoods, particularly in Greece and pre-Christian Rome.

With the transition to Christian Rome, the situation changed drastically, as reflected in the rejection from the canon of Holy Scripture of most books by or about women, particularly in the suppression of the Gnostic sects with their special mystical knowledge. In the Gnostic Gospel of Mary Magdalene, it's especially evident why the early male-and-law-dominated church wouldn't want such teachings to spread. Jesus is depicted as saying to Mary Magdalene, seen by many as Jesus' primary disciple, "The Son of Man already exists within you. Follow him, for those who seek him there will find him... Beyond what I have already given you, do not lay down any further rules nor issue laws as the Lawgiver, lest you too be dominated by them." This certainly wasn't a message that a religious hierarchy centered on creed and law wanted anyone to hear.

Such norms have been all the more impenetrable when they have been cast as God's will, word, or law. One would be hard pressed to name any mainstream religion that hasn't been dominated by the patriarchal system. Moreover, the criterion of male dominance appears to define what's considered mainstream in the first place. This is reflected in the fact that the important primal deities are nearly all male. The canons of sacred texts were also generally formulated by men. When the writings of a woman are featured, it's usually in a manner that reflects either the traditional role of women or the celibate woman. Even celibacy can be understood as a male fear of woman as temptress. Still today in many religions, this male-dominated view is internalized by women, who then claim that their station in life is their own choice.

So the woman's role is set. No matter what she does she will always be a woman—a view strengthened by creation mythologies in the Jewish, Christian, and Islamic traditions, which encompass 64% of all religious people worldwide.[101] Religions in which creative roles in myth are fulfilled primarily by women are few, limited to various far-flung indigenous traditions or extinct religions such as those of ancient Mesopotamia.

Reflecting the quite different role of the magic-mythic lens in Western versus Eastern religions, the revealed religions of the West are rooted in male-dominant creation stories, while those of the East such as Buddhism and Taoism might be classified as androgynous, characterized by stories involving cosmic energies.

The Western tradition is still largely dominated by a mythology of a "mistake" by just one of the sexes. The notion of Eve in the Garden of Eden typifies the attitude of other creation stories in which a male hero must tame the chaos of earth in the form of woman. Since primordial times, this problem has been tied to the menstrual cycle. In

---

[101] adherents.com.

so many religious traditions, during this most natural of cycles the woman is shunned or forbidden to appear in this or that social role. Such restrictions have designated the onset of menstruation as a time to educate young women about their proper roles as mothers and housekeepers. The connection of evil to sexuality, and especially the role of open sexuality, was central to the fables of witches and other concepts of female evil, such as the primal image being the woman engaging in sex with a demon. Even the womb itself has been seen as an image of death and the grave. The torture and killing of scores of thousands of women worldwide for "witchcraft" is one of the saddest heritages of this legacy.

Nearly all the world's secular law flows from earlier religious law in which the position of women tended to be secondary. Such religious law particularly influenced secular laws concerning inheritance, stipulating smaller portions for women than men. Similar rules have affected the value of testimony given by men and women in jurisprudence.

Men have also been favored in the domain of writing and publishing, while another consequence has been the domination of the social sciences by the male viewpoint because most of the research was carried out by men who recorded the views and opinions of mainly males. In fact, the field of sociology eventually had to establish rules and procedures to equalize this imbalance. This said, the situation can turn on its head when the gender roles of women as wives and mothers lead to stringent laws concerning alimony and child support, unfair as these may seem to many men.

The overall import of this predicament is that although the feminine sees life through a different lens from the masculine, this view has not yet been well represented or even defined.

The Beginning of Transformation

A myth from ancient India, the story of the goddess Durga in the Hindu sacred texts, illustrates the primal nature of the emerging feminine voice after millennia of patriarchy. When, as in nearly all sacred texts, good is confronted by evil, and humankind and their gods are challenged by all that would try to tempt, malign, or defeat them, the male gods are beset by a dilemma. However, they are blessed to have an important insight. They realize that when they are confronted by evil (in the form of male demons), to defeat this evil they must give their powers to a woman. Why? Because the male hero and the male demons share the same shadow. Only the woman could see clearly enough to defeat the demons.

The Durga story is evidence of a flip side to the characterization of women in myth. Along with every negative caricature that has been attached to women in mythology, woman is also the eternal mother, often earth itself as in the modern characterization of Mother Earth in the GAIA theories of modern science. In Greek mythology, Gaia was the eternal mother not only of earth but also of all the gods. The woman is further seen as the giver of ongoing or eternal life, as in the Egyptian iconography of Isis. The recognition that all birth came through the woman—so essential to the carrying on of lineages in ancient times—led to a fuller recognition of the pivotal role of the woman in all that represents the transformative or ultimate culmination.

Similarly, in many sacred stories the woman is the earthbound or celestial guide for the male hero, particularly representing the wisdom that imbues the realm in which he walks. Such transformative roles of goddesses are common throughout the traditions, such as Isis and Hathor (of Egypt and later of Rome), Ishtar (of Assyria and Babylonia), Inanna (of Sumeria), and Kali and Durga (of the ancient Eastern texts). From this root we can understand why in most traditions, from the Greek to the Buddhist, wisdom is mostly cast in the feminine voice. Examples include Athena (of Greece), Metis (of Greece and Rome), Isis (of Egypt and later Rome), Sarasvati (of India), and Tara (of Buddhism). They represent the root of the emerging understanding of the feminine as bringing wholeness to the species.

In the classic Heart Sutra of the East, the complementary elements are wisdom cast in the feminine, along with skillful means cast in the masculine. Such views are the polar opposite of the witch, and form the beginning of what appears to be a journey to a masculine-feminine mutuality. This is the archetypal role that's emerging in the Interspiritual Age. Coincidentally, science has also come to this understanding. As we noted previously, at the base of modern physics and cosmology are principles of complementarities or dual essentialities.

In many ways the search for a modern voice for the divine feminine parallels the stages secular feminism has journeyed. Globally the feminist movement can be seen as progressing through three waves. The first and second waves were basically First World phenomena. First wave feminism began to address major structural inequalities in the status of women. However, the common social lens of most people was so entrenched that other inequities weren't at first raised and had to wait for the second wave. Both of these waves were huge steps for humanity, even though in the main they involved First World women, particularly those of the upper and middle classes.

The Feminine Voice Today

Third wave feminism is generally acknowledged as what became of the global feminine movement once women of the First, Second, and Third Worlds were involved. The roles of the individual woman, together with the challenges facing her, were inevitably different from culture to culture. The differences encompassed not only matters of daily life, but also cultural assumptions. Even within a particular nation, culture, religion, or ethnic group, it was necessary to simultaneously address, in possibly quite different ways, the nature of roles and positions for women in everyday life. These range from the roles their societies permit, to their relation to cultural myth, including the subtleties of how these are portrayed in the media or through advertising.

Likewise, in the rise of the feminine voice within religions, one can identify three stages. The third and most recent is probably the most promising because it reflects the central realizations of the emerging integrative and holistic era. Of the three general directions women have taken worldwide in approaching the waves of emerging feminism within the context of the world religions, the first has been to retrieve from the past history of spirituality and religions the elements of matriarchy and feminine mythology that could serve the modern purpose. There has been a wide variety of such endeavors, from the reconstruction of ancient matriarchal practices (sometimes followed strictly in their primal forms), to separatist varieties of feminine religion that allow only female members, and new theologies or interpretations of the old that aim toward masculine–feminine balance.

The second direction has involved addressing the position of women within each particular current religion, with a mind to correcting what has been deficient in the old patriarchal structures and seeing how these can be altered to achieve balance. This kind of activity has gone on in nearly every religion currently active on the planet.

The third direction is the search for, and emergence of, fresh voices concerning the divine feminine, unconstrained by reference to the past and in step with the integrative and holistic era.

All of these trends, but particularly the latter, have been written of eloquently in some of the most recent books of the feminist movement, including *Why Women Need the Goddess* (Carol Christ), *The Spiral Dance* (Starhawk), and *The Goddess* (Christine Downing). A search of internet websites reveals nearly 5,000 books concerning the divine feminine, over 10,000 on goddesses, and 1,000 on emerging concepts of feminine spirituality.

The background to this current growth is, as with the evolutionary consciousness movement, both long and complex. As the voice of women began to arise worldwide, there existed niches already suitable for women to take important, and sometimes prominent, roles. Examples were the New Thought movement, Unity Church, Religious Science, and the Church of Divine Science. Each of these contributed to new and wider opportunities for the maturation of the emerging feminine voice. Men also contributed. Andrew Harvey's 1995 book *The Return of the Mother* is often considered a classic. Recently, influential theologian Matthew Fox has written on the emerging voice of the feminine in his books *The Hidden Spirituality of Men* and *Hildegard of Bingen—A Saint for Our Times*.

In the end, humankind can't avoid the implications of the role of the woman as mother—that which births space and time and every element of causality. It's implicit because it's inherently bound up with what we are, which is mostly water. This is true not only of the womb, but also of the primal languages of the creation stories that attribute genesis to the everlasting waters. All things material—earth, sky, and life—are what's left of the shell of the egg that's broken when the world is born.

The word "mother" has always been synonymous with destiny. In the end of nearly every myth is the hero at death who, as he passes over, is counseled by the woman in whatever guise she appears. Of course, being old myths, these still inculcate the shade of preference for the importance of the male. But what has been emerging is what scholars refer to as the "twin pillars," the balanced relationship of masculine and feminine. Each is only a part of the complete enigmatic image of humankind, and each is limited.

Thus arises the vision of the emergence of the feminine voice as finally bringing wholeness and completion. This is a huge shift, since for millennia the male hero has been the redeemer. In the new view, qualities long attributed to the feminine take on far more finely nuanced meanings, as do those of the masculine. These have to do with pointing together to our ultimate future. In the end, the voice of the feminine is also the voice of unity, which is crucial for a realized interspirituality.

26

Building and Living Interspirituality

"Take the path closest to your home"

His Holiness the Dalai Lama

THERE CAN BE NO COMPLETE DISCUSSION OF INTERSPIRITUALITY WITH-OUT addressing what it will look like if, as Brother Teasdale predicted, interspirituality becomes the natural path for religion and spirituality in the Third Millennium. As he made clear, "The real religion of humankind can be said to be spirituality itself because mystical spirituality is the origin of all the world's religions."[102]

Again drawing on the analogy of a tree, the world religions represent a vastly diversified human experience that has had at least 100,000 years to develop. It has always been in process of transformation, though the rate of transformation is more pronounced in today's tumultuous era. With expanding globalization and multiculturalism, the interrelations of the tree's parts will be in tremendous flux in the years ahead—something that will be intriguing to observe. While some changes will involve a slow evolution, others will be rapid—an example of which is the change in the status and role of women, occurring mostly in the last century.

---

[102] MH, p 26.

One obvious trend is from entrenched traditionalism and sectarianism to an appreciation of the world's interreligious landscape. This began in earnest with the cosmopolitan and pluralistic era unfolding after the world wars. The world's interfaith movements, and the melding of cultures in response to global public media, accelerated this process. With the unfolding of interreligious contact, there also emerged more and more communication between different paths. Not only could the world's spiritual traditions begin to understand their common experiential ground, but they also became open to exploration by ordinary individuals in larger and larger numbers.

Transformative theologian Matthew Fox has articulated the common elements people find in these deeper experiences of reality, identifying them as part of a collective path humanity is in the process of discovering. Included are deeper senses of delight, amazement, and awe (Fox's *Via Positiva*); the crucible of suffering, uncertainty, and even darkness (*Via Negativa*); our passion for birthing and creativity (*Via Creativa*); and our will to transform all forms of injustice that interrupt authenticity and fulfillment (*Via Transformativa*).

Two things are sure, and they can be said with some humor, framed by two vintage clichés. First, "Change happens one life at a time." Second, just as when the world's cosmopolitan and pluralistic age unfolded after World War II, "How are you going to keep 'em down on the farm after they've seen Parie?" People on every continent are dreaming boldly today.

Spirituality as Religion

Brother Teasdale identified spirituality *itself* as the potential global religion of this millennium. Obviously, he distinguished this spirituality from the creed-based exclusive religions that have dominated our planet. However, he didn't see these as at cross-purposes, only part of an evolving process.

Teasdale also recognized that the world's secular elites have for the most part discarded religion, seeing it only as the superstitions of our antiquated magic-mythic lens. Yet, as he said, this dismissal has been foolhardy, since six-sevenths of the world's population still holds religious views—and, especially in the West, they are powerful at the ballot box. Something more finely nuanced and holistic must arise, for it won't be sufficient for our planet's survival if these two cultures—the rational and the mystical—continue simply to coexist without communicating creatively concerning world problem solving.

The further evolution of religion and spirituality toward a more inclusive and holistic understanding has been the pattern of history and can be taken to be part of the ongoing evolution of earth itself. Consequently many feel that, with inevitable globalization and multiculturalism, "old-time" religion will either evolve in a holistic direction or become obsolete. Most also believe spirituality will remain a component of human life.

The most likely scenario is that interspiritual understanding will broaden and mature within all the world's religious and spiritual traditions, even as they continue their allegiance to their traditional paths. Arising as a realization *within* all religions, and maturing as a part of ongoing internationalization and multiculturalism, the interspiritual message would strengthen and enrich the globalization process. Its emphasis on heart and tolerance intensifies the *experience* of unity consciousness, thereby breaking down the boundaries that have for so many centuries caused religions and spiritual practices to be exclusive. It could even loosen the fears that underpin the separation of world religions, especially in terms of the notion of everlasting rewards or punishments, such as heaven and hell. Modern consciousness is capable of putting such fear behind us, and many individuals worldwide have already done so. The trend is so apparent that studies of modern religions now distinguish between "hotter" and "cooler" religions, with nearly 80% in the First World falling into the latter category.[103] "Hotter" religions still take their theologies so seriously that they believe followers of other beliefs are eternally doomed, whereas the "cooler" religions have tempered such beliefs so they are no longer active in interpersonal or intercultural exchange. This trend reflects

---

[103] Pew, 2008.

the world's general transition from reactive behavior to accommodating behavior. A popular understanding of this in the interspiritual community is represented by the "many tents in the valley" metaphor articulated by Sufi teacher Llewellyn Vaughan-Lee. According to this metaphor our shared divine nature—"true nature," "Christ-Buddha" nature, or the like—is one great valley in which are welcome the tents of all the world's religious expressions. In this valley can be pitched tents of any color and shape, myriads of foods cooked and shared, and innumerable varieties of music, dance, and story celebrated without end.

It's already apparent that a growing climate of tolerance has erased many fears across cultural and religious boundaries. We see it in inter-religious and international marriage, which is common, as well as in interracial marriage, which is becoming more and more so. We see it in sex and gender issues. Throughout history, old boundaries and categories have consistently dissolved, allowing cross-cultural, transnational, and trans-traditional melding. Interreligious union is particularly common at the interpersonal level in much of the world. Thus it's likely the deepening of heart and mystical understanding that characterizes interspirituality will become common in millions of people who will also continue to practice their traditional faith.

At the same time, it can be expected that interspiritually-inspired people will create new communities, as many already have. This could be an interesting and dynamic eventuality that might last decades, or even a century, while fear and an entrenched sense of boundaries gradually shake themselves out of our consciousness.

Accordingly, an aspect of interspirituality involves the creation of new directions and practices, including syntheses of trans-traditional practices, new religious lifestyles, and innovative modes of celebration, worship, and education. Pioneers who feel this calling will develop new dreams and visions.

Mirabai Starr has written a wonderful book, *God of Love: A Guide to the Heart of Judaism, Christianity and Islam,* in which she tackles many of the interspiritual challenges for the Abrahamic faiths. She skillfully addresses the dynamic of how interspiritual people can continue their traditional practice while also cultivating the enrichment that interspiritual understanding encourages. She depicts a heart-centered spirituality as it can actually arise within the varieties of religion that have in the past viewed themselves as distinct or even separate.

Given the patterns of history, Brother Teasdale's vision of interspirituality evolving fully within the current world's religions may well be on target. Evolution of more heart-centered and inclusive religion could also provide the platform for our species to meld the magic-mythic and rational lenses. This might create an environment in which our two currently different but coexisting cultures of inner and outer experience—religion and science—could also embrace a cooperative, synergistic, and ultimately holistic path. This kind of integration already characterizes the best of the Great Wisdom Traditions and the emerging integral paradigm, leading to a spirituality that, though for many will always be *somewhat* magic-mythic, understands the essential skills of rigorous learning and intellect that characterize science.

Consciousness has always been the arbiter of our successful evolution, and it will be the same with surviving today. Reaching a new threshold in dealing successfully with the problem of exclusive religious claims, together with the integration of scientific and spiritual knowledge, is no different from the integration that was necessary to give us food, fire, shelter, clothing, names, language, and so many other skills.

Centering Religion on Consciousness Itself

This "new earth," to borrow Eckhart Tolle's famous phrase, would require a new consciousness involving the wellbeing of all. Decade by decade, little by little, the integrative lens and integrative way of life would continue to evolve, balancing our interior and exterior experiences and gifts. Though utopian, it's the basic ethos of all the world's religions—at least in their original vision, if not so often lived out.

If such a new earth seems farfetched, a world no longer ruled by monarchs would have seemed unrealistic to most in the medieval period, as would having an individual opinion during our 70 centuries of God-Kings and totalitarian states. Just ask yourself what kind of a world we would have if millions expressed an ethos of unconditionality like that of His Holiness the Dalai Lama, Mother Teresa, Nelson Mandella, or The Most Venerable Thich Nhat Hanh.

Would this mean no one would have the kind of experiences that cause them to believe they have a special message? In this developing world, everyone would be *taught* they should expect this to be their reaction to subjective experiences after millennia of the magic-mythic. There would be an awareness that everyone naturally imagines their experience to be normative and other people's a variation. Exclusive beliefs might spring up from time to time, but most of the world would be on to the fact that this isn't the way it works anymore, just as nearly everyone today realizes it's natural to stop on red and go on green, or to form a line for food or tickets instead of fighting to get what you want. As interspirituality develops, there doubtless will be many experiments in terms of how it works in practice, just as there were when democracy emerged from monarchial systems.

A powerful testament to the naturalness of interspirituality was given by a young woman at an interspiritual conference sometime after Brother Teasdale's transition in 2004. She identified herself as an "experiential evangelical Christian," but said she was also a committed "interspiritual." Her story went something like this: "As a Christian, before I realized what interspirituality is, I used to wonder how I had been lucky enough to be born into the right religion, the one where I would naturally go to heaven. I wondered about that for some time. Then I began to wonder how my friends were unlucky enough to get born into a religion that was wrong and thus would be going to hell. Because I was so close to all these people, sharing my everyday life with them in such intimate ways, I began to think, 'There must be something wrong with this picture.' Suddenly I realized that my spirituality was really about loving and embracing these people, not just the narrative about reality that I'd been told by my religion—or they by theirs. Then I wondered, 'Why be a Christian at all?' But that worked out too. I read the Scriptures in a new way, and what I saw there, in Jesus' words, was this deeper message and not one about which card I needed to carry to get into heaven. And I heard the Dalai Lama speak on television. A young Christian was asking him, 'Which direction, which tradition, should I take up to be the best kind of person I can be?' He replied, 'Take the path nearest your home; you're a Christian, right?' Following this, my deepest feelings about ultimate reward and punishment shifted from any concern with creed and toward really looking at the kind of person I was. I'm still a Christian, but I realize I might be telling this same story had I been brought up in Islam, Judaism, Hinduism, or Buddhism."

It's this simple vision that's springing up around the world that fuels the interspiritual movement. Often it's just a matter of love plus common sense. In the winter of 2012, an internet video by a young Christian who had also had this realization went viral to over 15 million viewers worldwide. The video was audacious. He proclaimed that he was disavowing religion in the name of Jesus' original teachings of love, fellowship, and compassion. The video obviously touched a nerve in multimillions.

Interspirituality is simply religion aimed at deconstructing the destructive tendencies embedded in the exclusivity of religion. In a sense, it's a sudden realization that previous conflict resulted from pre-global consciousness itself, no different than the story of blindfolded people touching an elephant and claiming that the part of the elephant they are touching is what the whole elephant is like.

Interspirituality is also the natural way in which an arising unity consciousness will affect the world. Many are actually engaging in interspirituality without realizing this is what they are doing. They simply stumble across it. Seen through the lens of unity consciousness, exclusive religious claims suddenly appear rather irrelevant. Those caught in the mindset of "who's right" become aware that this wasn't the primary message the founder of their religion was teaching, whether that be Jesus, Buddha, Mohammed, or whoever. The original message was about love and the recognition of the divine nature in everything.

Does this mean all religions have, at their base, taught unconditional love? Most have, though not all. There have always been deluded or even dangerous teachings in the name of religion. But with a higher consciousness and a deeper heart, these can easily be seen for what they are. As one person who discovered the universality in interspirituality recounted of his epiphany: "I was so happy, I just lay on the ground and laughed. It was as if I had realized that I was actually so free, I had been free not to be free."

A Convergence of Faiths

Interspirituality is an inevitable convergence, the path to which is similar for a great many. Most start their lives in a religious tradition, most often the one of their family or culture. They are brought up in the ways of that religion and naturally identify themselves as Christian, Jewish, Moslem, Buddhist, Hindu, Sikh, Jain, Taoist, humanist, agnostic, atheist, and so on. However, in our cosmopolitan era, they are also increasingly aware of the religion of others.

Since the dawn of the cosmopolitan and pluralistic period arising after World War II, most also know it's important for people to get along—a realization that leads to what has been dubbed "interfaith." It's been big in the world since our last global conflict. If you go to nearly any international gathering or watch one on television, it's likely you'll see some kind of interfaith blessing featuring a rabbi, an imam, and a minister or priest. In our cosmopolitan world, we often work alongside, know well, or are even close friends with people of other faiths. In these ways, along with movies and television, we get a sense of what everyday life is like in various religious traditions.

Today nearly 60% of Americans have had some kind of positive experience with a neighbor or friend sharing their different religious faith.[104] A 2010 *New York Times* poll indicated that across nine different religions, up to 20% of people interviewed could answer questions about other religions with some intelligence. A Pew Survey of the same year indicated direct religious study was the basis for most people's religious knowledge, with learning from conversations with

---

[104] *Newsweek,* 2010.

other people ranked second. A study by Global Social Survey[105] indicated 25% of marriages in America or Europe are between people of different religions, with those of minority religions married to a person of another faith 60% of the time. This same poll indicated 60% had dated a person of another religious background.

There's a perception, particularly put forth by some elements of the media, that Islam and Christianity are at loggerheads. However, a 2008 Gallup Poll indicated that among Europeans and Americans, 50% of Christians spoke highly of Moslems they knew personally. An independent poll by Gallup indicated 30% of Moslems responded similarly. An Interfaith Alliance poll in 2009 indicated 78% said their favorable view of those of another religion came from personal contact, precisely the view put forward by Brother Teasdale in *The Mystic Heart*.

This doesn't mean there aren't entire sectors of societies entrenched in centuries-old bitter divisiveness and hatred. No one is naive about the obstacles confronting any kind of holistic human endeavor. For instance, a recent attempt to join some Middle Eastern Jews and Palestinians in an everyday "laughter experiment" on New York television ended in utter failure. The participants ended up having to bow to threats of harm and political ultimatums, eventually asserting that they couldn't occupy the same stage. The original sponsors wished to remain anonymous, as they themselves had to abandon the project. A psychologist commenting on the venture noted that, if we're honest, entire world populations still suffer from severe post-traumatic stress disorder (PTSD) due to hurt and injury from the past, which has a huge impact on how people relate. The psychologist wasn't at all surprised the experiment went awry.

In its most fundamental sense, interspirituality is the sharing of ultimate experiences across traditions, making accessible to more and more people an expansion of consciousness through the many forms the human spiritual journey offers. As Brother Teasdale predicted, as the interspiritual experience matures, it will facilitate a new kind of interreligious dialogue worldwide.

---

[105] 2006.

From Interfaith to Interspirituality

As people begin to taste other religious experiences and appreciate the rich historical backgrounds behind them, they find the interfaith experience increasingly meaningful. As a person's spiritual path matures, they often begin to harvest the riches of varied religious practices, experiences, and insights. Truly valuing this richness is often referred to as a "trans-traditional spirituality." Worldwide, large numbers today utilize the practices of more than one religion. In some cases this has resulted from direct inquiry, though it's increasingly happening as a result of globalization and multiculturalism.

If we consider Eastern meditation techniques and yoga, a full 40% of Americans now utilize meditation techniques originally from the East.[106] As a result, 30% of Americans today have highly individualized religious practices involving activity at home as well as in their communities, and identifying themselves as "spiritual but not religious."[107]

Trans-traditional spirituality is especially common in large cities in which cultural diversity is high. Interfaith celebrations, music, chant, dance, and inter-mystical meditation are commonly advertised. In North America's and Europe's more than a dozen interfaith seminaries, virtually every graduate ordained as an "interfaith" or "interspiritual" minister has said their interest in interfaith or interspiritual ministry followed a fulfilling experience with trans-traditional spirituality.

It's important to further distinguish each of the steps that seem to characterize the natural movement from traditional spirituality to interfaith, trans-traditional spirituality, and interspirituality. There are subtle but important differences that may not be apparent.

In terms of the tree of world religions, traditions can be viewed horizontally as just the variety of religions that are on the planet right now, or they can be seen vertically as a single unified venture of our species involving our collective human experience. When seen horizontally, inevitably the question arises, "Who's right and who's

---

[106] ABC News, 2011.
[107] *Newsweek,* 2009.

wrong?" This approach also spawns concern about the participants' ultimate fate if they make a wrong choice in their beliefs.

Sectarian religions, along with interfaith or conventional ecumenism, start with the "given" that our planet has various religions, each providing a different narrative concerning who we are, where we came from, and where we may be going. Each religion also naturally believes that its understanding is most likely "true" or normative. Interfaith, or conventional ecumenism, encourages discussion among these varied views with the hope of promoting mutual understanding, tolerance, and as a spin-off world peace. However, when the chips are down, there remains an overriding concern with the differences, stemming from the question of who's actually right.

The difference between interfaith or ecumenical approaches lies in valuing more than one tradition, which is the phenomenon of trans-traditional spirituality. Though it begins with the same assumption of differences between the religions as does the interfaith approach, it emphasizes the value of sharing the varied experiences of many faiths. In enjoying more than one religion, it temporarily sets aside the concern of who is ultimately "right" or "wrong," though the issue remains. If you inquire, a trans-traditional adept will usually answer along the lines of, "I try not to go there." The concern lingers in the background, because this religious experience is shallow enough that there's still mental concern about who's ultimately "right" or "wrong." When plumbed, this concern is almost always linked to deeply hidden fear about ultimate rewards or punishment. In other words, the sense of separateness continues in most trans-traditional experience.

As one develops in trans-traditional experience, one begins to understand that there is a common "knowing" at the core of all religious experience. This awareness of a deeper holistic spirituality, interconnectedness, unconditional love, and non-separation becomes the basis of truth, not the mental concern about which religious narrative, story, interpretation, speculation, prophecy, practice, method, leader, or messiah is ultimately "right." This happens only in a mystical or contemplative understanding in which simple "right" and "wrong" (and thus rewards and punishments) are no longer at play. Love itself has become the arbiter. Rumi speaks of "beyond right and wrong" in his famous poem *Out Beyond Ideas*. Because interspirituality is a great leap into freedom, it amounts to awakening to our most primal level of unconditional love.

Interspirituality, then, starts from a different understanding of religion. Even as a teaching, it begins with the view that the entire religious experience of our species has been *a single experience* that has been unfolding through many lines and branches, together empowering our species for ever-higher evolution. In other words, interspirituality recognizes a common *experience* within all spirituality. It acknowledges a shared origin, shared process, and shared maturing. In such authentic "awakening," the individual loses the sense of separation and instead becomes aware of a profound interconnection and continuum among all things. For interspirituality, this common *experience* is the "absolute truth." From this perspective, history is in a sense irrelevant because interspirituality's primary experience concerns "right here, right now." This is why interspirituality is so profoundly connected to the awakening process.

It comes down to the fact that everyone is dreaming a different dream, and can this be okay? What actually connects us in this unfolding? How does interspirituality see this?

A prominent rabbi recently spoke to his congregation about a meeting he had with a Buddhist Zen master. They sat down together in meditative silence and quiet dialogue. Being a learned man, the rabbi said he was very aware of the huge gulf between what each had been taught to believe and what each actually believed. The rabbi felt he was sitting there aware of, if not representing, God, the entire tradition of the laws and precepts of his faith, and the identity of his people. For the Zen Master, a Buddhist who doesn't personify God, "no one was listening." There was even "no such thing" as an identity, laws, and concepts.

Being a learned man, the rabbi reported he was aware enough of the holistic lens to see that he and the Zen master, just like the seven other billion people on our planet, were simply "dreaming a different dream." Their being together felt so good, the clarity of their contact and recognition so moving, that he began to cry. There was no problem with the two different dreams.

This led the rabbi to reflect on his own life and the world of his dreams—how many simultaneous threads come and go in dreams, even causing discomfort. Then we awaken and realize all is okay. For the first time, the rabbi had a sense of humanity's collective consciousness and an awareness that our dreams don't need to be identical. In fact, he concluded that maybe they were never meant to be the same.

The story of Earth is a narrative that has simply run through the consciousness of those 106.5 billion people who have come and gone since humanity arose. We're just at the threshold of understanding a new freedom, involving mutual recognition, within the collective dream.

27

Interspirituality Before Interspirituality

"It is important to be rooted, but not stuck"

Brother Wayne Teasdale

WHAT HAS BECOME INTERSPIRITUALITY IN NAME AROSE FROM BROTHER Teasdale's association with Father Bede Griffiths, who was born Alan Richard Griffiths in Britain in 1906. Griffiths attended Oxford to study literature and philosophy, where he was tutored by C.S. Lewis. The two became close friends, sharing their exploration of ultimate reality.

Following a period of experimenting with spiritual and community life in the 1930s, Alan was drawn to Christianity and its mystical roots, which led him to apply for ministry in the Church of England. However, before he could make this move, he became involved in work with the poor and, after that work, found himself embracing the monastic life of the Roman Catholic Church. Becoming a Benedictine novice, he received the religious name of "Bede," meaning "prayer." In 1937 he took his perpetual vows as a Benedictine monk and was ordained a priest in 1940.

During the ensuing years in a number of European monasteries, and especially meeting monks of Indian origin, Father Griffiths found himself compelled to explore the Eastern mystical traditions, yoga, Indian scripture, and Jungian analysis. In 1955, a year after writing *The Golden String*, Father Bede moved to Bombay and, after visiting Elaphantes and Mysore, settled in Kengeri, Bangalore. In 1958 he joined other monks in Kurisumala, where he remained for ten years, during which time he developed activities and liturgies that acknowledged both Hindu and Christian mystical roots.

It was during this period that Father Griffiths entered into the tradition of Indian "Sannyasa," a life of utter simplicity and dependence on grace. This lifestyle later became the seed for the vision of Brother Wayne Teasdale. When in India, Griffiths dressed in the Kavi (the orange robes of the Sannyas) and went by the Sanskrit name Dhayananda (meaning "the bliss of prayer"). During this time, he wrote *Christ in India*. He also began returning to the West with some regularity to initiate East-West dialogues, a practice that was gaining in interest at that time. He sought to bring forth the mystical heritage of the world's spiritual traditions as an authentic reservoir of wisdom, not merely the conflicting ideas, narratives, and dogma of religion.

To further cement this cross-traditional work, Griffiths dedicated himself to the work of Shantivanam, an ashram in Tamil Nadu that had been founded by pioneer Christian monks working within the Hindu culture and mystical traditions. Included among these were Father Jules Monchanin and Father Henry le Saux (also known by the Hindu guru name Abhishiktananda). Griffiths worked with numerous other pioneers in the Christian-Hindu dialogue, including Raimon Panikkar, and published the books *Vedanta and the Christian Faith* and *Return to the Center*.[108]

Following this period, Father Griffiths lectured widely around the world—work that culminated in *The Cosmic Revelation* and *The New Vision of Reality,* which together with *The Marriage of East and West* are his best-known works.[109] During these last years, he was also a pioneer, especially on his lecture tours, in discussing the implications of the new physics and quantum theory for the mystical understanding

---

[108] See Griffiths, B. 1973 and 1976 respectively in Bibliography.
[109] See Griffiths, B. 1981 and 1989, 1952 respectively in Bibliography.

of reality. Shantivanam was a petri dish from which came numerous other pioneers in trans-traditional mysticism, including Father Griffiths' association with holistic scientist Rupert Sheldrake and his mentoring of close colleagues such as Brother Teasdale, Russill Paul, and Andrew Harvey. Father Griffiths transitioned on May 13, 1993 in his monastic hut in Shantivanam.

The Roots of Interspirituality

Because interspirituality is a state toward which we tend naturally as spirituality evolves, many were engaging in interspirituality before Brother Teasdale coined the word in 1999. For example, in the 1980s A.H. Almass (the pen name of Hameed Ali) authored the bestselling book *Essence*. This teaching, now also known as The Diamond Heart Work, combined the mystical Sufi message from Islam, modern psychology, and Tibetan Buddhism.

As that decade turned to the 1990s, Francisco Varela, Evan Thompson, and Eleanor Rosch wrote a popular guide entitled *The Embodied Mind,* melding the message of Buddhism, French phenomenological philosopher Maurice Merleau-Ponty, and cognitive and immunological science. Later in the 1990s, but before Brother Teasdale's *The Mystic Heart*, integralists Michael Murphy and George Leonard began a program by the name of Integral Transformative Practice, combining meditation practice, affirmative visioning, attention to physical exercise and nutrition, study of world spiritual traditions, and collective sacred service. Also in the 1990s, a prominent trans-traditional teacher Lex Hixon (whose Sufi name was Nur al-Anwar al-Jerrahi) endeared himself to many. Imbued with the messages of mystical Islam, Christianity, Hinduism, Buddhism, and the Lakota indigenous tradition, his 1995 book *Coming Home: The Experience of Enlightenment in Sacred Traditions* is now considered a classic.

One of the greatest injustices in the history of developing interspirituality involves the early contributions of theologian Matthew Fox who, following two official Vatican inquiries into his forward-looking views, and dismissal from the Dominican Order in 1993, moved his ministry and work to the Episcopal church. Fox's pioneering writing in the areas of creation spirituality, the understanding of a cosmic Christ, and what he called "deep ecumenism," reflected the heart of the interspiritual message before it could easily be popular and well in advance of Brother Teasdale's coining of the word in 1999. In hindsight, Fox's classic works, such as *The Coming of the Cosmic Christ* and *One River, Many Wells,* are among the great precursors of the interspiritual message. Early on, he pointed out the central interspiritual message in such great Christian figures as St Francis, Julian of Norwich, Meister Eckhart, Nicholas of Cusa, and most recently Hildegard von Bingen. Fox's work, ongoing now through over thirty books that have reached millions of readers, amply reflects the tug of war that has gone on historically between visionary thinking and the constraints of ecclesiastical authority. Even the discussions of the post-Vatican II foundationalist theologians, none of whom were forced to leave the Roman Church, also fell to the censors of ecclesiastical authority in proclamations of the Vatican's Congregation for the Doctrine of the Faith in 1984 and 1986. Fox joins Teilhard and Aurobindo in this respect, and his work now is able to stand out in the greater light that recent decades have brought.

The roots of interspirituality go even deeper in secular society. The same ethos that marks interspirituality was at the heart of the 19th century American enlightenment flowing from the pens of Ralph Waldo Emerson, Henry David Thoreau, and Walt Whitman, who identified the insights of interconnectedness and the praxis of love—in line with the central message of the world's Great Wisdom Traditions, but freed from the exclusive theological claims and end-time scenarios of organized religion. Outstanding figures followed in the wake of America's civil rights movement as well. A prominent, truly interspiritual figure among them was Howard Thurman who, as Dean of Chapel at Howard University, crystallized the teachings of Gandhi for the movement that surrounded Dr Martin Luther King.

With the culmination of the 19th century and the beginning of the 20th, the same ethos became the message of humanism, which has both a religious and a secular brand. The motto "deed over creed" was coined by Ethical Culture founder Dr Felix Adler, whose universal view of Judaism had led to his dismissal from the New York City rabbinate. When one examines the literature of Ethical Culture, the views of religious humanism and interspirituality are uncannily similar—as long as the humanists aren't caught up in a need to identify solely with atheism. Adler, an ethical philosopher by post-rabbinic profession, was a mystic, whereas subsequent generations of humanist leaders moved toward reductionism and atheism. One can read Felix Adler and Brother Teasdale and find many of their words are virtually the same. People versed in Adler often remark that if his version of humanism had survived and prospered, the interspiritual movement wouldn't have been necessary.

Variety and Interspirituality

After the initial success of his book, Brother Teasdale commented that the most common question he was asked concerned how interspirituality would come into wider practice. Accordingly, Teasdale and a circle of colleagues in New York City founded Interspiritual Dialogue in 2002 in association with the Spiritual Caucus of nongovernmental organizations at the United Nations, a network that became Interspiritual Dialogue 'n Action (ISDnA) after Teasdale's passing in 2004. The name and acronym were suggested by indigenous shaman and anthropologist Don Oscar Miro-Quesada, an early friend of Teasdale, who felt the letters DNA had special significance.

As mentioned earlier, the 2004 program was to provide a half-day introduction to the interspiritual vision at the 2004 Parliament of the World's Religions, the same Parliament where the World Commission on Global Consciousness and Spirituality proposed its global manifesto. Teasdale was to be the keynote speaker, but because of his failing health was unable to attend. Father Thomas Keating, who with Teasdale and others had shared intermystical understanding through the Snowmass Initiative, in 2002 founded the Spiritual Paths Foundation with other friends and colleagues of Brother Teasdale. Members of both these groups joined for Common Ground conferences at The Crossings retreat center in Austin, Texas. These meetings had been inaugurated by leaders such as Teasdale, Wilber, Keating, and His Holiness the Dalai Lama before the publication of *The Mystic Heart*. A tribute event was held for Teasdale by the Common Ground gathering following his passing. The nine-point platform put forward by the Snowmass Inititative became a centerpiece of these original interspiritual associations. The nine points are:

1. The world religions bear witness to the experience of Ultimate Reality to which they give various names: Brahma, Allah, (the) Absolute, God, Great Spirit.

2. Ultimate Reality cannot be limited by any name or concept.

3. Ultimate Reality is the ground of infinite potentiality and actualization.

4. Faith is opening, accepting, and responding to Ultimate Reality. Faith in this sense precedes every belief system.

5. The potential for human wholeness—or in other frames of reference, enlightenment, salvation, transformation, blessedness, nirvana—is present in every human.

6. Ultimate Reality may be experienced not only through religious practices but also through nature, art, human relationships, and service to others.

7. As long as the human condition is experienced as separate from Ultimate Reality, it remains subject to ignorance, illusion, weakness, and suffering.

8. Disciplined practice is essential to the spiritual life; yet spiritual attainment isn't the result of one's own efforts, but the result of the experience of oneness (unity) with Ultimate Reality.

9. Prayer is communion with Ultimate Reality, whether it's regarded as personal, impersonal (transpersonal), or beyond both.

After Teasdale's passing, the East-West integral journal *Vision in Action* published a retrospective by other close friends of Teasdale summarizing aspects of his vision of interspirituality he hadn't the opportunity to record. Additionally, a book entitled *The Common Heart* appeared in 2006, summarizing the vision of the Snowmass conferences. It isn't the history of these events or their participants that's so important (lists are readily available across the internet and in the various writings mentioned), but the clarification of interspirituality that emerged.

Further guidelines for interspirituality came with the creation of The Community of The Mystic Heart. A large but far-flung association centered on many of Brother Teasdale's personal friends, it originally aimed to fulfill his dream of a universal order of *sannyasa* (renunciates) engaged in interspiritual work. With an ordaining authority for interspiritual ministers, brothers, sisters, and wisdom keepers through its allied Order of Universal Interfaith, it remains a center for dynamic discussion and promulgation of the Teasdale vision. However, the monastic mission in its modern setting, together with the redefining of whole life commitment to spiritual practice and sacred service, currently involves more the New Monasticism discussion, along with those who trace their work to the lifestyle and structures that typified Father Bede Griffiths' Shantivanum ashram in India.

Witnessing the speedy growth of the interspiritual vision in the decade since Teasdale's seminal writings, it's fair to say that today anything goes in creating the structures and activities that will ultimately serve this vision. We are in a time of experimentation, open to anyone. Even the ordaining authority for creating interfaith and interspiritual ministries now emerging from the increasing number of interfaith seminaries and associations is an exploration of how interspirituality might best unfold.

The Message of Interspirituality After *The Mystic Heart*

After Brother Teasdale's passing, to their surprise many discovered that he had talked about quite different matters to different people. Part of this may be because, in his contemplative humility, he tended to be rather selective and compartmentalized in his sharing. In discussions across his coterie of friends and acquaintances, it was noticeable that to some who knew him well, he had spoken of many personal matters but not necessarily in detail about his vision for interspirituality. On the other hand, with colleagues he had assembled to advance this work, he was more likely to talk less about personal matters and more about the details of the interspiritual dream. For instance, it was several years after Teasdale's passing when many of his friends learned that Seven Pillars House of Wisdom, an interspiritual organization with headquarters in upstate New York, had been dedicated to Teasdale's memory because of his friendship with its founder, Pir Zia Inayat-Khan. Other examples were the founding of Claritas Institute for Interspiritual Inquiry by Joan Borysenko and Brother Teasdale's work as a Founding Patron of the Edinburgh International Center for Spirituality and Peace. As a result, many of Teasdale's friends didn't meet each other until interspirituality began to grow, especially as assisted by today's frequent gatherings of contemplatives from many traditions—a practice that was only in its infancy when Teasdale was alive.

Prior to his death, Teasdale made further clarifications to his friends following publication of *The Mystic Heart* in answer to what he said was the most common response he received: "This is a beautiful vision, but how will it be achieved?" In New York, in preparation for the 2004 Parliament of the World's Religions, he further distinguished what he called a "primary" and "secondary" interspirituality. These may sound like academic terms, but they come from ecological jargon Teasdale had picked up from Thomas Berry. In *The Mystic Heart*, Teasdale wrote copiously about nature and nature-based religion, making many references to Berry's pioneering work. The message about primary and secondary interspirituality is important and easy to understand.

In ecology, "primary" (as in primary forest or primary habitat) means undisturbed or virgin habitat. "Secondary" (secondary forest, secondary habitat) refers to what comes after disturbance, separation, and a history of use. Teasdale recognized a paradox in the identity of interspirituality as heart-based and unity consciousness-based. In traditional spiritual terms, he knew he was speaking of awakening. In *The Mystic Heart*, he singled out this spiritual awakening of humankind as the definitive revolution for our species. Knowing such awakening would occur in the context of the existing religious and spiritual traditions, he identified the primary work of interspirituality as the cultivation of that innate element in our human nature—the mystical endeavor.

In this pursuit, one meets only what's right here, right now—as if there was *no* history of differences between all the myriad paths of spiritual seekers. When individuals explore their inner space with meditation or contemplation—call it what you may—or assemble and share this exploration, they are no longer relating in the context of concepts or ideas. They are plumbing the subtle realms of reality, whether understood in spiritual language or the language of science's quantum fields. This territory essentially has no history, occurring only in the "now." This is the primary habitat of our nature.

Brother Teasdale also recognized the historical differences of the various traditions and saw that they required a reaching out from the unity consciousness of primary interspiritual sharing, involving a full recognition and embracing of each other in what's right here, right now, with a view to the healing of these past experiences of disagreement. Teasdale explores this healing process in what is perhaps his most important book, *Bede Griffiths: An Introduction to His Interspiritual Thought*. This distinction of primary and secondary interspirituality has also been noted by spiritual teachers familiar with Teasdale's writings but unaware of his conversations after *The Mystic Heart*. For instance Loch Kelly, a Buddhist meditation teacher and founder of Awake Awareness Institute, has used the term "intraspirituality" for Teasdale's "primary interspirituality," since *intra* implies within, while *inter* implies between. Raimon Panikkar made a similar distinction about the internal spiritual journey in a 1999 book entitled *The Intra-Religious Dialogue*.

In practice this means interspirituality has two kinds of initial work to accomplish:

- Cultivating the Presence found in the pristine contemplative experience, as if there had never been a history of divisions among us.

- Working through interreligious gatherings, discussions, dialogues, and discourse to heal the divisions of this fractured past.

The first need is being met by the numerous meetings of active contemplatives everywhere in the world, as well as by the myriad teachers and students of the contemplative pursuit. The mystical pursuit should be encouraged by all the traditions and not relegated to a special activity for only a few.

The second need is met whenever interfaith and interreligious groups recognize their need to gather, discuss, learn, understand, and work for mutual understanding among the world's religions. Teasdale emphasized that the special quality of such gatherings is the personal connection between religious adherents simply as people—something always mentioned by His Holiness the Dalai Lama. Relating as human beings beyond conventional boundaries enables us to discover how alike we really are. In this spirit, The Order of Universal Interfaith, developed by associates of Brother Teasdale, hosts a "Big I" conference annually, emphasizing "Interfaith, Interspirituality, and Integral."

28

Interspiritual Life and Practice

"The Interspiritual Age will require institutions and structures to carry, express, and support it"

Brother Wayne Teasdale

BROTHER WAYNE TEASDALE'S STATEMENT THAT THE INTERSPIRITUAL AGE must be supported by appropriate institutions and structures[110] presents both a challenge and a mandate to anyone attracted to interspirituality.

If interspirituality is to emerge as the anchor for earth's religions of the future, it requires structures, even institutions, to develop, foster, and carry its message. Addressing what these will be is a discussion that will go on for a long time. Brother Teasdale would have had no desire to own or guide this process. He was simply the one who set the vision down in writing at an early stage. Like His Holiness the Dalai Lama, he referred to himself simply as a "monk."

Many are already living an interspiritual life, having integrated into their daily routine and spiritual practice aspects of more than one tradition—a move that has enriched their lives immeasurably. However,

---

[110] MH, p 248.

although interspirituality is deeply identified with the more intimate, personal "I" and "We" experiences of reality, it desires a world in which institutions—the enigmatic "It" and "Its" space—reflect the sensitivity, values, and vision of the more intimate spaces.

At a recent Gathering of Young Contemplatives sponsored by The Contemplative Alliance, one of the distinctive traits of younger people pursuing the interspiritual path was their desire to live in a world in which spirituality and everyday life are no longer divorced in the way they so often are in the business world. Not only do they understand the inherent schizophrenia in the more pathological institutions of our planet and wish to remedy this, but they also identify commercial greed and lack of any sense of the collective as among the greatest dangers facing our planet. These are not just spiritual do-gooders, but in many cases the cream of the crop of universities and colleges.

Because interspirituality is such a natural vision, its principles can't be separated from the common search of the evolutionary consciousness movement, the Integral movement, and the foundationalist discussions following Vatican II. This is the search for realistic unifying principles—the Archimedean points. The central unifying point is, of course, unity consciousness and the realization that a trend toward unity consciousness is apparent in history. This reflects the trend toward higher consciousness and skill set in modern scientific studies of the brain-mind.

The variety of spiritual teachings is dizzying, each with its own "take" and a committed following who have found that particular way the best for them, at least for now. Unfortunately, many fall into the trap of the "myth of the given," which is the belief that their way is the best for everyone. While the conversation may be shifting away from a monolithic understanding of religion toward the smorgasbord of trans-traditional spirituality—or even toward the innate unity consciousness in interspirituality—this is going to be a lengthy process that will move in fits and starts.

It's crucial that interspirituality always serves to balance and integrate. The magic-mythic lens is alive and well in the burgeoning New Age movement, and it often turns anti-intellectual and even anti-factual. When this happens and the toolbox of the mind is discarded, people can believe almost any fanciful idea that appeals to their emotions, creating another form of information-proof fundamentalism. The same is true of an over-reliance on just the rational lens. The rational lens often requires ignoring the entire spectrum of subjective experience, discarding spiritual experience as unreal, even delusional, and thereby becoming just as information-proof. An integrative lens promotes balance among our natural human skill sets.

An integrated lens can take in interior and exterior, objective and subjective, emotional and intellectual, and learn to navigate these with balance, employing a skillful yin-yang. It's essential that people speak out for this in all circles.

Interspirituality Isn't a New "Blend Religion"

When people look at interspirituality without going deeply into the heart and considering the implications of an actual unity consciousness, they are tempted to think interspirituality is an attempt at a new "blend religion." In theological terms this is called "syncretism," a blend that isn't exactly this and not exactly that. This can be confusing for people who equate religious belief with the "faith phenomenon" and the latter with absolute truth. If interspirituality is just a blend, what has become of absolute truth, and especially people's concern with ultimate rewards and punishments, their destiny in a heaven or a hell?

As we have noted, throughout history the "faith phenomenon" has motivated loyalty to countless nations, leaders, and religions. Faith in this sense is a matter of energy and will connected to something believed to be true. The 9/11 terrorists showed that dark side of "faith" when they crashed their passenger-filled airplanes into their intended targets. Here, the insights of the integralist Wilber Combs Lattice, mentioned by us earlier, are helpful and important. The vertical experience of devotion and faith is a shared and powerful element in all human nature. When it's attached to a certain idea or belief, it can motivate extraordinary behavior. But a sweeping view of history, especially remembering the devotion of millions of people to thousands of religions that are now extinct, calls us to keep in mind that innate, ineffable, and powerful subjective experiences are simultaneously filtered through cultural lenses. How else, for instance, are we to understand that, for centuries, slavery was taken for granted as moral and ethical, and supported by many of history's great religions?

The holistic age and the experience of interspirituality—the very awakening Brother Teasdale was speaking of—calls us to go deeper into the world of the heart. Certainly not everyone will immediately understand this subtle but important difference between faith in a particular religious context, or even faith based on some kind of a personal mystical experience, yet still *exclusive* and not inclusive in nature. The heart of interspirituality is a unity consciousness which is innately inclusive. This is why interspirituality is ultimately an experiential matter.

Fortunately, the true interspiritual experience is itself synonymous with the nature of true spiritual, moral, and ethical maturity in the context of *any* of the world's spiritual traditions. Interspirituality is actually *spiritual maturity* and thus quite in tune with all the world's existing traditions. It's far from "just a new blend."

Holarchy and Hierarchy

Central to a grassroots experiential spirituality are intimate circles of colleagues in associations that must grow in size and capability. This kind of development reflects how life itself matured on our planet, from cells to colonies, and finally to organisms. A simple assemblage of people as a circle offers a way to experiment dynamically with grassroots, experiential, horizontal, holarchical ways of doing things, constituting a break from the old hierarchical structures. Hierarchy is also a part of nature, of course, but the emphasis of institutions on rigid hierarchy—which has often been connected to patriarchy—has generated many problems. Brother Teasdale called the transition to circles the "democratization" of spirituality.

Circles have a rich history. We don't hear about them because they were replaced so soon by hierarchies that dominated during the many centuries of monarchy and dictatorship, but the circle model was common in the early indigenous and nature-based religions, and still is. The Circle of Elders met as equals and problem-solved together. The first active democracies were actually among pirates. The motivation was far from idyllic, but to make sure no one got cheated, most pirate groups used a voting system. Hence the expression "honor among thieves."

Teasdale wrote about circles as a structure in which mutual trust and authentic friendship could generate radical personal and collective empowerment. He attributed the energy of circles to the reality of collective consciousness and pointed out how such circles underpinned many of the great reform and revival movements down through history. He believed the recognition of interspirituality had grown out of circle work as the culmination of many years of discussion among contemplatives and sacred activists about their shared experience. Although these circles didn't directly intend to birth a new paradigm, he noted that it has happened anyway as an emergent phenomenon. This was another reason Teasdale chose the prefix "inter" when he authored the words "interspiritual" and "intermysticism."

Writing in 1999, it was probably impossible for Teasdale to be aware that by the new millennium an entire movement would develop around circles or "holarchies." It has swept through the business community, into the modeling of group and governance process, and has itself put new terms in our vocabulary the likes of "group think," "collective consciousness," and "synergistics." The simple realization that nearly everything is at once a whole and a part has become a game changer. We are holons, and the entire cosmos is a holon. Interspirituality holds that the world's religions are also holonic.

The discussion about holarchies is today very sophisticated. If you follow thinkers like Ken Wilber, Andrew Smith, Don Beck, Chris Cowan, Gerry Goddard, Mark Edwards, or Fred Kofman, you'll see that the discussion is influencing global transformation. A Google of "holarchy" or holarchical models will bring up 100,000 entries, while a search for holarchical business models will bring up nearly a million, as will a search under "circle-style leadership" or "circle work." This is a far cry from the old Robert's Rules of Order and its Sergeant-at-Arms to eject anyone not in line with the hierarchy. Again, it's testimony to "you have to admit it's getting better."

The kind of activities that appear naturally across the interfaith, trans-traditional, and interspiritual landscape now number in the thousands, as can be discovered through internet search engines. To try to create a worldwide list would be nearly impossible. However, they include the following:

Shared Meditation, Deep Listening, and Deep Dialogue Satsang. Contemplative practices address the inherent need all have for what Teasdale called primary interspirituality—sharing consciousness and heart together "right here, right now." East and West, such gatherings have gone on for centuries and today are extremely common. The most well known word for such meditative circles, whereby you can find out about gatherings in your area, is "*satsang*," which is Sanskrit for a circle of truth. Authentic satsang is about open inquiry into, and experience of, consciousness itself, and not about the teachings of this or that tradition. Ed Bastian of Spiritual Paths Institute has provided a wonderful book on cross-traditional meditation methods, entitled *Interspiritual Meditation: A Seven-Step Process from the World's Spiritual Traditions*. An advantage of these kinds of formulations is that they draw on time-tested processes from the world's traditions and can be adopted and adapted by multiple interfaith and interspiritual communities.

Formats for circle work are rapidly developing. Loch Kelly, a spiritual teacher associated with Adyashanti, proposed a format for *Lateral Satsang* in 2004, and this has been employed by several interspiritual circles (or "intraspiritual" circles, in Loch's terms). Other experiments with circle formats have included the well-known *Snowmass Inter-religious Initiative* of Fr Thomas Keating, the *Interspiritual Dialogue Circles, Aspen Grove,* and *Light Circles* formed around friends of Brother Teasdale—and even an exotically named *Nondual Dinner* among the community of spiritual director Greg Goode. Today there is an Institute for Circle Work on America's East coast, in the Sacred Activism community a network of *Circles of Grace*, and in the Integral community the *Ken Wilber Meetup*. This is only the beginning.

Mystical Celebration and Sharing. These may take as many forms as the traditional religions have to offer, as interfaith, trans-traditional, and interspiritual practitioners gather for mystical sharing. Zikr (or Dhikr, "Remembrance of God") and Kirtan (Kirtana or Sankirtan, "Praise or Eulogy") are two popular forms of chanting or praying silently, aloud, or with music, and even sometimes dance, that come respectively from Islam and from the traditions of India. The Passover Seder from the Jewish tradition and Eucharist from the Christian tradition are also often celebrated in an interspiritual context. The same is true of Pipe Ceremony and other traditions from the world's indigenous communities. Sacred pop music is also popular with millions today. A look at your local listings of spiritual and religious events will readily tell you what kind of activities are going on in your area.

Interspiritual Education. Interfaith seminaries in both North America and Europe rapidly evolved toward trans-traditional spirituality, then interspirituality, as Brother Teasdale's book became available to elaborate the path. Many of these seminaries now ordain both interfaith and interspiritual ministers. Such ordinands often find ministries serving the cross-traditional community, especially in colleges, hospitals, and hospices. Other interfaith and interspiritual ministers have become entrepreneurs, establishing their own interspiritual churches, centers, and communities, or even new seminaries. Included are experimental programs in interspirituality, interspiritual education, and masters and doctoral level dissertations on the development of interspiritual life and ministry.[111]

New Community. Particularly in response to Brother Teasdale's second book, *A Monk in the World*, the definition of complete commitment to spiritual practice and sacred service—the traditional role of monasticism—is also changing. Inspired interfaith and interspiritual pioneers worldwide are experimenting with new kinds of communities involving both actual community and more far-flung associations.

---

[111] See graduate programs and interspirituality under "O'Brien", "Pennington", and "Wright" in the Bibliography; see Interspiritual Education programs at three of the institutions first associated with Br Wayne Teasdale: www.onespiritinterfaith.org, www.spiritualityandpractice.com, www.spiritualpaths.net, and at www.thecominginterspiritualage.com.

Interspiritual Dialogue. The number of interreligious gatherings involving sharing and discussion of worldviews, theology, contemplative practice, and sacred service is nearly overwhelming. This sharing addresses Brother Teasdale's secondary interspirituality, aiming at trans-traditional and cross-cultural discussion that can promote the healing of past divisions and wounds. Almost every association, seminary, or other institution that has sprung from the interfaith, transtraditional, and interspiritual movements sponsors regular or annual interfaith and interspiritual discussions.

Circles in Practice: the Creation of Effective Collectives

It's one thing to teach about awakening and quite another to produce awakened behavior. The proof will be in the pudding when it comes to the interspiritual community actually being able to create an exemplary collective. For all the wonderful words about awakening and unity consciousness—and for all the inspiring teachers whose focus is oneness—if such teachings aren't reflected in an ability to work together with new skill, it will be cause for pause, even skepticism.

The failure of communities to create institutions that reflect their professed values has been epidemic throughout history. The interspiritual, integral, and evolutionary consciousness movements need to look at this soberly. For all the high-end talk and theory about "oneness," it can be hard to get past all the advanced egos in the room. This is where the rubber meets the road. Because there are so many variables at play with collectives, time and many experiments are going to be necessary to discover processes that work. Below are some examples of the thresholds that need to be met.

The Meaning of "We." It's often joked that, to some in leadership, "We" means "more people working with *me*." One circle pioneer reported that in forming an initiative, he reached out to a certain individual of note and received the reply, "I don't really have the inclination or time to put into this, but if you get something going, I'll be happy to lead it."

Conflict between the magic-mythic and the rational also often comes to the fore. While one would think everyone might appreciate the need for balance, there can be disagreement between the "be"-ers and the "do"-ers in the group. Also, magic-mythic or transcendently inclined individuals often insist that all structures are bad, then wonder why they can never achieve long-term results.

Misunderstanding of the transcendent lens can lead people to preach "we don't need to do anything," "it will just happen," or "we don't need a plan." At the opposite pole, pure activists or individuals not into spiritual practice often form circles with no standards for basic behavior such as kindness and cordiality. One of the criticisms of the Occupy Wall Street movement has been that some of its groups appear so stuck in their own methods that they can't learn from the lessons of past activists, especially anyone over 50. They simply repeat old missteps.

Discussing these foibles of cooperative work might seem silly, but it unfortunately reflects many realities of group process. Brother Teasdale addressed this by noting that work in our three-dimensional world always involves an integration of heart, head, and hands. If you leave any of these out, you neglect a crucial element. This is exactly the kind of omission that characterizes the dead ends so many circle initiatives end up in.

Psychologists point out that most people find identity and fulfillment either from validation by others or validation from within themselves. These tendencies result in different ways of pursuing fulfillment and working with others to do so. Other-validated individuals put great emphasis on group process, while self-validated individuals favor structures that coordinate while maximizing individual gifts and creativity. These personality types are often at odds in associations and organizations of our "green" epoch.

Creative Energy: Balancing Input and Output. Another challenge in circle work is to get people, especially leadership, to put as much energy into a collective effort as they do toward promoting their own work or ministry. This reflects the centuries-long embedment of ego and serving one's "I-space" first. A challenge that's particularly difficult is the habit of claiming to have neither time nor resources to share, while asking why others in the group "aren't doing anything." In many cases, the second law of thermodynamics is being overlooked: if energy isn't constantly input into the system, it will run down. Hence when any circle forms, there not only needs to be clear discussion of the need for proactive input, and no blame, but also an awareness that continual energy will need to be injected into the circle for anything to be sustained. As Brother Teasdale said, everyone has to be willing to provide that *extra*ordinary energy.

Experiencing Collective Consciousness. Another challenge with the development of the "We" collective space is to actually experience collective consciousness. Everyone who has had the experience of a group arriving at creative synergy knows this experience is palpable. Successful group synergy is often not repeatable each time a group meets, perhaps due to the enigmatic nature of the subtle realms. Most people feel this is because we are at the beginning of the discovery process with respect to synergy, circles, collectives, and collective consciousness.

We also have a lot of bad habits, one of which in the spiritual community is the competition among leaders. This is what the integralists have identified as "myth of the given"—that it's utterly natural for everyone to assume the experience they are having is the one everyone is having, or should have. It can be especially subtle because most leaders and teachers lead and teach from their own experience, which is of course completely natural. The reality of the myth of the given needs to be factored in as one of the subtle shadows in the group process.

A Clash of Eras. One aspect of us all sharing the same process of development—humorously referred to in science as all being "victims of evolution"—is that we carry problems embedded from earlier levels of human experience. The integral movement has done a great service in pointing out the dynamics of how our most recent integrative and holistic eras are still at odds with things taken for granted since the earlier pluralistic period. Subtle conflicts that arise from this are so common and dicey that they need to be mentioned.

The pluralistic epoch emphasized everything that's good about radical freedom and equality. However, how many times have we been at gatherings where giving everyone "equal time" and listening to every individual's story, pet theory, or pet solution bogged the process down into a going-nowhere mediocrity? As the developmentalists point out, although the worldwide movement to freedom and equality was an essential step, it resulted in the problem of how to discern what has higher value. It's crucial to have equality and freedom while also discerning higher value and collective direction.

Holarchical business models take this into account by balancing the roles of the individual in circles and the role of the circle itself. The circle designates individuals to move the agenda forward on behalf of the sense of collective value and direction. Oddly, this is just what the old-time pirates were doing in their early quasi-democracies. They voted for the leaders they felt best understood and could effectuate the common good. But this can also present problems as it seeks its skill sets. Most of us have experienced what is maybe best called the "I know better group" within the group. This group will wait until hell freezes over for everyone else to agree with them. As a result, how does anyone decide who's really got the balance in a group? It can be difficult, but often it has to do with who's willing to do the work.

In the long run, the world will either see effective collectives emerge from all these international attempts at integration and holism or it won't. Whether humankind can actually reach the threshold of expressing a skilled collective has to be one of the major questions of the Interspiritual Age.

Democratizing Spirituality: Everyone Is a Pioneer

What could be more appropriate in our age of growing fear of multinational corporations and financial institutions than a call by religion to experiment with holarchies and circles?

Experimenting with circle work and holarchy is essential to interspirituality and grassroots spirituality, for it explores the human potential to build global structures that serve the wellbeing of all. Nearly every world problem results from ineffective collective structures that serve only self-interest groups—structures to which we have repeatedly returned in response to past failure of collective models.

Two points regarding the future are pivotal. First, in the past we could fall back on self-interest models because the world was still large enough and resources plentiful enough that inequity appeared sustainable. In our era of globalization and finite resources, this is no longer the case. Second, our avoidance of identifying and creating successful collective structures postpones the necessary evolutionary leap that our species must make if it is to survive long-term on a crowded and resource-scarce planet.

We are being asked to cross the same threshold we failed to cross in past experiments involving capitalism versus socialism. In terms of the common good and the wellbeing of all, socialism had the right goal. However, a key missing ingredient was mature, conscientious individuals who wouldn't abuse the collective. Another missing ingredient was the reality that if the individual isn't motivated, stimulated, and fulfilled, socialist structures fall apart from within. Accordingly, socialist or collective failures in the past were characterized by rampant corruption, lack of respect for public property, and lack of an incentive for individuals to succeed through their own energy and creativity.

When you speak to young people from the socialist societies of Europe, they often express resentment that their system requires motivated individuals to carry uninspired, unproductive people. But no sooner do they express a preference for what they call the "animal-style economic freedoms" of the United States than they see the growing division between rich and poor, which leads them to conclude that neither is this model sustainable. The search for balance between these different social models characterizes the political dynamic worldwide as we move through the integrative and holistic period.

A provocative summary of this challenge appeared in a book by an American author championing "conservative" values. The book is subtitled *Recapturing Conservative Pessimism*, and its thesis is that only pessimism protects humanity from, to paraphrase, "running off a cliff" as we pursue our desire to make the world better. The author concludes that conservatism loses its political punch when anyone becomes optimistic. He advises that it's best for everyone to feather their own nest and take as a maxim that it's folly to have any sense of the collective or collective value. This book was wildly popular in the conservative movement.

Experimentation in balancing holarchical forms with traditional hierarchical forms has been widespread in education since the pluralistic era. One of the well-known pioneers is writer Parker Palmer, a sociologist associated for many years with the American Association of Higher Education. He was an early advocate of processes that generate multiple perspectives, encourage proactive listening and feedback, and view leadership as best informed and empowered by a collective consisting of quality relationships among all the individuals within a group. Palmer also became influential in interreligious circles because his writing directly addressed balancing the interior and exterior concerns of life, together with the mutuality of being and doing. His influential writings view teaching and learning as a dance, a dynamic yin-yang. Other approaches to generating multiple perspectives characterize the important progress made in recent decades by methods for amiable conflict resolution. David Cooperrider's Appreciative Inquiry and Marshall Rosenberg's Non-Violent Communication have been landmark contributions.

This same sense of balance and dance is typical of successful business holarchy models, about which nearly 30,000 entries are available on the search engines. In these models, ego is replaced by the sense of the evolutionary purpose and goals of the group. The circle tasks individuals within it to address how to best dynamically steer the group toward its vision and goals. Holarchy has played an important part in the development of the Arab Spring, the Occupy movement, and also house church movements worldwide among religious people who, especially in the wake of financial and ethical scandals, desire to remain true to their religious roots but step away from organized religion.

Organizing the Interspiritual Dream

Nothing happens without someone who has a vision to which they are committed. But everyone is busy, so it's rare for collectives to come about as a result of a group stepping up to work together to form an institution. Usually a few people committed to the vision work in an ad hoc way to keep the vision "out there," positioning it more and more. Eventually a vision whose time has come gains traction, from which an institution may later arise.

Brother Teasdale was aware of this and spoke of the importance of central figures moving a vision along during its infancy. He believed that many people worldwide are prepared—preconditioned actually —for stepping up to the unfolding interspiritual vision.

This principle is also known in science, where it's referred to as being "pre-adapted." In evolution, some things developed rapidly because certain plants or animals had already developed attributes that could easily make a second leap. Flying is a good example. Feathers developed in the dinosaurs for regulating body temperature, not for flying. But they became the perfect pre-adaptation to eventually make flight possible.

Teasdale felt that many traditions and individuals were pre-adapted to make the leap to a spirituality for the Third Millennium. He saw this as part of the mystical process that underpins how the natural search for unifying principles and Archimedean points among the world's spiritual traditions would result in the emergence of an Interspiritual Age. This was why he advocated person-to-person contact among mystics and contemplatives. He suspected they would recognize each other's experience of unity consciousness. Since they were respected by the leadership of their own tradition, they might be able to turn organized and exclusive religion toward a more universal understanding.

Teasdale used to say such shared commitment was far more important than money or initial administrative structures. He saw a special empowerment in what he called "authentic friendship in the context of a shared mission" and felt such personal connections and the shared energy of commitment were a special part of the global interspiritual unfolding. Asked how the interspiritual vision could become a reality, he replied, "We have to believe that extraordinary people will come forward and establish extraordinary relationships."

For those who may feel called to build new models, structures, and institutions to carry the interspirituality vision, a simple model is quite powerful, especially when viewed in a diagram and seen as a process to be repeated over and over. The model involves either imagining or drawing a four-pointed diamond that in geometry is called a "rhombus." A rhombus has a central point at the top, two points (one left and one right) at the middle, and another central point at the bottom below the central pair. Think of the point at the top as the *inspiration*. If you are a person who believes in spiritual inspiration, such as guidance from God or spirit, think of the top point as God or your "spirit guide" inspiring you to do something and giving you a plan.

The first step is for the inspiration to find *you* and convey the idea. You perhaps have an "aha moment," maybe even the beginnings of a plan. You can represent this on your diagram by drawing an arrow to connect the top point and the middle left point. You and the inspiration are connected. The next step is that, just as the inspiration found you, *you* need to link with someone who "gets" the vision as clearly as you. On your diamond, imagine yourself as the left of the two middle points, looking for the point on the right to join with you. Now imagine you have found a co-visionary or even several who are as excited about the plan as you. Join these left and right middle points of your diamond with an arrow. Also draw an arrow from the inspiration point, connecting it with the entire middle of your diamond. You have just manifested your vision, and it's bigger than you. You now have your base.

The next step is to expand your base to more and more people, represented by the bottom point of your diamond. In each case such expansion is a repeating of the process of the left-hand point finding the right-hand point and joining. The diamond is just repeating itself over and over. Now draw an arrow from the top of your diamond down through the middle and to the bottom. There's no end to how many levels you can expand to by simply repeating the pattern. You'll just need an inspired central figure and inspired followers at each step.

There's nothing new about this strategy, and both good and bad causes have used it. The early democratic cells of a transforming medieval Europe used the model, as did the American Revolution, the Communists, and Al Qaeda. So did McDonalds, which began as a single enterprise, not as a full-blown franchise. If you recognize that each step of growth is a repeat of central figures finding followers and solidifying their base, it's all rather simple. However, without a strong central figure to take responsibility for the *inspiration* and be dedicated to its expansion, little will happen.

Conclusion

Reflections on Today's Interspirituality

INTERSPIRITUALITY IS THE WAY AUTHENTIC SPIRITUALITY HAS INHERENTLY responded to humankind's advancing sense of unity and the inevitable processes of globalization and multiculturalism. In other words, it's a phenomenon that has a life of its own quite apart from the particular individuals who pioneered its expression.

Two other movements, each with their own particular relationship to Brother Teasdale, also represent the same spirit and have lives of their own, evolving in tandem with the interspiritual movement. One is the Sacred Activism movement, the other the Integral and Integral Life Practice movements.

Sacred Activism has been championed by another leader with roots going back to Father Bede Griffiths and the Christian ashram at Shantivanum—Andrew Harvey, whose decades as a mystical writer have featured the pivotal figures of spirituality with universal appeal and a clear passion for transformation of the world. These have included Buddha, the mystical Jesus as depicted in the Gnostic Gospel of Thomas, the Sufi and Indian poets Rumi and Kabir, and the two great interspiritual figures of India, Sri Ramakrishna and Sri Aurobindo. Harvey's other passion has been the divine feminine, and his book *The Return of the Mother* is considered a classic.

Beginning in 2005, Harvey has championed the vision of interspirituality in sacred activism across the globe. His book *The Hope: A Guide to Sacred Activism* detailed this vision in 2009. His Institute for

Sacred Activism, headquartered in Oak Park, near Chicago, serves as a teaching center. Central to the vision of Sacred Activism is the warning that spirituality as a transcendent pursuit is inadequate, and that the bliss of transcendent consciousness is only an aspect of the meaning of our species. A mature understanding of awakened spirituality involves both the transcendent and the transformation of what's right here, right now.

Brother Teasdale warned of the same partial understanding, as did Aurobindo. Teasdale said the danger of a heightened transcendent experience is it can overlook the yearning of the heart. He explained that from knowledge of this yearning comes "will," which is the element that can bring together transcendent experience and world transformation.

Anyone who reads Ken Wilber's *Integral Spirituality* and knows Brother Teasdale's thinking immediately recognizes the linkage of interspirituality and the integralists. The message of the developmentalists, Integral, and Spiral Dynamics is indispensable to the interspiritual vision. The two form a yin–yang at the heart of unity consciousness and the skill sets needed to move that heart and consciousness into tangible transformation. They are inseparable because they go beyond the vision of blend, dialogue, or simple relative pluralism. Integral and Spiral Dynamics provide the big, meta picture of all aspects of the experience of *Homo sapiens* and our journey through history. There are several videos of discussion between Ken Wilber and Wayne Teasdale in the year before Brother Teasdale's passing, which were Teasdale's last public appearances. We have already noted that he was seriously ill at the time, which caused his friends to urge him not to tire himself with the trip to Colorado to make these videos with Wilber, but he insisted.

Brother Teasdale was tying a number of threads together in the last months before he was eventually too ill to travel and was essentially homebound with friends and caregivers in Chicago. Along with his professional caregivers, his friends Gorakh Hayashi, Russill and Asha Paul, Martha Foster, and others, were able to spend significant time with him during those last months.

Brother Teasdale began to mention the work of Wilber in his last books. Wilber wrote the Foreword to *A Monk in the World,* in which Teasdale spoke of integral in a generic sense. The *Bede Griffiths* book, which Teasdale worked hard to complete before his passing, makes substantial reference to the integral vision. These inclusions reflected Brother Teasdale's emerging sense of the importance of the integral view and explain his interest in doing the Wilber videos even though he was so ill.

The connection of Brother Teasdale to integral in many ways grew out of the most common response he received from the public about his books, as mentioned earlier: "Great book, but now how do we accomplish this vision?" There was also a pivotal meeting with Lama Surya Das, the American Buddhist writer who Teasdale's friend the Dalai Lama called "the American lama," in which the importance of creating initial structures through which Teasdale's vision could continue to be pursued was discussed. These led to further activities of the association Teasdale helped found in New York City, as Lama Surya Das' Dzogchen Center was situated in nearby Massachusetts. At the nearby Omega Institute in upstate New York, discussions of the future of Brother Teasdale's vision after his transition were held with Sufi leader Llewellyn Vaughan-Lee and several leaders of American Advaita Vedanta.

It must be said that all these gatherings, including those with Wilber, were cut short by Brother Teasdale's health. In a note received from Teasdale in those last weeks, he expressed his regret that he hadn't been able to return to the East Coast since 2004. This was particularly saddening, since anyone who has read the *Bede Griffiths* book knows that Brother Teasdale experienced a short-lived remission of cancer, during which he imagined he would soon be able to continue his work. He had his dream of the Omega Vision at the same time, along with a poignant dream of himself as an Eastern monk falling from a mountain, then being caught up in an embracing peace at its foot. Many of his friends interpreted the latter as a premonition of his own passing.

Redefining Spiritual Commitment and Lifestyle

It's amazing how the world has progressed since Brother Teasdale as a monastic wrote *The Mystic Heart*. It's as if the world has already passed through a period wherein a monastic like Teasdale was advising us about a saner and more balanced life, into a world where monasticism itself might become obsolete. We noted earlier that while Teasdale sought to be a part of the world of organized religion, and monasticism in particular, so much of his vision was aimed at deconstructing it. Today, with unity consciousness arising in the secular world and an awakening to interspirituality happening in religion and spirituality, we must take a new look at what complete dedication to spiritual practice and sacred service now mean.

We already know that people with a growing interspiritual understanding can remain within their traditional religion, transforming and enriching its practice and empowering a deeper heart-sense of unity and goodwill in all the world's religions. We also know that some will be called to create new structures that reflect trans-traditional spirituality and interspirituality in more specific ways. In this new demography of religious people, associations and groups that seek a more complete spiritual and service commitment will have the same role traditional monastic communities and orders always had among the world's religions—that of service, inspiration, and empowerment. But these communities will inevitably reflect the way modern people live their lives—celibate and non-celibate, single and married, with families or not, activist or contemplative, and combinations of all of these.

Brother Teasdale painted this future in broad brushstrokes, but he also described more specific ways this life might be lived. Constantly mentioned by Teasdale was his dream of a Universal Order of Sannyasa (*sannyas* referring to someone who gives up all for the sake of serving the whole). This would characterize any association, order, or community committed to spiritual practice and sacred service on behalf of the larger mutual goals of the species. It includes the role monastic and service orders have always had in the world—one still entirely relevant to an emerging Interspiritual Age.

When we think of monks, nuns, or committed clergy within any tradition, we often think simply of this lifestyle as we have run across it in our own lives. However, there is a deeper meaning beneath the role monastics have often played. Throughout history, individuals have always questioned the assumptions and narratives of the culture of which they were a part. Their experience led them to ask new questions—or at least to recognize that new questions were needed. This tended to happen when their own daily lives ceased to make sense for them. Historically, the common reaction to this was to separate from their society and take time to ask questions and seek answers. Although few realize it, the role of monastics, and even the origin of the word, refers to this action of being "set apart." The English word "monk" comes from the Greek word for "solitary."

The term "monk" carries the connotation of "separation from those not sharing the same purpose." Thus, when the word monastic is evaluated in any language, be it the Sanskrit word *bhikkhu* for Buddhists and Hindus, *lama* in Tibet, *phongyi* in Burma, or *pigu* in Korea, a primordial meaning implies separating oneself for some kind of search for meaning. Throughout history, and in all cultures, the word has also been used generically for women as well as men, although most languages also had a separate word for this pursuit by women. The most universal of these is the word "nun" (a word so ancient and common to many cultures that, except for its affinity to words meaning "renunciant," it's generally considered to be of uncertain origin).

Of course, the words "monk" or "nun" have also had meanings that were unconnected with searching for new questions and new answers. In this context, within strict adherence to a religious or cultural tradition, the words referred to a life of strict devotional activity solely within the conventions of that tradition. In certain periods, social conditions were such that people also took refuge in monastic communities for all kinds of other reasons, even simple safety.

Today the role of the monastic—be it the monk, nun, cenobite, hermit, anchorite, or hesychast—is changing. Still, thousands worldwide feel called to a life of spiritual devotion and sacred service. Eastern cultures have traditionally supported such lifestyles as a part of their social norms; such support has been less common in the West. Well-known historical figures East and West emerged from this tradition, the Buddha being one whose tradition continues today. The monastic life is common throughout Hinduism and much of Asia. It was also the life of St Francis of Assisi, along with so many other leaders venerated by Christianity whose role as pivotal world figures continues today.

The moral example of modern monks is one of great influence on world culture: His Holiness the Dalai Lama, Thich Nhat Hanh, Mother Teresa, Brother Wayne Teasdale, Thomas Merton, and Father Thomas Keating being examples that readily come to mind. When asked in a CNN interview about the commanding economic, population, and military positions of mainland China and its leadership, His Holiness the Dalai Lama commented that the problem with the Chinese leadership is they don't understand kindness. CNN.com requested a response to His Holiness from a Western theologian. A university professor, who was also taking the opportunity to advertise his latest book, suggested that the Dalai Lama was "wrong" and "naïve," asserting that, like it or not, religions are about power and who will control the world. It shows the predicament we are in.

The difference between the Dalai Lama and the theologian is that one represents the heart-centered nature of interspirituality, whereas the other reflects the realities of global "business as usual." They also represent different "levels," to borrow a term from the developmentalists. His Holiness reflects the ethos of a future Global Age that will be our Seventh Great Advance, while the professor represents the best that the post-World War II era has to offer.

But there is something else. It may be that the monastic lifestyle offers the ethical advantage of living a simple life, which enables the monk to be an optimist on behalf of humankind. There is an advantage in being free to look to the wellbeing of all, as well as to cultivate what it means to treat others in the way one would want to be treated (the Golden Rule, common to dozens of the world's spiritual traditions). This distinction seems to characterize the newer meaning of being "set apart." If it's the medium that makes the difference, this attests to Marshall McLuhan's maxim "the medium is the message" (a maxim that dates to the integrative age).

What would the world be like today if no one in the past had heard a calling to set themselves apart, go deeper, and ask new questions about "where we came from, why we are here, and where are we going"? What if Jesus hadn't gone into the desert to ponder before his ministry? What if the one who became the Buddha hadn't left his royal household to become an ascetic, later sitting under the Bodhi tree to contemplate why his years as an ascetic hadn't given him the answer he sought?

Brother Teasdale envisioned emerging communities and collectives doing the work of interspirituality in all kinds of forms. This is already unfolding in the new monasticism movement. An internet search of "new monasticism" or "new monastic communities" brings up nearly two million entries. Wikipedia summarizes the views of many across a number of traditions. Envisioned are communities of all kinds, celibate or not, married or not, sharing property or not, creating shared business and livelihood or working in the wider community. Many of these models already exist, especially in the Sufi communities of Islam and groups in the Christian evangelical community. Members of the interspirituality community are part of an effort to create visions and guidelines for such communities.[112]

Interspiritual Education

What should interspiritual education be about? The most important goal of interspiritual education is the cultivation of experiential unity consciousness. This involves all the traditions that emphasize the individual search for direct contemplative and mystical experience. It also involves the continuance of the hundreds of gatherings of mystics and contemplatives worldwide.

At these gatherings, not only is the unity of the contemplative

---

[112] In 2012 meetings were hosted by Fr Keating and produced a vision statement; see McEntee and Bucko 2012 in bibliography.

understanding discussed, but this sharing together of contemplative practice also invites incomparable engagement with the subtle realms of reality. Participants report this as the deepest form of sharing, a direct transmission of knowledge of the other as an aspect of oneself. As Brother Teasdale emphasized, these gatherings are also important because all the religious and spiritual traditions respect their mystics and contemplatives, who are looked to as a source of wisdom. It was from such gatherings that interspirituality arose, and it's from similar gatherings that it will continue to grow.

Another priority for interspiritual education is what Brother Teasdale referred to as the "second" activity required by interspirituality, the dialogue and study required if we are to heal the divisions and wounds of the past. This involves stressing the ethical and behavioral standards that all the traditions hold in common, the most obvious of which is the Golden Rule. From this stems the entire list of values that accompany such a high ethos: kindness, compassion, understanding, consolation, and every variety of loving service imaginable. As Brother Teasdale pointed out, these values must be practiced not just with regard to other human beings, but toward all beings and the earth and cosmos itself.[113]

Such teachings are not only unifying principles but should be the message of the bully pulpits of authentic religion worldwide. The emphasis should be on the great ethical and wisdom teachings of the religions, with their stress on the grandeur of humanity—a grandeur that lies at the heart of the arts, including literature, poetry, music, art, dance, and all the other manifestations that mark *Homo sapiens* as an unparalleled species.

We can summarize the elements of interspiritual education as follows:

- Teaching interspirituality itself (the journey from inter-faith to experiential interspirituality)

- Teaching sacred activism (the inherent connection of being and doing)

---

[113] A wonderful example from the interspiritual community is a volume written for presentation at the United Nations Rio+20 summit in 2012; see Harland and Keepin in Bibliography.

- Cultivating higher consciousness (unity consciousness as an actual experience)

- Nurturing individual formation (personal maturation in authentic universal spirituality)

- Teaching Integral (the integral vision and the developmental view of history)

- Community building (building authentic communities of all kinds)

- Ministry development (developing interfaith and interspiritual ministry from conventional roles—in religious institutions, chaplaincy, hospice—to entrepreneurial initiatives, creating new roles for interfaith and interspiritual ministry).

The educational elements of interspirituality are intimately connected to Brother Teasdale's Nine Elements of a Universal Spirituality. These nine elements provided the structure of his first book on interspirituality, *The Mystic Heart*. Each not only represents an aspiration of authentic spirituality but also a description of the goal and fruits. Each circumscribes a realm of spiritual and ethical inquiry and responsibility. Each also contains multiple aspects that are critical to spiritual education:

- Actualizing full moral and ethical capacity

- Living in harmony with the cosmos and all living beings

- Cultivating a life of deep nonviolence

- Living in humility and gratitude

- Embracing a regular spiritual practice

- Cultivating mature self-knowledge

- Living a life of simplicity

- Being of selfless service and compassionate action

- Empowering the prophetic voice for justice, compassion, and world transformation.

The balancing of individual maturity and collective evolution is central to interspirituality, as well as being an Integral principle. When Brother Teasdale imagined the work of interspirituality, he set it out along those two lines.

A Call to Universal Exploration

Not even the closest colleagues among today's interspiritual circles and communities, or among those who knew Brother Teasdale well, have a universal understanding of what interspirituality is or might become. Yet, with backgrounds from across all the world's religions and often reporting vastly different spiritual and inspirational experiences, they have found together a profound peace, friendship, and sense of a common human destiny. They may not understand every detail of each other's conversations, but they profoundly understand the meaning of being together. This "raw feel" of oneness among them may actually be the central message! It's probably the message to be discovered by a successfully globalizing world.

The call to interspirituality is a call for radical and universal exploration into the subtle realms of consciousness and the deepest regions of the heart. This involves plumbing exactly what unifying principles—what Archimedean points of unity—lie beneath the societal history of our species.

After billions of years, there's still a society on this planet participating in the decisions that will ultimately determine our destiny. This is why interspirituality is so important and so timely. This is ultimately what propels the tale—not this group or that, this citizen or that. The message is always about unity, about ultimate togetherness—earth and cosmos, earth and animal, animal and animal, animal and human, human and human, religion and religion. In the end the message is about the end of separateness, as in all the myths and sacred texts. This is the heart of unity consciousness.

Appendix I

Synopsis of the Developmental Periods

I. Origin of Modern Humans

Time Period—100-50,000 years ago

Developmental Features:

Integral Tags—Archaic & Instinctive (e.g. clan structures, survivalistic, automatic, reflexive)

Integral Color—Beige (Spiral Dynamics); Infrared (Integral)

Brain-Mind Features: reflexive, more animal-like, relatively non-conscious

Consciousness Tags—primitive nondualistic, bicameral spiritual-religious

Spiritual-Religious Features—nature spirits, ancestors

2. First Great Advance: Humans Populate the Old World

Time Period—from 50,000 years ago

Developmental Features:

Integral Tags—Magical & Animistic (e.g. tribalist with magical relations with spirit world)

Integral Color—Purple (Spiral Dynamics); Magenta (Integral)

Brain-Mind Features—slightly more analytic, introspective, and reflective mind

Consciousness Tags—early dualistic, bicameral

Spiritual-Religious Features—direct experience of "the gods"

3. Second Great Advance: from Towns to Cities to Empires

From Towns to Cities

Time Period—from about 7000 BCE

Developmental Features:

Integral Tags—Egocentric & Exploitive (e.g. dominionist, the era of power gods and heroes)

Integral Color—Red

Brain-Mind Features—more self aware, intentional, strongly ego- and ethno-centric

Consciousness Tags—developing consciousness, declining bicamerality, increasingly dualistic

Spiritual-Religious Features—local and regional God-Kings

From Cities to Empires

Time Period—from about 3000 BCE

Developmental Features:

Integral Tags—Absolutist & Authoritarian (e.g. purposefully authoritarian; obedience and myth-based order)

Integral Color—Blue (Spiral Dynamics); Amber (Integral)

Brain-Mind Features—more self-aware but ethno-centrically identified and conformist with control-driven hierarchies

Consciousness Tags—developing consciousness, increasingly

dualistic but with emergent nondual mysticism (unity consciousness)

Spiritual-Religious Features—emergent Axial Age, rise of
the world's Great Religions and Church-State Empires

4. Third Great Advance: Rationalism

Time Period—from about 1000 CE (and spurred by the
European catastrophe, "The Black Plague")

Developmental Features:

Integral Tags—Multiplistic, Achievist, Scientific & Strategic
(e.g. rational, analytic, inquiring)

Integral color—Orange

Brain-Mind Features—conscious with analytic, introspective, reflective mind; free-thought movements challenging
religious dogmas but coexisting within rigid old hierarchical
social structures

Consciousness Tag—more advanced dualistic, subcultures of
nondual mysticism (unity consciousness)

Spiritual-Religious Features—alternative social structures
and free thought movements growing in, co-existing with,
and gradually replacing rigid old hierarchical systems.

5. Fourth Great Advance:
Toward a Worldwide Civilization

Planetary Cosmopolitanism

Time Period—from about 1850 CE (surging in 20th century)

Developmental Features:

Integral Tags—Relativistic (e.g. personalistic but also

communitarian, pluralistic, and egalitarian; early Modernism)

Integral color—Green

Brain-Mind Features—conscious with more analytic, computational, inventive, introspective mind

Consciousness Tag—advanced dualistic

Spiritual-Religious Features—contact between the differing world religions, early mixing of East-West subjective views, emerging new syntheses (including religion and 19th century science), early interreligious discussion, experimentation with trans-disciplinary, transcultural ideas; strong subcultures of nondual mysticism (unity consciousness)

Meeting the Demands of an Integrated World

Time Period—from about 1950 (spurred by the aftermaths of the world wars)

Developmental Features:

Integral Tags—Systemic & Integrative (e.g. Modernism per se)

Integral Color—Yellow (Spiral Dynamics); Teal (Integral)

Brain-Mind Features—conscious and highly analytic, computational, introspective, reflective, creative, exploratory, tolerant mind

Consciousness Tags—advanced dualistic with emergent nondual initiatives (the new physics, etc.)

Spiritual-Religious Features—regular contact among the world's religions, cosmopolitan mixing of East-West subjective views, distinguishing religion from spirituality, emerging new syntheses (including spirituality and the new science), growing interreligious discussion, experimentation with boundaries and meaning of consciousness; strong subcultures of nondual experience (unity consciousness)

6. Fifth Great Advance: The Dream of Holism

Time Period—from about 1970 CE

Developmental Features:

Integral Tags—Integrative & Holistic (e.g. search for broad syntheses of human knowledge, post-modernism, multiculturalism)

Integral Color—Turquoise

Brain-Mind Features—conscious with analytic, computational, post-rational, introspective, reflective, creative skills

Consciousness Tag—advanced dualism with emerging advanced nondualism

Spiritual-Religious Features—emerging Interspiritual Age, movement of spiritualities toward the experiential and heart-based, with dialogue and sharing across the religions; exploration of consciousness in scientific arena; worldwide subculture of nondual experience (unity consciousness); backlash of fundamentalism across many religions

7. The Sixth Great Advance: Our Future?

Time Period—following the current Turquoise Epoch

Developmental Features:

Integral Tags—Planetary Integral & Holistic (e.g. implications of increasing percentages of persons being of Turquoise integral worldview)

Integral Color—Coral (Spiral Dynamics); Indigo (Integral)

Brain-Mind Features—advanced consciousness with analytic, computational, post-rational, introspective, reflective, creative mind

Consciousness Tag—increasingly nondual

Spiritual-Religious Features—religion and spirituality are about experiential consciousness, anthropomorphic and magic-mythic religious views are obsolete, science and spirituality are in accord about reality, nondual experience (unity consciousness) becomes more and more universal

8. A Seventh Great Advance?

The promise of our future earth having met the thresholds of the Planetary Integral & Holistic Epoch and advanced beyond

Appendix II

Magic-Mythic and Apocalyptic Views of 2012

In descending order of probable credibility

Mayan Calendar plus Mayan, Aztec, and Hopi Myth, Astrology, and Astronomy

Sources:

Several decades of scholarly and popular speculation concerning the Mayan calendar have been joined with elements of Aztec and Hopi legend and astrological and astronomical prediction.

Twenty Predictions:

Earth and cosmic calamities due to geometric alignments, including (from various authors) galactic alignment, total synchronization, galactic entrainment, galactic synchronization, collision with the phantom planet "Nibiru," reversal of the earth's magnetic field, reversal of the earth's rotation axis, a 90-degree flip of the earth's axis, massive displacement of the earth's crust, solar storms peaking an 11-year cycle in 2012, solar debacle by combined effect of our sun and a nearby supernova "Sirius B," bombardment by comets and asteroids due to alignments influencing the "Ort cloud" (source of comet and asteroid debris), lethal rays from the center or "dark rift" of the Milky Way galaxy, earthquakes and super-volcanoes, collision with or gravitational effects of the black hole at the center of the Milky Way, return of the Mayan star-god Bolon Yokte and the Aztec god Quetzalcoatl (both portended by crop circles), return of the Phoenix (of Egyptian legend) and discovery of lost ancient records of the Egyptian civilization, return or appearance of the Blue Star Kachina (Hopi Indian legend thought by many to refer to the star Sirius B).

Puzzles and Problems:

Puzzles—some of these catastrophes have been documented by science in the past or can be seen happening elsewhere in the universe; moreover, scholars disagree about whether the Mayans and Aztecs actually knew of "precession" and other galactic-level perspectives.

Problems—scholars disagree on details of both the math and the mythological narratives of the Maya, Azctecs, and Hopis. Further, many of the disaster scenarios represent unprecedented events, so possible outcomes would be uncertain. However, of those seen before, most scientists say pole shifts occur over thousands of years, not suddenly; Nibiru, if it existed, would be easily spotted by astronomers; and Sirius B, if it did explode into a supernova, is too far away from the Milky Way to affect our solar system.

The King-Wen Sequence of the *I-Ching* and the Timewave Zero Computer

Sources:

Some scholars, but mostly popularizers, have articulated a symbolic event sequence from the Eastern spiritual classic, the *I-Ching*. Elements of this sequence have been combined with complex data analyses and simulations involving historical dates and events on the Timewave Zero computer program. Versions of the sequence, and this computer program, were devised by the late Terence McKenna and his associates. McKenna, also an early pioneer in psychedelic drugs, was a controversial scholar-popularizer who synthesized numerous mytho-logical and historical data sets into a vision of historically emerging phenomena, or "novelty." Aside from the controversy about his life and views, McKenna did influence the thinking of many mainstream philosophers and anthropologists, and his archives were kept by Esalen Institute.

Twenty Predictions:

Generally, all twenty of the consequences predicted for the Mayan calendar scenario.

Puzzles and Problems:

Puzzles—some of the elements of the scenario pointing to 2012 are compelling, as they parallel many well-supported views regarding epochs of world history and development.

Problems—The King-Wen sequence is a modern interpretation of the ancient I-Ching, incorporating many new and novel elements of the later New Age movement. Further, data for the computer compu-tations was also selected through modern interpretations (for instance, including dates like the bombing of Hiroshima as a benchmark). The computer program was also later revised to fit data from the Mayan calendar scenarios once they were known. Some scientists also have problems with so much of the data having been generated through the use of psychedelic drugs.

The Web Bot Computer Program

Sources:

The "Web Bot" computer program, originally developed for pre-dicting the stock market from myriads of simultaneous data, was adapted to analyze historical events and measures of trends in internet chat and blogs by New Age pundits Clif High and George Ure. The predictions are marketed worldwide. Conceptually, Web Bot is similar to what we have previously called "discursive theory," the view that trends in human thinking and awareness are followed subsequently by arising behaviors. The program has claimed success in predicting numerous sociological and natural events and, although extremely controversial, some of these claims are being evaluated by the scientific community, especially those curious about the mathematics of the method—"ALTA" (Asymmetric Language Trend Analysis).

Five Predictions:

Calamity is predicted for 2012, including either a reversal of the earth's magnetic poles, a series of expanding nuclear wars, a world financial collapse, devastating solar activity wiping out earth's electronic technology, or a near collapse from various causes followed by a productive and innovative human rebound.

Puzzles and Problems:

Problems—Because so few people understand the mathematics, there is considerable controversy about the nature of the predictive value of the computer program. Some suggest it's useful for predicting human-generated events that could be seen as "trending" in world communications content patterns. Many doubt the program has real value with regard to predicting natural calamities, and suggest such claims are simply sensationalized coincidences.

Nostradamus

Sources:

Various current interpretations of *The Prophecies* by French seer Michel de Nostredame ("Nostradamus," 1503-1566).

Six Predictions:

Calamities vary with author, but of the 20 calamities above, six are also attributed to Nostradamus, based primarily on cosmic collision (with attendant earthquake, volcanic, and tsunami disasters), final world war or alien encounter end-time scenarios.

Puzzles and Problems:

Problems—Predictions for 2012 attributed to Nostradamus did not exist before the 2012 prediction frenzy began. Depending on interpretation of his texts, Nostradamus predicted the world would end by a comet hitting in July 1999, but he also made predictions into the future at least as far as 3797.

Appendix III

Institutions, Organizations, Associations, and Centers Advancing the Vision of Interspirituality Worldwide

See:

The Interspiritual Multiplex Resource Website
http://multiplex.isdna.org/newpage1.htm

and

The Coming Interspiritual Age Website
www.thecominginterspiritualage.com

Bibliography

**Books and articles consulted or referred
to in *The Coming Interspiritual Age*** .

Adler, Felix. *Life and Destiny*. Kila MT: Kessinger Publishing, [1903] 2007.

_____. *Reconstruction of the Spiritual Ideal*. Kila MT: Kessinger Publishing, [1923] 2010.

Alighieri, Dante. *The Divine Comedy*. New York NY: Simon & Brown, [1555] 2011.

Almass, A. H. [Hameed Ali]. *Essence: The Diamond Approach to Inner Realization*. Yorkbeach MA: Red Wheel Weiser, 1986.

Argüelles, José. *The Transformative Vision: Reflections on the Nature and History of Human Expression*. Lyon FR: Muse Publications, 1992.

Armstrong, Karen. *The Great Transformation: The Beginning of Our Religious Traditions*. New York NY: Anchor, 2007.

Aurobindo Ghose [Sri Aurobindo]. *The Life Divine* [translated] [7th Ed]. Twin Lakes WI: Lotus Press, [1914-1919] 2010.

_____. *The Synthesis of Yoga* [translated] [US Ed.]. Twin Lakes WI: Lotus Press, [1914-1921] 1990.

_____. *Savitri: A Legend and a Symbol* [translated] [New US Edition] Twin Lakes WI: Lotus Press, [1946-1951] 1995.

_____. *"Essays Divine and Human"*, in *Collected Works of Sri Aurobindo* [re: lead-in chapter quotation for our "The Great Coming Together": vol. 12, p.158]. Sri Aurobindo Ashram Trust, 1972.

Bailey, Alice A. *Esoteric Psychology: A Treatise on the Seven Rays*. New York NY: Lucis Publishing Company, [1936-1960] 2002.

Bani Sadr, Abu al-Hasan. *L'espérance trahie* [*Hope Betrayed*]. Paris FR: Papyrus Editions, 1982.

Barnhart, Bruno. "Bede Griffiths and the Rebirth of Christian Wisdom". Talk given at Osage Monastery, Sand Spring OK, May 21, 2000.

Barušs, Imants. "Speculations about the Direct Effects of Intention on Physical Manifestation". *Journal of Cosmology* 3, pp. 590-599, 2009.

_____. *Science as a Spiritual Practice*. Thorverton UK: Imprint Academic, 2007.

_____. *Authentic Knowing: The Convergence of Science and Spiritual Aspiration*. Purdue IN: Purdue University Press, 1996.

Bastian, Edward. *Interspiritual Meditation: A Seven-Step Process from the World's Spiritual Traditions*. Charleston SC: CreateSpace, 2010.

Beck, Don and Christopher Cowan. *Spiral Dynamics: Mastering Values, Leadership, and Change*. Oxford UK: Blackwell Publishing Ltd., 1996.

Becker, Katrin, Melanie Becker and John H. Schwarz. *String Theory and M-Theory: A Modern Introduction*. Cambridge IK: Cambridge University Press, 2007.

Bergson, Henri. *Creative Evolution* [translated]. New York NY: Henry Holt and Company, 1911.

Berry, Thomas. *The Dream of the Earth*. San Francisco CA: Sierra Club Books, [1988] 2006.

Bhaktivedanta, A. C. *Bhagavad-Gita As It Is* [Revised Ed.]. Alachua FL: Bhaktivedanta Book Trust, 1997.

Bohm, David. *Wholeness and the Implicate Order*. London UK: Routledge, [1980] 2002.

Book of Mormon [Joseph Smith]. Manchester UK: Empire Books, 2012.

Bourgeault, Cynthia. *The Wisdom Way of Knowing: Reclaiming An Ancient Tradition to Awaken the Heart*. Hoboken, NJ: Jossey-Bass, 2003.

Brockman, John. *The Third Culture: Beyond the Scientific Revolution*. New York NY: Simon & Schuster, 1995.

Brown, Peter G. and Geoffrey Garver. *Right Relationship: Building a Whole Earth Economy*. San Francisco CA: Berrett-Koehler Publishers, 2009.

Buber, Martin. *I and Thou*. New York NY: Charles Scribner's Sons, [1937] 2000.

Burroughs, William S. *Naked Lunch*. New York NY: Grove Press, 1959.

Byrd, Kavita. Shakti Interspiritual Centre: Articles on the Divine Feminine by Kavita. http://shakticentre.blogspot.com/p/essays-on-divine-feminine.html

Byrne, Rhonda. *The Secret*. New York NY: Atria Books, 2006.

Calleman, Carl Johan. *Mayahypotesen*. Sweden: Garev Publishing International, 2001.

_____. *The Mayan Calendar and the Transformation of Consciousness* [4th Ed.]. Rochester VT: Bear & Company, 2004.

Campbell, Joseph. *The Hero with a Thousand Faces*. Princeton NJ: Princeton University Press, 1968.

Capra, Fritjof. *The Tao of Physics: An Exploration of the Parallels between Modern Physics and Eastern Mysticism* [5th Ed.]. Boston MA: Shambhala, 2010.

Carson, Rachel. *Silent Spring.* Boston MA: Houghton Mifflin Company, 1962.

Castaneda, Carlos. *The Teachings of Don Juan: A Yaqui Way of Knowledge.* Berkeley CA: University of California Press, 1968.

_____. *A Separate Reality.* New York NY: Pocket Books, 1971.

Chopra, Deepak. *Quantum Healing.* New York NY: Bantam, 1989.

Christ, Carol. *Why Women Need the Goddess [aka Womanspirit Rising, A Feminist Reader in Religion].* New York NY: HarperOne, 1992.

Cobb, John. *"The Beginning Dialogue between Christianity and Buddhism, the Concept of a 'Dialogical Theology' and the Possible Contribution of Heideggerian Thought", Japanese Religions* [Sept] pp. 87-91, 96, 1980.

Cohen, Andrew. *Evolutionary Enlightenment: A Spiritual Handbook for the 21st Century.* New York NY: Select Books, 2011.

Cooperrider, David L., & Diana Whitney. *Appreciative Inquiry: A Positive Revolution in Change.* San Francisco CA: Berrett-Koehler Publishers, 2005.

Cox, Harvey. *The Secular City: Secularization and Urbanization in Theological Perspective.* New York NY: Collier Books, 1965.

_____. *Religion in the Secular City.* New York NY: Simon & Schuster, 1985.

Darwin, Charles. *On the Origin of Species* [150th Anniv. Ed.]. New York NY: Signet Classics, [1859] 2003.

Dawkins, Richard. *The God Delusion.* Boston MA: Houghton Mifflin, 2006.

de Chardin, Pierre Teilhard. *The Phenomenon of Man.* New York NY: Harper Perennial, 1959.

de Nostredame, Michel [Nostradamus]. *The Prophecies.* Western MA: Wilder Publications, [1503-1566] 2009.

de Salzmann, Jeanne. *The Reality of Being: The Fourth Way of Gurdjieff.* Boston MA: Shambhala, 2011.

Dennett, Daniel. *Consciousness Explained,* New York: The Penguin Press, 1991.

Derbyshire, John. *We Are Doomed: Reclaiming Conservative Pessimism.* Three Rivers MI: Three Rivers Press, 2010.

Dianetics [L. Ron Hubbard]. Los Angeles CA: Bridge Publications, [1950] 2007.

Divine Principle [Sun Myung Moon]. New York NY: HSA-UWC, 1977.

Dowd, Michael. *Thank God for Evolution: How the Marriage of Science and Religion Will Transform Your Life and Our World.* New York NY: Penguin Group, 2009.

Downing, Christine. *The Goddess: Mythological Images of the Feminine.* Lincoln NE: Authors Choice Press, 2007.

Ehrlich, Paul R. *The Population Bomb.* New York NY: Ballantine Books, 1968.

Eisenstein, Charles. *Sacred Economics.* New York NY: Evolver Editions, 2011.

Eliade, Mircea. *Patterns in Comparative Religion* [translated]. London UK: Sheed and Ward, 1958.

_____. *The Sacred and the Profane: The Nature of Religion* [translated]. Paris FR: W.R. Trask, Harvest/HBJ Publishers, 1957.

Ellul, Jacques. *The Meaning of the City* [translated]. Eugene, OR: Wipf & Stock Publishers, [1970] 2011.

Esbjorn-Hargens, Sean and Michael E. Zimmerman. *Integral Ecology: Uniting Multiple Perspectives on the Natural World*. Boston MA: Integral Books, 2011.

Evolutionary Biology Portal: *http://en.wikipedia.org/wiki/Portal*

Fabella, Virginia and Sergio Torres. *Doing Theology in a Divided World*. Maryknoll NY: Orbis Books, 1985.

Faraday, Ann and John Wren-Lewis. "*The Selling of the Senoi*", *Lucidity Letter* 3 (1) 1984.

Fox, Matthew. *The Coming of the Cosmic Christ*. New York NY: HarperOne, 1988.

_____. *One River, Many Wells*. New York NY: Tarcher, 2004.

_____. *The Hidden Spirituality of Men*. Novato CA: New World Library, 2009.

_____. *Hildegard of Bingen: A Saint for Our Times*. Vancouver CN: Namaste Publishing, 2012.

Ginsberg, Allen. *Howl and Other Poems*. New York NY: City Lights Publishers, [1956] 2001.

Goldberg, Philip. *American Veda: From Emerson and the Beatles to Yoga and Meditation How Indian Spirituality Changed the West*. New York NY: Harmony, 2010.

Golding, William. *Lord of the Flies*. London UK: Hodder & Stoughton, [1954] 2002.

Greene, Brian. The *Fabric of the Cosmos: Space, Time, and the Texture of Reality*. New York NY: Alfred A. Knopf, 2005.

Griffiths, Bede. *Return to the Center*. Springfield IL: Templegate Publishing, 1982.

_____. *Vedanta and Christian Faith*. Middletown CA: Dawn Horse Press, 1991.

_____. *A New Vision of Reality: Western Science, Eastern Mysticism and Christian Faith*. Springfield IL: Templegate Publishers, 1990.

_____. *The Cosmic Revelation: The Hindu Way to God*. Springfield IL: Templegate Publishers, 1983.

_____. *The Marriage of East and West*. Norwich UK: S C M Canterbury Press, 2003.

Gurdjieff, G. I. *Meetings with Remarkable Men [transalted]*. Eastford, CT: Martino Fine Books, [1963] 2010.

Hamilton, Matthew. *Population Genetics*. Oxford UK: Wiley-Blackwell, 2009.

Harland, Maddy and Will Keepin. *Song of the Earth: A Synthesis of the Scientific and Spiritual Worldviews (with Keys to Sustainable Communities)*. Sag Harbor NY: Permanent Publications, 2012.

Harman, Willis. *Global Mind Change: The Promise of the 21st Century [2nd ed.]*. San Francisco, CA: Barrett-Koehler Publishers, 1998.

Harvey, Andrew. *The Return of the Mother*. Berkeley CA: Frog Books, 1995

_____. *The Hope, A Guide to Sacred Activism*. Carlsbad, CA: Hay House, 2009.

Hawken, Paul. *Blessed Unrest, How the Largest Movement in the World Came into Being and Why No One Saw It Coming*. New York NY: Penguin Books, 2007.

Hayashi, G. and K. Johnson. "The Heart of Brother Wayne Teasdale's Vision of the Interspiritual Age", *Vision in Action*, separatum 2008 and http://www.via-visioninaction.org/via-li/ArticlesEssays.php

Hermansen, Marcia K. "*The Academic Study of Sufism* at American Universities" *American Journal of Islamic Social Sciences* 24 (3): 23-45, 2007.

Hesse, Hermann. *Siddartha*. Mineola NY: Dover Publication, [1922] 1998.

_____. *Steppenwolf.* Mattituck NY: Amereon House, [1927] 2010.

Hick, John H. and Paul F. Knitter. *The Myth of Christian Uniqueness: Toward a Pluralistic Theology of Religions* [7th Ed.]. Maryknoll NY: Orbis Books, 1998.

Hixon, Lex. *Coming Home: The Experience of Enlightenment in Sacred Traditions*. Burdett, NY: Larson Publications, 1995.

Holy Bible [Revised Standard Version]. New York NY: Meridian/ Plume, 1974.

Homer. *The Illiad and The Odyssey* [translated]. London UK: Grafton, 1938.

Hume, David. *Dialogues Concerning Natural Religion*. Charleston SC: BiblioBizaar, [1779] 2008.

Huxley, Aldous. *The Doors of Perception: Heaven and Hell*. New York NY: Fontal Lobe Publishing (Tower), [1954] 2011.

_____. *Brave New World Revisited*. New York NY: Harper Perennial Modern Classics, [1958] 2006.

James, William. *The Varieties of Religious Experience*. Des Moines IA: Library of America, [1901] 2009.

Jantsch, Eric. *The Self-Organizing Universe: Scientific and Human Implications of the Emerging Paradigm of Evolution*. Oxford UK: Pergamon, 1980.

Jaspers, Karl. *The Origin and Goal of History* [translated]. New Haven, CT: Yale University Press, [1949] 1953.

Jaynes, Julian. *The Origin of Consciousness in the Breakdown of the Bicameral Mind*. Boston MA: Houghton Mifflin, 1976.

Johnson, Phillip E. *The Wedge of Truth: Splitting the Foundations of Naturalism*. Nottingham, UK: IVP Books, 2002.

Jordan, Michael. *The Encyclopedia of Gods: Over 2,500 Deities of the World*. Darby PA: Diane Books Publishing Company, 1998.

Keating, Thomas. *Open Mind, Open Heart* [20th Ed]. New York NY: Continuum, [1986] 2006.

Kerouac, Jack. *On The Road*. New York NY: Penguin, [1957] 1999.

Knitter, Paul F. "Toward a Liberation Theology of Religions". *Servicios Koinonia* [February] pp. 178-218, 1998.

Korten, David. *The Great Turning: From Empire to Earth Community*. San Francisco CA: Berrett-Koehler Publishers, 2007

Kubler-Ross, Elizabeth. *On Death and Dying*. New York NY: Scribner, [1969] 1997.

Kuhn, Thomas S. *The Structure of Scientific Revolutions*. Chicago IL: University of Chicago Press, 1996.

Laing, R. D. *The Divided Self: An Existential Study in Sanity and Madness*. London UK: Routledge Reprint Editions, [1960] 1998.

_____. *The Politics of Experience and the Bird of Paradise*. New York NY: Pantheon, [1977] 1983.

Lakoff, George. *Metaphors We Live By* [2nd Ed.]. Chicago IL: Chicago University Press, 2003.

Leary, Timothy, Ralph Metzner and Richard Alpert. *The Psychedelic Experience: A Manual Based on the Tibetan Book of the Dead*. New York NY: Penguin Modern Classics, [1964] 2008.

Lévi-Strauss, Claude. *Structural Anthropology* [translated]. Grundfest Schoepf. New York NY: Basic Books, [1958] 1963.

Lindbeck, George A. *The Nature of Doctrine: Religion and Theology in a Postliberal Age*. Philadelphia PA: Westminster Press, 1985.

Lipton, Bruce H. *The Biology of Belief: Unleashing the Power of Consciousness, Matter & Miracles* [13th Ed.]. Carlsbad, CA: Hay House, 2011.

_____. *Spontaneous Evolution: Our Positive Future and a Way to Get There From Here* [3rd Ed.]. Carlsbad, CA: Hay House, 2011.

Lovejoy, Arthur O. *The Great Chain of Being: A Study of the History of an Idea.* Cambridge MA: Harvard University Press, [1936] 1976.

Lovelock, James. *Gaia, A New Look At Life on Earth.* Oxford UK: Oxford University Press, [1979] 2001.

Loy, David. *Nonduality: A Study in Comparative Philosophy.* Amherst NY: Humanity Books, 1997.

Luther, Martin. *The Ninety-Five Theses.* New Milford CT: FQ Books, 1517 [2010].

Maslow, Abraham. *Towards a Psychology of Being* [3rd Ed.], New York NY: Wiley, 1998.

McEntee, Rory, Adam Bucko, Rob Renahan and Kurt Johnson. "The New Monastic Conversation: Guidelines for the 2012 Snowmass Abbey Meetings and a Permanent Colloquy on New Monasticism". Draft document prepared for 2012 Snowmass Initiatives and New Monastic Conversations, St. Benedicts Abbey, Snowmass CO, June 2012.

McEntee, Rory and Adam Bucko. *The New Monasticism: An Interspiritual Manifesto for Contemplative Life in the 21st Century.* Illustrated PDF from Snowmass Interreligious Discussions, 2012.

Meadows, Donella H., Dennis L. Meadows, Jorgen Randers, and William W. Behrens III. *The Limits to Growth.* New York NY: Universe Books, 1972.

Merton, Thomas. *The Seven Storey Mountain.* New York NY: Harcourt Brace, 1946.

_____. *Seeds of Contemplation*, New York NY: New Directions, 1949.

_____. *The Tears of Blind Lions*, New York NY: New Directions, 1949.

_____. *The Waters of Siloe,* New York NY: New Directions, 1949.

Michaelson, Jay. *Everything is God: The Radical Path of Nondual Judaism.* Boston MA: Trumpeter, 2009.

Miles-Yepez, Netanel [Ed.]. *The Common Heart: An Experience of Interreligious Dialogue.* Brooklyn NY: Lantern Books, 2006.

Milton, John. *Paradise Lost* [Norton Critical Editions]. New York NY: W. W. Norton & Company, [1667] 2004.

Mother [The], [Mirra Alfassa]. *Collected Works of The Mother* [17 vols.]. Sri Aurobindo Ashram Trust, 1978.

Murphy, Michael. *The Future of the Body: Explorations into the Further Evolution Of Human Nature.* New York NY: Jeremy P. Tarcher, 1993.

Nasr, Seyyed Hossein. *Knowledge of the Sacred.* Albany NY: State University of New York Press, 1989.

Needleman, Jacob. *What is God?* New York NY: Tarcher/Penguin, 2009.

Newberg, Andrew B., Eugene d'Aquili and Vince Rause. *Why God Won't Go Away: Brain Science and the Biology of Belief.* New York NY: Ballantine Books, 2002.

Newberg, Andrew B. and Mark Robert Waldman. *Why We Believe What We Believe: Our Biological Need for Meaning, Spirituality, and Truth.* New York, NY: Free Press, 2006.

O'Brien, Shawn W. "Responding to Contemporary Religious Diversity in the United States: Mitigating Religious Conflict by Emphasizing Pluralism and Interfaith Dialogue" Thesis; Honors Baccalaureate of Arts in Philosophy, Naropa University, May 20, 2011.

O'Connor, Flannery. *Everything that Rises Must Converge.* New York NY: Farrar, Straus and Giroux, 1965.

Olson, James. *The Whole-Brain Path to Peace*. San Raphael, CA: Origin Press, 2011.

Osborn, Fairchild. *Our Plundered Planet*. Glasgow UK: R. MacLehose and Company Limited, The University Press, 1949.

Ott, Heinrich. *Beyond Dialogue: Toward a Mutual Transformation of Christianity and Buddhism*. Philadelphia PA: Fortress Press 1982.

_____. "Buddhist Emptiness and the Christian God," *Journal of the American Academy of Religion*, 45: 11–25, 1979.

Ouspensky, P. D. *The Fourth Way*. New York NY: Vintage Books, [1957] 1971.

Paddock, Willam and Paul Paddock. *Famine 1975! America's Decision: Who Will Survive*. New York NY: Little Brown and Company, 1967.

Panikkar, Raimon. *The Unknown Christ of Hinduism: Towards an Ecumenical Christophany*. Maryknoll NY: Orbis Books, 1981.

_____. *The Intra-Religious Dialogue*. Mahwah, NJ: The Paulist Press, 1999.

_____. *Christophany: The Fullness Of Man*. Maryknoll NY: Orbis Books, 2004.

Paul, Russill. *Jesus in the Lotus*. Novato CA: New World Library, 2009.

Pennington, T. S. "Interspiritual Dialogue: Encountering the Other as a Sacred Practice". Ph.D. dissertation [in process]. Wisdom University, CA.

Penrose, Roger. *Shadows of the Mind: A Search for the Missing Science of Consciousness*. Oxford UK: Oxford University Press, 1994.

_____. *The Emperor's New Mind: Concerning Computers, Minds and The Laws of Physics*. Oxford UK: Oxford University Press, 1989.

Pinker, Stephen. *The Better Angels of Our Nature: Why Violence Has Declined*. New York NY: Viking, 2011.

Posner, Michael I. and Mary K. Rothbart. *Educating the Human Brain*. Washington DC: Amer. Psychological Assn, 2006.

Price, Huw. *Time's Arrow and Archimedes' Point: New Direction for the Physics of Time*. Oxford UK: Oxford University Press, 1997.

Prigogine, Ilya. *Order Out of Chaos*. Boston MA: Shambhala, 1984.

Prothero, Stephen. *God Is Not One: The Eight Rival Religions That Run the World and Why Their Differences Matter*. New York NY: HarperOne, 2011.

Puthiadam, Ignace. *"Christian Faith and Life in a World of Religious Pluralism,"* in *True and False Universality of Christianity,* Claude Geffre and Jean-Pierre Jossua, ed.'s. New York NY: Seabury, 1980.

Qur'an [The *Koran*]. Oxford UK: Oxford University Press [Reissue Ed.], 2008.

Ray, Paul H. and Sherry Ruth Anderson. *The Cultural Creatives: How 50 Million People Are Changing the World*. New York: Harmony Books, 2000.

Ressler, Peter and Monika Mitchell. *Conversations with Wall Street: The Inside Story of the Financial Armageddon & How to Prevent the Next One*. Sacramento CA: FastPencil Premiere, 2011.

Rohr, Richard. *Everything Belongs: The Gift of Contemplative Prayer*. Chestnut Ridge, NY: The Crossroads Publishing Company, 2003.

_____. *The Naked Now: Learning to See How the Mystics See*. Chestnut Ridge NY: The Crossroads Publishing Company, 2009.

Rosenberg, Marshal L. and Arun Gandhi. *Nonviolent Communication: A Language of Life*. Encinitas CA: PuddleDancer Press, 2003.

Rounder, Leroy S. *Religious Pluralism. Notre Dame IN*: University of Notre Dame Press, 1984.

Salinger, J. D. *Franny and Zooey.* New York NY: Back Bay Books, [1961] 2001.

_____. *The Catcher in the Rye.* New York NY: Back Bay Books, [1951] 2001.

Santayana, George. *The Life of Reason.* [5 vols.] New York NY: Prometheus Books, 1905–1906.

Schnarch, David M. *Constructing the Sexual Crucible: An Integration of Sexual and Marital Therapy.* New York NY: W. W. Norton, 1991.

_____. Christopher Ryan and Cacilda Jetha. *Sex at Dawn: The Prehistoric Origins of Modern Sexuality.* New York NY: Harper Collins, 2010.

Schuon, Fritjof. *The Transcendent Unity of all Religions.* Wheaton IL: Quest Books, 1948.

Schwerin, David A. *Conscious Capitalism: Principles for Prosperity.* Oxford UK: Butterworth-Heinemann, 1998.

Segundo, Juan Luis. *The Liberation of Theology.* Maryknoll NY: Orbis Books, 1976.

Sheldrake, Rupert. *The Science Delusion: Freeing the Spirit of Enquiry.* London UK: Coronet, 2012.

Shepard, Philip. *New Self, New World: Recovering Our Senses in the Twenty-First Century.* Berkeley, CA: North Atlantic Books, 2010.

Smith, Wilfred Cantwell. *The Meaning and End of Religion.* Novato CA: New American Library, 1964.

Snow, C.P. *The Two Cultures.* London UK: Cambridge University Press, [1959] 2001.

Snow, C. P., and Stefan Collini. *The Two Cultures* [Commemorative Ed.]. London UK: Cambridge University Press, 1993.

Starhawk. *The Spiral Dance:* A *Rebirth of the Ancient Religion of the Goddess* [20th Anniv, Ed.]. New York NY: HarperOne, [1979] 1999.

Starr, Mirabai.*God of Love: A Guide to the Heart of Judaism, Christianity and Islam.* Rheinbeck NY: Monkfish Book Publishing, 2012.

Suzuki, Shunryu. *Zen Mind, Beginners Mind.* Boston MA: Shambala, [1970] 2011.

Swidler, Leonard. *Toward a World Theology of Religions.* Maryknoll NY: Orbis Books, 1987.

Szasz, Thomas. *The Myth of Mental Illness: Foundations of a Theory of Personal Conduct.* New York NY: Harper Perennial, [1960] 2010.

Tart, Charles. *Altered States of Consciousness* [3rd Ed]. New York NY: Harper, 1990.

Tattersall, Ian. *Masters of the Planet: The Search for Our Human Origins.* New York NY: Palgrave Macmillan, 2012.

_____. *The Fossil Trail: The Search for Our Human Origins.* [2nd Ed.]. Oxford UK: Oxford University Press, 2008.

Templeton, Alan Robert. *Population Genetics and Microevolutionary Theory.* Hoboken NJ: John Wiley & Sons, 2006.

Teasdale, Wayne. *The Mystic Heart: Discovering a Universal Spirituality in the World's Religions.* Novato CA: New World Library, 1999.

_____. *A Monk in the World.* Novato CA: New World Library, 2002.

_____. *Bede Griffiths: An Introduction to His Interspiritual Thought.* Woodstock VT: SkyLight Paths Publishing, 2003.

Thomas, Wendell Thomas. *Hinduism Invades America.* Boston MA: The Beacon Press, Inc., 1930 [2003].

Tolle, Eckhart. *The Power of Now.* Vancouver BC: Namaste Publishing, 1997.

_____. *A New Earth: Awakening to Your Life's Purpose.* New York NY: Dutton, 2005.

Toynbee, Arnold. *"The Task of Disengaging the Essence from the Non-essentials in Mankind's Religious Heritage,"* in *An Historians Approach to Religion,* Arnold Toynbee. Oxford UK: Oxford University Press, 1956.

Trompf, G. W., *Cargo Cults and Millenarian Movements: Transoceanic Comparisons of New Religious Movements.* New York NY: Mouton de Gruyter, 1990.

University of South Florida. *Mysticism and Modernity* virtual resource at: http://pegasus.cc.ucf.edu/~janzb/mysticism/

Varela, Francisco, Evan Thompson, and Eleanor Rosch. *The Embodied Mind: Cognitive Science and Human Experience.* Princeton MA: MIT Press, 1992.

Varela, Francisco and Humberto Maturana. *Tree of Knowledge: The Biological Roots of Human Understanding* [Rev. Ed.]. Boston MA: Shambhala, 1987 [1992].

Watson, James D. *DNA: The Secret of Life.* New York NY: Alfred A. Knopf Borzoi Books, 2004.

Watts, Alan. *This Is It: and Other Essays on Zen and Spiritual Experience.* New York NY: Vintage Books, [1960] 1973.

_____. *Psychotherapy East and West.* New York NY: Vintage Books, [1961] 1975.

Wedge [The]. "The Wedge Strategy" [aka "The Wedge", attributed to The Center for the Renewal of Science and Culture [aka The Center for Science and Culture]. Seattle WA: Discovery Institute, 1998 [leaked 1999] (see also Johnson, Phillip E. herein) and http://www.antievolution.org/features/wedge.html

Weinberg, Steven. *Cosmology.* Oxford UK: Oxford University Press, 2008.

West, Morris. *The Shoes of the Fisherman.* New York NY: William Morrow Company, 1963.

Whitehead, Alfred North. *Process and Reality.* New York NY: The Free Press, [1929] 1979.

Wilber, Ken. *The Spectrum of Consciousness* [20th Anniv. Ed.]. Wheaton IL: Quest Books TPH, [1977] 1993.

_____. "An Integral Theory of Consciousness". *Journal of Consciousness Studies,* 4 (1): pp. 71-92, 1997.

_____. *Sex, Ecology, Spirituality: The Spirit of Evolution* [2nd Ed.]. Boston MA: Shambhala, [1995] 2001.

_____. *Integral Spirituality: A Startling New Role for Religion in the Modern and Post-modern World.* Boston MA: Shambhala, 2007.

Wilson, E.O. *Consilience: The Unity of Knowledge.* New York NY: Alfred A. Knopf, 1998.

_____. *The Future of Life.* New York NY: Vintage Books, 2003.

Wren-Lewis, John. "*The Dazzling Dark*" from *What is Enlightenment?* [1995] and http://www.nonduality.com/dazdark.htm

Wright, Matthew. "Reshaping Religion: Interspirituality and Multiple Religious Belonging". M.Div. Thesis. Protestant Episcopal Theological Seminary in Virginia, VA. 2012.

Wright, Robert. *The Logic of Human Destiny.* New York NY: Vintage, 2001.

_____. *The Moral Animal: Why We Are the Way We Are: The New Science of Evolutionary Psychology.* New York NY: Vintage, 1995.

Yogananda, Paramahansa. *Autobiography of a Yogi.* Los Angeles CA: Self-Realization Fellowship, 1973.

Zukav, Gary. *The Dancing Wu Li Masters.* New York NY: HarperOne, [1979] 2001.

About the Authors

Kurt Johnson

 Kurt Johnson is well known internationally as a scientist, comparative religionist, social activist, and former monastic. With a PhD in evolution, ecology, systematics, and comparative biology, plus extensive training in comparative religion and philosophy, he was associated professionally for twenty years with the American Museum of Natural History and the One Spirit Interfaith Seminary in New York City. Ordained in three spiritual traditions, he is widely regarded as the closest organizational associate of Brother Wayne Teasdale, the founder of the modern "interspiritual movement." He also works with the international Contemplative Alliance, Father Thomas Keating, (founder of the Centering Prayer movement) and the international Integral community. In science, Dr Johnson has published over 200 professional articles and seven books on evolution and ecology. His popular book *Nabokov's Blues: The Scientific Odyssey of a Literary Genius* (co-authored with *New York Times* journalist Steve Coates) was a "ten best" book in science in 2000 at *Booklist, Library Journal*, the *Washington Post* and *HMS Beagle* and "Editor's Choice for 1999" at *The Seattle Times*. Johnson, Teasdale, and colleagues cofounded the international Interspiritual Dialogue association in 2002, which presented at the 2004 Parliament of the World's Religions and then expanded to become the virtual Interspiritual Multiplex web resource.

Dr Johnson resides in Brooklyn, New York.

David Robert Ord

David Robert Ord is a former Presbyterian (USA) minister and Graduate of San Francisco Theological Seminary. He coauthored along with Dr Robert B. Coote the books *The Bible's First History—From Eden to the Court of David with the Yahwist*, *In the Beginning—Creation and the Priestly History*, and *Is the Bible True? Understanding the Bible Today*. David is also author of the Namaste Publishing book *Your Forgotten Self: Mirrored in Jesus the Christ* and the audiobook *Lessons in Loving—A Journey into the Heart*. He is Editorial Director for Namaste Publishing and resides in the United States.

namaste
PUBLISHING

books that change your life

Our Service Territory Expands

Since introducing Eckhart Tolle to the world with *The Power of Now* in 1997 (and later with *Stillness Speaks, A New Earth,* and *Milton's Secret*), NAMASTE PUBLISHING has been committed to bringing forward only the most evolutionary and transformational publications that acknowledge and encourage us to awaken to who we truly are: spiritual beings of inestimable value and creative power.

In our commitment to expand our service purpose—indeed, to redefine it—we have created a unique website that provides a global spiritual gathering place to support and nurture ongoing individual and collective evolution in consciousness. You will have access to our publications in a variety of formats—including some available exclusively on our site—as well as a myriad of multimedia content.

We invite you to explore our authors, our blogs on health, consciousness, and parenting, as well as the timely guidance found in our Compassionate Eye blog. Enjoy the wisdom of Bizah, a lovable student of Zen, dished up in daily and weekly doses. And because we are all teachers and learners, you will have the opportunity to meet other Namaste Spiritual Community members and share your thoughts, update and share your "spiritual status," and contribute to our interactive online spiritual dictionary.

What better way to come to experience the reality and benefits of our Oneness than by gathering in spiritual community? Tap into the exponential power to create a more conscious and loving world when two or more gather with this same noble intention.

We request the honor of your presence at
www.namastepublishing.com